SITUATING INDIAN WOMEN

ACHYUTANANDA PANDA

ABHIJEET PUBLICATIONS
DELHI 110094

ABHIJEET PUBLICATIONS
2/46 Tukhmeerpur Extension
Delhi 110094
Phones: 011-22960492, 65698474
e-mail: abhijeetpublication@gmail.com
abhijeet_singh1@indiatimes.com

SITUATING INDIAN WOMEN

First Published 2008

ISBN 978-81-89886-32-5

Price: Rs. 880/- (INR)

PRINTED IN INDIA

Published by J.K. Singh fo Abhijeet Publications, Delhi 110094, Lasertypeset by Gaurav Graphics, Delhi and Printed as Himanshu Printers, Delhi.

Preface

It is a common feature in all societies that women have not been given their due status and in many countries they have remained alienated from the mainstream socio-economic-political process since time immemorial. In spite of the vociferous defence of gender equality women have become the largest marginalized group in the world.

The condition of women in traditional societies is much more precarious. In those societies, the male dominated social orders have evolved customs and practices suitable to perpetuate the male dominance in all spheres of the social systems. Women are forbidden from taking part in the decision making process and as a result, the interests of women have continued to be neglected.

The position of women in India is no better. In spite of many reform movements launched by different social reformers during different periods and enactment of innumerable legislations aiming at improving the conditions of women the lot of women in India is yet to be uplifted to the desirable extent. Though the Indian Constitution makes provisions for establishing equality between men and women and provides for affirmative actions in favor of women to rectify their adverse position, the fate of women in India continues to be in a bad shape and it is imperative to take additional steps for achieving the goal of operational equality between men and women in India.

All these factors necessitate discussing and understanding the different issues related to women for appreciating the problems of women in India. The present volume is a modest attempt in that direction.

The present volume is the result of the untiring efforts of some scholarly persons who are genuinely interested in studying and analyzing women issues. It is believed that the articles included in this book will throw some lights on different aspects related to women and be helpful in grasping the problems of women to some extent.

The final product of a scholarly work, however small it may be, requires the cooperation and help of many well wishers, friends and supporters. It is also true in the case of this volume.

I must express my gratitude and appreciation to all the learned contributors who responded to my requests and spent their valuable time and energy to write their informative and analytical articles. Without their kind help it would not have been possible for me to produce this volume. I am obliged to all of them.

I sincerely thank Dr. A.D. Mishra, Prof. J.N. Sharma, Prof. A. Nag, Dr. D.K. Padhi and Dr. B.K. Dash for their inspiration, valuable suggestions and help at different stages of the preparation of the manuscript.

I earnestly express my thanks to Smt. S. Mohapatra, Principal, Panchayat College, Bargarh and my friends, wellwishers and colleagues Dr. M. Sahu, Prof. P.C. Mallick, Dr. S.K. Dash and Dr. D.K. Rout for their kind help and encouragement for pursuing this task.

I thank the members of my family, especially my wife Mili and my daughters, Mama and Niki, for their encouragement and backup during the long hours of work for this volume.

I also appreciate the difficult task of Sri P.K. Pattnaik who has done all my typing works without any complain.

Last but not the least I thank my publisher for publishing this volume, without whose help the entire efforts would have been wasted.

A.N. PANDA

Contents

1

Introduction

A.N. Panda

Women in general and women in traditional societies in particular have been given a secondary status and their problems have continuously been neglected. If their difficulties have been given attention in any occasion then these have been considered along with the difficulties of other sections of society. The shortcomings of women have rarely been regarded as the shortcomings of a group which has a separate identity and in need of a special contemplation. Women have always been regarded as the recipients of the consequences of any policy decision. They are generally excluded from the decision making process and not encouraged to initiate any move which is likely to challenge the prevailing social notions and destabilize the social order.

Even in those countries which boast of having egalitarian social systems and democratic political orders the cause of women has not been given due importance. There also women have been marginalized in different spheres. In those countries also women have not been able to reach positions of authority, especially in political fields. For example, in a democratic country like the United States of America, till now there has not been an occasion when a woman has been elected as the President of the country. Likewise, it is not Great Britain, which has been practising democracy for several centuries and commands the credit of being the mother of Parliamentary democracy, to become the first country in the world to grant the voting right to women; the honour of enfranchising women goes to a country like New Zealand, which began the era of introducing liberal democracy in the world by granting voting right to women in 1893.

Political participation of a group is conditioned to a great extent by its status in the social system. Though other aspects like education, occupation, economic standard, exposure to outside world, political socialization, individual aptitude, nature of the political system, etc. affect the involvement of a person in the political activities in the country these factors are also controlled by the social environment. Therefore, the position of women in society has a corresponding effect in their political engagements. As women are generally accorded a secondary social rank, they are normally not found to be more active in the political sphere. In short, it can be said that social status of a woman is instrumental in creating a positive or negative environment for her political participation.

Different scholars have time and again raised the issues concerning women and tried to analyze the problems of women from women's perspectives. However, there is always a need for such a study as the problems of women remain unsolved and many queries continue to remain unanswered. In spite of the sincere efforts of many researchers and writers many aspects of women's involvement in political arena go unexplored and those concerned with women studies still find the women issues fascinating and challenging. Making a study of the status, empowerment and political participation of women still provides an interesting area of political enquiry.

It is more interesting to be familiar with the problems of women of a traditional society such as India. India presents the example of a society divided and sub-divided into many castes, creeds, religions, linguistic groups, ethnic groups and such other divisions and sub-divisions. People in this country are swayed by many primordial considerations and even now different groups retain their own separate identities and cultures. It is well remarked that India is a country divided by itself. However, in spite of these factors which are responsible for dividing the country into many groups and sub-groups, it still continues as a country where unity is also a discerning fact. Therefore, it is also remarked that 'there is unity in diversity in India'.

The position of women in India has varied from one of high social status and dignity to a secondary rank. In the ancient period women had perfect equality with their male counterparts and they used to enjoy power and prestige in all spheres. Their contributions to the continuity and progress of the Indian society have been eulogized and many verses are written in their honour. But gradually they lost their importance and social standing due to the wrong decisions imposed by the male dominated social order.

However, this discrimination in the social system against women has not gone without protest. Many a time, social activists have raised their voice against the evil practices practised against women in the Indian society. Many social reformers have attempted to ameliorate the bad condition of women and tried to elevate women from a position of degradation to that of reverence. They had, time and again, tried to emphasize the importance of women and make people aware of the positive contributions made by women towards the existence and welfare of the human race. In this respect, both male and female reformers were actively championing the cause of women. The contributions of social reformers like Dayanand Saraswati, Keshab Chandra Sen, Raja Ram Mohan Rai, Sarojini Naidu, Annie Besant, Pandita Rama Bai, Rama Bai Ranade and others can be cited as examples.

During the freedom struggle women got an opportunity to show their mettle against the foreign rulers; but more importantly, this opportunity enabled them to make the society aware of their plight as well. As they continued to make contributions towards attaining the national goal they also put forth their demands in different forums. As a result, many reforms were affected to improve the conditions of women in India and some scopes were provided to them in a limited way. The result can be seen in the legislative enactments like laws against Sati or the provision for giving them limited voting rights in the later stages of the British rule.

A turning point in the women movement in India was the independence of the country from the British in 1947. With independence came the possibility for enabling women to have equality in the socio-economic-political sphere. The Constitution of India guaranteed gender equality and positive discrimination in favor of women at one stroke; it liberated them from the many age old practices, at least theoritically. In the later years, the Government of India in its various policies and plans took different measures to provide women their rightful dues in India and empower them by passing various laws; especially, the 73rd and 74th Constitutional Amendments helped women in their march towards political empowerment while making provisions for one third reservation of seats for women at the grassroots levels.

All these developments in India present new vistas of women studies. The glorious period of gender equality, the intervening period of subjugation of women and the emerging trends in women's participation in the political field as a result of their empowerment offer many interesting aspects of study concerning the women in India.

In this present volume, consisting of many enlightening and investigative articles, many writers have tried to comprehend some problems concerning women in India and put forward their own ideas. They have studied different aspects of the problems of women in this country and analyzed those problems from their own points of view. This volume contains academic inputs offered by different research scholars ranging from the study of the position of women in ancient India to the position of women in modern India to the efforts of the Government to empower the women in India to the political involvement of Indian women in the political process of the country.

The first article, "Situating Indian Women in Proper Perspective: A Framework for Analysis" by Dr. A.N. Panda deals with the concepts of Status, Political Participation and Empowerment and suggests these three concepts are linked in the context of Indian women. It gives a picture of the status of women in the Indian society. From this article a description of the women movement in the world for gender equality and political empowerment can be found. While describing the Indian situation the author narrates the movement in India for removing the shortcomings of women. He also discusses the various provisions in the Indian Constitution, the different legislations made in India, the different efforts made and the policies adopted by the Government in various five year plans and the executive actions taken concerning the women of the country.

The article ends with the highlights of the need for empowerment of the Indian women for removing their handicaps. It suggests making the legal provisions operational so that women in India are really benefited.

Professor J.N. Sharma has traced the status of women in ancient period in India in his paper "Status of Women in Ancient India" by presenting a description of the position of women as depicted in the scriptures like Rigveda and Manusmriti and argued how women of that period enjoyed freedom and equality in society like their male colleagues. He has further stated that the Indian tradition regards a woman as the other half of a man and it visualizes both man and woman complementary of each other. He has emphasized how without his female partner a man is not permitted to perform religious rites. The position of women during ancient period was never a position of degradation or neglect. During that period there were many great persons who longed for a daughter. Substantiating his points of view by ample evidences cited from many scriptures and reputed works he has ably presented his analysis of the status of women in ancient India. He has proceeded to affirm that the vested interests of some sections of society were responsible for degrading the position of women and curtailing their liberty and rights.

Dr. D.K. Padhi has dealt with the status of women through the ages in his paper "Women in India, Down the Ages" and has outlined the position of women at different periods in India. In his paper he has covered the status of women in

Vedic period and shown with the help of sufficient proofs quoted from the ancient Indian scriptures that women in that age though enjoyed virtue sometimes they were denigrated. In later periods they were relegated to a secondary position.

In modern India the worth of women is not given proper recognition. The Constitution of India grants women equality with men and allows them all facilities for their uplift. However, in spite of the Constitutional provisions and efforts of Government the status of women has not improved. Women in India continue to be malnourished, their literacy rate remains low, their health problems remain unattended and their contribution to society remains unrecognized. On the contrary, women are subjected to maltreatment; they are open to hazards of technological development and face threats in the form of dowry deaths, divorce and deprivation of inheritance rights. He has argued for taking remedial measures to rectify the disadvantageous social rank of women.

Dr. H.N. Pradhan in his paper "Working Women and Law in India" has tried to present a picture of the laws related working women in India. He has begun his paper by pointing out the changing position of women in India at different times. He has highlighted how the Indian situation is unfavourable to women. He has attempted to justify his contention by giving the example of the provisions existing in India concerning to marriage.

He has proceeded to analyse the working condition and the existing laws in India which regulate the situation at workplace. He has dealt with the judgements of Supreme Court of India in sexual harrassment cases and other laws which provide for maintaining a healthy condition for women at workplace. He has discussed the Constitutional stipulations, the Equal Remuneration Act, the Maternity Benefit Act and the Factory Act to narrate the provisions for women at workplace.

The paper of Dr. Gautam Vir "Status of Women in Rural India and their Role in Rural Development" deals with the status of women in rural India and the contribution they make in rural development. The author has narrated the position of women in different religions, especially in Hinduism and

Islam and he has pointed out the disadvantages faced by women in society. He has also given a description of the various provisions mentioned in the Indian Constitution with regard to women.

The article goes on to describe the different schemes launched by government for the benefit of women. The author argues that without the involvement of women it is not possible to achieve rural development. Moreover, he emphasizes on the positive role the voluntary organizations can play in improving the condition of women in India.

Dr. Ashutosh Pandey and Smt. Archana Pandey in their article, "Empowerment of Rural Women through Development: Need for a Changing Perspective in India" begin with a brief presentation on the condition of Indian women and the need to frame a development strategy taking into account women's perspective in the development approach, especially while proposing development measures in the rural areas. They go on to argue how women's productive efforts have been ignored down the ages and how without their involvement no development effort can succeed.

The paper brings to light the accomplishments of many women leaders and in spite of the exemplary performance of these leaders how the potentialities of women have been sidelined. They give a narration of the condition of Indian women, particularly the women of rural India and champion for the imperative need for removing the deficiencies of these women to achieve true development. They also emphasize that private initiatives can be made to bring a positive result in the development of the country.

Prof. Sushma Yadav begins her article "Women and Development: Innovative Strategies" with a detailed description of the concept of development and emphasizes the need for adopting a gender approach in the process of development to really help women. She argues that development process should be women related so that it can remove the inadequacies of women. She points out the necessity for adopting specific policies for the development of women.

She further adds that there is a shift in the focus of development strategy. Presently, more attention is given in the development process to the issues at the grassroots level. In this context there is a growing importance of the involvement of women in grassroots politics. The State has adopted the Empowerment approach to remove the handicaps of women. As a result of the various proactive steps taken by the Government there are a large number of women leaders at the grassroots level, though they encounter some problems while functioning as the representatives of people.

She has highlighted that it is imperative to involve women in the development projects at lower level and to make them partners in the development process and for this, it is necessary to make them genuinely empowered and overcome their difficulties. She has called for adopting an innovative approach to involve the women at the grassroots level to make the development process successful.

The article of Dr. M.V.S. Koteswara Rao and Dr. B.P.C. Bose, "National Policy for the Empowerment of Women 2001—An Appraisal" has begun with a description of the pitiable condition of the women in India. It describes the concept of empowerment and how the needs of empowerment of Indian women are felt in the post-independence period and how various steps have been taken towards this goal in this country. Against this background it analyses the "National Policy 2001" for the empowerment of women.

The "National Policy 2001" has been divided into 17 sections. After recognizing the gap between the development goals and the situational reality in India, it proceeds to emphasize the necessity for introducing various changes into the legal system to make it gender sensitive and more responsive. It underlines the development process and socio-economic-political empowerment of women and the different steps to be taken to achieve these goals. It also acknowledges the positive role of the voluntary organizations to achieve this objective. The writers not only deal with these aspects but also point out the defects of the policy and raise different relevant questions with regard to the prospects of the policy.

Dr. K. Chandra Kumar's article "Strategies for

Empowerment of Women in India—A Review" has begun by presenting a picture of the poor in India and painted a grim picture of women in India, particularly those who live in rural areas. At the same time he has appreciated the different plans implemented by the Government for the uplift of women, specifically he has described the different policies adopted by the Government in different Five Year Plans.

He has also praised the other different schemes such as the Functional Literacy of Adult women, the scheme for setting up Women's Training Centers for the rehabilitation of Women in Distress etc. to help the cause of women. He has presented a detailed list of the efforts of the Government in this direction. He ends his article with a positive note and expects that the Indian women are at the cross road and they can play an instructional role in the development process of the country and their life as well.

The article of Dr. V. Divya Thejo Murthy, "Women Empowerment: New Initiatives in Voluntary Action" begins by emphasizing on the need for searching for an appropriate approach to bring development to India in the 21st Century. He argues that India should make efforts in this direction like China. He has called for the need of international cooperation to end the problems of mankind. He has drawn the attention of the readers to the important role of voluntary organizations to solve the problems of the needy people and the part they can play in empowering women. He has pointed out that these organizations can be very effective in checking the violation of the rights of women.

He has made a study of Andhra Pradesh in this context and described how the Self Help Groups and DWCRA groups have played their significant role in the fields of literacy, health, hygiene, nutrition, income, popularizing small family norm and empowerment of women. He has concluded that these groups have brought transformation in Andhra Pradesh, particularly in the countryside of the state. He has also appreciated the role of the Government of Andhra Pradesh.

In their article, "Empowerment of Indian Women: The Case of Self Help Groups in Andhra Pradesh", Prof. M Bapuji and Dr. Md. Mastanvali have addressed the impact of the latest strategy of Self Help Groups pursued by the Government for women empowerment in India with a particular reference to Andhra Pradesh. The authors have analyzed the concept of empowerment in the context of the Indian women and how it helps in increasing their capacity. They have narrated the lower status of women in India and stressed their less participation in the political process of the country. They have traced the history of empowerment of Indian women and discussed the different steps taken by the Government for this purpose.

After briefly examining the concept of empowerment the article presents a picture of the special initiatives including the Self Help Groups strategy for the empowerment of women in India. The achievements of Self Help Groups and their impact on the women of Andhra Pradesh is the main thrust of this article. The article argues that the Self Help Groups strategy in Andhra Pradesh is a success story and a valuable experience. The authors have discussed how the government of Andhra Pradesh has utilized the services of these groups in poverty alleviation efforts, particularly in removing the poverty of the rural women. The authors have argued that these Groups can play a more crucial role in empowering the poor women if the lapses in this scheme are identified and rectified.

Dr. A.D. Mishra in his paper "Empowerment through Political Participation" highlights the secondary position of women and how they have been subjected to different kinds of exploitation and how they have been sidelined in the political field. He has analyzed the concept of political participation from the perspective of women and stated how women have been marginalized in spite of the increasing amount of participation by them. He has summarized that the involvement of women in political field is essential for overall socio-economic changes.

He has dealt with the participation of women in the political process of India and presented the picture of women's participation in different elections in different capacities. He has discussed the various problems women face in course of their participation. He has also suggested the different ways for removing the hurdles in women's political participation.

Dr. Rajendra Bharti's paper "Political Participation of Women in Local Administration in India and Globalization" begins with a discussion of the status of women and deals with the concepts of political participation, local administration and globalization. He has described the changing picture of local administration in view of the new incorporations made in the Indian Constitution in the shape of the 73rd and 74th Amendments.

In his article Dr. Bharti has tried to find out the new challenges local administration faces in an era of globalization and what role women can play in the changing situation. In this context he has emphasised the importance of the involvement of women in local administration. He has concluded that local administration has to be overhauled to make it more effective and be useful to meet the new challenges in the period of globalization.

Dr. Sweta Mishra's article, "Women and Political Participation in India" begins with a presentation of the deploring state of women in India and depicts how women in India have been living in a state of neglect. It describes the concept of political participation, its meaning and purpose and explains how participation is necessary in the context of removal of the various shortcomings of women. While presenting the historical background of participation of women she points out how women of India had participated in the freedom struggle of the country under the leadership of Gandhi. She has also underlined the role of women in trade union movement, principally the participation of women under the leadership of Ambedkar. In her paper, she has given importance to the contributions of women leaders like Sarojini Naidu, Annie Besant, Bi Amma, Kasturba Gandhi, Kamaladevi Chattopadhyay and Rajkumari Amrit Kaur.

She has dealt with the participation of women in different positions after independence. She has described the percentage of women in the legislatures, in the councils of ministers, in the political parties and their effectiveness in these political institutions.

Though women have played many effective roles in the

political system their contributions are not duly recognized and other women are not given encouragement to enter into the decision making institutions. She has made suggestions for more women participation and argued for making reservation for women in different political bodies.

Dr. M.M.S. Negi, in his article "Voting Participation of Women in India: A Case Study of Uttaranchal with Special Reference to Garhwal" has highlighted the different events leading to the attainment of voting rights by the women of India. After dealing with the concept of voting participation he has proceeded to describe the voting participation of women in Garhwal, a district in Uttaranchal.

After describing the universe of study he has presented an analysis of voting participation of women by age, marital status, caste, education, family income, occupation, family structure, political socialization and political awareness. He has tried to give a picture of voting participation of the women in the Garhwal region.

Smt. Gayatri Mishra and Dr. A.N. Panda in their article "Political Participation of Women Leaders: A Case Study in Orissa" present a picture of the participation of the positional women leaders at the district level by making a case study of Sundargarh district in Orissa.

After briefly explaining the concept of political participation and giving a broad picture of the universe of study, they proceed to describe the various political activities of the women leaders at the Zilla Parishad level. Adopting an empirical method of data collection, which is also supported by library works, they have attempted to give the description of the involvement of women leaders in different political activities. They have studied the participation of women during the time of voting as well as at the time when there is no election. They have analyzed the data, drawn conclusions and presented the findings in a tabular form.

In her article "The Problems of Working Women in India" Dr. Ashu Pasricha has paid attention to the changed nature work setting and how women have to work outside their home and how they have been marginalized in the occupational hierarchy due to professionalisation of occupation. She has discussed the changing nature of occupation and its effects on women, chiefly in the context of the rural women in the developing countries. She has discussed the relationship between women and economy and highlighted how the importance of women has been overlooked in the past.

She has also objected to clubbing together the entire working women into one group and the lack of understanding with regard to the problems of the working women. She has discussed the problems of both the skilled and unskilled women. She has analyzed the problems of working women from socio-psychological points of view and the different hardships faced by women in the work place.

Dr. Parvathy, A. in her article "Uniform Civil Code and Gender Justice: A Critical Perspective" analyses the need for a Uniform Civil Code from women's perspective. She points out that a Uniform Civil Code in India is very intimately connected with the issue of gender justice and despite its importance the basic issue of ensuring justice and equality to women is getting enmeshed in many other issues like religion, secularism, freedom and so on. She argues that the main issue can not be swept away under the carpet and gender issue need to be dealt with all seriousness.

In her paper she has explained the constitutional position of Uniform Civil Code and discussed the debates in the Constituent Assembly on the issue. Then she has proceeded to examine the Supreme Court cases related to women which have prompted the court to give direction to the Government for the implementation of the Uniform Civil Code. After giving the description of the initial attempts made by the legislature to bring about a Uniform Code in the form of the Hindu personal Code she has presented a general and critical perspective on various questions raised in connection with gender injustice and inequality. Dr. Parvathy has concluded the paper with a suggestion that it is necessary to have a Uniform Civil Code from the point of view of bringing equality between communities and between men and women.

Dolly Phukhon's paper "Women and Politics of Peace Process in North-East India" has dealt with the problems of women in the North East India. She has described the ethnic conflict in the North-east and its negative impacts in the area. She has highlighted the plights of women because of the conflicts among different groups in the region and the heavy price they have been paying as a result of the conflicts.

She has emphasized the role women have played in the peace process in the area. She has described the women movements in different states in the region and how the women groups have been active in the area to sutain peace and development. She has also stressed the role of some individual women in this regard. She has concluded her observation by making a reference to the need for further reseach in this direction.

The last article "Prospects for Indian Women" by Dr. A.N. Panda describes the important role women have played in the country and how they can be more effective if they are given proper scope in the socio-economic-political process of the country. He concludes his paper with a positive note by saying that women in India have suffered a lot but gradually their worth has begun to be recognized and there are better prospects in future for women in India.

2

Situating Indian Women in Proper Perspective: A Framework for Analysis

A.N. Panda

Status, Political Participation and Empowerment of Women

It is agreed by the demographers that women constitute about half of the population of the world. It is also a world phenomenon that their importance and status are not duly recognised in most of the countries. Though the civil societies in different countries vary in terms of their nature of formation, customs and social practices, manner of stratification, socio-economic-political arrangements and legal-judicial provisions for providing rights and liberties to the people, one aspect which is common to most countries is that women are not given due importance in their civil societies. In this respect there is no difference between the societies in many developing countries and those in many developed nations.

The inferior status of women in society is sanctioned by different religions. While describing the role and functions of women different religions have enjoined women to play a supplementary role and follow their male counterparts. "According to Manu (Laws of Manu, Chapter 10, p. 51), a woman is never fit for independence, because her father protects her in childhood, her husband in youth, her sons in old age. Hindu religion considered sons as essential to the family since sons alone could offer oblations to their departed ancestors and save them from suffering a spell in hell. The daughter could not perform these rites and was therefore considered as inferior to the son. The ancient Roman, Greek, and Egyptian civilisations were no exception wherein the status of women was inferior to that of man. England, which boasts of an ancient democratic tradition, gave its women a right to vote only in the year 1918. Like Hindu religion, other religions such as Islam and Christianity also placed women on a much lower pedestal than that of men."[1]

Thus, the secondary status of women is based on religious beliefs and social practices and the importance of women is not properly recognised in almost all countries. The nations have not accorded women a position of dignity consonant with their numerical strength and the valuable contributions made by them towards the continuity of the social order have been continuously ignored. Women constitute the largest neglected group in the world and suffer varieties of constraints in different countries in different respects. But when the relative rank of the women of the western and non-western countries is compared the women of the third world states lag considerably behind their equals in the western countries. They remain backward, uneducated and neglected in these countries. The male dominated social orders supported by traditions, customs and religious faiths do not acknowledge the principle of gender equality. The effects of the women's disadvantageous social position are also reflected in these countries in their less participation in economic and political spheres. The male-female participation in the socio-economic-political sphere is marked by a high degree of inequality and an utter disregard for the sacrifice made by women. India is no exception to this practice.

Though many attempts have been made in the past by different persons in different countries to affect gender equality, nothing concrete has been achieved. The different movements for bringing social reforms in this direction have not improved the social status of women. Women have been continuously relegated to the position of suppliants and their demands have been continually ignored by the masters of the social systems. The decisions concerning women have been taken without their consent and as a result they continue to suffer because of the unfavourable decisions taken by the male decision-makers.

One way of rectifying this adverse position of women is to give them adequate representation in the decision-making system in the political field. If women have an equal share of political power with their male equivalents and are able to take decisions which affect their life, they will be able to overcome their shortcomings and can be truly equal with their male collea A congenial form of government based on the equality of all citizens is a prerequisite to attain this goal and among all the existing systems of government, democracy is best suited for this purpose. A democratic form of government is citizen oriented; it gives importance to the affairs of the individual and allows popular participation in the decision making process.

Participation of citizens in the political process of a country constitutes the basic foundation of modern democracies. It ensures the enjoyment of political rights by citizens and protects their interests while decisions are made and executed. Through their political participation the citizens of a country can propose alternative solutions to public problems. Without the involvement of all sections of people in the political system democracy in a country can not function satisfactorily and survive for a long period. Political participation helps in building a healthy political culture within a country. "Participation has developmental or educative effects to the extent that the process of participation itself changes participants by developing in them new values, attitudes, skills, knowledge and beliefs."[2] Political participation is the best safeguard against the erosion of democratic values in society. However, in all most all countries of the world, all groups are not given their justified share of political power and women constitute such a group in many countries.

Though the significance of participation in the political, process is acknowledged by all, the political theorists have not forwarded a definition or a meaning of political participation which is acceptable to all. The views of the scholars differ with regard to the definition, meaning, content and purpose of political participation. But it is agreed that participation is 'an episodic public act of private individuals in the pursuit of their wants.'[3]

While participating in the political process of a country citizens perform certain activities for a definite objective. "Political participation refers to those activities by private citizens that are more or less directly aimed at influencing the selection of governmental personnel and/or the actions they take."[4] Political participation is a process by which people engage themselves in political activities to show their preferences. While participating in the political activities of the country people assert themselves and try to protect their own interests against the interests of their opponents.

The competition among the citizens prevailing in the political system is reflected in their participation. They try to motivate the decision makers to consider their demands positively and get a favourable result. In this process they not only seek to influence the decision makers but also support the latter as long as the latter contribute towards protecting their interests. Thus, political participation means "those activities of citizens that attempt to influence the structure of government, the selection of government authorities, or the policies of government. These activities either may be supportive of the existing policies, authorities, or structure, or they may seek to change any or all of these."[5]

Though in political participation much emphasis is put on voting by individuals and for the laymen, political participation generally means selecting the rulers through voting, the act of political participation is not limited to only voting. "Most discussions of citizen action equate the public's participation in politics with the act of voting. Although voting is the most visible and widespread form of citizen action, it certainly is not the only means of citizen input."[6] Citizens also remain politically active at a time when there is no election. Political participation is a continuous process in which people remain engaged even during a time when there is no election. Besides voting at the time of election, citizens perform other political activities to show their political choices and influence the decision makers to extract a preferred judgement.

Hence, whenever citizens are involved in the process of decision making they take part in the political process. Numerous activities are performed by the people while they remain active in the political system of a country. "Participation consists of many things, such as voting, conducting revolutions, forming parties and leading them, managing bureaucracies and rioting. Despite this diversity, however, all forms of participation consist of action and therefore, involve that kind of decision –making which is the selection of one action out of a set of alternative actions."[7]

Political participation can be of different types. It may be active or passive. It is active when it is goal-oriented or instrumental and passive when it implies or means mere observation; for example, the act of following some political developments attentively without being involved can be regarded as passive political participation. It may also be conventional or unconventional.[8] When participation is according to the accepted norm of the dominant group it is regarded as conventional; if not, it is regarded as unconventional; in the unconventional sense, though the form of participation is legal it is not accepted by the dominant group as permissible. A distinction is also made between symbolic and instrumental political participation;[9] some acts, such as, saluting the national flag, singing the national anthem, reciting the pledge of allegiance, etc. are examples of symbolic political participation. Instrumental participation deliberately attempts to achieve a definite goal. "Political participation as instrumental action is performed with a view to obtaining a specific personnel or policy out come."[10]

In addition, political participation can be broader or narrower taking into account the nature and extent of involvement in the political process and the issues at stake. While one is very involved in all kinds of political activities it can be regarded as political participation in the broader sense, but when it is limited to only some definite activity like voting in the election or performing an activity to achieve a specific goal it can be regarded as narrower political participation.

Political participation can also be violent and peaceful. When the act of participation is associated with violence it is violent political participation; for example, the act of rioting for or against some political goal can be considered as violent political participation. But political participation is peaceful when it is devoid of violence; for example, peaceful demonstration in support or against some public policy can be regarded as peaceful political participation.

Political participation serves many useful purposes. It links the individuals with the political system of a country as citizens select the leaders who man the decision making centre and is instrumental in channelling the demands of the people to the decision-makers. Through their participation citizens communicate their preferences to the decision-makers. Further, political participation generates a sense of involvement of the individual with the decision making system of a country. It plays such a pivotal role in the political system of a country that it is considered as an end in itself. "Participation is important not only because it communicates the citizen's needs and desires to the government, but because it has other, more direct benefits. Some have argued that it is, in itself, a prime source of satisfaction—satisfaction with the government and satisfaction with one's role. Furthermore, it has been viewed as an educational device through which "civic virtues" are learned."[11] It not only politically socialises the individual to be an effective citizen of the state but also gives continuity to the political culture of a country. Political participation gives more credibility to the political process of a country because the citizens do not feel alienated.

Hence, it is essential to encourage political participation of all the people of society to ensure their involvement in the mainstream political process and make them a part of the political system of a country, to provide continuity to the political culture of the country and induct new members into its political tradition and finally, inculcate among the people a healthy trend of becoming the effective citizens of the state. But in reality, due to a variety of reasons, all sections of society do not enjoy equal opportunity to be active in the political process of a country.

In almost all countries, women constitute one of such groups who encounter many constraints in the political sphere and are prevented to be active participants. As the political system is a sub-system of society, the social position of women has an effect on their chance for getting involved in the political field. "The ubiquity of women's secondary political status demonstrates how politics is intertwined with other aspects of life. We see politics, economics, culture, religion and law as mutually constitutive, each creating itself and the others at the same time. The secondary status of women in each realm is reinforced by the total pattern of men's privileges. But each sphere of society also creates unique elements of gender inequality and its own opportunity for resistance, innovation, and transformation."[12]

The extent to which citizens participate in the political process is determined by their social background. Their status in the social sphere very often influences their engagement in different political activities. "Citizens of higher social and economic status participate more in politics."[13] "Individuals of higher social status develop such civic orientations as concern for politics, information and feeling of efficacy, and these orientations in turn lead to participation."[14] Likewise, it depends on the political situation of a country to allow more or less participation by its citizens. If the political environment is congenial for the greater involvement of people the level of participation by citizens is more.

Though women comprise about half the population, they are not adequately represented in the decision making systems in almost all countries. Their secondary social status is reflected in the scope available to them to perform in the political field. It is forgotten that if the interests of women are neglected the maintenance of social order is negatively affected, because not only women account for about half of the population but also they are the backbone of the social system as they support the other half of society in different ways. Their cause can be neglected only at the peril of the social system itself.

To make women a part of the political process some countries have expected the various machineries of the political system to evolve their own mechanism to give due representation to women. In some states, it is made binding on the political parties to recruit women leaders. Still in some other countries, the law takes a proactive stand by making provisions for women's association in the political field. One sure way of ensuring their political participation is to empower them.

The empowerment approach is considered as the best approach because through empowerment, a special provision is made in the legal system and a particular section is given an additional chance to take part in the decision making process where the traditional practices impede its participation. By enacting some legislation protective discrimination is made in favour of the disadvantaged section. Besides, various agencies of the state are required to provide the necessary scope to the neglected category on a compulsory basis. It is also suitable to reach quick results because in the normal course, the disadvantaged people get the opportunity only at a much later stage or sometimes, they may not get it at all.

Therefore, the empowerment approach has been followed in many countries to rectify the defects of the social system and enhance the prospects of women's political participation. As a consequence, women in many countries have gained entry into the centres of decision-making. But the attainment of political power by the women has not been a smooth affair. They had to wage a stiff struggle to attain this goal and that too it has been achieved after a pretty long period.

Movement for Equality in Europe

The women liberation movement began in the late 1960s primarily in America.[15] The earlier women leaders, since the colonial period up to 1920, had followed a masculine model. They had accepted the male version of the role of women with regard to education, work and democracy and considered the superiority of men as rational.[16] From 1920s through 1950s feminism remained dormant. But in 1960s feminism adopted an aggressive posture and demanded equality with men.[17] "The 1960s witnessed a rapid increase in the creation or growth of organisations that expressed the policy concerns women and worked to gain an effective public policy on issues of particular interest to women."[18] During the twentieth century women fought for civil rights and equality. State concentrated on women as biological reproducers and emphasised on their wider role within the family.[19]

The demand for equality between men and women began early in the form of different social movements. Later it took the form of franchise movement for women. The different social movements aimed at improving the status of women facilitated the enfranchisement movement because the women acted as powerful pressure groups in different contexts. The importance of women and the rights of women were recognised as a result the different movements and revolutions though those were not primarily aimed at either equality between men and women or the political rights of women. For example, during the French Revolution, demand was made for freedom and equality in general. The ideals of liberty, equality and fraternity were considered as the basic rights of all human beings. Later these ideals formed the basis of different social movements in different countries for protecting the interests of different oppressed classes.[20]

America has also made certain contributions towards the political rights of women. The feminist movement in America began as early as 1848 as a result of the women rights convention called in Seneca-Falls, New York.[21] The women movement in America basically grew out of the anti- slavery movement.

"Women's acquisition of political and legal rights has been the result of two distinct women's political movements, each of which has two phases. In the first phase of the first women's movement (the first six decades of the nineteenth century), women demanded basic rights. Perhaps best known is the wide range of policy demands contained in the Declaration of Rights issued by Seneca Falls Convention in 1848. This phase culminated in the unsuccessful drive to include guarantees of legal and political rights for women in the post-Civil War amendments to the United States Constitution, which conferred the legal rights of citizenship, including the right to vote, on black males."[22]

"The second phase of the first women's movement, which

was dominated by disputes about both the issue agenda that should be pursued and the most appropriate means for seeking policy change, culminated in the ratification of the women's suffrage amendment to the Constitution in the 1920. Women have acquired other rights as a result of court decisions and the enactment of federal and state laws during the nineteenth and twentieth centuries."[23]

'Though women movement remained dormant during the period from 1920 to 1960 many changes took place in American society during this period which gave rise to the first phase of the second women movement in the 1960s. This phase raised women's political and social consciousness about policy problems and the denial of their basic rights. Women became aware of the effectiveness of collective actions in bringing about political and social change. The 1960s also saw the growth of organisations that expressed public concerns of women and emphasised on issues of particular interest to women; for example, the National Organisation for Women was established on October 29, 1966 and this could be regarded as the beginning of the second phase of the second women movement. The National Organisation of Women highlighted the issues like enforcement laws prohibiting gender discrimination in employment, provision for adequate child care for families of employed women, maternity leave for employed women, fair tax treatment for employed women and equal access to all fields of education.'[24]

However, New Zealand had begun the process of granting political rights to women much earlier. "Modern liberal democracy came into being in 1893, when New Zealand offered the franchise to women. The Commonwealth state was the first to institutionally open up the public sphere to both men and women."[25]

By the end of the Nineteenth century, New Zealand was the only country to have given women the right to vote; but by 1945, nearly half of the 51 original members of the United Nations had guaranteed women the right to vote. In 1966, 114 out of the 125 countries of the world had granted right to vote to women. Presently, all modern democracies grant women the right to vote.

But women are poorly represented in political field throughout the globe. "Women make up less than five per cent of the world's heads of the State, heads of major corporations and top positions in international organisations."[26] "In Britain, where women were granted franchise way back in 1918, the first woman member took her seat in 1919. In 1970 election, only 26 were returned to the House of Commons, which constituted only 4.1 per cent of the total membership. In US, where women got franchise as far back as August 1920, there were only 10 members, 2.03 per cent only, in House of Representatives, which was comprised 435 members in the early 1970s."[27]

The Indian Scenario

The position of women in India has varied from one period to another. At the early period of the Indian society women were accorded due prestige and they enjoyed equal rights with their male counterparts. The importance of women had been recognised in different contexts and they had attained positions of prestige and power. They could venture into the fields of education and wealth and had the liberty to choose their life partners. However, later their position deteriorated in society and they were generally assigned a secondary position.

In this male dominated society, women were regarded as performing a subordinate role and they were to supplement the efforts of their male counterparts in society. Accordingly, the process of induction of the girl child into the social system was determined to enable her to perform her secondary role in the society. Gradually she was excluded from positions of power, prestige and dignity. She was prevented from taking decisions and she became not the initiator of a decision rather the subject of the decision made by the male dominated decision making system. "Socialisation of the girl child in our country has followed a set pattern for millennia, where she has been trapped and moulded by deep –rooted combined cultures of patriarchy and hierarchy. Women are considered a population at risk because of their limited access to resources and opportunities and their systematic exclusion from positions of decision making."[28] Women had to fit into the male version of social and moral orders.

The fundamentalists of different religions imposed their own decisions on the female population and expected women to obey their decisions without any objection. These vested interest groups formulated the yardsticks of society keeping in view their own interests and kept the women folk subjugated. In India "in the name of supporting traditional law and custom, Muslim and Hindu fundamentalists have tried to reinforce the loosening shackles of medieval paternalistic morality and preserve male supremacy"[29]

Because the contribution of women to mankind has been continuously ignored by the male dominated society women have been relegated to an inferior position. "Women continue to be regarded as secondary to men because of the historical devaluation of their productive and reproductive roles."[30] The opponents of the women liberation movement influenced the decision makers and as very often they themselves were the decision makers, they did not to allow women to have equality with their male counter-parts. "The progress of women's movement toward socioeconomic justice and the end to women's subordinate status are seriously threatened by the fundamentalist and communal backlash."[31] It was difficult on the part of women to protest against their opponents as the opponents were their own men.

However, in spite of this handicap, the fight for equality and protection of women rights began long back and the struggle was continued and slowly it bore positive results. Steps were taken by the rulers to ameliorate the defects in the Indian society with regard to women. Decisions were taken to protect the interests of women and give them some respite from their suffering.

During the British rule some acts were passed to provide some relief to the Indian women. For example, the Hindu Widow Remarriage Act of 1856 and the Child Marriage Restraint Act of 1929 aimed at putting an end to the inhuman practice of condemning a Hindu widow to lead a life of misery and prohibiting the practice of getting innocent girls married at an early age or even during their infancy.

Some women leaders themselves had taken a lead to fight for the rights of women. These women became politically involved to safeguard their interests. In this respect, some male leaders also helped the women leaders. "Indian women's involvement in politics in the modern era started in the late eighteenth and early nineteenth centuries. Although British imperialism profoundly influenced the political engagement of both the elite and nonelite women during this period, its impact on the character and purposes of their engagement was different. Nonelite women fought against the British colonialists.... Elite women were mainly involved in the Indian Renaissance—the social reform movement of the nineteenth century."[32] While the non-elite women fought for their material benefits the elite women worked for different social causes under the leadership of their male equals and they put emphasis on various women related issues like female education, end of female infanticide, sati, child marriage and widow remarriage.[33] The emphasis of the movement of the elite women was "not on women's equality but, rather, on the separateness and complementarity of the roles of women and men in society"[34]

Movements for educational and social reforms had begun in India much earlier than the Movement for Independence of the country. In this respect, both male and female social reformers had taken the lead. In India, women organisations were established during the last two decades of the 19th century and the early part of the 20th century. The Ladies Association under the patronage of Brahmo Samaj at Calcutta (1886), Sri Zorostrian Mandal at Bombay (1903), Bharat Stri Mahamandal (1910), Women's India Association at Adyar, Madras (1917-37), The National Council for Women in India (1925), All India Women's Conference (1926-1932) were a few such organisations.[35]

The women leaders were also active in this regard. "Several Indian women leaders like Pandita Rama Bai (1858-1922) of Karnataka, Rama Bai Ranade (1862-1922) (wife of reformer Justice Mahadev Govind Ranade) of Maharashtra, Madam Cama (1861-1936) of Bengal, worked for the emancipation of women in the 19th century."[36]

In the 19th century, reformers like Raja Rammohan Rai,

Keshab Chandra Sen, Dayananda Saraswati and Iswara Chandra Vidyasagar worked relentlessly to bring about many changes in social, legislative and educational fields to improve the condition of women in India. Because of their persistent efforts many significant changes were brought in the condition of the Indian women.

But majority of the organisations had emphasised on educational and social reforms in general; these were not women specific. There were a few associations like the Bombay Graduate Women's Union or the Women's Branch of the Home Rule League, which were outside the realm of social refoms.[37] However, most of these organisations had neither a large following nor a national appeal. Only two organisations, the Women's Indian Association established in 1917 and the All India Women's Conference established in 1927 had branches in different parts of the country. Though initially they were working for the educational opportunities for women and improving their position through social and legal reforms, later they became interested in political rights and political participation of women.[38]

The contributions of some individual women leaders, who had made attempts to improve the condition of women in India, can not be ignored. 'In 1913, Saroj Nalini Dutt founded mahila samitis in many towns; she also started women's institutes in Bengal. In 1910, Sardadevi Choudhurani, founded Bharat Stree Mahamandal to assert an independent identity for the Indian women.'[39]

Some non-Indian women leaders also promoted the cause of emancipation of the Indian women. The first attempt to organise women on an all India basis was made by some British women like Dr. Annie Besant and Margret Cousins among others, when they formed the Women's Indian Association. Dr. Annie Besant was especially interested in the education of Indian women and she also worked for their social and political rights.[33] The formation of the Women's Indian Association was a result of the impact of the feminist movements in the west.

The Women's Indian Association was founded by Besant in 1913 in Madras. She encouraged the Indian women to join the Home Rule League and the Swadeshi movement. Another such association, the National Council of Women in India was founded in 1925 by Lady Aberdeen, Lady Tara and others. The All India Women's Conference was also founded in 1927 by Margaret Cousins and others.[41]

Before 1917 women enjoyed limited franchise in the presidencies of Bombay and Madras. As a result, it failed to make any impact on their political consciousness in Madras.[42]

The association established by Annie Besant, Women's India Association, raised the issue of women suffrage with Lord Montague and as a result, limited franchise was granted to women in India.

The Government of India Act, 1919 gave power to the Provincial Legislature to remove the inequality between men and women with regard to enfranchisement and accordingly, some Provincial Legislatures passed resolutions to enfranchise women; for example, such resolutions were passed in Madras and Bombay in 1920, in United Provinces in 1923, in Central Provinces, Bengal and Punjab in 1926.[43] But under the Act of 1919, women got only limited franchise in India. Thus, in the first election held under this Act in 1926, the enfranchised women were less than one per cent in India. In that election, the proportion of female voters to the total adult female population was one per cent in Madras, in Bombay 0.8 per cent, in Bengal 0.3 per cent, in United Provinces 0.4 per cent and in Assam 0.2 per cent. Bihar, Orissa and Central Provinces did not adopt women franchise.[44] Further, the qualifications prescribed for men and women voters were based on age and property.

However, to enlarge the female electorate, the efforts of the politically conscious women continued.[45] With this aim, an organisation named as All India Women's Conference was formed and it appointed a committee to look into the matter of enfranchising more women. This committee recommended, besides the existing qualifications of age and property, three more qualifications for giving voting right to women. The additional qualifications for granting voting right were (a) wife of a man who had property qualification and was over 25 years of age, (b) a widow of over 25 years age, if her husband was franchised at the time of his death, and (c) graduate over 25 years of age.[46]

The support for empowering women through enfranchisement continued in India. The Congress Party had supported women enfranchisement. This point of view was reflected in the Nehru Report which endorsed the principle of universal adult suffrage as the best way to emancipate women.[47]

When the Act of 1935 was passed women franchise was allowed in the election to the Central Assembly. "But the property and literacy qualifications were retained along with the age qualification in the Government of India Act 1935. According to this Act, women over 25 years of age could vote provided they were literate and owners of property or wives and widows of men having property."[48]

During the freedom struggle, the women of India had taken an active role and worked for the independence of the country. One such woman leader, Sarojini Naidu, Congress president in 1925, was responsible for building a mass support for the cause of Indian women. The women leaders believed that the emancipation of Indian women was linked to independence of India. Thus, there was involvement of a large number of women in different stages of the freedom movement such as the Non-cooperation Movement, Civil Disobedience Movement and the Quit India Movement. Under the leadership of Gandhi the women of India fought against the British. Though some women did not directly bear the brunt of the protest against the British, they suffered for the freedom of the country as they had to support their families when their husbands were away fighting against the British.

The involvement of the women in the political process of the country and their protest against injustice continued even after independence. "As a kind of continuum from the pre to postindependence and as a bridge between the political and the socioeconomic, some vary militant peasant movement of both women and men need special mention. The Tebhaga movement (1946-50) in Bengal and the Telengana (1948-51) movement in Andhra Pradesh were launched to obtain a more equitable distribution of land. In both movements women formed "women brigades" to protect villages, homes and children against police atrocities and were given guerrilla training for self defence. These two movements led to the passing of zamindari (landlordism) abolition acts in many states in the early 1950s, which granted some rights to the tillers of the land."[49]

As a result of the various efforts made by innumerable male and female leaders for bringing about positive changes in the deplorable condition of women in India, independent India adopted a number of legal provisions in the country to rectify many defects of the Indian society with regard to women. This spirit is reflected in its Constitution and different policies decided after independence.

Constitutional Provisions for Women in India

Independent India is one among the few countries where women did not have to fight for getting their political and civil rights. Independence brought with it equality in social and political spheres. It was only after independence of the country that social and political equalities were accorded to women in India along with their male counterparts while the Constitution adopted the principle of universal adult franchise and several provisions in the chapters enumerating the Fundamental Rights and the Directive Principles of State Policies. Some provisions of the Constitution are women specific whereas from some other provisions the women get benefits indirectly or by implication. If any thing, the Constitution did sanction positive discrimination in their favour and in later years also several laws have been enacted and some other policies have been adopted to provide them more scope for overcoming their age old handicaps.

The Constitution of India, besides mentioning in its Preamble that the people of India have resolved to secure all its citizens justice, liberty, equality and fraternity assuring the dignity of the individual, provides in its different articles equality for both men and women. At the same time, it makes provisions to offer special scope to the women of India for enabling them to better their position and acquire capability to be equal with the male folk of the society.

The several articles of the Constitution[50] which directly or indirectly make provision for gender equality are as follows

Article 14 – The State shall not deny to any person equality before law or equal protection of law within the territory of India. This article is the bedrock of the principle of equality guaranteed to all, men and women.

Article 15(1) – The State shall not discriminate against any citizen on grounds only of religion, race, caste, sex, place of birth or any of them. Article 15(2) – The State can make special provision for the benefit of women and children. This article provides for positive discrimination in favour of women and children.

Article 16(2) – This article provides for equality of opportunity for all citizens in matters relating to public employment. 'The State is prohibited to discriminate against women while an employment is given under any State or the Central government.'

Article 21 – In this article the Constitution guarantees right to life to all citizens.

Article 23 – The Constitution prohibits traffic in human beings.

Article 32 – This article provides for the protection of fundamental rights of the citizens of India. Thus, the Constitution not only makes provisions for fundamental rights to be enjoyed by the citizens of the state but also guarantees remedies for their enforcement.

Article 38 – The Constitution directs the state to secure a just socio-economic-political order to promote a welfare state in India. It also gives a direction to the state to remove inequalities in status, facilities and opportunities among individuals.

Article 39 – The state shall direct its policy for security of the citizens, men and women: (a) equal right to an adequate means of livelihood, (b)equal pay for equal work, (c) preservation and promotion of health and strength of workers, men, women and children against abuse.

Article 40 – The Constitution provides for the organisation of village Panchayat to promote self government in the country.

Article 41 – The state is directed to provide right to work, education and public assistance in cases of unemployment, old age, sickness, disablement and other types of undeserved wants.

Article 42 – The Constitution directs the state to make provision for just and human conditions of work and for maternity relief.

Article 43 – This article directs the state to make provision for just and human condition of work, a living wage, condition of work ensuring a decent standard of life for workers, social and cultural opportunities for all workers and the promotion of cottage industries.

Article 44 – A direction has been given to the state to secure for its citizens a uniform Civil Code throughout the territory of India.

Article 45 – The Constitution directs the state to provide free and compulsory primary education to all children up to the age of 14.

Article 51 – The Constitution has given a directive to the state to end gender based discrimination in India. It directs the citizens to renounce practices derogatory to the dignity of women.

Article 243 – In this article, a provision for one third reservation in local bodies for women has been made.

Article 326 – The principle of universal adult franchise is provided in this article.

As a consequence of independence of India from the British and the enforcement of a democratic constitution in the country women in India got the right to universal franchise and equality with their male counterparts. The constitution guarantees liberty, equality and justice to all individuals in the Indian society and promises to protect their dignity. It directs the state to safeguard the interests of all men and women.

Legal Changes in India

Apart from the different provisions of the Constitution, which are directly and by implication applicable to women, several laws have also been enacted in India before and after independence and these laws have a direct bearing on women. "Following the clear enunciation of the state's approach to women issues, the Indian legislatures have passed various laws from time to time to protect and promote the cause of women and remove their disabilities. Of course, many such laws were enacted in the earlier decades as part of the Government's efforts at social reform or labour welfare. But the post Independence era saw several of these laws being amended in response to the egalitarian urges of the new constitution."[51] The Indian Divorce Act (1869), the Married Women's Property Act (1874), the Guardians and Ward Act (1890), the Legal Practitioners (Women) Act (1923), the Indian Succession Act (1925), the Child Marriage Restraint Act (1929), the Payment of Wages Act (1936), the Muslim Personal Law (Shariat) Application Act (1937), the Minimum Wages Act (1948), the Special Marriage Act (1954), the Hindu Marriage Act (1955), the Hindu Adoptions and Maintenance Act (1956), the Immoral Traffic (Prevention) Act (1956), the Hindu Minority & Guardianship Act (1956), the Hindu Succession Act (1956), the Dowry Prohibition Act (1961), the Equal Remuneration Act (1976), the Family Court Act (1984), the Juvenile Justice Act (1986), the Child Labour (Prohibition and Regulation) Act (1986), the Commission of Sati (Prevention) Act (1987) and the Pre-Natal Diagnostic Techniques (Regulation & Prevention of Misuse) Act (1994)[52] are a few such laws.

All these laws have attempted to safeguard the interests of women in India in different respects and set right the defects of the Indian society with regard to women. These laws have tried to enhance the status of Indian women by guaranteeing them legal protection and by opposing the age old practice of keeping women subjugated by the male dominated social order. These laws have also outlawed many evil social customs which were derogative and disadvantageous to women and responsible for reducing the higher status of women to a secondary position.

Through these laws, the state has tried to remove the shortcomings of the Indian women by assuring them legal safeguards. Through these laws the state has provided the manner in which marriage can be solemnised, how women can inherit property, how a girl child can be protected even before her birth, how a woman can be protected from being exploited in different ways and such other protections concerning women.

As a result of the demands from women and pressure worldwide different countries have taken steps to make legislation in this direction and India is not an exception in this respect. The process of removing different hurdles in the path of women liberation movement accelerated with independence of India from the British. Special efforts have been made in India to help women to enhance their position.

During the period of the UN Decade for Women, 1976–85, the Equal Remuneration Act was passed in 1976, which guarantees women equal pay for equal work. Some administrative changes were also made in the Government. A Women's Department in the Ministry of Labour and Employment was created. Likewise in the Ministry of Welfare a Coordinating Bureau for Women was created. The National Commission for Women Act was passed in 1990 and the Commission was set up on 31st January, 1992. "The primary mandate of the National Commission for Women (NCW) is to seek justice for women, safeguard their rights, and promote women's empowerment. The Commission monitors the proper implementation of all the legislations enacted to protect the rights of women so as to enable them to achieve equality in all spheres of life."[53]

The Government declared the National Policy for the Empowerment of Women in 2001. This policy emphasised on economic, social and political empowerment of women and removal of the different hindrances in the path of progress of women by providing them opportunities in different fields and protecting their rights. It emphatically declared to induct women perspectives in the developmental schemes and give women importance in different levels of the decision making system.

Five Year Plans

In the different Five Year Plans also the Government made many provisions for the benefits of women. Though during the initial phases there was no direct emphasis on the welfare of women, women got benefits as one of the marginalised groups in the Indian society. The focus in this direction also varied with the passage of time. "It is convenient to divide this journey into three phases i.e. 1950s and 1960s—when the approach was welfare centred; 1970s and 1980s—when developmental issues came to the fore, and the 1990s—when the goal became women's empowerment."[54]

In the initial years of planning in India, the welfare of women was combined with the welfare of other sections of society. The cause of women was dealt along with the problems of such other under-privileged categories and all such problems were clubbed in the category Social Welfare. This approach continued more or less up to the Fourth Five Year Plan.

The developmental approach began with the Fifth Five Year Plan (1974-1979). Emphasis was given to employment of women and providing them many economic benefits. "However, in all this, the perception of the role of a woman still remained one of a homebound individual devoted to the care of the family and she was seen a client of development i.e. as the beneficiary of various services."[55]

The Sixth Five Year Plan focused on economic uplift of women and aimed at creating more opportunities for them. The importance of women was recognised and steps were taken to provide them more facilities in the employment sector. But the real shift was made in the Seventh Five Year Plan when it was realised that without the involvement of women no real development could be achieved and efforts were made to bring women into the mainstream of the developmental process. A new Department was set up namely the Department of Women and Child Development to deal with the issues concerning women.

In the nineties, empowerment was the key word and emphasis was given to empower women. It was realised that though economic benefit was essential for the development of women, mere economic advancement would not bring the desired results. Therefore, it was felt, political empowerment coupled with economic self-reliance was necessary to effect the emancipation of women. Especially, the Ninth Five Year Plan (1997-2002) gave special emphasis to the empowerment of women. "For the first time, Empowerment of Women has been mentioned as one of the nine objectives of the national Plan."[56]

The Constitution of India puts emphasis on spreading democracy at the grassroots level. It also envisages greater involvement of women in different local bodies. But as the past experiences in this regard did not reveal an encouraging result the Government wanted to rectify the defects by incorporating amendments into the Constitution. The 64th Amendment Bill of the Constitution, introduced in Lok Sabha in July 1989 proposed for reservation seats for women, but this bill was defeated in Rajya Sabha. After the defeat of this Bill another bill, the 74th Amendment Bill was introduced in Lok Sabha in 1990 which also included a provision for reservation for women. But this bill could not be passed due to the dissolution of the 9th Lok Sabha in March 1991.

But the milestone in this regard is the 73rd Amendment Act of 1993. Passed by Parliament on 22nd December 1992 and notified through Official Gazette on 20th April 1993, this Act covers a wide range of issues concerning Panchayatiraj. It provides for reservation of seats for SCs, STs, and one third reservations of seats for women. It also provides that the post of Chairman can be reserved for SCs, STs and women.

The 73rd Constitutional Amendment Act has improved the scope for political participation by women. The 73rd Amendment to the Constitution of India has brought structural changes in the grassroots democratic bodies by providing that not less than one third membership/chairpersonship be reserved for women in local self government at the rural level.

"Empowerment entails developing the ability to organize and influence the direction of social change to create a more just socio-economic order. This can be facilitated by more women becoming active and visible—in other words, with an increasing participation of women in politics."[57]

"It is important to note that these provisions bestowing absolute equality in the women in the matter of their civil or political rights were far ahead of the position prevailing in many of the western countries, where bitter battles had to be fought to extend suffrage to women."[58] However, though these provisions have been incorporated in the basic law of the country and aim at providing equal opportunity to women in all spheres, in reality the status, position and political participation of women show that a lot more has to be done in this direction. "While substantial gains have been made by the women's movement over the decades in India, this has not been adequately reflected in the representation of women in position of power."[59] To make the political rights functional mere written laws are not sufficient. Sincere efforts are needed to be made by persons with power so that the legal principles are made operative.

This point of view was corroborated by the Committee on the Status of Women which was appointed in 1975 to enquire into the condition of women. It examined the nation building process from women's perspective. The Committee concluded that as the women lacked political power commensurate with their numerical strength, they were gradually emerging as a minority group. To remedy this adverse condition, the Committee recommended that the political parties set a quota by themselves for women. It suggested for constitution of commissions both at the Centre and State level to look into the affairs of women and it made it binding on the Government to obey the recommendations of the women commissions.

Voting Participation of Women in Lok Sabha Elections

Election	*Total voters*	*Female voters*	*Male percentage*	*Female percentage*	*Total percentage*
1952	173213635				61.2
1957	193652069				62.2
1962	216372215	102427981	63.31	46.43	55.42
1967	249003334	119434730	66.73	55.48	61.33
1971	274094493	130619662	60.90	49.11	55.29
1977	321174327	154155176	65.63	54.91	60.49
1980	355590700	170380385	62.16	51.22	56.92
1984	379540608	182810109	68.18	58.60	63.56
1989	498906429	236861287	66.13	57.32	61.95
1991	498363801	236531302	61.58	51.35	56.93
1996	592572288	282756512	62.06	53.41	57.94
1998	605884103	289191475	65.72	57.88	61.97
1999	619559944	295723180	63.97	55.64	59.99
2004	671524575	322030439	61.84	53.47	57.82

Source: Election Commission of India.

But in spite of the various laws enacted by the State and different policies adopted by the Government the participation of women in political field has remained very low. If the voting participation of women in different elections to Lok Sabha can be taken as an example, as the above table shows, it has not been very encouraging.

The political parties firmly declare to give representation to the women in the political affairs. "However, women constituted a mere 3.1% of the total contestants in the 1996 election and did not occupy more than 6-10% of the total seats in State Legislative Assemblies and Parliament. Women's participation in local political institutions—village Panchayats and municipal bodies—has also remained low, in spite of the Government's policy of cooption and reservation of seats for women."[60]

In the recently held election to the lower house of Parliament, in the 2004 Lok Sabha election, the total candidates were 5435 for 543 seats out of them the number of women candidates was only 354.[61]

The representation of women in the political field is far less than what it was before independence of the country. "The irony of women's exclusion from formal politics is aptly conveyed by the situation of women in India before and after the ouster of the British. In the decades before independence, women constituted 10 per cent of those jailed for anti-British activities. In the decades since independence, however, women have never held more than 8 per cent of the seats in the Lok Sabha, the lower house of Parliament. It was easier to get arrested for supporting democracy than it is to get elected to the democratic institutions that Indian nationalists were fighting to obtain."[62] Though it has been proclaimed in the Constitution to give equality to women in every sphere with their male colleagues, in reality the picture is totally different.

It has to be realised that unless women are given their due place in society and allowed to participate in the decision making process neither society nor women are benefited. "Impressive participation in the political process, formal and informal, is not goals in themselves, they are means and strategy for achieving something more fundamental, which the group can do, only when its participation touches upon the structure of politics itself."[63] To remove the handicaps in the path of progress of women and elevate their social position it is imperative to grant women political rights which are truly operational. "Women's political empowerment and equal participation in all decision-making institutions are critical elements in the struggle against their subordinate status within the family and the society not with standing the Constitution of India guaranteeing equal rights to men and women."[64]

Even the limited number of women who are fortunate enough to have got decision making power should be more active to help their less fortunate fellow women. "Since decisions at the policy-making level affect women's lives and have a significant impact on them, it is important that more women occupy decision-making positions and those who are already there are gender-sensitized."[65] The women in power should be friendlier towards the less fortunate women.

Thus, though women are gradually coming to the forefront to claim their legitimate share in political power there is a lot to be done in respect of giving women their due place in the political field. To attain the goal of ensuring political participation by women in proportion to their number in society what is imperative is greater awareness among the political leaders of the need to make women equal partners in the development process of the country and the realisation that involvement of women is more vital for the progress of the social order. Then only the structural changes brought by the legislative measures and government policies can be truly functional. There is a necessity to bring about an attitudinal change in both men and women; without this attitudinal transformation true participation of women will be a distant dream.

References

1. *Search for a Vision Statement on Women Empowerment vis-à-vis Legislation & Judicial decisions*, National Commission for Women, New Delhi, p. 17.
2. Muller, Edward, *Aggressive Political Participation*, Princeton University Press, Princeton, New Jersey, 1979, p. 13.
3. Schwartz, Joel I., "Political Participation and Multi-subjective Understanding: An Interprotivist Approach to the Study of

Political Participation", *Journal of Politics*, Vol. 46, 1984, p. 117.

4. Verba, Sidney and Nie, Norman H., *Participation in America, Political Democracy and Social Equality*, The University Press of Chicago, Chicago, 1987, p. 2.
5. Conway, M. Margaret, *Political Participation in the United States*, Congressional Quarterly Press, Washington, 1985, p. 2.
6. Dalton, Russell J., *Citizen Politics*, Chatham House Publishers, Inc., New Jersey, 1988, p. 35.
7. Riker, Wiliam H. and Ordeshook, Peter C., *An Introduction to Positive Political Theory*, Prentice-Hall, Inc., Englewood Cliffs, New Jersey, 1973, pp. 45-46.
8. Conway, M. Margaret, *Political Participation in the United States*, Congressional Quarterly Press, Washington, 1985, p. 3.
9. *Ibid.* p. 8.
10. *Ibid.* p. 10.
11. Verba, Sidney and Nie, Norman H., *Participation in America, Political Democracy and Social Equality*, The University Press of Chicago Press, Chicago, 1987, p. 5.
12. Chowdhury, Najma; Nelson, Barbara J. and others, "Redefining Politics: Patterns of Women's Political Engagement from a Global Perspective" in Nelson, Barbara J. and Chowdhury, Najma edited *Women and Politics Worldwide*, Oxford University Press, Delhi, 1997, p. 3.
13. Verba, Sidney and Nie, Norman H. *Participation in America, Political Democracy and Political Equality*, The University of Chicago Press, Chicago, 1987, p. 125.
14. *Ibid.* p. 126.
15. Harlambos, Michael, *Sociology: Themes and Perspectives*, Oxford University Press, New Delhi, 1991, p. 403.
16. Poonacha, Veena, *Economic and Political Weekly*, October 9, 1993, p. 2193.
17. Yates, Gayle Graham, *What Women Want: The Ideas of the Movement*, Havard University Press, Cambridge, 1975, pp. 33-34.
18. Conway, M.M.; Ahern, D.A.; Steuernagel, G.A.; *Women and Public Policy*, Congressional Quarterly Press, Washington D.C., 1995, p. 7.
19. Bland, Lucy; Brunsdon, Charlotte; Hobson, Dorothy; Winship, Jenice; "Women Inside and Outside, the Relation of Reproduction" in Women Studies Group, Centre for Contemporary Cultural Studies, University of Birmingham edited *Women Take Issue, Aspects of Women Subjugation*, Hutchinson of London, 1978, p. 47.

20. Mies, Maria, "Class Struggle or Emancipation: Women's Emancipation Movement in Europe and the US", *Economic and Political Weekly*, 1973, pp. 2221-2250.
21. Good, Barbara J. "Significance of Women's Organisations in the Advancement of Women in the US", *Indian Journal of American Studies*, Vol. 13, No. 2, p. 98.
22. Conway, M.M.; Ahern,D.A.; Steuernagel, G.A.; *Women and Public Policy*, Congressional Quarterly Press, Washington DC, 1995, p. 5.
23. *Ibid*. pp. 5-6.
24. *Ibid*. pp. 6-7.
25. Reynolds, Andrew, "Women in the Legislatures and Executives of the World", *World Politics*, John Hopkins University Press, New Jersey, Vol. 51, Issue 4, July 1999, p. 547.
26. Mohanty, K.T., "Empowering Women—A Catalyst in Indian Development ", *Employment News* (Weekly) September 16, 2000, p. 1.
27. Kumari, Ranjana, "Introduction" in Stifung, Friedrich Ebert, edited *Women in Politics—Forms and Processes*, Har-Anand Publications, New Delhi, 1996, p. 5.
28. Parthasarathi, Vibha, Foreword to *A Decade of Endeavour (1990-2000)*, National Commission for Women, New Delhi, 2001.
29. Swarup, Hem Lata; Sinha, Niroj; Ghosh, Chitra; Rajput, Pam; "Women's political engagement in India: Some Critical Issues" in Nelson, Barbara J. and Chowdhury, Najma edited *Women and Politics Worldwide*, Oxford University Press, New Delhi, 1997, p. 377.
30. *A Decade of Endeavour (1990-2001)* Vol. II, National Commission for Women, New Delhi, p. 61.
31. Swarup, Hem Lata; Sinha, Niroj; Ghosh, Chitra; Rajput, Pam; "Women's Political Engagement in India: Some Critical Issues" in Nelson, Barbara J. and Chowdhury, Najma edited *Women and Politics Worldwide*, Oxford University Press, New Delhi, 1997, p. 377.
32. *Ibid*, p. 365.
33. *Ibid*, p. 365.
34. *Ibid*. p. 365.
35. Sharma, Radhakrishna, *Nationalism, Social Reform and Indian Women*, Janaki Prakashan, Patna, 1981, pp. 105-135.
36. Kuppuswamy, B., *Social Change in India*, Konark Publishers Pvt. (Ltd.), Delhi, 1994, p. 322.
37. Agnew, Vijaya, *Elite Women in Indian Politics*, Vikas Publishing House, Pvt. Ltd., New Delhi, 1979, p. 104.

38. *Ibid*, p. 104.
39. Swarup, Hem Lata; Sinha, Niroj; Ghosh, Chitra; Rajput, Pam "Women's Political Engagement in India: Some Critical Issues" in Nelson, Barbara and Chowdhury, Najma ed. *Women and Politics Worldwide*, Oxford University Press, New Delhi, 1997, p. 366.
40. Devi, Rukmini, "Dr. Annie Besant and the Indian Women's Movement", *Women's Indian Association: Golden Jubilee Number, 1917-1967*, p. 35.
41. Ali, Aruna Asaf, "Women Suffrage in India" in Nehru, Shyam Kumari ed. *Our Cause*, Kitabistan, Allahabad, 1935, p. 349.
42. Report of the Franchise Committee quoted in Agnew, Vijaya, *Elite Women in Indian Politics*, Vikas, New Delhi, p. 110.
43. Menon, Lakshmi, *The Position of Women*, Bombay, Oxford University Press, 1944, p. 27.
44. Agnew, Vijaya, *Elite Women in Indian Politics*, Vikas Publishing House Pvt. Ltd., New Delhi, 1979, p. 113.
45. *Ibid.*, pp. 112-113.
46. *Ibid.*, p. 120.
47. *Memorandum on Certain Questions affecting the Status and Welfare of Women in the Future Constitution of India*, p. 8.
48. Agnew, Vjaya, *Elite Women in Indian Politics*, Vikas Publishing House Pvt. Ltd., New Delhi, 1979, p. 124.
49. Swarup, Hem Lata; Sinha, Niroj; Ghosh, Chitra; Rajput, Pam, "Women's Political Engagement in India: Some Critical Issues" in Nelson, Barbara and Chowdhury, Najma edited *Women and Politics Worldwide*, Oxford University Press, New Delhi, 1997, p. 367.
50. Basu, Durga Das, *Introduction to the Constitution of India* (19th Edition, Reprint 2004) Wadhwa and Company, New Delhi, 2004.
51. *Gender Equity*, National Commission for Women, New Delhi, 2001, p. 4.
52. *A Decade of Endeavour (1990-2000)*, National Commission for Women, New Delhi, p. 232.
53. *Legal Awareness Programme*, National Commission for Women, New Delhi, p. 1.
54. *Gender Equity*, National Commission for Women, New Delhi, 2001, p. 15.
55. *Ibid.*, p. 27.
56. *Ibid.*, p. 21.
57. *A Decade of Endeavour (1990-2000)*, National Commission for Women, New Delhi, p. 57.

58. *Gender Equity*, National Commission for Women, New Delhi, 2001, p. 2.
59. Kumari, Ranjana, "Introduction", in Stiftung, Friedrich Ebert edited *Women in Politics—Forms and Processes*, Har-Anand Publications, New Delhi, 1996, p. 1.
60. *A Decade of Endeavour, (1990-2000)*, National Commission for Women, New Delhi, 2001, p. 57.
61. *Election Commission of India*.
62. Chowdhury, Najma; Nelson, Barbara J. and others, "Redefining Politics: Patterns of Women's Political Engagement from a Global Perspective" in Nelson, Barbara J. and Chowdhury, Najma ed. *Women and Politics Worldwide*, Oxford University Press, Delhi, 1997, p. 15.
63. Kaushik, Susheela, "Women and Political Participation" in Stiftung, Friedrich Ebert edited *Women in Politics—Forms and Processes*, Har-Anand Publications, New Delhi, 1996, p. 40.
64. *Annual Report 1996-97*, National Commission for Women, New Delhi, p. 41.
65. *Ibid*, p. 41.

3

Status of Women in Ancient India

Jai Narain Sharma

Contemporary feminist discourse in India has come a long way in putting an edge on feminist consciousness and thought. With a fair measure of success, it has tried to expose the gender bias present in many of our literary texts, political treatises and historical documents. Nor has it failed to show that patriarchal bias all along vitiates the very ways in which questions about women are posed and answered.

Such attitudes have to be examined with care. But because they themselves may be tainted with prejudice, our way of looking at them has to be balanced and impartial. We can neither merely acquiesce in all that the traditional texts say, or are supposed to say about women, nor reject it impatiently *in toto*. We have to discover and seize the basic human values in them and to reject what is offensive to common sense and disrespectful to human dignity.

Care has to be exercised, not only in respect of the study of our ancient texts but quite as much in our concern with modern writing on feminism; for, most of our scholars and researchers today have accepted and built upon Western models a bit too glibly, at times to the extent of blind acceptance. Such uncritical following has not only led to misreading of our ancient texts that are unduly faulted, but to suggestions and views that are neither warranted by these texts which are unfairly held responsible for the plight of women, nor are helpful to the preservation of values that still sustain our family life today.[1]

Western thought holds the field in almost every region of intellectual activity, and quite a few of our scholars today find it convenient to fit the Indian social reality to borrowed (Western) frameworks of thought, with scant regard for our own history of social theory and practice. In doing so, many of us have unquestioningly accepted all western assumptions and constructions. This, in turn, has distorted the proper tenor of our discourse and methodology. The scholars in question first arbitrarily select such extracts from our philosophical texts as appear to lend point to western theory, and then pick, at their convenience, such emphases from modern western theory and thought as serve to highlight what is admittedly condemnable in our attitude to our women today. These self-styled spokesmen of modernity are quite uninformed about the essentials of traditional Indian sociological thought. Any sociological criticism will be inadequate if it restricts itself only to the level of phenomena and does not pay due attention to their conceptual foundations.[2]

It seems imperative, at this point, to briefly highlight some of the cardinal features of Indian cultural tradition. It advocates an integrated working of the body, mind and spirit, without which attainment of the ultimate end of life, that is, self-realization is not possible. It is quite different from the predominantly material civilization like that of the West today. By and large, our emphasis has been on the need to rise up to a fuller vision of the Eternal by following the dictates of conscience, morality and dharma and higher psychological practices. Our whole social system and our philosophy, religion and yoga, art and literature—all are, in principle directed at this end. This is to be seen not only in our most ancient scriptures and books of knowledge and sastras like the Vedas and the Upanisads, but in the Smritis which are products of a much later period. To quote *Manusmriti:*

> Let man discriminate between good and evil, right and wrong, the true and false, the real and the unreal; and thus discriminating, let him yet one–pointedly ever behold everything in the self, the transitory as well as that which abides. He who beholdeth all in Self...his mind strayeth not into sin.

In such a social set-up, it is obvious that women could never be regarded as inferior to men. Our traditional texts, in fact, accorded her a very high position in society, mainly because of her exceptional nurturing abilities. But the trouble with contemporary feminist theory is that on the one hand, it glibly equates all that is traditional with conservatism, repression, blind faith and backwardness and on the other hand, sheer rationality and freedom and progress in science and technology—which hold the field today—are regarded as the only marks of true modernity. What is worse, the two words, tradition and modernity, have been generally so interpreted as to favour imperialism, exaggerated individualism, and blind nationalism. Such an impatient and ill balanced attitude has led to gross indifference to the details of truth and reality.

This attitude however, has not sprung of itself. The colonial bias has been at work. It is this which has led to an overall misinterpretation of the role and value of women in our ancient texts and to a wholesale distortion of our educational curricula towards western literature and values, and away from the Indian cultural traditions. However, such defects can be remedied. We have only to realize that our word for tradition—that is, *parampara*—does not exclude progress, but only signifies continuity of progress in the light of without being tied down to past experience. Further, this *parampara* has always rejected that anthropology which promotes alienation; that ontology which believes in pure naturalism; that epistemology which believes in sheer empiricism and that motivation which aims at repression of others, as against eliciting their willing cooperation. Positively, it has always stood for participation, care for spiritual values and idealism and wisdom as against mere scholarship. These are the values that have existed since times immemorial and have all along provided coherence and stability to the Indian society. It is only the greed-centered people who impose their selfish will on others and treat them as mere tools and instruments, to the total neglect of the ideals laid down in Sastras. It is these people only who should be blamed for the distortion of the texts to serve their own selfish ends.[4]

Therefore, there is an obvious need to turn to our time-honoured view of parampara, which has never been indifferent to spiritual values. It is in this connection heartening to note that the once fashionable modes of thinking have already been outgone in some fields of learning. Psychology, for instance, has recently taken a leap from its experimental and cognitive forms to clinical, then humanistic and finally, transpersonal psychology. Indifference to the ethico-religious slant of our tradition as outlined above has resulted in a gross underestimation of the value of our texts leading incidentally to quite a few blunders in scholarship, both Indian and western. Who does not know that the RgVedic verse X.18.7 was interpreted for long in such a way that it could be taken to prove that Sati Pratha had the sanction of *RgVeda*.[5] Several mantras which did not support this interpretation were tactfully ignored. The truth, on the contrary, is that *RgVeda* not only allowed re-marriage, but encouraged it for the clear purpose of individual welfare, social cohesion and stability. Besides, other mantras *RgVeda* (X.18.8)[6] clearly direct the widows to arise from the front of the husband's dead body and resume their household duties. A similar wrong has been done to *Manusmriti*. Scholars quote those verses from it freely which appear to impose some restrictions on women, but tactfully ignore those verses where she is provided with innumerable rights and privileges.

The truth is that the Indian tradition visualizes the woman as the other half of a man. In other words, it emphasizes the complementarity of the relationship between a man and a woman. In a proper social order, they would not be competing but cooperating. In fact, the whole idea of a competitive society is a peculiar feature belonging to the modern western society and being sought to be emulated by non-western societies, though in a very imperfect manner. In India, for example, the principle of reverse discrimination largely offsets the competitive principle. Traditional societies, by and large, are not based on competition. The principle of the value of economic production has been the offspring of an individualistic and capitalistic industrial system. It needs to be adopted with much modification.

Women, again, have been viewed in the Indian tradition as the image of loveliness and delight. It is said that Mother Sarada once asked Sri Ramakrishna Paramahansa what she was to him. His reply was "*Sudhu Anandamayee*"—pure delight. All arts and literature are focused on this aspect of womanhood.

Dr. S. Radhakrishnan, our philosopher President asserts that woman has an important part to play in the renewal of the social order, as she is the "missionary of civilization".[7] Since he considers the status of woman as an index of a country's culture and its spiritual maturity, it is not surprising that he has dealt with her nature, her status, her subjection, her emancipation and issues connected with it.

Apart from the basic biological difference that a woman alone can bear a child, a woman is a man's equal—intellectually and spiritually. Hence in all human beings, irrespective of their sex, "the same drama of the flesh and the spirit, of finitude and transcendence takes place."

Whilst some have derided women, majority think that women have more virtues than they claim. Women are great lovers, educators par excellence, pillars of strength and sources of inspiration to men. Brutality, violence and anger are not their typical features. Above all they are self-effacing and self-sacrificing with immense powers of patience and endurance. Centuries of tradition and social and religious cultures have made Indian women acquire and possess these traits in a superlative degree. At the same time, the traits that men and women acquire are largely due to environmental factors (hence there are women combatants, mountaineers, etc.) and women are different from men not by nature but by contrivance. It will be appropriate to point out here the opinion of G. Dietrich regarding the altruistic characteristics of a woman. She says that whilst these traits may have been useful when directed against a common enemy, in the absence of an enemy or a foreigner, these values can only contribute to a woman's oppression.[8]

Women generally love children which "is not a product of social conditioning though some women lack the maternal instinct. The Indian woman in particular is essentially a mother. It is a calling in which she finds fulfillment and the love and care she bestows on her children are irreplaceable. Jacobson[9] has referred to the dual character of the Hindu female—"the wife is the woman under male control; the mother is the woman in control of herself and children". In ancient texts, the Hindu wife has generally been regarded as her husband's complement and help-mate. She is *sahadharmini* and without her the house is not a home but a wilderness. The wife is man's *ardhangi* or half-self. Together they constitute a unity even though they may perform diverse functions. Even God is regarded as *Ardhanarisvara*.

Women were held in high esteem in ancient India and were granted the same privileges as men. They had intiation rites and carried out sandhya rites and Vedic duties with the husband or independently. They were provided with educational opportunities and training according to their class and the practice of co-education prevailed. They were not forced to marry. Some Brahamavadinis devoted themselves to sacred wisdom and were highly acclaimed for their learning. Women enjoyed property rights and chose their life–partners as is evident from the practice of swayamvara in the epic period. According to the Narada Smriti, widows could remarry if the husband died, was impotent or for such other reasons and property would be granted if the widow married a person approved by her father-in-law.

However, there are diverse views with regard to women's status in ancient India. If it means the Vedic Age, there are some scholars like A. S. Altekar[10] and K. M. Kapadia[11] who hold that women did enjoy a high status. P. S. Aiyer[12] contends that this was so except for rights to property and inheritance and that the position of women deteriorated in the Sutra period. O. F. M. Bernard's[13] view is that women's status declined at the time of the Brahmanas. Subbamma and Sharma assert that women were eulogized in some texts in the Vedas and depreciated in others. I. Mahindra[14] thinks that the privileges and honour the Rig Vedic women enjoyed had to be commensurate with the Aryan patriarchy. Jawaharlal Nehru[15] thinks that the position of women in India, for hundreds of years, was not a good one, neither according to law nor in public and social life.

Radhakrishnan regards ancient Indian tradition as constituting the whole of Indian tradition and says that "Indian tradition has generally respected womanhood, though occasionally we find derogatory references to women."[16] He considers the low status of woman to be a "recent occurrence" which must also be considered part of the Indian tradition, though it is not Indian tradition at its best.

The passages of Manu, which speak highly of women, are in conformity with the Vedic ideology which gives women a noble position in society. But later, subjugation of woman came to stay and we find derogatory references of her.

A woman, according to Manu, should be protected and honoured at all stages of her life. Manu starts, with the fundamental principle that "day and night women must be kept in dependence by the males of their families. Her father protects her in childhood, her husband protects her in youth, and her sons protect her in old age; a woman is never fit for independence".[17] Narada justifies this on the ground that women, having no knowledge of shastras, are unable to discern what is good and what is bad.

The main reason for the guarding of the wife is to preserve the purity of the offspring.[18] There is confirmation of these prescriptions in later texts also. In Daksa the following view is expressed. 'Women are like the leech; but while the poor leech draws blood only, the woman draws your riches, your prosperity, your flesh, your vitality and your strength. During adolescence, she is in fear of the man; during youth she demands excessive pleasure and when her husband becomes old, she does not care a straw for him'.[19] Manu gives the circumstances under which a woman is likely to go astray. Drinking, associating with immoral people, separating from her husband, roaming around, sleeping late, and dwelling with other men—these are the six causes of her ruin.[20] She may neglect her appearance, develop an artificial passion, becomes heartless, disloyal to her husband, gives to excessive love of bed and ornaments, may harbour impure desires, be wrathful, dishonest or malicious. In the company of such women no sacramental rite should be performed. That is the law. If they are destitute of moral strength and know not the Vedas and are impure and false, there are no rites for them. Women should not perform any sacrifice or vow, no fast must be performed by them apart from their husbands and no girl or young woman has the right to offer agnihotra.

In contrast to these observations, women are highly honoured and praised in other passages by Manu. There is no difference between the housewife and the Goddess of Fortune, both illumine the home and are to be adored as such.[21] Where women are honoured, there the Gods revel, where they are not honoured, all religious acts become futile;[22] that home perishes in which the daughter-in-law suffers; homes cursed by them go to grief.[23] In that home in which husband and wife are mutually happy, there is invariably auspiciousness.[24] No religious rite could be performed without the wife. Indeed the husband and wife are one.[25] That man obtains his wife as a gift from the gods is the teaching of the law; that, he who does not treat her well falsifies the world of men and gods alike, is stated in the Mahabharata text. According to Manu, the mouth of a woman is always pure.[26] Men should always honour women for their own prosperity and interest.[27]

Yajnavalkya says that women should be honoured with ornaments, clothes and food by their husbands, brothers, fathers, parents, relations, mothers-in-law, brothers-in-law and maternal relations.[28] According to Visnu, the person who is ready to die for the sake of a woman gets heavenly blessing.[29] Special privileges were given to the newly married and pregnant women. They were allowed to eat even before the guests were served.[30] For a woman, her husband should be everything. Through devotion and love for him, she fulfils her duty and develops her highest personality. Whatever be the qualities of the husband with whom she is lawfully united, such qualities she assumes, like a river united with the sea. Akshamala, a woman of the lowest birth, united with the sage Vasista, and Madanpala united with the sage Sarangi became worthy of honour. These and other women of lower birth have attained eminence by following their husbands' good qualities.[31] If a wife obeys her husband, she will for that reason, exalted in heaven.[32]

Woman has a duty in the social order, the arduous task of motherhood. To be mothers, women were created and to be fathers, men were created; religious rites are therefore ordained to be performed by the husband with the wife.[33]

In his famous eulogy of women in the *Brhat-Samhita*, Varahamihira (sixth century) cites Manu in support while lauding women.

Varahamihira (6th century AD) in his *Brhat-Samhita* chap. 74 (ed. By Kern) makes a spirited defence of women and eulogises them highly. He first says that on women depend dharma and artha and from them a man derives the pleasures of sense and the blessing of sons; that they are the Laksmi (goddess of Prosperity) of the house and should be always given honour and wealth. He then condemns those who following the path of asceticism and other-worldliness proclaim the demerits of women and are silent about their virtues and pertinently asks 'tell me truly, what faults attributed to women have not been also practiced by men?' Men in their audacity treat women with contempt, but they really possess more virtues (than men). He then cited the dicta of Manu in support (verses 7-10). "One's mother or one's wife is a woman; men owe their birth to women; ungrateful wretches, how can happiness be your lot when you condemn them?"[34]

It is widely believed that women do not possess the right to inherit according to the Manusmriti and moreover, that women did not have the right to inherit in RgVedic period.[35] It seems, however, that "there was a school of jurists representing a small minority, which favored the recognition of the right of inheritance of the daughter along with the son as early as c. 500 B.C."[36] One of the authorities it relied upon is a passage in the *Nirukta* (III.4), a passage which is attributed by Yaska to Manu: "This verse does not, however, occur in the present *Manusmriti* and it contradicts its views on this point".[37] So we now experience yet another moment of "cognitive dissonance". First we found Manu, denounced for his negative portrayal of women, being cited in the tradition for his positive portrayal of the same women. Now we find Manu, branded as the denier of rights to women, being cited within the tradition as an upholder of the daughter's right to inherit.

The *Manusmriti* is regularly cited as the classical proof text of the Hindu caste-system. This same caste-system is the subject of discussion between Nahusa (in the form of a snake) and Yudhisthira in the *Mahabharata*.

When Yudhisthira, the incarnation of Righteousness, is asked by the snake, to define a Brahmana, he answers, "He is considered a Brahmana in whom one can see truth, liberality, forgiveness, character, non-violence, self-control and pity "*Satyam danamksamasilam anrsamsyam damo ghrna Drsyante yatra nagendra sa brahmana iti smrtah*". At this, the snake logically points out that these qualities may be found in a Sudra. Yudhisthira then goes on to declare, "In that case the Sudra is not a Sudra, nor the Brahmana a Brahmana, where this conduct can be discerned, he is a Brahmana, where it is not found that one is to be indicated a Sudra." In that case, the snake argues, jati would be quite meaningless. Yudhisthira replies by saying that jati is impossible to discern since all men constitute a single species. Hence, according to Yudhisthira, Manu rightly stated that all are Sudra by birth till they are spiritually regenerated. It is conduct, therefore, that really distinguishes the varnas. Otherwise, their confusion is unavoidable.[38]

It is worth noting that the view, that all are sudras by birth, is attributed by Yudhisthira to Manu—a view highly subversive of the caste system. G. C. Pande notes that "The view attributed to Manu does not occur in the present Manusmriti but may be traced in other dharma-sastra authors."[39]

The Manuvada presentation of Manu is for me an illustration of how information without context can lead to or at least contributes to, alienation. It provides scope for ideologies to provide the context or scope for speculation or worse to provide the context. Information in context, by contrast, promotes analysis.

When read holistically on its own terms, the *Manusmriti*

is not as formidable an obstacle to social reconstruction as it has been made out to be. Individual verses can be used to draw toxic conclusions, generate synthetic outrage and magnify it into a generalized fear about the future. When judged by selective quotations, one tends to look upon *Manusmriti* with an air of excited horror, while evidence to the contrary from the same text is tactfully or perhaps I should say tactlessly, withheld. Reading the text as a whole helps us to break out of the circumscribing limited hermeneutical circles, in which people have been going in circles for two centuries now.

Similarly characters woven in the *Mahabharata* reflect the vision of the society about women. There are house-wives, there are ladies in search of their identity and there are ardent devotees, devoted to notable characters. While Draupadi reveals a most serene and touching profile of an Indian woman, Gandhari, Kunti, Devayani, Savitri and Damyanti are the most inspiring characters. They visualize the undeterred spirit of struggle and perseverance as well as the nobility of character. In fact, the *Mahabharata* attains the grandeur and sublime through such women characters.

The girl child was given a special position of honour in the society during that period. After momentary disappointment at the birth of a daughter, the parents lavished affection on her and were even proud of her, as was the case with Savitri[40], Damayanti[41], Draupadi[42] etc. and Gandhari, even after the birth of a hundred sons, longed for a daughter.[43] There were a number of fathers like the Brahmana in Bakavadha parva who asserted that for him, the son and the daughter were equal;[44] Bhishma expressed a similar opinion.[45] Nor were such ideas of appreciation applicable to women of royalty alone; others like Devayani[46], Subhru[47], Suvarchala[48] and Gadhi's daughter Satyavati[49] were also a source of joy to their fathers.

Girls were often adopted by childless persons. The king of Vidarbha adopted Lopamudra[50], Kuntibhoja adopted Kunti[51]. Even sages adopted girls such as Shakuntala[52], Pramadara[53] and Kripi[54] and brought them up with affection and care. Even the fisherman Dasa adopted Satyavati, who was found in the belly of a fish and was given to him by the king.[55]

The daughter's son, just like one's own son, could bring religious merit and enabled his grandfather to attain the desired world, as in the case of Yayati.[56] Moreover a childless person could make his daughter a Putrika, whose son would belong to family of his maternal grandfather, rather than to the family of his parental side. Chitrangada was made a Putrika by her father Chitaravahana of Manalura.[57] The daughter's son could offer pinda and perform the Shraddha of his maternal grandfather. Thus, daughters, even without being Putrikas, could be mothers of sons who were offering Pinda, and were thus equal to any son that the grandfather might have had.[58] That daughters were indeed a source of religious merit is clear from the fact that even today, *Kanya Dana* (giving a daughter in marriage) is deemed to bring immense Punya.

The *Mahabharata* declares; *'Niyam nivaste' lakshmih kaniyakasu pratish pratishthia'*. *'Kanyeyamkula-jivitiam'* — 'the girl is very life of the family', observed Kalidas.[59] In the person of a girl, resides ever steadily fortune as well as grace. The greatest homage paid by Manu to women is expressed thus:

yatra naryastu pujyante ramante tatra devatah
yatraitastu na pujyante sarvastatraphalah kriyah.[60]

'Where women are worshiped, there Gods roam around.'

From time immemorial, India has always honoured women. Manu and his six commentators viz., Medhatithi, Govindaraja, Sarvajnanarayana, Kullukabhatta, Raghavananda, Nandana Ramachandra have paid eloquent testimony to the greatness of Indian womanhood. Besides these, Yajanvalkaya, Vatsyayana, Narada and others have paid glowing tributes and honoured women.

References

1. Chandrakala Padia, *Feminism Traditions and Modernity*, Shimla, IIAS, 2002, p. 1.
2. *Ibid.*
3. Manu, XII, 118.
4. Chandrakala Padia, *Feminism Traditions and Modernity, op. cit.*, p. 3.
5. *Rig Veda* X 18.7

6. *Ibid.*, X 18.8
7. S. Radhakrishnan, *Religion and Society,* London, Allen and Unwin Ltd., 1947, p. 154.
8. G. Dietrich, "Culture, Religion and Development" by J. Mahakal on behalf of the Centre of Social Action, Madras, 1978, p. 47.
9. W. S. Jacobson, *Women in India,* New Delhi, Manohar, 1978, p. 119.
10. A. S. Altekar, *The Position of Women in Hindu Civilization,* New Delhi, Motilal Banarsidas, 1966, pp. 337-38.
11. K. M. Kapadia, *Marriage and Family in India,* Calcutta, Oxford University Press, 1966, p. 252.
12. P.S. Aiyer, *Evolution of Hindu Moral Ideals,* Calcutta, 1935, p. 57.
13. O. F. M. Bernard, *Indian Mind,* Rome, Gregorian University, 1962, p. 233.
14. I. Mahindra, *The Rebellious Homemakers,* Bombay, SNDT Women University, 1980, pp. 39-40.
15. *Ibid.*, p. 124.
16. S. Radhakrishnan, *Occasional Speeches and Writings,* October 1952-January 1956, p. 371.
17. Manu IX, 2-3.
18. *Ibid.*, IX, 6.
19. Quoted in *Vivadaratnakara,* p. 413.
20. Manu IX, 13.
21. *Ibid.*, IX, 26.
22. *Ibid.*, III, 56.
23. *Ibid.*, III, 57, 58.
24. *Ibid.*, III, 60.
25. *Ibid.*, IX, 45.
26. *Ibid.*, V, 130.
27. *Ibid.*, III, 56-59.
28. Yajnanalkya, 1.82.
29. Visnu XXII, 32.
30. Manu III, 114.
31. *Ibid.*, IX, 21-24.
32. *Ibid.*, V, 155.
33. *Ibid.*, IX, 96.
34. P. V. Kane, *History of Dharmasatra,* Poona, Bhandarkar Oriental Research Institute, 1974, Vol. II, Part I, p. 579.
35. A.S. Altekar, *The Position of Women in Hindu Civilization, op. cit.*, p. 239.
36. *Ibid.*
37. *Ibid.*, p. 240.

38. G. C. Pande, *Dimensions of Ancient Indian Social History*, New Delhi, Books and Books, 1984, p. 162.
39. *Ibid.*, p. 174.
40. *Mahabaharata*, Aranyaka Parva 277.23-24.
41. *Ibid.*, 50.8.
42. *Mahabharata* Adiparva, 155.45-46.
43. *Ibid.*, 107.34.
44. *Ibid.*, 145.36-37.
45. *Mahabharata*, Anushasana Parva, 45.12
46. *Mahabharata*, Adiparva, 75.8.9.
47. *Mahabharata*, Shalya Parva, 51.3-4.
48. *Mahabharata*, Shanti Parva, 36.50.
49. *Mahabharata*, Anushasana Parva, 4.7.
50. *Mahabharata*, Aranyaka Parva 277.23-24.
51. *Mahabharata*, Adiparva, 75.8.9.
52. *Ibid.*, 66.12.
53. *Ibid.*, 8.9.
54. *Ibid.*, 120.16.
55. *Ibid.*, 57.54.
56. *Mahabharata*, Udyoga Parva, 119.23.
57. *Mahabharata*, Adiparva, 207.19.
58. *Mahabharata*, Anushasana Parva, 45.13
59. Kalidas, *Kumara-Sambhava* 6.63.
60. *Manu-Smrti* 3.56.

4

Women in India, Down the Ages

Dilip Kumar Padhi

Bharta cha Rama, Janaka Cha Pita Guru madhye Basista Cha
Tahapi na Sita khanake na sukham

The meaning of the Sanskrit copulates shows vividly the status of women in India through the ages. 'Sita was having Rama as her husband; she was the daughter of Raja Janaka, one of the most learned and richest king, Brahamshree Basistha was her Guru; despite all she had, she could not get peace for a while'.

If we study the history of human race, we can find that men are perennially in competition with women. At the first opportunity man wants to show women down. Men are more creative; may it be scientific development, may it be in the field of fine art, may it be anything when it comes to creativity men always have a dominance over women. It is not because women are born not to be creative. They are endowed with the most wonderful gift of nature; capacity to conceive and have a baby. Only a woman can give birth to a child, the best and the most wonderful creation in the entire world. Since men cannot give birth to a child, they want to show they are also superior and in that process they have become more assertive. We Indians have a great tradition of treating women differently at different times. Sometimes they were respected in society and at other times they were given a very low status.

During the Rig-Vedic period women enjoyed a very high status. The Rigveda is the only scripture, among the scriptures of all religions in which the divine Truths are revealed to women sages also. Some of these hymns, which describe the revelations find a prominent place in the Rigveda Samhita like the hymn 10.125 (tenth mandala, 125 sukta or hymn) and are attributed to the woman sage Vak Ambrini. There are more than thirty women sages mentioned in Rigveda with specific hymns associated with them. In all the Semitic religions like Christianity, Islam etc. there is no mention of any revelation to women and no woman is listed among the prominent disciples of the founders or prophets of those religions.

There are numerous hymns in the Rig Veda indicating the high status accorded to women in the Vedic society. For instance, the hymn 10.85, the so called marriage hymn, explicitly states that the daughter-in-law should be treated in the family as a queen, *samrajni,* by all members especially the mother-in-law, husband, and father-in-law etc.

Of course, some critics have a very different view that 'women were oppressed in Hindu society even during the Vedic times'. The role of Women in Hinduism is often disputed, and their positions range from a quite fair one to an extremely intolerant one. Hinduism is based on numerous texts, some of which date back to 2000 BC or much earlier. They vary in authority, authenticity, content and theme, with the most authoritative being the Vedas. The position of women in Hinduism is widely dependent on the specific text and the context. Positive references are made to the ideal woman in texts such as the Ramayana and the Mahabharata, while some other texts such as the Manu Smriti advocate a restriction of women's rights.

While studying the Hindu pantheism, we often come across the wide variety of viewpoints within the different schools and sects of Hinduism concerning the exact nature and gender of the Supreme person or being; there are even sects that are sceptical about the existence of such a being. The Shakti traditions, for example, focus their worship on the goddess Durga as the supreme embodiment of power and feminine strength (a female form of God). Vaishnavism and Shaivism both worship Lakshmi with Vishnu and Parvati with Shiva respectively as beings on an equal level of magnitude (the male and female aspects of God). In some instances, such as with Gaudiya Vaishnavism, specific emphasis is placed on the worship of God's female aspect (Radharani) even above that of her paramour Krishna. Thus, it could be said that Hinduism considers God to have both male and female aspects, as the original source of both.

Male deities (such as Shiva and Indra) are believed, in some traditions, to themselves offer worship to the Goddess, Durga:

"O Parameshwari, (The supreme Goddess) who is praised by the husband of the daughter of Himalayas (Shri Shiva)..." "O Parameshwari, who is worshipped with true feelings by the husband of Indrani (Indra) please give us the spiritual personality, the victory, the glory and destroy our enemies."

Elsewhere Shiva and Vishnu are also described as possessing feminine qualities represented through their Ardhanarishvara and Mohini forms respectively.

In the marriage hymn (*RigVeda* 10.85.26), the wife "should address the assembly as a commander."

A *Rig Veda* hymn says: I am the banner and the head, a mighty arbitress am I: I am victorious, and my Lord shall be submissive to my will *(Rig Veda*, Book 10). These are probably the earliest references to the position of women in Hindu society.

Several women sages and seers are mentioned in the Upanishads, the philosophical part of the Vedas, notable among them being Gargi and Maitreyi. The Sanskrit word for female teachers as Acharyaa (as opposed to Acharya for teacher and Acharyini for teacher's wife) reveals that women were also given a place as Gurus.

The *Harita Dharmasutra* (of the Maitrayaniya school of Yayurveda) declares that there are two kind of women:

Sadhyavadhu who marry, and the Brahmavaadini who are inclined to religion, they can wear the sacred thread, perform rituals like the agnihotra and read the Vedas. Bhavabhuti's Uttararamacharita 2.3 says that Atreyi went to Southern India where she studied the Vedas and Indian philosophy. Shankara debated with the female philosopher Ubhaya Bharati, and Madhava's Shankaradigvijaya (9.63) mentions that she was well versed in the Vedas. Tirukkoneri Dasyai (15th century) wrote a commentary on Nammalvar's Tiruvaayamoli, with reference to Vedic texts like the Taittiriya Yajurveda.

Katyayana's *Varttika* 125, 2477 mentions that there were female teachers of grammar. Patanjali writes in his comments to *Ashtadhyayi* 3.3.21 and 4.1.14, that women undergo the thread ceremony before beginning their education, and says that women studied grammar.

In the Hindu system of marriage in ancient time women were given higher status. Both the husband and wife were two parts of one, complementing each other and becoming one in their spiritual journey. The most sacred part of the ceremony involved circumambulating the sacred fire in seven steps to a Vedic mantra which the groom used to address his wife.

Rigvedic verses suggest that the women married at a mature age and were probably free to select their husband. The wedding hymn in the *Rigveda* (*Rig Veda* 10.85.37-38) speaks of "husbands" (plural) for a single wife, but this may have a mythological character.

In the *Mahabharata,* Satyavati, a poor and lowly fisherman's daughter exercised her freedom of choice in marriage. Even Shantanu (the great Kuru king) could not just go and marry her. He had to seek permission for her hand in marriage from her and her father (a lowly fisherman). He even had to agree to a pre-nuptial agreement with her promising that her own sons would inherit his throne eventually. This indicates that in ancient India a poor and lowly girl was able to exercise her power and freedom even while marrying a king.

Also Satyavati's marriage to Shantanu did not require any dowry from her father, which is another indication that there was no dowry system. Moreover, she did not have to commit suicide or sati after Shantanu died which shows that sati as a custom did not exist then. After her husband's death, Satyavati remained very active in running the affairs of his kingdom (Kuru dynasty) and even helped her sons in performing their royal duties efficiently. This shows that women used to have a very active and fruitful social life when they became widowed or old and they certainly were not put to death prematurely through sati etc.

The Hindu system of marriage also allowed divorce and remarriage. Both *Manusamhita* and *Arthashastra* say that, if the husband is impotent, a traitor, evil-liver, has become an ascetic or an outcast or is missing for a prescribed number of years, then the wife can leave him without blame and marry again. Arthashastra also declares that in other circumstances, divorce can take place only by mutual consent. Manu discusses situations where the wife wishes to return to her first husband whether she has simply deserted him or had married another.

The system of Sati is also a very ancient practice. Sati, is an act of immolation of a woman on her husband's funeral pyre. Sati is the one who immolated either self-willingly or by societal inducement and compulsion. This was also practiced by the ancient peoples of Scythia, Egypt, Scandinavia and China. Though no scripture mandates it, the Puranas, part of the Hindu Smriti, mention sati as highly meritorious in several instances. A few instances of sati are recorded in the Hindu epics, which are otherwise replete with influential widows. Some examples from the Mahabharata include: Madri, second wife of Pandu, who held herself responsible for his death, performed sati. His first wife Kunti did not commit sati. (*Mahabharata* Adiparvan 95.65]

Moreover, Kunti in the *Mahabharata*, even had a son before marriage (albeit by accident or through her naivete) but went on to become a queen by marrying another man (king Pandu). It shows that the society used to value women more for their overall qualities of intelligence, determination, loyalty and leadership etc. rather than some personal and private issue such as the pre-marital virginity. Needless to say, Kunti, in spite of her pre-marital indiscretion, not only married a king but also remained highly respected and loved by all (family and others) throughout her entire and long life and did not have to commit sati at the time of her husband's death.

In India, the practice of Sati began around the inception of the Moghul Empire in 13th century. From 13th century onward, because of the death of their husbands, Hindu women (who avowed to remain true to their husbands as part of the sacred ritual of marriage) became targets of Muslim raiders and early conquerors of India. Since such women were vulnerable to molestation, rape and other atrocities, it became a societal means to deprive the conquerors of rape and pillage of the Hindu women. One account from the conquest of a Rajput town by Muslim invaders relates that the high-caste women burned themselves to death to preserve their honour and avoid abuse. That saw a significant increase in Satiism (especially among high-caste women) from mid-13th century until early-20th century, when the British Viceroy abolished the act of Satiism by the Order of The Empress Victoria. However, the actual practice of Sati continued by tacit endorsement of the British and was reduced significantly thanks to the social work of the Brahmo Samaj under Raja Ram Mohan Roy.

As told earlier in this article, some critics have a very different view that 'women were oppressed in Hindu society'. Lets us take the example of Sita. She was taken away forcibly by Ravana and was kept in captivity in a jungle surrounded by evil looking demons. After the war, after Ravana was killed and Sita was rescued, she was forced to prove her virtue by entering into the fire. Later after listening to the complaint of some washerwoman Rama deserted Sita again in the jungle despite her pregnancy. Yet we still call Rama as the Uttamapurusha. In the *Mahabharata* Draupadi was treated as a commodity and was shared by five husbands. Yudhisthira alias Dharmaraja lost her in the bet and she was asked to undress in the rajsabha by Dussasana. Such was also the status of women.

In the recent time the status of women is also the same. They are being discriminated at various levels. There are seven major areas of discrimination against women in India:

Malnutrition: India has exceptionally high rates of child malnutrition, because tradition in India requires that women eat last and least throughout their lives, even when pregnant and lactating. Malnourished women give birth to malnourished children, perpetuating the cycle.

Poor Health: Females receive less health care than males. Many women die in childbirth of easily avoidable complications. Working conditions and environmental pollution further impair women's health.

Lack of education: Families are far less likely to educate girls than boys, and far more likely to pull them out of school, either to help out at home or from fear of violence.

Overwork: Women work longer hours and their work is more arduous than men's, yet their work is unrecognized. It is thought that "women, like children, eat and do nothing." Technological progress in agriculture has had a negative impact on women.

Lack of training: There is no scope for training women to enable them to do their work. In women's primary employment sector—agriculture—extension services overlook women.

Mistreatment: In recent years, there has been an alarming rise in atrocities against women in India, in terms of rapes, assaults and dowry-related murders. Fear of violence suppresses the aspirations of all women. Female infanticide and sex-selective abortions are additional forms of violence that reflect the devaluing of females in Indian society.

Powerlessness: While women are guaranteed equality under the constitution, legal protection has little effect in the face of prevailing patriarchal traditions. Women lack power to decide who they will marry, and are often married off as children. Legal loopholes are used to deny women inheritance rights.

India has a long history of activism for women's welfare and rights, which has increasingly focused on women's economic rights. A range of government programs have been launched to increase economic opportunity for women, although there appear to be no existing programs to address the cultural and traditional discrimination against women that leads to her abject conditions.

The greatest tragedy facing humanity today is the persistence of chronic hunger—an intolerable phenomenon that takes the lives of 24,000 of us every day. For fully one-fifth of humanity, life is a daily struggle for survival in conditions of relentless poverty. Day after day, the lives of one billion individuals are cut short or terribly diminished by chronic and persistent hunger. Day after day, one billion people are denied the opportunities they need to lead healthy and productive lives.

People living with chronic hunger exist in conditions of severe poverty. What they lack is the chance to improve their situation, to develop their own self-sufficiency. The most potent confirmation of this fact can be seen in the lives of women. They, along with their children, are the main victims of hunger, and they are also deprived of the opportunities to end their own and their families' hunger.

The Hunger Project acknowledges the fact that the persistence of hunger in India—and elsewhere in the world where hunger is still an overriding social issue—is, to a large degree, due to the subjugation, marginalization and disempowerment of women. Furthermore, women's suppression is rooted in the very fabric of Indian society — in traditions, in religious doctrine and practices, within the educational and legal systems, and within families.

Ironically, much of the essential work of ending hunger rests in women's hands.

Traditionally, women bear primary responsibility for the well-being of their families. Yet they are systematically denied access to the resources they need to fulfil their responsibility, which includes education, health care services, job training, and access and freedom to use family planning services.

In order to gain a shared understanding of the condition of the status of women in India and its impact on the persistence of hunger, this document surveys papers done by leading scholars in Indian development issues. It is organized in a framework of seven issues that characterize the plight of resource-poor women, with a focus on rural women in India: malnutrition, poor health, lack of education, overwork, lack of skills, mistreatment and powerlessness.

The link between these issues and the persistence of hunger in India was underscored in a 1996 study: *The Asian*

Enigma, by Vulimiri Ramalingaswami: In short, the poor care that is given to girls and women by their elders and by their husbands is the first major reason for high levels of child malnutrition that are markedly higher in South Asia than anywhere else in the world. We can take an overview of India.

India, with a population of 989 million, is the world's second most populous country. Out of that number, 120 million are women who live in poverty.

India has 16 percent of the world's population, but only 2.4 percent of its land, resulting in great pressures on its natural resources.

Over 70 percent of India's population currently derive their livelihood from land resources, which includes 84 percent of the economically-active women.

India is one of the few countries where males significantly outnumber females, and this imbalance has increased over the years. India's maternal mortality rates in rural areas are among the world's highest. From a global perspective, Indian accounts for 19 percent of all live births and 27 percent of all maternal deaths.

"There seems to be a consensus that higher female mortality between ages one and five and high maternal mortality rates result in a deficit of females in the population. It is estimated that deaths of young girls in India exceed those of young boys by over 300,000 each year, and every sixth infant death is specifically due to gender discrimination." Of the 15 million baby girls born in India each year, nearly 25 percent will not live to see their 15th birthday.

"Although India was the first country to announce an official family planning program in 1952, its population grew from 361 million in 1951 to 844 million in 1991. India's total fertility rate of 3.8 births per woman can be considered moderate by world standards, but the sheer magnitude of population increase has resulted in such a feeling of urgency that containment of population growth is listed as one of the six most important objectives in the Eighth Five-Year Plan."

Since 1970, the use of modern contraceptive methods has risen from 10 percent to 40 percent, with great variance between northern and southern India. The most striking aspect of contraceptive use in India is the predominance of sterilization, which accounts for more than 85 percent of total modern contraception use, with female sterilization accounting for 90 percent of all sterilizations.

The Indian constitution grants women equal rights with men, but strong patriarchal traditions persist, with women's lives shaped by customs that are centuries old. In most Indian families, a daughter is viewed as a liability, and she is conditioned to believe that she is inferior and subordinate to men. Sons are idolized and celebrated. 'May you be the mother of a hundred sons' is a common Hindu wedding blessing.

The origin of the Indian idea of appropriate female behaviour can be traced to the rules laid down by Manu in 200 B.C.: "by a young girl, by a young woman, or even by an aged one, nothing must be done independently, even in her own house". "In childhood a female must be subject to her father, in youth to her husband, when her lord is dead to her sons; a woman must never be independent."

The primary issue with which all women are concerned is struggling with everyday survival. Insufficient incomes and the lack of employment are reported to be their most pressing concerns. Survival is a constant preoccupation and at its most basic, survival means food. The most common problems are the lack of essential amenities such as food, water, fuel, fodder and health facilities. In addition, the deterioration of the natural environment and the fact that many of their traditional occupations are no longer viable, conditions make it increasingly hard for women to continue sustaining their families, as they had done in the past.

Women are Malnourished

The exceptionally high rates of malnutrition in South Asia are rooted deeply in the soil of inequality between men and women.

> "...the poor care that is afforded to girls and women by their husbands and by elders is the first major reason for levels of child malnutrition that are markedly higher in South Asia than anywhere else in the world."

This point is made in the article, The Asian Enigma, published by UNICEF in the 1996 *Progress of Nations,* in which the rates of childhood malnutrition in South Asia are compared with those in Africa. We learn that malnutrition is far worse in South Asia, directly due to the fact that women in South Asia have less voice and freedom of movement than in Africa. "Judgement and self-expression and independence largely denied, millions of women in South Asia have neither the knowledge nor the means nor the freedom to act in their own and their children's best interests."

> "Gender disparities in nutrition are evident from infancy to adulthood. In fact, gender has been the most statistically significant determinant of malnutrition among young children and malnutrition is a frequent direct or underlying cause of death among girls below age 5. Girls are breast-fed less frequently and for shorter durations in infancy; in childhood and adulthood, males are fed first and better. Adult women consume approximately 1,000 fewer calories per day than men according to one estimate from Punjab. Comparison of household dietary intake studies in different parts of the country shows that nutritional equity between males and females is lower in northern than in southern states."

Nutritional deprivation has two major consequences for women: they never reach their full growth potential and anaemia. Both are risk factors in pregnancy, with anaemia ranging from 40-50 percent in urban areas to 50-70 percent in rural areas. This condition complicates childbearing and result in maternal and infant deaths, and low birth weight infants.

One study found anaemia in over 95 percent of girls ages 6-14 in Calcutta, around 67 percent in the Hyderabad area, 73 percent in the New Delhi area, and about 18 percent in the Madras area. This study states, "The prevalence of anaemia among women ages 15-24 and 25-44 years follows similar patterns and levels. Besides posing risks during pregnancy, anaemia increases women's susceptibility to diseases such as tuberculosis and reduces the energy women have available for daily activities such as household chores, child care, and agricultural labor. Any severely anaemic individual is taxed by most physical activities, including walking at an ordinary pace."

Women are in Poor Health

Surviving through a normal life cycle is a resource-poor woman's greatest challenge.

> "The practice of breast-feeding female children for shorter periods of time reflects the strong desire for sons. If women are particularly anxious to have a male child, they may deliberately try to become pregnant again as soon as possible after a female is born. Conversely, women may consciously seek to avoid another pregnancy after the birth of a male child in order to give maximum attention to the new son."

A primary way that parents discriminate against their girl children is through neglect during illness. When sick, little girls are not taken to the doctor as frequently as are their brothers. A study in Punjab shows that medical expenditures for boys are 2.3 times higher than for girls.

As adults, women get less health care than men. They tend to be less likely to admit that they are sick and they'll wait until their sickness has progressed before they seek help or help is sought for them. Studies on attendance at rural primary health centres reveal that more males than females are treated in almost all parts of the country, with differences greater in northern hospitals than southern ones, pointing to regional differences in the value placed on women. Women's socialization to tolerate suffering and their reluctance to be examined by male personnel are additional constraints in their getting adequate health care.

Maternal Mortality

India's maternal mortality rates in rural areas are among the highest in the world.

A factor that contributes to India's high maternal mortality rate is the reluctance to seek medical care during pregnancy — it is viewed as a temporary condition that will disappear. The estimates nationwide are that only 40-50 percent of women receive any antenatal care. Evidence from the states of Bihar, Rajasthan, Orissa, Uttar Pradesh, Maharashtra and Gujarat find registration for maternal and child health services to be as low as 5-22 percent in rural areas and 21-51 percent in urban areas.

Even a woman who has had difficulties with previous pregnancies is usually treated with home remedies only for three reasons: the decision that a pregnant woman seek help rests with the mother-in-law and husband; financial considerations; and fear that the treatment may be more harmful than the malady.

It is estimated that pregnancy-related deaths account for one-quarter of all fatalities among women aged 15 to 29, with well over two-thirds of them considered preventable. For every maternal death in India, an estimated 20 more women suffer from impaired health. One village-level study of rural women in Maharashtra determined on the basis of physical examinations that some 92 percent suffered from one or more gynaecological disorder.

Contraception Use

Women's health is harmed by lack of access to and the poor quality of reproductive services.

"About 24.6 million couples, representing roughly 18 percent of all married women, want no more children but are not using contraception. (Operations Research Group, 1990). The causes of this unmet need remain poorly understood, but a qualitative study in Tamil Nadu suggests that women's lack of decision-making power in the family, opportunity costs involved in seeking contraception, fear of child death, and poor quality of contraceptive service all play an important role." (Ravindran 1993).

Some estimates suggest that some 5 million abortions are performed annually in India, with the large majority being illegal. As a result, abortion-related mortality is high. Although abortion has been legal since 1972 in India, "studies suggest that although official policy seeks to make pregnancy-termination services widely available, in practice guidelines on abortion limit access to services, particularly in rural areas. In 1981, of the 6,200 physicians trained to perform abortions, only 1,600 were working in rural areas."

Job Impact on Maternal Health

The tasks performed by women are usually those that require them to be in one position for long periods of time, which can adversely affect their reproductive health. A study in a rice-growing belt of coastal Maharashtra found that 40 percent of all infant deaths occurred in the months of July to October. The study also found that a majority of births were either premature or stillbirths. The study attributed this to the squatting position that had to be assumed during July and August, the rice transplanting months.

Impact of Pollution on Women

Women's health is further harmed by air and water pollution and lack of sanitation.

The impact of pollution and industrial wastes on health is considerable. In *Environment, Development and the Gender Gap,* Sandhya Venkateswaran asserts that "the high incidence of malnutrition present amongst women and their low metabolism and other health problems affect their capacity to deal with chemical stress. The smoke from household biomass (made up of wood, dung and crop residues) stoves within a three-hour period is equivalent to smoking 20 packs of cigarettes. For women who spend at least three hours per day cooking, often in a poorly ventilated area, the impact includes eye problems, respiratory problems, chronic bronchitis and lung cancer. One study quoted by WHO in 1991 found that pregnant women cooking over open biomass stoves had almost a 50 percent higher chance of stillbirth.

Anaemia makes a person more susceptible to carbon monoxide toxicity, which is one of the main pollutants in the biomass smoke. Given the number of Indian women who are anaemic—25 to 30 percent in the reproductive age group and almost 50 percent in the third trimester—this adds to their vulnerability to carbon monoxide toxicity.

Additionally, with an increasing population, diseases caused by waste disposal, such as hookworm, are rampant. People who work barefooted are particularly susceptible, and it has been found that hookworm is directly responsible for the high percentage of anaemia among rural women.

Women are Uneducated

Women and girls receive far less education than men, due both to social norms and fears of violence.

India has the largest population of non-school-going working girls.

India's constitution guarantees free primary school education for both boys and girls up to age 14. This goal has been repeatedly reconfirmed, but primary education in India is not universal. Overall, the literacy rate for women is 39 percent versus 64 percent for men. The rate for women in the four large northern states—Bihar, Uttar Pradesh, Rajasthan and Madhya Pradesh—is lower than the national average: it was 25 percent in 1991. Attendance rates from the 1981 census suggest that no more than 1/3 of all girls (and a lower proportion of rural girls) aged 5-14 are attending school.

Although substantial progress has been achieved since India won its independence in 1947, when less than 8 percent of females were literate, the gains have not been rapid enough to keep pace with population growth: there were 16 million more illiterate females in 1991 than in 1981.

Sonalde Desai in *Gender Inequalities and Demographic Behaviour* asserts that "parents' reluctance to educate daughters has its roots in the situation of women. Parents have several incentives for not educating their daughters. Foremost is the view that education of girls brings no returns to parents and that their future roles, being mainly reproductive and perhaps including agricultural labour, require no formal education. As more and more boys are engaged in education, there is a growing reliance on the labour of girls. Girls are increasingly replacing their brothers on the farm while carrying on their usual responsibilities in housework. A large proportion of the roughly 40 million "nonworking" girls who are not in school are kept at home because of responsibilities in housework."

The role of parents is to deliver a chaste daughter to her husband's family. Sonalde Desai goes on to point out that "another disincentive for sending daughters to school is a concern for the protection of their virginity. When schools are located at a distance, when teachers are male, and when girls are expected to study along with boys, parents are often unwilling to expose their daughters to the potential assault on their virginity."

There is little response to counter these obstacles: school hours remain inflexible to the labour demands of girls; many villages do not have a school; and less than 1/3rd of India's primary and middle-school teachers are women.

According to Mapping Progress, "educational funds were cut by 801.3 million rupees in the 1991-92 budgets. Funds for the mass literacy movement, in which women participate enthusiastically, have been reduced by 5 percent from the previous year. Budgetary provisions for non-formal education have been cut by 17 percent, leading to closure of many night schools and adult education programs in which working-class women participate. Reduction in government expenditures on higher education and encouragement to private colleges will reduce women's opportunities for higher education since privatization in education promotes only male-dominated professional and technical courses, as they are lucrative."

Women are Overworked

Women work longer hours and their work is more arduous than men's. Still, men report that "women, like children, eat and do nothing." Women work roughly twice as many hours as men.

Women's contribution to agriculture—whether it be subsistence farming or commercial agriculture—when measured in terms of the number of tasks performed and time spent, is greater than men. "The extent of women's contribution is aptly highlighted by a micro study conducted in the Indian Himalayas which found that on a one-hectare farm, a pair of bullocks works 1,064 hours, a man 1,212 hours and a woman 3,485 hours in a year."

In Andhra Pradesh, (Mies: 1986) it is found that the work day of an woman agricultural labourer during the agricultural season lasts for 15 hours, from 4 am to 8 pm, with an hour's rest in between. Her male counterpart works for seven to eight hours, from 5 am to 10 am or 11 am and from 3 pm to 5 pm.

Another study on time and energy spent by men and women on agricultural work (Batliwala: 1982) found that 53 percent of the total human hours per household are contributed by women as compared to 31 percent by men. The remaining contribution comes from children.

The linking of agricultural activities to male dominance is described by Roy Burman (in Menon: 1991):

> The anxiety of man to monopolize his skill in plough culture is reflected in the taboo that is observed almost all over India, against the women's handling the plough. In many societies, she is not even allowed to touch it.

Mies further observed that "whereas operations performed by men were those that entailed the use of machinery and draught animals, thereby using animal, hydraulic, mechanical or electrical energy, women almost always relied on manual labour, using only their own energy." Rice transplantations, the most arduous and labour intensive task in rice cultivation, is carried out entirely by women without the help of any tools.

"Girls learn to assist their mothers in almost all tasks, and from the age of 10 years participate fully in the agricultural work done by women. Mies cites the case of Laxmi, a three-year-old infant who, along with her mother, pulled seedlings for transplanting. Boys on the other hand were seldom seen transplanting or weeding though they did help out in ploughing or watering the fields."

"Not only do women perform more tasks, their work is

also more arduous than that undertaken by men. Both transplantation and weeding require women to spend the whole day and work in muddy soil with their hands. Moreover, they work the entire day under the intensely hot sun while men's work, such as ploughing and watering the fields, is invariably carried out early in the morning before the sun gets too hot. Mies argues that because women's work, unlike men's, does not involve implements and is based largely on human energy, it is considered unskilled and hence less productive. On this basis, women are invariably paid lower wages, despite the fact that they work harder and for longer hours than do men."

In contrast, a study in Uttar Pradesh reports that men "only reluctantly conceded that their womenfolk really work. The researchers in this area were repeatedly told that women, like children, simply eat food and do nothing."

Women's work is rarely recognized.

Many maintain that women's economic dependence on men impacts their power within the family. With increased participation in income-earning activities, not only will there be more income for the family, but gender inequality should be reduced. This issue is particularly salient in India because studies show a very low level of female participation in the labour force. This under-reporting is attributed to the frequently held view that women's work is not economically productive.

In a report of the National Commission on Self-Employed Women and Women in the Informal Sector, the director of social welfare in one state said, "There are no women in any unorganized sector in our state." When the Commission probed and asked, "Are there any women who go to the forest to collect firewood? Do any of the women in rural areas have cattle?" the director responded with, "Of course, there are many women doing that type of work." Working women are invisible to most of the population.

If all activities—including maintenance of kitchen gardens and poultry, grinding food grains, collecting water and firewood, etc.—are taken into account, then 88 percent of rural housewives and 66 percent of urban housewives can be considered as economically productive.

Women's employment in family farms or businesses is rarely recognized as economically productive, either by men or women. And, any income generated from this work is generally controlled by the men. Such work is unlikely to increase women's participation in allocating family finances. In a 1992 study of family-based textile workers, male children who helped in a home-based handloom mill were given pocket money, but the adult women and girls were not.

The Impact of Technology on Women

The shift from subsistence to a market economy has a dramatic negative impact on women.

According to Sandhya Venkateswaran, citing Shiva, the Green Revolution, which focused on increasing yields of rice and wheat, entailed a shift in inputs from human to technical. Women's participation, knowledge and inputs were marginalized, and their role shift from being "primary producers to subsidiary workers."

Where technology has been introduced in areas where women worked, women labourers have often been displaced by men. Threshing of grain was almost exclusively a female task, and with the introduction of automatic grain threshers—which are only operated by men—women have lost an important source of income.

Combine harvesters leave virtually no residue. This means that this source of fodder is no longer available to women, which has a dramatic impact on women's workload. Moreover, as cattle dung is being used as fertilizer, there is less availability of fuel for cooking.

"Commercialization and the consequent focus on cash crops has led to a situation where food is lifted straight from the farm to the market. The income accrued is controlled by men. Earlier, most of the produce was brought home and stored, and the women exchanged it for other commodities. Such a system vested more control with the women."

Women are Unskilled

Women have unequal access to resources.

Extension services tend to reach only men, which perpetuates the existing division of labour in the agricultural sector, with women continuing to perform unskilled tasks. A World Bank study in 1991 reveals that the assumption made by extension workers is that information within a family will be transmitted to the women by the men, which in actual practice seldom happens. "The male dominated extension system tends to overlook women's role in agriculture and proves ineffective in providing technical information to women farmers."

Mapping Progress, states, "in the farm sector, the process of mechanization of agricultural activities has brought in tendencies for gender discrimination by replacing men for a number of activities performed by women and also by displacing the labor of women from subsistence and marginal households. Women are employed only when there is absolute shortage of labor and for specific operations like cotton-picking.

"To supply food-processing industries being set up with foreign collaboration, there has already been a major shift from subsistence farming method of rice, millet, corn and wheat to cash-crop production of fruit, mushrooms, flowers and vegetables. This shift has led to women being the first to lose jobs."

A number of factors perpetuate women's limited job skills: if training women for economic activities requires them to leave their village, this is usually a problem for them. Unequal access to education restricts women's abilities to learn skills that require even functional levels of literacy. In terms of skill development, women are impeded by their lack of mobility, low literacy levels and prejudiced attitudes toward women. When women negotiate with banks and government officials, they are often ostracized by other men and women in their community for being 'too forward.' Government and bank officials have preconceived ideas of what women are capable of, and stereotypes of what is considered women's work.

Women are Mistreated

Violence against women and girls is the most pervasive human rights violation in the world today.

Opening the door on the subject of violence against the world's females is like standing at the threshold of an immense dark chamber vibrating with collective anguish, but with the sounds of protest throttled back to a murmur. Where there should be outrage aimed at an intolerable status quo there is instead denial, and the largely passive acceptance of 'the way things are.'

Male violence against women is a worldwide phenomenon. Although not every woman has experienced it, and many expect not to, fear of violence is an important factor in the lives of most women. It determines what they do, when they do it, where they do it, and with whom. Fear of violence is a cause of women's lack of participation in activities beyond the home, as well as inside it. Within the home, women and girls may be subjected to physical and sexual abuse as punishment or as culturally justified assaults. These acts shape their attitude to life, and their expectations of themselves.

The insecurity outside the household is today the greatest obstacle in the path of women.

In recent years, there has been an alarming rise in atrocities against women in India. Every 26 minutes a woman is molested. Every 34 minutes a rape takes place. Every 42 minutes a sexual harassment incident occurs. Every 43 minutes a woman is kidnapped. And every 93 minutes a woman is burnt to death over dowry.

One-quarter of the reported rapes involve girls under the age of 16 but the vast majority are never reported. Although the penalty is severe, convictions are rare.

Selective Abortions

The most extreme expression of the preference for sons is female infanticide and sex-selective abortion.

A study of amniocentesis in a Bombay hospital found that 96 percent of female fetuses were aborted compared with only a small percentage of male fetuses.

> "Government officials even suspect that the disproportionate abortion of female fetuses may be a major underlying cause of the recent decline in the nation's sex ratio. In 1971 there were 930 females for every 1,000 males. A decade later this figure had increased to 934, but by 1991, instead of continuing to rise, the ratio dropped to 927, lower than the 1971 figure. This sex ratio is one of the lowest in the world."

Sonalda Desai reports that there are posters in Bombay advertising sex-determination tests that read, "It is better to pay 500 Rs. now than 50,000 Rs. (in dowry) later."

Government has passed legislation to curb the misuse of amniocentesis for sex selection and abortion of female fetuses. Women activists have been critical of this act because of its provision that calls for punishing the women who seek the procedure. These women may be under pressure to bear a male child.

Women are Powerless

Legal protection of women's rights have little effect in the face of prevailing patriarchal traditions.

Marriage: Women are subordinate in most marriages.

Exposure to and interactions with the outside world are instrumental in determining the possibilities available to women in their daily lives. The situation of women is affected by the degree of their autonomy or capacity to make decisions both inside and outside their own household.

"The position of women in northern India is notably poor. Traditional Hindu society in northern rural areas is hierarchical and dominated by men, as evidenced by marriage customs. North Indian Hindus are expected to marry within prescribed boundaries: the bride and groom must not be related, they have no say in the matter, and the man must live outside the woman's natal village.

"Wife givers" are socially and ritually inferior to "wife takers", thus necessitating the provision of a dowry. After marriage, the bride moves in with her husband's family. Such a bride is "a stranger in a strange place." They are controlled by the older females in the household, and their behaviour reflects on the honour of their husbands. Because emotional ties between spouses are considered a potential threat to the solidarity of the patrilineal group, the northern system tends to segregate the sexes and limit communication between spouses—a circumstance that has direct consequences for family planning and similar "modern" behaviours that affect health. A young Indian bride is brought up to believe that her own wishes and interests are subordinate to those of her husband and his family. The primary duty of a newly married young woman, and virtually her only means of improving her position in the hierarchy of her husband's household, is to bear sons.

Sonalde Desai points out that the perception that sons are the major source of economic security in old age is so strong in the north that "many parents, while visiting their married daughters, do not accept food or other hospitality from them. However, given women's low independent incomes and lack of control over their earnings, few can provide economic support to their parents even if parents were willing to accept it."

In the south, in contrast, a daughter traditionally marries her mother's brother or her mother's brother's son (her first cousin). Such an arrangement has a dramatic impact on women. "In southern India, men are likely to marry women to whom they are related, so that the strict distinction found in the north between patrilineal and marital relatives is absent. Women are likely to be married into family households near their natal homes, and are more likely to retain close relationships with their natal kin."

"Over the past several decades, however, marriage patterns have changed markedly. Social, economic, and demographic developments have made marriages between close relatives less common, and the bride price has given way to a dowry system akin to that in the north. Nevertheless, as long as the underlying ethic of marriage in the south remains the reinforcement of existing kinship ties, the relatively favourable situation of southern Indian women is unlikely to be threatened."

Child Marriages: Child marriages keep women subjugated.

A 1976 amendment to the Child Marriage Restraint Act raised the minimum legal age for marriage from 15 to 18 for young women and from 18 to 21 for young men. However, in many rural communities, illegal child marriages are still common. In some rural areas, nearly half the girls between 10 and 14 are married. Because there is pressure on women to prove their fertility by conceiving as soon as possible after marriage, adolescent marriage is synonymous with adolescent childbearing: roughly 10-15 percent of all births take place to women in their teens.

A May 1998 article in the New York Times states:

Child marriages contribute to virtually every social malaise that keeps India behind in women's rights. The problems include soaring birth rates, grinding poverty and malnutrition, high illiteracy and infant mortality and low life expectancy, especially among rural women.

The article cites a 1993 survey of more than 5,000 women in Rajasthan, which showed that 56 percent of them had married before they were 15. Barely 18 percent of them were literate and only 3 percent used any form of birth control other than sterilization. Sixty-three percent of the children under age 4 of these women were severely undernourished.

"Each year, formal warnings are posted outside state government offices stating that child marriages are illegal, but they have little impact."

One man interviewed for the article has seven daughters. He borrowed some 60,000 rupees to pay for the dowries for six of his daughters, ranging in age from 4-14. He reported that "the weddings mean that he can now look forward to growing old without being trapped in the penury by the need to support his daughters."

Dowries

Women are kept subordinate, and are even murdered, by the practice of dowry.

An opposing opinion is however, that the evil of dowry is conspicuous by its absence in the entire range of authoritative religious literature of Hindus. Scholars (Such as Veena Talwar Oldenburg) have shown that dowry amongst Hindus started as a result of peculiar conditions created during the British rule in India, and that this practice is actually attested quiet well in medieval Europe. In lieu of dowry however, brides were gifted lavishly by her father and brothers upon her wedding. These gifts constituted her personal property not subject to use or control by her husband or her in-laws. Upon her death, it passed onto her daughters. A bride's or a wife's personal wealth was called 'stridhana' or the woman's wealth. If the bride's father was no longer alive, her brothers were obliged to grant her a share of their own inheritance to create her stridhana and for her marriage.

In the *Manusmriti,* on the other hand, 8 types of marriage are specified; two involve bedecking the bride with costly garments and ornaments before giving her away, two involve the groom's family giving a gift to the bride's and the other four do not involve an exchange of gifts.

The *Manusmriti* enjoins 'Let mutual fidelity continue until death,' this may be considered as the summary of the highest law for husband and wife. [Manu IX 101]

In the recent times in India, 6,000 dowry murders are committed each year. This reality exists even though the Dowry Prohibition Act has been in existence for 33 years, and there are virtually no arrests under the Act. Since those giving as well as those accepting dowry are punishable under the existing law, no one is willing to complain. It is only after a "dowry death" that the complaints become public. It is estimated that the average dowry today is equivalent to five times the family's annual income and that the high cost of weddings and dowries is a major cause of indebtedness among India's poor.

A December 1997 article in *India Today,* entitled, Victims of Sudden Affluence states, "A woman on fire has made dowry deaths the most vicious of social crimes; it is an evil endemic to the subcontinent but despite every attempt at justice the numbers have continued to climb. With get-rich-quick becoming the new mantra, dowry became the perfect instrument for upward material mobility." A study done by a policy think-tank, the Institute of Development and Communication, states, "the quantum of dowry exchange may still be greater among the upper classes, but 80 percent of dowry deaths and 80 percent of dowry harassment occurs in the middle and lower stratas."

The article goes on to state, "So complete is the discrimination among women that the gender bias is extended even toward the guilty. In a bizarre trend, the onus of murder is often put on the women to protect the men. Sometimes it is by consent. Often, old mothers-in-law embrace all the blame to bail out their sons and husbands."

Despite every stigma, dowry continues to be the signature of marriage. Says Rainuka Dagar, "It is taken as a normative custom and dowry harassment as a part of family life."

Divorce: Divorce is not a viable option

Divorce is rare—it is considered a shameful admission of a woman's failure as a wife and daughter-in-law. In 1990, divorced women made up a miniscule 0.08 percent of the total female population.

Maintenance rights of women in the case of divorce are weak. Although both Hindu and Muslim law recognize the rights of women and children to maintenance, in practice, maintenance is rarely set at a sufficient amount and is frequently violated.

Both Hindu and Muslim personal laws fail to recognize matrimonial property. Upon divorce, women have no rights to their home or to other property accumulated during marriage; in effect, their contributions to the maintenance of the family and accumulation of family assets go unrecognized and unrewarded.

Inheritance

Women's rights to inheritance are limited and frequently violated.

Ancient Indian scriptures like the *Arthashastra* and *Manusamhita* are sources about the woman's right to property or 'Stridhan', (literally meaning, property of wife). It is of two types: maintenance (in money or land given by the husband), and anything else like ornaments given to her by her family, husband, in-laws and the friends of her husband. Manu further subdivides this into six types—the property given by parents at marriage, given by the parental family when she is going to her husband's house, given by her husband out of affection (not maintenance which he is bound to give), and property given separately by brother, mother and father [Manu IX 194]. Pre-nuptial contracts are also mentioned where the groom would agree to give a set amount of bride price to both parents and the bride. Such property belonged to the wife alone and was not to be touched by the groom or her parents except in emergencies (in sickness, in famine, threatened by robbers, or for performing holy deeds). At the same time, the Manu Smriti contradicts itself by declaring that a wife has no property and the wealth earned is for the husband [Manu VIII.416].

Daughters and sons equally inherit their mother's property; but some scriptures insist that a mother's property belongs solely to the daughters [Manu IX 131], in order of preference: unmarried daughters, married but poor daughters, married and rich daughters. When a father dies, unmarried daughters have to be given a share in their father's property, equal to one-fourth from every brother's share [since it is assumed that the married daughter had been given her share at marriage] [Manu IX. 118]. If the family has no sons, the (appointed) daughter is the sole inheritor of the property [Manu IX 127].

In the mid-1950s the Hindu personal laws, which apply to all Hindus, Buddhists, Sikhs and Jains, were overhauled, banning polygamy and giving women rights to inheritance, adoption and divorce. The Muslim personal laws differ considerably from that of the Hindus, and permit polygamy. Despite various laws protecting women's rights, traditional patriarchal attitudes still prevail and are strengthened and perpetuated in the home.

Under Hindu law, sons have an independent share in the ancestral property. However, daughters' shares are based on the share received by their father. Hence, a father can effectively disinherit a daughter by renouncing his share of the ancestral property, but the son will continue to have a share in his own right. Additionally, married daughters, even those facing marital harassment, have no residential rights in the ancestral home.

Even the weak laws protecting women have not been adequately enforced. As a result, in practice, women continue to have little access to land and property, a major source of income and long-term economic security. Under the pretext of preventing fragmentation of agricultural holdings, several states have successfully excluded widows and daughters from inheriting agricultural land.

Women in Public Office, Panchayat Raj Institutions

The highest national priority must be the unleashing of woman power in governance. That is the single most important source of societal energy that we have kept corked for half a century.
—Mani Shankar Aiyar, *India Today*

Through the experience of the Indian Panchayati Raj Institutions (PRI) 1 million women have actively entered political life in India. The 73rd and 74th Constitutional Amendment Acts, which guarantee that all local elected bodies reserve one-third of their seats for women, have spearheaded an unprecedented social experiment which is playing itself out in more than 500,000 villages that are home to more than 600 million people. Since the creation of the quota system, local women—the vast majority of them illiterate and poor–have come to occupy as much as 43% of the seats, spurring the election of increasing numbers of women at the district, provincial and national levels. Since the onset of PRI, the percentages of women in various levels of political activity have risen from 4-5% to 25-40%.

According to Indian writer and activist Devaki Jain, "the positive discrimination of PRI has initiated a momentum of change. Women's entry into local government in such large numbers, often more than the required 33.3%, and their success in campaigning, including the defeat of male candidates, has shattered the myth that women are not interested in politics, and have no time to go to meetings or to undertake all the other work that is required in political party processes...PRI reminds us of a central truth: power is not something people give away. It has to be negotiated, and sometimes wrested from the powerful."

Contrary to fears that the elected women would be rubber stamp leaders, the success stories that have arisen from PRI are impressive. A government-financed study, based on field work in 180 villages in the states of Uttar Pradesh, Rajasthan and Madhya Pradesh, and coordinated by the Center for Women's Development Studies in New Delhi, has found that a full two-thirds of elected women leaders are actively engaged in learning the ropes and exercising power. Says Noeleen Heyzer, executive director of UNIFEM, "This is one of the best innovations in grass-roots democracy in the world."

Women leaders in the Panchayati Raj are transforming local governance by sensitizing the State to issues of poverty, inequality and gender injustice. Through the PRI, they are tackling issues that had previously gone virtually unacknowledged, including water, alcohol abuse, education, health and domestic violence. According to Sudha Murali, UNICEF Communications Officer in Andhra Pradesh, women are seeing this power as a chance for a real change for them and for their children and are using it to demand basic facilities like primary schools and health care centres.

The PRI has also brought about significant transformations in the lives of women themselves, who have become empowered, and have gained self-confidence, political awareness and affirmation of their own identity. The panchayat villages have become political training grounds to women, many of them illiterate, who are now leaders in the village panchayats. Says Sudha Pillai, joint secretary in India's Ministry for Rural Development, "It has given something to people who were absolute nobodies and had no way of making it on their own. Power has become the source of their growth."

By asserting control over resources and officials and by challenging men, women are discovering a personal and collective power that was previously unimaginable. This includes women who are not themselves panchayat leaders, but who have been inspired by the work of their sisters; "We will not bear it," says one woman. Once we acquire some position and power, we will fight it out...The fact that the Panchayats will have a minimum number of women [will be used] for mobilizing women at large." It is this critical mass of unified and empowered women which will push forward policies that enforce gender equity into the future.

An observation by Deepak Tiwari in *This Week,* displays the promising future made possible by the PRI. He notes, "'Learning politics' is the latest fad for young village girls, who dream of joining the growing band of women panchayat representatives, 164,060 at last count, in the state."

As UN Secretary General Kofi Annan has stated, "Gender equality is more than a goal in itself. It is a precondition for meeting the challenge of reducing poverty, promoting sustainable development and building good governance."

This recognition is currently missing in India. Transforming the prevailing social discrimination against women must become the top priority, and must happen concurrently with increased direct action to rapidly improve the social and economic status of women. In this way, a synergy of progress can be achieved.

As women receive greater education and training, they will earn more money.

As women earn more money—as has been repeatedly shown—they spend it in the further education and health of their children, as opposed to men, who often spend it on drink, tobacco or other women.

As women rise in economic status, they will gain greater social standing in the household and the village, and will have greater voice.

As women gain influence and consciousness, they will make stronger claims to their entitlements—gaining further training, better access to credit and higher incomes—and command attention of police and courts when attacked.

As women's economic power grows, it will be easier to overcome the tradition of "son preference" and thus put an end to the evil of dowry.

As son preference declines and acceptance of violence declines, families will be more likely to educate their daughters, and age of marriage will rise.

For every year beyond 4th grade that girls go to school, family size shrinks 20%, child deaths drop 10% and wages rise 20%.

As women are better nourished and marry later, they will be healthier, more productive, and will give birth to healthier babies.

Only through the actions to remedy the discrimination against women the vision of India's independence, an India where all people have the chance to live a healthy and a productive life, can be realized.

Bibliography

Abbe Jean Antoine Dubois, *Hindu Manners, Customs, and Ceremonies*, translated from the French by Henry King Beauchamp, (Oxford: Clarendon Press, 1897).

Abzug, Bella., and Davis, Susan, "India." Mapping Progress: Assessing Implementation of the Beijing Platform, 1998.

ARGALA STOTRUM.

Brahma Purana.

Bunch, Charlotte. "The Intolerable Status Quo: Violence Against Women and Girls." The Progress of Nations 1997, New York: UNICEF

Burns, John F. "Though Illegal, Child Marriage is Popular in Part of India." *The New York Times*. May 11, 1998.

Carr, Marilyn, and Chen, Martha, and Jhabvala, Renana, Speaking Out: Women's Economic Empowerment in South Asia. Southampton Row, London: Intermediate Technology Publications Ltd., 1996.

Desai, Sonalde, *Gender Inequalities and Demographic Behavior: India*. New York: The Population Council, Inc., 1994.

Gandhi and Status of Women, Article on how Mahatma Gandhi's experiments with truth involved and affected women's status in the 20th century in India.

Mahabharata.

Neft, Naomi, and Levine, Ann D., *Where Women Stand: An International Report on the Status of Women in 140 Countries*. New York: Random House, 1997.

Omvedt, Gail, *Violence Against Women: New Movements and New Theories in India*. Kali Primaries, 1990.

Purushothaman, Sangeetha, *The Empowerment of Women in India: Grassroots Women's Networks and the State.* New Delhi: Sage Publications, 1998.

R.C. Majumdar and A.D. Pusalker, editors, *The History and Culture of the Indian People.* Volume I: The Vedic age, (Bombay: Bharatiya Vidya Bhavan, 1951).

Rajan. "Will India's Ban on Prenatal Sex Determination Slow Abortion of Girls?" Internet.

Ramalingaswami, Vulimiri, and Jonsson, Urban, and Rohde, Jon, "The Asian Enigma." The Progress of Nations, 1996, New York: UNICEF.

Reardon, Geraldine, *Power and Process,* Oxford: Oxfam, 1995.

Rig Veda.

Sindhi Culture by U.T. Thakkur, Univ. of Bombay Publications, 1959.

Tanika Sarkar, *Hindu Wife, Hindu Nation: Community, Religion and Cultural Nationalism,* (New Delhi: Permanent Black, 2001).

Times of India. "Protest Against Atrocities in Women." Internet. p.3

Tinker, Anne, Improving Women's Health in India. Development in Practice Series. The World Bank, 1996.

Vasuda Narayanan, *Women of Power in the Hindu Tradition.*

Venkateswaran, Sandhya, *Environment, Development and the Gender Gap.* New Delhi: Sage Publications, 1995.

Vinayak, Ramesh "Victims of Sudden Affluence." *India Today.*

Manu Smriti, Manu, Aryavartta, 4400 B.C-1500 B.C. ? translations exist, see eg.

The Laws of Manu, W. Doniger and B.K. Smith, Penguin India, N. Delhi 1991.

Garuda Purana.

Vishnu Smrti.

Bhagavata Purana.

Vasishta's *Padma Purana.*

D.C. Ganguly 'Some aspects of the position of women in Ancient India'.

5

Working Women and Law in India

H.N. Pradhan

The Indian society prcsents an example of diametrically opposite points of view with regard to the status of women. Sometimes women are worshiped like goddess and accorded the status of divinity and at times they are despised like demons and regarded as the symbol of frailty. But it is fact that the discrimination meted to women is endemic in the Indian society. The unequal treatment given to women is sanctified by tradition and even law has seldom taken note of the adverse situation of women in the Indian society. In fact, the laws applicable to women are framed by the male section of society and women in India have little chance of participating in the making of laws. The most important laws relating to women such as marriage, divorce, inheritance, maintenance etc. have been under the control of the leaders of different religions and without the consent of these religious heads no change can be introduced in the personal laws of respective religious groups. Therefore, though independent India grants freedom and equality to women those provisions have practically little meaning for women in India.

In the nineteenth century many social reformers in India had shown their concern for the cause of women. They urged the colonial rulers to make legislations to improve the condition of women. As a consequence, the British gradually took interest in the position of women. Up to 1858 the British had concentrated on consolidating their rule in India, none the less they had taken certain steps towards removing the disadvantages of women in India. Thus, the Bengal Sati Regulation Act of 1829, the Caste Disabilities Removal Act of 1850 and the Hindu Widow Remarriage Act of 1856 were passed with an aim to remove some of the disabilities of Indian women. Though after 1858 the British pursued a policy of non-interference in the religious affairs of the Indians they nevertheless took initiatives in this direction; for example, a law was passed in 1870 to prevent female infanticide among the Rajputs and the Age of Consent Act was passed in 1891.

The Indian Succession Act of 1925 is yet another act which favoured women in India. Other such acts were the Hindu Women's Right to Property Act of 1937, the Muslim Personal Law (*Shariat*) Application Act of 1937, the Dissolution of Muslim Marriages Act of 1939 and all these enactments granted limited rights to women.

After independence of India, there was a trend for rapid social change in India. The Constitution of India incorporated into it several provisions pertaining to gender equality and those provisions gave rise to many new developments in India. Though the Hindu traditionalists in their own ways challenged the liberals much legislation were passed for giving different rights to women. The introduction of Hindu Code Bill saw a lot of controversy in India. Later the same was passed in piecemeal basis. The Hindu Marriage Act of 1955, the Hindu Adoption and Maintenance Act of 1956, the Hindu Minority and Guardianship Act of 1956 and the Hindu Succession Act of 1956 were passed to give effect to the provisions of the Hindu Code Bill.

In India several laws have been made to codify the principles which regulate different aspects of Hindu society that concern women directly or indirectly. If the single aspect of marriage can be taken as an example it can be seen that there have been changes in the position of women in India according to legal provision, though not in actual practice.

According to the Indian law all Hindu marriages are treated as monogamous and if he/she deviates from this practice he/she is liable to be punished if his/her act is challenged in the court of law. The aggrieved party can drag the other party to the court and has a right to initiate criminal proceedings against the erring party. But in reality women in India do not normally recourse to challenge the acts of their husbands because of their financial dependence on others, lack of education and social taboo. Even if a woman is in the right she does not go to the court as her action is viewed with suspicion. Further, the court normally takes the stand that to nullify the marriage it must have been solemnised, i.e. it must have been according to all the required paraphernalia; so a consensual staying together by two man and woman does not have the sanctity of marriage in the eyes of law.[1] But in reality the price is paid by the woman who looses her husband, family and other related benefits such as security, financial benefits and social prestige. Thus, the offender, if he is a male, has an added advantage to benefit from this ambiguity in law. It is provided in India that the marriageable age for a girl and a boy is 18 and 21 respectively. But in reality many marriages are solemnised where both the grooms and the brides are under the stipulated age. In the name of social custom and religious independence many such acts are committed with the approval of the masters of society which ultimately ends in many cases in sexual exploitation, torture, divorce and death of the child brides at the time of child birth.

However, one of the major problems which are faced by women in recent years is the problem of getting a protected atmosphere at their workplace. It has become a source of anxiety for policy makers, employers and other concerned persons, especially women, to create a friendly atmosphere at the workplace for women. There is increasing incidence of violence against women and the fate of working women who venture outside their home to achieve economic independence is not good. They are forced to tolerate the exploitation of other people outside their homes. How to protect the interests of women in such places has become a vital issue in contemporary period.

Due to various changes taking place in modern time women are willingly or unwillingly taking up different professions to be self sufficient and self reliant. No longer are they considered as the captives of the four walls of their houses and under the control and supervision of the male members of their families. Education, new economic avenues, emerging employment opportunities, professional competence, etc. have encouraged women to be engaged in many professions and earn their own means of livelihood. This has led to employment of a large number of women in different places.

Thus, in the changed context the protection of women at workplace has assumed greater importance and necessitated legislation and vigilance not only to provide them a congenial working condition with benefits like equal pay with their male counterparts and maternity leave but also to protect the life, dignity and honour of women. Women at the workplace have been subjected to different kinds of exploitation at the hands of their male colleagues and supervisors. In a male dominated society like ours, women are always put in a disadvantageous position and various offences are committed without any fear of punishment. Protection of women at the workplace is a major concern which directly affects the working women. Therefore, there is a need to analyse the provisions relating to sexual harassment of women and working condition of women at their workplace.

A. Sexual Harassment

Biologically women are susceptible for sexual harassment, but there is no clear definition of the term 'sexual harassment'. However, it can be assumed that when somebody forces him on an unwilling woman then it amounts to sexual harassment and can be regarded as a sexual offence. The Supreme Court has described sexual harassment in its landmark judgement[2] that "sexual harassment includes such unwelcome sexually determined behaviour, directly or by implication, as physical contact and advances, demand or request for sexual favours, sexually coloured remarks, showing pornography and any other unwelcome physical, verbal or non-verbal conduct of sexual nature."

The Supreme Court has considered sexual harassment as a form of sex discrimination when it pronounced in another case[3] "An analysis of the above definition, shows that sexual harassment is a form of sex discrimination projected through unwelcome sexual advances, request for sexual favours and other verbal or physical conduct with sexual overtones, whether directly or by implication, particularly when submission to or rejection of such a conduct by the female employee was capable of being used effecting the employment of the female employee and unreasonably interfering with her work performance and had the effect of creating an intimidating or hostile working environment for her."

The Constitution of India has guaranteed equality to all citizens, male and female, in Articles 14, 15 and 19 in the matters of law, employment and right to select one's occupation. It has made provision for the protection of life and personal liberty of all citizens. A citizen can knock the doors of the higher Courts in India, the High Court in a state and the Supreme Court in the country, to get his or her fundamental rights protected according to Article 32, which itself is a fundamental right. Article 42 of the Constitution provides that "the state shall make provisions for securing just and humane conditions of work and maternity relief." The Constitution has also enjoined all citizens to protect the dignity of women according to Article 51A, which is a fundamental duty of all citizens of India. Thus, on the one hand, women are given some rights to protect their interests in the event of their violation; on the other hand, the state has been given the responsibility to maintain certain condition to ensure a better standard for women.

The Indian Penal Code also provides "whosoever assaults or uses criminal force to any woman intending to outrage or knowing it to be likely that he shall thereby outrage her modesty, shall be punished with imprisonment of either description of a term which may extend to 2 years or fine or both"[4] and whosoever intending to insult the modesty of any woman utters only word, makes any sound or gesture or exhibits any object, intending that such gesture or object shall be seen by such women or intrudes upon the privacy of such women shall be punished with simple imprisonment for a term which may extend to one year or with fine or with both".[5]

However, these provisions are not always effective to check sexual harassment of women. Very often the employers or the male colleagues of the working women give help or other benefits on a quid pro quo basis; as a result, the criminal laws are not applicable in such situations. It has been observed that "criminal law includes only one type of non consensual sexual act as offensive, it excludes men who use economic, social or organisational power rather than actual or threatened use of force to overcome an unwilling but subordinate, and therefore, vulnerable women."[6]

As there is no clear law to protect women from sexual harassment the judiciary has become proactive and taken steps to give relief to the victims, especially in the two historic cases, Vishaka vs. State of Rajastan and Apparel Export Promotion Council vs. A.K.Chopra. The judiciary has asserted that "In a case involving charge of sexual harassment or attempt to sexually molest, the Courts are required to examine the broader probabilities of a case and not to get swayed by insignificant discrepancies or narrow technicalities or dictionary meaning of the expression 'molestation'. They must examine the entire material to determine the genuineness of the complaint."[7] These decisions have widened the scope of the meaning of sexual harassment. The Supreme Court has also enlarged the scope of the issue by lying down that sexual harassment does not necessarily include physical contacts. Even an insinuation can be considered an act of sexual harassment.

As the follow up actions in this regard it was also suggested by the Court to take steps to protect women from sexual harassment. The Court observed that it would be the duty of the employers and other responsible persons in workplaces to prevent or deter the commission of the acts of sexual harassment. When such acts have been committed it would be the duty of the employer to initiate criminal proceedings against the erring person by making a complaint to the appropriate authorities. The employer is also duty bound to initiate disciplinary actions against the wrong doer. There should also be a grievance Redress Cell or a complaint mechanism to check the occurrence of sexual harassment. Moreover, awareness should be created within the organisation and at the workplace against sexual harassment. Where the act of sexual harassment is committed by an outsider, all possible steps should be taken to prevent it.

B. Protective Labour Legislation

In India, several laws have been enacted to benefit women workers in their workplace. The Constitution has provided equal protection of law to all and promised end of discrimination in the country on the ground of sex. It has also pledged socio-economic-political justice to all citizens along with equality of status and opportunity. Hence, according to our Constitution women enjoy the same position and are treated equally with their male colleagues in the workplace. There have also been enactments of some protective legislation specifically made for working women. The Constitutional provisions along with the legislative enactments protect the interests of women in workplace.

(i) Constitutional Provisions

The constitution in its Preamble promises justice in social, economic and political fields. It guarantees equality to all citizens irrespective of their sex. But the most notable constitutional provision in this respect is Article 39 of the Constitution which directs the state to secure equal pay for equal work for both men and women. This stipulation of the Constitution ends discrimination in the workplace with regard to unequal payment to male and female if they do same kind of and same amount of work. The Constitution in Article 42 directs the state to make provision for maintaining a just and humane condition of work and for maternity benefit. It directs the state to make legislation in these regards.

(ii) Equal Remuneration Act 1976

To give respect to the Constitutional provision there has also been legislation, the Equal Remuneration Act 1976 to end disparity in payment to male and female and protect the interests of women at workplace. According to this Act its "provisions shall have effect notwithstanding anything inconsistent therewith contained in any other law or in terms of any award, agreement or contract of service, whether made before or after the commencement of this Act, or in any instrument having effect under any law for the time being in force."[8]

The Act makes the employer duty bound to pay equal remuneration to his workers, both male and female, if they perform same amount of work or work of similar nature.[9] It also provides that if there is prevalence of two pay scales for males and females for same work or work of similar nature then the higher pay scale shall be retained and applicable to women.

This Act provides that there should be no discrimination regarding the recruitment against any woman. As per this provision, 'at the time of making recruitment for the same work or work of similar nature or in any condition of services subsequent to recruitment such as promotions, training or transfer, make any discrimination against women except where employment of women in such work is prohibited or restricted by or under any law for the time being in force.'[10]

The Act makes a provision for the constitution of an Advisory Committee consisting of ten members of whom five members should be women to advise the Government on the matters relating to employment of women in any establishment or employment.[11] The Government on its part may appoint an authority for hearing complaints against non-payment or unequal payment to women. The employer is obliged to maintain records relating to the workers employed by him. In case of non-compliance of these provisions the employer is liable for punishment.

(iii) Maternity Benefit Act, 1961

The Maternity Benefit Act, 1961 was enacted to 'regulate the employment of women in certain establishments for periods before and after child birth and provide for maternity benefit and certain other benefits.' The Act is applicable to "every establishment being a factory, mine or plantation including any such establishment belonging to Government and to every establishment wherein persons are employed for the exhibition of equestrian, acrobatic and other performances."[12] Further the Act applies to 'every shop or establishment within the meaning of any law for the time being in force in relation to shops and establishments in a state, in which ten or more persons are employed or were employed, on any day of the preceding twelve months.'[13]

Every woman is entitled to this benefit if she has worked in the establishment for a period not less than eighty days of the twelve months immediately preceding the date of her expected delivery and the maximum period for which any woman shall be entitled to maternity benefit shall be twelve weeks of which maximum six weeks shall precede the date of her expected delivery.[14]

(iv) The Factory Act, 1948

The Factory Act 1948 contains some provisions which are specifically related to women. According to this Act in every factory separate enclosed accommodation shall be provided for male and female workers.[15] It also provides that the State Government may prescribe the number of latrines and Urinals to be provided in any factory in proportion to the number of male and female workers ordinarily employed therein and provide for such other matters in respect of sanitation in factories.[16]

The Act makes provisions for maintenance of accommodations for the women employees and children of working women in the factories.

Women are also protected from working in places which expose them to security risks.

Thus, these laws aim at providing a healthy working condition to women. While the Constitution emphasises on the establishment of a welfare state in the country it does not ignore the welfare of the working women. It proposes to maintain a congenial atmosphere so that women can have full security in their workplace and have other benefits necessary for their special needs. The Constitution and the

State are not blind to the specific requirements of working women. For this purpose Acts have been passed and provisions have been made for punishment in case of their violation.

However, in spite of these Acts it is often reported that women suffer at their workplace. There have been instances cruelty against women and many cases are reported where the interests of women have been ignored. This leads one to conclude that only legislative enactments can not ameliorate the unfavourable condition of women, though those laws may be instrumental in removing some disadvantages of women if properly applied. Legislations are necessary to act as catalysts for making others act. Legal sanctions may deter some individuals to behave in a derogative manner. Some may be afraid of the likely punishment given for violation of a law. But what really matters is the change of attitude of the persons associated with the working condition of women and then only women will get a better working atmosphere and feel protected.

References

1. Bhaurao Shankar Lokhande and Another vs. The State of Maharastra, AIR, 1965 SC 1564.
2. Vishaka vs. State of Rajasthan, AIR 1997 SC 3011.
3. Apparel Export Promotion Council vs. A.K.Chopra, AIR 1999 SC 625.
4. IPC, Section 354.
5. IPC, Section 509.
6. Box, Steven, *Power, Crime and Mystification*, Tavistock Publications, New York, 1983, p. 10 as quoted by Singh, Subhash Chandra, in "Sexual Harassment of Women in the Workplace: Need for a Comprehensive Legislation", *Supreme Court Journal*, 1998, p. 52.
7. Apparel Export Promotion Council vs. A.K.Chopra, AIR 1999 SC, 625.
8. Equal Remuneration Act, 1976, Section 3.
9. Equal Remuneration Act, 1976, Section 4.
10. Equal Remuneration Act, 1976, Section 5.
11. Equal Remuneration Act, 1976, Section 6.

12. Maternity Benefit Act, 1961, Section 2 (1) (a).
13. Maternity Benefit Act, 1961, Section 2 (1) (b).
14. Maternity Benefit Act, 1961, Section 5.
15. The Factory Act, 1948, Section 19 (f) (b).
16. The Factory Act, 1948, Section 19(3).

6

Status of Women in Rural India and their Role in Rural Development

Gautam Vir

The prevailing status of women in society has now been recognized all over the world as an important indicator of the progress of a nation and its development. It is also felt that the problem of poverty cannot be tackled without providing opportunities of productive employment to women. Productive employment to women would provide necessary economic base to improve their social status. The position of women in any given society serves not only as an index of its civilization, but also it influences to a great extent the socio-economic development of the country. The position of women acquires a greater importance in a democratic welfare state like India because it manifests the level of their wellbeing and the success of the country in achieving the goal of becoming a people centric state. It is needless to say that women can play their various roles properly only when they possess the necessary awareness, knowledge and skill. But all these depend upon the scope they are given and the status they enjoy in society. This explains the interest of social scientists studying the problems connected with the status of women.

Women all over the world suffer from certain disabilities and possess a status lower than that of men. In both the industrially advanced countries and less developed ones, women are burdened with cumulative inequalities as a result of socio-cultural and economic discriminatory practices, which until recently have been taken for granted as though they were part of the immutable scheme of things established by nature. It was only when the status of women was raised by removing their disabilities that they started playing their roles properly in various walks of life and contributing their might to the development of society. The advanced nations of the world were then convinced that the nation's well-being as well as that of its women depended upon development policies, programmes and research that fully utilized women's potential.

It was due to this experience of other countries that our leaders and policy makers wanted to take steps to raise the status of Indian women. Various writers referred to the inferior position of Indian women before independence. Even Gandhiji admitted that Indian women were subjected to all sorts of injustice at the hands of men and society. It is really shocking to note that our women possessed a very degrading and humiliating position in society before independence.

The status of women in a given society cannot be assessed in isolation from the social framework in which they live. Their status is closely related with the social structure, religion, family and kinship, cultural norms and value systems; these are important determinants of their position and behavior patterns in society as individuals as well as in relation to others inside and outside the family. This is truer in the context of the status of rural women in India where the process of modernization is rather very slow. The life and behavior patterns of the rural women and the attitude of the society towards them are shaped and guided by traditional socio-cultural norms and values which are so deep-rooted in the minds and hearts of the people that there seems a wide gap between the position the Constitution accords to women and the position they actually occupy in the traditional society. Religion, family and kinship, cultural norms, moral values etc. delimit the sphere of women's activities in the family and society. The rural women are yet to overcome the handicaps imposed by traditional norms and taboos and they are yet to enjoy a position of 'equality' with their male counterparts as individual citizens as acknowledged by the Constitution.

Indian society consists of different religious communities. The Hindu community constitutes an overwhelming majority of the total population of the country; in terms of percentage it is 82.72. The Muslim community is the largest religious minority, accounting for 11.21% of the total population. About 6% of the total population is comprised by the communities of the Christians, Sikhs, Buddhists, Jains and others. These different religious communities have their own religious faiths, socio-cultural norms and values and due to this fact women of the different communities differ in their position and behavior pattern.

Religion provides ideological, moral, cultural and traditional bases for the accorded status and role of women in a given society. Each religion has numerous myths and legends emphasizing certain values and guiding the conducts of its followers since their birth till their death. Each religion depicts the position, status and role of the two sexes in the process of social interactions and in the performance of the rituals at different occasions. The different social restrictions imposed on women, the different activities they are expected to perform in the domestic and extra-domestic spheres, people's notions about them and the different norms and taboos observed in society pertaining to women are largely derived from the religious conceptions prevailing in society. The basic notions of the tasks of women in society, their assumed virtues, limitations, voices, strengths, weaknesses etc. are also regulated by the religious precepts. All these, taken together, direct and outline their status and role in the family as sisters, wives, mothers etc. and as females in society. It is because of the enormous impact of religion on the lives of people, particularly in a traditional society like India that women of different religious groups possess different kinds of positions in family and society; the rank given to women varies from one religion to another. Religion not only demarcates the spheres of women's activities and prescribes their responsibilities, but also it exercises a determining influence on the attitude of men towards their womenfolk. Hence, for a better understanding of the status of women, it is necessary to analyze the position of women as laid down by different religions.

Status of Women in Hinduism

During the centuries of its existence, the image of women according to Hinduism has undergone many changes and their status has been shifting from period to period and from epic to epic. It is said that the women in Vedic period enjoyed a very high and honorable rank in society and they were provided with equality with their male counterparts.

After the Vedic period, the position of women considerably deteriorated and they were put under many restrictions as illustrated by the epics, Purans and Dharmasastras. The Hindu law giver Manu had made a woman entirely dependent on men and subjected her to the authority of her father, husband and son in different periods of her life as a daughter, a wife and a mother. According to him, there could be no freedom for a woman at any stage in her life.

Tulsidas also had a very poor opinion about women and compared a woman with a drum, a moron, a Shudra and an animal and considered her as an object fit to be beaten.

On the other hand, there are a number of honorable and praise-worthy attributes acknowledged in women in Hindu religion and women have been given highly respectable designations and considered as persons possessing commendable qualities. Many prestigious terms, such as the creator of mankind, a person full of piety, the centre of affection and love, a faithful companion, an individual full of character and chastity etc. have been used to refer a woman. It is a famous dictum in Hindu community that God resides where women are worshipped. A mother is a Goddess and fit to be worshipped and she should not be disobeyed by her sons in any respect and in any situation. Lord Rama willingly and happily followed his stepmother Kaikei and went to jungle for 14 years. Thus, a woman as a mother has been elevated to a very high position in many Hindu religious books.

However, a woman in Hinduism has different positions at different stages of her life. As a daughter she is trained for her future role in her married and family life. She is regarded as a property of an unknown male and is preserved and shaped in such a way that she happily performs her duties in her ensuing married life. At this stage, she is given all training so as to enable her to shoulder her new responsibility. As a wife, a woman is expected to love and serve her husband faithfully and give due respect to her in-laws. The moment she becomes the mother of a son, her status is raised in the family. A sonless mother does not get due care and is often ignored. She herself thinks that she is deprived of the most important treasure of her life. Thus, after marriage, the first and most important wish of her life is to become the mother of a son and not of a daughter since a daughter is regarded as inferior to a son.

The Hindu mythology narrates a number of stories relating to the sacrifices made by women for their husbands. Some of the well known women characters in Hindu mythology are Sita, Ahilya, Draupadi, Gandhari, Mandodari, Damayanti, Savitri etc. who are completely submissive and devoted to their husbands and who continue to guide and inspire the Hindu women to dedicate their life for the sake of their husbands. The faithfulness of wives to their husbands has been glorified and culminated in the expectation of immolation on the deceased husband's pyre (Sati) by the widow. This bad practice of Sati was banned by the British rulers. This, however, proves that a woman, without her husband, has no worth to live in the world. This feeling, by and large, prevails in the minds of Hindu womenfolk even today.

Marriage and motherhood are the most valuable and honorable goals for Hindu women for which they observe Vratas, fasts and worship in many ways. Significantly, a Hindu male does not observe any Vrata or fast and worship for the long life and welfare of his wife, whereas a Hindu female observes them for securing long life and prosperity of her husband. This again portrays an inferior and subordinate status of Hindu women.

The position of a Hindu widow is much inferior to a Sumangali woman or a woman whose husband is alive and as such she is denied of many of the facilities those are enjoyed by a Sumangali. For example, a widow is not welcomed in receiving a bride at the door of her husband. Similarly, she is not allowed to put vermilion on the forehead of a bride. Besides, there are many restrictions on the widow's dress and life style. They are not expected to use items of decoration and cosmetics, to wear glass bangles, flowers and attractive ornaments and coloured clothes. Plain, simple and white colour is always associated with her. These curbs are imposed on her with a view to enabling her to suppress her natural desires and to pass the life without any worldly pleasure.

Status of Women in Islam

The Shariat is regarded as a complete set of rules governing the whole life of both male and female in the Muslim community; their relationship, marriage, divorce, remarriage, property, inheritance, education, religious performance, social relationship etc. are governed by the Shariat. In some respects, both male and female are equal in Islam and in other respects women are regarded as inferior to their male counterparts. A Muslim woman, like a man, is an individual with a full right to worship the Khuda and to seek redemption. Islam does not consider a woman as an impediment in the path of religion and as a cause for the downfall of a man; she has the right as well as duty to recite Quran, to read Namaj and to go on fast for one month in Ramjan. In spite of this equality, a woman, however, can not be a priest and can not lead the prayer. She has no place in formal religious organizations and legal affairs of the community. She can not be appointed a Kazi.

The Purdah system in the Muslim community has made women much inferior to men and a series of constraints have been imposed on them. Some of the very common restrictions are – they should not converse with other men and if it is at all necessary to converse, they should converse under Purdah or with the help of a mediator; they should not talk so loudly that others can hear; they should not receive guests in the house without the permission of their husbands; they should not freely move in society and so on. Due to this Purdah system, Muslim women perform prayer and Namaz in their houses. They can join in the prayer at the mosque only when there is a separate and secluded arrangement for women.

In the Muslim community marriage is not a permanent bond of a male and a female. Although marriage is a contract among the Muslims it gives very unequal right to a man and a woman. The right of repudiation of marriage contract is with the husband. The contract, on the one hand, permits polygamy and on the other hand, restricts polyandry. Religion permits a man to have four wives at a time and a woman is not permitted in any case to have more than one husband. A wife, therefore, has a distinctly inferior status. After divorce, a woman can not claim subsistence allowance under the civil law except the Mehr which is the security for the wife against the possibility of a divorce made at the husband's free will.

Thus, the rural women in India, governed by the tenets of religions, have a very unequal position in society and very often they lead the existence of slaves wholly depended on men since birth till their death. The secondary status of women has been sanctified by different religions and the protagonists of different religions interpret the religious principle to suit their vested interests. As a result, different religions sometimes become instruments of suppression of women in India.

Constitutional Position of Women

After independence, the Constitution of India made a sincere attempt to rectify the adverse position of women in the country. The preamble of the constitution refers to "We the people of India" who mean both male and female and resolves to "all citizens of India equality of status and opportunity and liberty of thought and expression, besides bestowing social, economic and political justice to all.

In the Fundamental Rights chapter, Article 14 of the Constitution promises equality before law. Article 15 prohibits any discrimination on ground of sex. Article 16 ensures and guarantees equality of opportunity in matters of public employment. Article 17, abolishing untouchability and making it an offence punishable in accordance with law, provides an equal status to all those males and females of the scheduled caste people who were regarded as untouchables for so many centuries due to socio-religious complexities. Article 19 guarantees numerous freedoms to all citizens under some reasonable restrictions. Articles 20 and 21 provide protection to every person, both male and female, in respect of conviction for offences and guarantees protection of life and personal liberty of all.

The Directive Principles of State Policy contain some 'women-specific' principles and concern women directly; these have a very special bearing on their socio-economic status. Articles 40, 41, 43, 44, 45 and 47 relate to many welfare measures which are concerned with women indirectly.

Status of Women within the Family

In a traditional society, the rural family is the most prominent area of women's activities. In fact, women have practically no role outside the family in traditional, middle and upper class families and their whole life is spent within the four walls of their families. Even the women, who work outside the family due to economic pressures, concentrate on the family activities before and after their work. In fact, a woman with no activity in home is simply an exception. Therefore, the family provides the most suitable area for evaluating the status of women, whether they are working women or non-working women. In traditional rural India, a man is the head of the household and makes most of the family decisions. The traditional position of women is inferior to men in the family and they generally follow their male counterparts in the family matters.

But it does not always mean that the male are the 'masters' and the females are the 'servants'. In fact, due to changing socio-economic compulsions the attitude towards women has been changing and women have gradually been recognized as equal partners of men and they have begun to gain considerable freedom in family matters. The modern life and economic hardships and pressures are loosening the sex-ascribed roles in the family and women are enjoying considerable latitude in family matters and therefore, the male-dominance is gradually declining.

On its part, the government has also launched several schemes for improving the status of rural women and has invested huge amounts of money on these schemes.

Beneficiary-oriented Schemes for Women: Sector/Schemes

Category A – Schemes Exclusively for Women

I. Rural Development

1. Development of women and children in rural areas.

II. Education

2. Non-formal education exclusively for girls.

III. Family Welfare

3. Training of ANMs, Midwives and LHVs.
4. Training of Dais.
5. Immunization with TT for expectant mothers.
6. Village Health Guides Schemes.

IV. Labour and Labour Welfare

7. Vocational Training for Women.
8. Diversification and extension of the vocational training programmes for Women (including RVTIs).
9. Establishment of RVTI at Hissar in Haryana.
10. Establishment of placement cell and conducting training needs assessment surveys at RVTIs/HVTIs.
11. Establishment of additional RVTIs.
12. Strengthening of NVTI for women at New Delhi and RVTIs at Bombay and Bangalore.
13. Grants-in-aid to State Governments for establishing women ITIs.

V. Employment Services

14. Rehabilitation of handicapped women

VI. Development of Backward Classes

15. Girls' Hostels.

VII. Social Welfare

16. Hostels for working women
17. Employment and income generating training- cum-production centres

18. Condensed courses of education for women
19. Socio-economic Programme.
20. Training of rural women in distress.
21. Women's Development Corporations.
22. Rehabilitation of women in distress.
23. Short Stay·Homes
24. Crèches.

VIII. Science and Technology

25. Application of science and technology for women.

Category B – Schemes where Percentage has been fixed for Women

I. Rural Development

1. Integrated Rural Development Programme.
2. Training of Rural Youth for Self-employment.

II. Agriculture

3. Backyard Poultry Development.

III. Social Forestry

4. Tree Pattas.

Category C – Schemes which already cover adequate number of Women Beneficiaries

I. Rural Development

1. Rural Landless Employment Guarantee Programme.
2. National Rural Employment Programme

II. Education

3. Non-formal Education
4. Rural Functional Literacy
5. Khadi and Village Industries

III. Social Forestry

6. Rural Fuel Wood Plantation.
7. Soil Water and Tree Conservation in the Himalayas

Women's Involvement in Rural Development Programmes

A good part of rural economic activities are carried out by

women. According to our census reports, a significant portion of our rural workforce consists of women. Women are mostly engaged in agriculture either as agricultural labourers or cultivators, in household industries as artisans, in mining and construction activities as workers and to a small extent, they are engaged in other services. Thus, women are already participating in the rural economic activities. Without their co-operation, and effective involvement, no programme of rural development can succeed.

Women can specially play an important role in the institutional programme because they are directly involved in cooking food for the family and the children. They have a special role to play in making the family planning programme effective and successful. The Sixth Plan realized that to make their participation and involvement in rural development effective, "it would be necessary to remove all types of impediments which stand in the way of participation of women of all socio-economic groups as equal partners in the development process". According to the Seventh Plan document also women play an important role in the various economic activities of the country. Although out of the total female population in India, only 14 percent of them constitute workers their contribution to G.N.P. varies between 25 to 40 percent if their unpaid work is also taken into account. Their work participation adds significantly to the national output and family incomes.

In order to make them effective partners in the process of economic development they need to be properly educated and trained, made conscious and self-confident. They need to develop a scientific temper and thus made equal partners in the developmental process.

Conditions for Effective Participation and Involvement of Women

The Sixth Plan has rightly pointed out that to enable women for effective participation in rural development, there is the need for creating a sense of awareness and responsibility among them, and proper education and training and inculcating in them scientific spirit and temper to make them more productive in whatever fields they work. But this is not enough. Proper conditions have to be created by which women could be enthused and involved in the developmental work on their own. For this, the programmes of rural development must specify and elaborate the programmes of development of women. It is heartening to note that even a brief document like "the Approach Paper to the Seventh Plan" has devoted a paragraph enlisting schemes for development of women in the rural areas. According to this document it would be necessary to "adopt an integrated inter-disciplinary developmental approach consisting employment, health, family planning, education, nutrition, application of science and technology, for economic and social development of women". This would require an effective co-ordination of the sectoral programmes at the block, district, Sate and Central level.

The document also pointed out that in order to create a sense of awareness, responsibility and confidence among women efforts will have to be made for their economic and social advancement through grant of equal rights to economic resources, co-sharing of assets, social emancipation and their overall development as a group. The Plan has further promised preferential treatment to women in matters of employment, education and training, schemes of integrated rural development, TRYSEM schemes and facilities for women entrepreneurs. We believe that these are not only promises, pious wishes or hopes; these are not only to be worked out in details in the form of concrete and specific programmes and targets but also to be effectively implemented.

Conclusions

No doubt, the government has launched several schemes for improving the status of rural women and has invested huge amounts of money on these schemes. Still their impact is negligible or marginal at the most, due to the faulty implementation of these schemes. Efforts should, therefore, be made to implement the various schemes for ameliorating the conditions of women with due sincerity.

Government efforts alone are not sufficient for raising

the status of rural women. While the Government has a big role to play, attempts should also be made to involve as many voluntary organizations as possible. If found suitable, the services of such organizations as Christian Missionary Organization, Rama Krishna Mission, Sat Shri Sai Baba Mission, Lions Club, Rotary Club and other social organizations can be utilized for this purpose. Women's organizations like All India Women's Conference can also extend a lot of help in increasing the awareness of rural women. The Government should, therefore, contact and persuade these organizations to offer their help in this regard.

The rural women have no easily available proper medical facilities in the rural areas and they still depend upon road side physicians and other local treatments. In the process very often they pay a heavy price and sometimes there is loss of valuable lives. The Governments should, therefore, see that the services of qualified lady doctors, nurses and midwives are made available to the rural women.

Integrated rural development implies not only integrated implementation of various programmes but also integrated development of various target groups including women and weaker sections and their active participation and involvement in the developmental process. The Sixth and Seventh Five Year Plans have envisaged an important role of women in rural development and for this purpose creation of a sense of confidence, awareness and responsibility among women through a process of education and training is necessary. The Sixth Five Year Plan has made a modest beginning in this direction. But much more needs to be done; proper working conditions have to be created for them, economic and social impediments have to be removed if women are to play the role of equal partners in the developmental process.

The laws enacted for the well being of women and regulating different women problems like marriage, divorce, dowry, widow marriage etc. should be strictly implemented and the defaulters should be severely punished. Side by side, there should be a sustained publicity through mass media to educate the people to shake-off the age old traditional attitudes prejudicial to the position of women in society.

To sum up, all efforts should be made to improve the status of rural women who constitute 80 percent of India's female population. International women's Year and the consequent women's movements have no relevance to this large number of Indian women if their lot can not be improved. Different techniques to suit the socio-economic-cultural background of rural women should be employed to better their condition.

Notes and References

A. De Souza, *Women in Contemporary India,* Delhi : Manohar Book Service, 1975.

M.K. Gandhi, *Women and Social Justice,* Ahmedabad : Navjeevan Publishing House, 1968.

Draft Five Year Plan, 1978-83, Government of India, Planning Commission, New Delhi, p. 159.

The Approach to the Seventh Five Year Plan 1986-90, Govt. of India, Planning Commission, New Delhi, p. 32.

The Seventh Five Year Plan 1985-90 Vol. II, Government of India, Planning Commission, pp. 322-323.

J.J. Biddle and E.J. Thomas, *Role Theory : Concepts and Research,* New York : John Wiley and Sons Inc. 1966.

P.F. Secord and C.W. Backman, *Social Psychology,* New York : McGraw Hill, 1964.

E.E. Jones and H.B. Gerard, *Foundation of Social Psychology,* New York: Wiley, 1967.

K. Gould and Kolb, "Role" in *Dictionary of Social Sciences,* New York: The free Press, 1967.

L.J. Nieman and J.W. Hughes, "The Problem of the Concept of Role: A Resurvey of Literature", *Social Forces,* Vol. 30, 1951-2.

P.H. Prabhu, *Hindu Social Organisation,* Bombay : Popular Books, 1958.

Thomas, *Indian Women through the Ages,* Bombay : Asia Publishing House, 1964.

M.A. Indra, *The Status of Women in Ancient India* (second revised ed.) Bombay : Motilal Banarsidas Publishers, 1955.

Ministry of Social Welfare, GOI, Programmes and Schemes for Women's Development, New Delhi : Women's Welfare and Development Bureau, 1979.

P. Oakely and D. Marsden, *Approaches to Participation in Rural Development*, Geneva: International Labour Office.

Pradipto Roy, "Extension with the Disadvantaged" in G.E. James and M.J. Rolls (Eds.), *Progress in Rural Extension and Community Development*. Vol. I, UK: Univesity of Reading, 1982.

Om Shrivastav and R. Tandon, *Participatory Training for Rural Development*, New Delhi Society for Participatory Research in Asia, 1982.

W.R. Tracey, *Managing Training and Development Systems*, Taraporevala Publishing Industries.

7

Empowerment of Rural Women Through Development: Need for a Changing Perspective in India

Ashutosh Pandey and Archana Pandey

Rural Development is viewed as a complex process of change in the rural system and its various sub-systems leading to the desired improvements in rural income, employment opportunities, income distribution and other aspects of rural life. In all these activities, women who constitute half of the total strength are involved either as partners in bringing about the changes or as the beneficiaries of these changes. Moreover, women should be considered as the core of the rural development strategy not only in view of the key roles they play as producers and as deliverers of the basic needs but also because of their disadvantageous status as a result of continuous discrimination perpetrated on them since time immemorial. Unless special attention is paid to the cause of women the inequality persisting between men and women can not be removed.

However, while rural development policies and strategies demand a great deal from women in production and in family care, their access to knowledge, resources and decisions, which is of utmost importance to enable them to perform these roles adequately, has not received due attention, except in the recent past. In view of their activities, their involvement and integration in development process are vital towards eradication of the problems of poverty, unemployment, illiteracy and other social and economic difficulties.

Since the beginning of the UN decade for women, attention has been focused on the role of rural women in development. However, it is said that like development in general, rural development is also regressive in effect in relation to women. As the UN decade for women has been over, it is pertinent to look into the Indian experience in involving and integrating women in rural development.

Women constitute nearly half of the work force in the rural areas in the developing countries though their contribution to economic and social development remained largely invisible. The issue has attracted attention in the world at large. A perceptive understanding of women's rural economic activities is necessary to evaluate the strategy aimed at involving women in rural development and their outcomes. Women's activities are broadly divided into three categories: (a) Income producing, (b) Income-substituting, and (c) Home-making and child care. To this, one must add an important activity like participation in decision-making.

Case studies conducted in various developing countries including India, as part of the inter-regional ILO project on 'Energy and Rural Women's Work', confirm that rural women tend to work longer hours than men over all, with about half of their working hours devoted to essential survival tasks such as fetching fuel and water, cooking and childcare which are generally not considered 'productive labor'. A time disposition study on work participation by landless poor revealed that the average number of work hours per day varied from 15.00 to 18.07 hours and the time spent on domestic work alone is more than 8 hours excluding child care. Thus, women as care takers of the home spend more than an 8 hour work day with little or no financial reward, a thankless job for many women.

Equating female leadership with the dynastic account of leadership of females in South and Southeast Asia does not adequately explain the varied paths to power that many female political leaders in India have followed, at least in the past two decades. It also does not reflect the changing political scene in India which has seen the growing importance of the state level parties, resulting in a regionalization of politics, thus allowing regional or sub national leaders to become more influential at the national level. Prominent female politicians demonstrate the diverse manifestations of female political leadership in India.

Structural gender bias and gender-biased perceptions and expectations are understood to have a significant impact on assessments of behavioral style and performance. Yet these sources of gender power can be utilized by leaders, reinforcing and legitimizing stereotypes in exchange for political power. Identity politics and political discourse play important roles in the exercise of leadership. However, the implications for women's political participation suggest little short-term benefits for women in politics. The changing political system has only worked to catapult a few women into positions of power.

Nevertheless, female political participation and leadership in the local panchayats does have potential implications for the future generation of political leaders and the political participation of women. Contemporary accounts differ somewhat in explaining a leader's path to power, but many accounts reproduce an insider/outsider dichotomy, which distinguishes between two sets of individuals. "Insiders" have risen through the ranks of the political institutional infrastructure whereas "outsiders" come to political leadership and/or perform 5 formal political activities with little experience of the "rules of the game", yet may possess popularity, expertise, ambition, or substantial interest in policy issues, or any combination of these.

Gendered accounts of leadership highlights an additional category, the political 'surrogate', which, while similar to the concept of 'outsider', takes on its own unique significance in dynastic accounts of female leadership. There are two features that are important in the accession to Indian leadership—those of winning mandates and a leader's pathway to power. The importance of an individual's pathway to power in determining his legitimacy is especially relevant to the critique of the dynastic account of female leadership because "the path taken to leadership in some part determines the power held by the leader, the legitimacy of his leadership, and, to some extent, support for his policies" Therefore, a leader's route to the top determines in part the legitimacy that he or she commands and has implications for the success and sustainability of that leadership.

The political mobilization of women during the fight for Independence has been identified as one of the key factors in determining women's political participation in contemporary times. Several accounts of the women's movement in India which accompanied the nationalist struggle for independence from British rule, note the lack of an emancipatory outcome and the enduring subservient nature of women's role in society. Women were welcome to join the resistance to British colonial rule, but their political activity was encouraged only in so far as to support the traditional gender hierarchy within Indian society. As long as their political activity supplemented but didn't sacrifice their traditional duties as wives, daughters and sisters, their political activism was encouraged. However, several male supporters of reform for women's issues supported women's franchise.

Crucially, the nature of the women's movement and the participation of women in politics in India must be understood in terms of the impact of colonialism. Women rejected the label of "feminist" for fear of being accused of as unpatriotic; the enemy in their understanding was not their male counterparts but the forces of colonial power and "foreign domination". While the nationalist leader M.K. Gandhi supported the notion of female suffrage, he emphasized the need for unity and solidarity against the British Raj.

Gandhi consistently mobilized the Hindu goddess Sita as the supportive and sacrificing wife; in the process, "Gandhi was constructing a new ideal for Indian women that rewrote passivity and self-suffering as strength". Despite successful mobilization of women's organizations such as the All-India Women's Conference (AIWC), these organizations largely benefited middle-class women by providing experience of working within organizational structures. There were however, significant advances in women's legal rights and progress in addressing the need for women's education and with Independence women did obtain the franchise. Furthermore, their demands for a place in the government of newly Independent India were legitimized by their involvement in the nationalist movement.

The role of Indian women in post-Independence and modern Indian politics is directly related to the lack of a significant outcome for the women's movement after the achievement of Independence from British rule by the nationalists. While a liberal discourse of equality ensued upon Independence in 1947, by 1974 the Committee on the Status of Women in India produced a commissioned report titled 'Towards Equality' which evaluated and acknowledged the enduring plight of Indian women.

In the past, women's political participation was largely manifested through the women's movement, itself fragmented as a result of differing ideologies and issue-based protests, with only token numbers of women participating in "formal" politics, many of whom were from higher class and caste backgrounds and had been supported by liberal progressive families. The present women's movement has been organized on diverse issues like torture for dowry, attack or violence (including rape) against women, equal economic and employment opportunities with men (SEWA), ecofeminism, and anti-development protests opposed to displacement as in the Narmada valley or due to similar state-sponsored developmental projects.

In the last two decades, the Hindutva movement has also become a site of women's right-wing political mobilization although with dubious potential for the empowerment of women and has become particularly militant around communal issues. Modern Indian politics has seen political parties' appropriate women's issues, such as the concerns of the anti-arrack movement and appear sympathetic towards them in order to capture the women's vote. By adopting the interests of what could be considered a subaltern group in India, they are, employing a populist strategy for gaining political mileage. Positive change may therefore prove elusive and sympathy may turn out to be pure rhetoric, as political U-turns on prohibition laws have demonstrated.

As a consequence of this appropriation, much of the women's movement has fragmented along ideological and political lines as women's organizations operate as offspring of the major political parties. Despite the movement-based nature of the women's political mobilization, women are engaged in electoral politics which manifests similar overall turnouts for men and women at assembly and Lok Sabha elections, with some regional variance. The Lok Sabha elections in May 2004 elected just over 8% of female candidates to the Lok Sabha, with proportions of contesting and elected women candidates varying considerably among political parties. Some point the finger at the changing political party system; others attribute this to India's vast diversity in terms of electoral demands, from the Dalit movement of Uttar Pradesh to the regional identity discourse of the southern states. Many see both as factors causing the change. The demise of the dominant Congress (I) party has seen the simultaneous dilution of the Congress-based dynastic succession through the Nehru-Gandhi dynasty; yet the dynasty still remains central to the party's core supporters, with Sonia Gandhi as Congress party chairwoman and the entry into politics of her children, Rahul and Priyanka.

Populist politics in India is driven by the discourse centered on the politics of identity, which fragments and destabilizes the political agenda. Politics of regionalism as a result of India's vast diversity and the federal structure of the Indian polity have also contributed to this fragmentation of the political agenda and have given rise to the emergence of a fickle and unstable coalition era based more on expediency than on any ideology or policy agenda. Traditionally, this has presented a complex picture in terms of electoral alliances and campaigns.

Recently, however, in states such as Andhra Pradesh, Tamil Nadu and the Northern Hindi states that have strong regional parties, founded on a cultural discourse of regional identity or a spatially concentrated representation base, these smaller parties have proved to be very crucial in the alliance and coalition-building process for the national catch-all parties to access supporters of these regional parties. In exchange for increased power and representation at the national level, state-level parties enter coalitions with the national parties and the latter in theory receive an amount of cooperation and support from the state level parties. As a result, changes in party politics in India present alternative opportunities for women in India.

Several prominent female political leaders have occupied many high political offices, including the office of Chief Minister in different states; 12 women leaders have become Chief Ministers simultaneously, some for a longer period than others. As James Manor states, state level politics thus provides a wealth of experience for female political leaders and recently five of India's states were governed by female chief ministers, totaling around half the population of India.

Despite their growing importance and political clout due to the changing Indian electoral politics, there is currently less published materials in academic circles on them with regards to their leadership, even less so in terms of the role gender has to play. Further, arguments are forwarded in favor of women's higher moral capital support and it is argued that effort should be made to increase women's presence in electoral politics in the light of India's apparent decaying morality in the political sphere.

A majority of the villages in India do not have sustainable economies and only through oppression of women and lower castes can the landlords, upper castes and government officials support a better life for themselves, The social injustice that underlines this perennial problem cannot be addressed without a frontal attack on women's issues by targeting women alone; but it requires a comprehensive endeavor in which communities develop through sustainable and integrated programmes that impact everyone. Issues of rural poverty and health have traditionally been the concern of governments; however, in the present context a new orientation is needed to change the outlook.

In the past and even today, most programmes designed to benefit rural India are funded and managed exclusively by the government. Private initiatives are lacking as the government, to preserve its power, has placed obstacles and disincentives at every step. For example, modern healthcare for all of rural India is a free government service, but the reality is that the delivery of primary health care has failed miserably. A number of charitable institutions and non-governmental organizations (NGOs) have played a positive role, often assisted by government grants and foreign donations.

The World Bank has been the major source of external funding through loans to governments for specific projects. Very few projects have ever met their goals; in fact, most rural projects have been dismal failures. Unbearable bureaucracy, terrible inefficiency and rampant corruption at all levels of the government have wasted much of the money allocated to rural development.

Furthermore, the local officials who manage projects that target women do not themselves believe in the potential of women. Yet the process continues, without an alternative. International agencies continue to pour money into these programmes, only to benefit the middlemen. Clearly, a new approach is required to have an impact on the lives of women in rural India.

Empowerment of women involves many things like economic opportunity, social equality and personal rights. Women are deprived of these human rights, often as a matter of tradition. In rural areas, women are generally not perceived to have any meaningful income generation capacity and hence, they are relegated mainly to household duties and cheap labour. Without the power to work and earn a good income, their voices are silenced; there is no easy or quick fix to the problems related to women's empowerment and reproductive health in rural India.

The real solution lies in a holistic approach that deals with all the major interrelated issues of economic welfare, social justice, education, health and traditions/spirituality. The three key ingredients of success are trust, infrastructure for delivery and financial incentives. Behavioral change can be initiated and promoted only by those who have earned the trust of the people they claim to serve; government officials are amongst the least trusted and hence, they are the most ill-suited for the task. People listen to those whom they trust, but still may not act without financial incentives that are offered through economic opportunities, and without actually seeing the infrastructure for delivery of services. Hence, projects run exclusively by private and non-governmental institutions (funded directly by government, international agencies and private donors) and without unwanted governmental interference, have better chances of success.

Private initiatives in rural areas need not always be charitable or non-profit. In fact, products and services, including education and health services, paid for through fees based on income levels can be very effective in stimulating a village's economy. Private companies need to be encouraged to deliver products and services for profit, but at affordable costs. When non-profit institutions work with profit-oriented private companies in a competitive environment, products and services are delivered at an economic cost that even most rural people can afford.

When villagers realize that they are indeed the beneficiaries of projects, they begin to trust and have confidence in those providing the services. This then opens up the opportunity to educate people on different delicate topics such as sexual behavior, use of condoms, family planning, alcoholism, abuse of women and children and many others. Institutions that are best suited for communicating these messages are the villages' health clinics, schools, community centers and religious institutions. When project leaders become part of these institutions, they come closer to the people they serve.

In most rural areas, the primary symbol of wealth and respect is in owning cultivable land and/or cattle. When a woman earns and saves enough to buy either one on her own, she automatically gains immense respect and voice in her family and within the community.

The greatest tragedy facing humanity today is the persistence of chronic hunger – an intolerable phenomenon that takes the lives of 24,000 of us every day. For one-fifth of humanity, life is a daily struggle to survive in conditions of relentless poverty. Day after day, the lives of one billion individuals are cut short or terribly diminished by chronic and persistent hunger. Day after day, one billion people are denied the opportunities they need to lead healthy and productive lives. People living with chronic hunger subsist in conditions of severe poverty.

In order to gain a deep understanding of the condition of the status of women in India and its effect on the persistence of hunger, organized in a framework of seven issues that characterize the plight of poor women, with a focus on rural women in India: malnutrition, poor health, lack of education, overwork, lack of skills, mistreatment and powerlessness. The link between these issues and the continuity of hunger in India was underscored. In short, the poor care that is afforded to girls and women by their husbands and by elders is the first major reason for levels of child malnutrition that are markedly higher in South Asia than anywhere else in the world.

India, with a population of 989 million, is the world's second most populous country. Of that number, 120 million are women who live in poverty. India has 16 percent of the world's population, but only 2.4 percent of its land, resulting in great pressures on its natural resources. Over 70 percent of India's population currently derives its livelihood from land resources, which includes 84 percent of the economically-active women.

India is one of the few countries where males significantly outnumber females and this imbalance has increased over time. India's maternal mortality rates in rural areas are among the world's highest. From a global perspective, India accounts for 19 percent of all live births and 27 percent of all maternal deaths.

"There seems to be a consensus that higher female mortality between ages one and five and high maternal mortality rates result in a deficit of females in the population. Deaths of young girls in India exceed those of young boys by over 300,000 each year and every sixth infant death is specifically due to gender discrimination." Of the 15 million baby girls born in India each year, nearly 25 percent will not live to see their 15th birthday. "Although India was the first country to announce an official family planning programme in 1952, its population grew from 361 million in 1951 to 844 million in 1991. India's total fertility rate of 3.8 births per woman can be considered moderate by world standards, but the sheer magnitude of population increase has resulted in such a feeling of urgency that containment of population growth is listed as one of the six most important objectives in the Eighth Five-Year Plan."

Since 1970, the use of modern contraceptive methods has risen from 10 percent to 40 percent, with great variance between northern and southern India. The most striking aspect of contraceptive use in India is the predominance of sterilization, which accounts for more than 85 percent of total modern contraception use, with female sterilization accounting for 90 percent of all sterilizations. The Indian constitution grants women equal rights with men, but strong patriarchal traditions persist, with women's lives shaped by customs that are many centuries old.

In most Indian families, a daughter is viewed as a liability, and she is conditioned to believe that she is inferior and subordinate to men. Sons are idolized and celebrated. May you be the mother of a hundred sons is a common Hindu wedding blessing. The origin of the Indian idea of appropriate female behavior can be traced to the rules laid down by Manu in 200 B.C.: "by a young girl, by a young woman, or even by an aged one, nothing must be done independently, even in her own house." "In childhood a female must be a subject to her father, in youth to her husband, when her lord is dead to her sons; a woman must never be independent."

A study of women in the Swayam Shikshan Prayog (SSP), based in 20 villages in four districts in Maharashtra state was introduced in this way: The primary issue all women in the SSP were struggling with was that of everyday survival. Insufficient incomes and the lack of employment were reported to be their most pressing concerns. Survival is a constant preoccupation and at its most basic, survival means food. The most common problems were the lack of basic amenities such as food, water, fuel, fodder and health facilities.

India's maternal mortality rates in rural areas are among

the highest in the world. A factor that contributes to India's high maternal mortality rate is the reluctance to seek medical care for pregnancy. It is viewed as a temporary condition that will disappear. The estimates nationwide are that only 40-50 percent of women receive any antenatal care. Evidence from the states of Bihar, Rajasthan, Orissa, Uttar Pradesh, Maharashtra and, Gujarat find registration for maternal and child health services to be as low as 5-22 percent in rural areas and 21-51 percent in urban areas.

Some estimates suggest that some 5 million abortions are performed annually in India, with the large majority being illegal. As a result, abortion-related mortality is high. Although abortion has been legal since 1972 in India, "studies suggest that although official policy seeks to make pregnancy-termination on services widely available, in practice guidelines on abortion limit access to services, particularly in rural areas. In 1981, of the 6,200 physicians trained to perform abortions, only 1,600 were working in rural areas; given the number of Indian women who are anemic – 25 to 30 percent in the reproductive age group and almost 50 percent in the third trimester – this adds to their vulnerability to carbon monoxide toxicity. Additionally, with an increasing population, diseases caused by waste disposal, such as hookworm, are rampant. People who work barefooted are particularly susceptible, and it has been found that hookworm is directly responsible for the high percentage of anemia among rural women.

Girls receive far less education than men, due both to social norms and fears of violence. India has the largest population of non-school-going working girls. India's constitution guarantees free primary school -education for both boys and girls up to age 14. This goal bas been repeatedly reaffirmed, but primary education in India is not universal. The overall literacy rate for women is 39 percent versus the male literacy rate of 64 percent. The rate for women in the four large northern states —Bihar, Uttar Pradesh, Rajasthan and Madhya Pradesh—is lower than the national average; it was 25 percent in 1991. According to the 1981 census, the attendance rates in schools suggest that no more than 1/3rd of all girls (and a lower proportion of rural girls) aged 5-14 were attending school. Women's contribution to agriculture —be it subsistence farming or commercial agriculture – when measured in terms of the number of tasks performed and time spent, is greater than men. "The extent of women's contribution is aptly highlighted by a micro study conducted in the Indian Himalayas which found that on an one-hectare farm, a pair of bullocks works 1,064 hours, a man 1,212 hours and a woman 3,485 hours in a year."

In Andhra Pradesh, it has been found that the work day of women agricultural laborers during the agriculture season lasts for 15 hours, from 4 am to 8 pm, with an hour's rest in between. Her male counterpart works for seven to eight hours, from 5 am to 10 am or 11 am and from 3 pm to 5 pm. Another study on time and energy spent by men and women on agricultural work found that 53 percent of the total human hours per household are contributed by women as compared to 31 percent by men. The remaining contribution comes from children. In a report of the National Commission on Self-Employed Women and Women in the Informal Sector, the director of social welfare in one state said, "There are no women in any unorganized sector in our state." When the Commission probed and asked, "Are there any women who go to the forest to collect firewood? Do any of the women in rural areas have cattle?" the director responded with, "Of course, there are many women doing that type of work."

Working women are invisible to most of the population. If all activities-including maintenance of kitchen gardens and poultry, grinding food grains, collecting water and firewood, etc. are taken into account, then 88 percent of rural housewives and 66% of urban housewives can be considered as economically productive.

Violence against women and girls is the most pervasive form of human rights violation in the world today. Opening the door on the subject of violence against the world's females is like standing at the threshold of an immense dark chamber vibrating with collective anguish, but with the sounds of protest throttled back to a murmur. Where there should be outrage aimed at an intolerable status quo there is instead denial, and the largely passive acceptance of 'the way things are.'

Male violence against women is a worldwide phenomenon. Although not every woman has experienced it and many expect not to, fear of violence is an important factor in the lives of most women. It determines what they do, when they do it, where they do it and with whom. Fear of violence is a cause of women's lack of participation in activities beyond the home as well as inside it. Within the home, women and girls may be subjected to physical and sexual abuse as punishment or as culturally justified assaults. These acts shape their attitude to life and their expectations of themselves. The insecurity outside the household is today the greatest obstacle in the path of women.

In recent years, there has been an alarming rise in atrocities against women in India. Every 26 minutes a woman is molested. Every 34 minutes a rape takes place. Every 42 minutes a sexual harassment incident occurs. Every 43 minutes a woman is kidnapped. And every 93 minutes a woman is burnt to death over dowry. One quarter of the reported rapes involve girls under the age of 16 but the vast majority is never reported. Although the penalty is severe, convictions are rare.

The most extreme expression of the preference for sons is female infanticide and sex-selective abortion. A study of amniocentesis in a Bombay hospital found that 96 percent of female fetuses were aborted compared with only a small percentage of male fetuses. "Government officials even suspect that the disproportionate abortion of female fetuses may be a major underlying cause of the recent decline in the nation's sex ratio. In 1971, there were 930 females for every 1,000 males. A decade later this figure had increased to 934, but by 1991, instead of continuing to rise, the ratio dropped to 927, lower than the 1971 figure. This sex ratio is one of the lowest in the world,"

Women's rights to inheritance are limited and frequently violated. In the mid-1950s, the Hindu personal laws, which apply to all Hindus, Buddhists, Sikhs and Jains, were overhauled, banning polygamy and giving women rights to inheritance, adoption and divorce. The Muslim personal laws differ considerably from those of the Hindus and permit polygamy. Despite various laws protecting women's rights, traditional patriarchal attitudes still prevail and are strengthened and perpetuated in the home. The highest national priority must be the unleashing of woman power in governance. That is the single most important source of societal energy that we have kept corked for half a century.

Through the experience of the Indian Panchayati Raj Institutions (PRI) 1 million women have actively entered the political arena in India. The 73rd and 74th Constitutional Amendment Acts, which guarantee that all local elected bodies reserve one-third of their seats for women, have spearheaded an unprecedented social experiment which is playing itself out in more than 500,000 villages that are home to more than 600 million people. Since the creation of the quota system, local women—the vast majority of them illiterate and poor—have come to occupy as much as 43% of the seats, spurring the election of increasing numbers of women at the district, provincial and national levels. Since the onset of PRI, the percentages of women in various levels of political activity have risen from 4-5% to 25-40%.

However, there is still a lot to be done to achieve the objective of women empowerment. It is imperative to give more emphasis to the causes of women and protect their interests in the larger interests of the mankind as women not only constitute about half of the population but also help the other half to lead a better life. What constitutes the real interest of a woman is not better known to any body than a woman. She must be given proper opportunity to take decisions which concern her. Therefore, it is absolutely necessary to empower women and provide them development in true sense of the terms and include them in the mainstream of socio-economic-political process of the country.

References

Acharya, S., (1984), Women and Rural Development in the Third World, Paper presented at Workshop on Women, Technology and Forms of Production held at Madras Institute of Development Studies, Madras, *October*.

Agarwal, Bina, "Work Participation of Rural Women in Third World. Some Data and Conceptual Biases," *Economic and Political Weekly, A* 155 - A 164.

Ahmad, Iftikar, (1983), "Technology and Rural Women in the Third World," *International Labour Review*, 493-505.

Ahmad, Z.M. and Martha F. Loutfi, (1984), "Women Workers in Rural Development" A Programme of the Rural Employment Policies Branch, Employment and Development Department, ILO, Geneva.

Anker, Richard (1983), "Female Labour Force Participation in Developing Countries: A Critic of Current Definitions and Data Collection Methods," *International Labour Review*, 709-124.

Avinashalingam, T.S. (ed.), 'Eradication of Rural Poverty,' Sri Ramakrishna Mission Vidyalaya, Coimbattore, 1977.

Balasubrahmanyam, Virnal (1986), "Towards Women's Perspective on Family Planning," *Economic and Political Weekly*, 69-71.

Bardhan K., (1979), 'Work as a medium of Earning and Social Differentiation: Rural Women of West Bengal, Paper presented at A.D.C. - ICRISAT Conference on Adjustment Mechanism of Rural Labour Markets in Developing Areas, Hyderabad, August 22-24.

Batliwala, Srilatha (1983), 'Women in Cooking Energy," *Economic and Political Weekly*, 227-30.

Boserap, Ester (1.970), 'Women's Role in Economic Development,' St. Martin's Press, New York.

Brandtzaeg, Brita, (1979), 'Women, Food and Technology—Case of India,' *Economic and Political Weekly*, 1921-24.

Chariton, Sue Ellon M. (ed.), *Women in Third World Development*, Westerview Press, London, 1984.

Christopher Colclough (1982), 'the Impact of Primary Schooling on Economic Development: A Review of the Evidence,' *World Development*, 167-185,

Croll, Elizabeth (1982), Rural Women's Organizations, ILO (ed.) *Rural Women Workers in Asia.*

Das, Parimal, (1959), "Women under India's Community Development Programme," *International Labour Review*, (July-December), 27-45.

Deere, Carmen, Diana, (1982). "The Division of Labour by Sex in Agriculture: A Peruvian Case Study," *Economic Development and Cultural Change*, 795-811.

Devadas, P. Rajammal (1977), "Role of Women in Agricultural Productivity and Home Improvement," in Avinashlingam, T.S. (ed) *Eradication of Rural Poverty.*

Dhillon, Gurmeet, (1980), "Rural Women in Decision-making Action," *Kurukshetra*, 19-21.

Dixon, Ruth B., (1978), *Rural Women at Work-strategies for Development in South Asia*, John Hopkins University Press, London.

Dube., S.C., (1955), *Indian Village*. Routledge and Kegan Paul, London. Epistein,

Etienne, Gilbert, *India's Changing Rural Scene: 1963-1979*, New Delhi Oxford University. Press-1982.

Scarlet, (1962), *Economic Development and Social Change in South India*, Oxford University Press, India.

Government of India (1980), Planning Commission, Sixth Five Year Plan, New Delhi.

Government of India (1985), Seventh Five Year Plan, 1985-90.

Huntington, Suellen (1975), "Issues in Women's Role in Economic

Development: Critic and Alternatives," *Journal of Marriage and Family*, 1001-12.

Indira Devi, M., "Caste and Women's Participation in Labour Markets:

A Study of Landless Poor," Paper presented at the 2nd National Conference on Women's Studies, Trivandrum.

ILO - ARTEP (1981), *Women in the Indian Labour Force*, Bangkok.

ILO - (1982), *Rural Women Workers in Asia*, Geneva.

Jain, S.P. and Krishna Murthy Reddy, V, (1977), "Role of Women in

Rural Development (A Study of Mahila Mandals)", National Institute of Rural Development, Hyderabad,

Johnston Bruce F. and William, C. Clark, (1982), *Redesigning Rural Development—A Strategic Perspective*, The John Hopkins University Press, London, 102-104.

Kala, C.V., (1976), 'Female Participation in Farm Work in Central Kerala,' *Sociological Bulletin*, 185-206.

Lakshmi Devi Achanti, (1982), "Role of Rural Women in Agricultural Development," *Kurukshetra*, 15-20.

Lee, Man-Gap (Ed), towards a new Community Life—Reports of International Research Seminar on the Saemaul Movement, Institute of Samaeul Undong Studies, Seoul National University, Seoul, 1981.

Lele, Uma, (1986), 'Women and Structural Transformation', *Economic Development and Cultural Change*, 195-222.

Lisa Leghorn and Parker Catherine, (1981), *Women's Worth: Sexual*

Economics and the World of Women, Routledge and Kegan Paul, London.

Majumdar, Vina, (1978), *Role of Rural Women in Development*, Allied Publishing Pvt. Ltd., Bombay.

Marothia, D.K. and Sharma, S.K., (1985), 'Female Labour Participation in Rice Farming Systems of Chattisgarh Region,' *Indian Journal of Agricultural Economics*, 235-39.

Mukhopadhyay, Swapna, (1981), "Women Workers of India: A Case of Market Segmentation," ILO-ARTEP, Women in the Indian Labour Force.

Nagabrahman, D. and Sambrani, Sreekanth. (1983), 'Women's Drudgery in Firewood Collection,' *Economic and Political Weekly*, 33- 38.

Naik, J.P., (1983), *Relevance of Education to Development Especially in Rural Areas in Education and New International Order*, Concept Publishing House, New Delhi,

Narain, Dheerendra, (1970), "Interpersonal relationship in Hindu Family," in Reuben Hill and Rene Konig (ed), *Families in the East and West Paris*, The Hague Monton and Co.

Oppenheimer Valerie, Kincade, (1977), the Sociology of Women's Economic Role in the Family, *American Sociological Review*, 387-406.

Palmer, Ingrid, (1977), "Rural Women and the Basic Needs Approach to Development," *International Labour Review*, 97-107.

Parthasarathy, G. and Dasaratharama Rao, G., (1981), "Women in Indian Labour Force," ILO-ARTEP (ed.), Bangkok, 121-37.

Rolthschild, Constantina Safilios, (1984), "The Role of the Family in Development," in Sue Ellen M. Chariton (ed.), *Women in Third World Development*.

Rothschild, Constantina Safilios, (1985), "The Persistence of Women's Invisibility in Agriculture: Theoretical and Policy Lessons from Lesotho and Sierra Leone," *Economic Development and Cultural Change*, 299.

Sawer, J. Barbara, (1973), "Predictors of the Farm Wife's Involvement in General Management and Adoption Decisions," *Rural Sociology*, 412-426.

Sen, A.K., (1986), Women, Technology and Sexual Divisions, UNCTAD, Trade and Development, 195-223.

Sen, A.K. and S. Sengupta, (1983), 'Malnutrition of Rural Children and the Sex Bias,' *Economic and Political Weekly*, 855-864.

Sharma, Miriam, (1985), "Caste, Class and Gender Production and Reproduction in Rural North India," *The Journal of Peasant Studies*, 57-88.

Sisodia, J.S., (1985), "Role of Farm Women in Agriculture: A Study of Chambal Command Area of Madhya Pradesh," *Indian Journal of Agricultural Economics*, 223-230.

Suryawanshi, S.D. and Kapase, K.M., (1985), "Impact of Ghat Irrigation Project on Employment of Female Agricultural Labour," *Indian Journal of Agricultural Economics*, 240-244.

Tinker Irene and Cho Hyoung, (1981), "Women's Participation in Community Development of Korea," in Man-Gap Lee., (ed.) *Towards a New Community Life*, 343-386.

Thakur, Ramesh, *The Government & Politics of India*, New York: St. Martin's Press, 1995.

Wilson Fiona, (1985), "Women and Agricultural Change in Latin America: Some Concepts Guiding Research," *World Development*, 1017-1035

Weiner, Myron, *The Indian Paradox: Essays in Indian Politics*, Edited by Ashutosh Varshney, New Delhi; Sage Publication, 1989.

8

Women and Development: Innovative Strategies

Sushma Yadav

Women's role in development is an indispensable factor. Community development is incomplete without their participation and contribution. Development projects that tend to ignore women's needs and contributions have often miserably failed. Women are usually not involved in the process of developmental activities, which affect their lives. If development is understood as an improvement in the lives of all, than the improvement in the status of women should be an indicator. Unless and until women are empowered to fully participate in the national programmes and projects by gaining access to and control of both material and information resources they will not be able to transform the structures and institutions that perpetuate gender discrimination and social inequality.

Development is a multi-dimensional and multi-faceted phenomenon. It is a continuous and complex process which involves diverse agencies and people with different hierarchic levels of living, professing different occupations and having a variety of cultural identities. It encompasses myriad intervention strategies depending upon the social, economic, political and cultural status of the people. Exogenous models of development alien to the local genius can go up to a point but remain ineffective in the long run to solve the chronic deficiencies and socio-institutional imbalances. Real development can take place only by solving the problems of poverty of all kinds and of all shades of people, men and women, high and low and advantaged and disadvantaged. So development is incomplete without developing women who constitute about 50 per cent of the population.

Even broad concepts of development, which include the achievement of self-respect as well as growth of national output, remain focused on the production of goods and services which are sold in the market. The reproduction and maintenance of human resources is taken for granted. This is the result of an utter neglect of gender relations. The way in which children are raised, sick people nursed, old people cared for, as a non-commodified process undertaken without pay, is left out of account. They are not accepted as assets which can be sold and so, not taken as a part of human capital formation. This reasoning is a fall out of the ways in which development is conceptualized and 'strategy' is formulated. Both these processes are inimical to women's work and render their major work/activity as unpaid and unproductive.

During the last decade, the concept of human development has received much attention in development economics because it provides a link between growth and development. Development is more than just expansion of income and wealth. Human Development is being perceived as an end and growth as a means. The Human Development Report 1990 has defined development as a process of enlarging people's choices. The most crucial of these wide-ranging choices are to live a long and healthy life, to be educated and to have access to resources needed for a decent standard of living. Human capabilities can be formed through good health, knowledge and skills. The formation of human capabilities and the use people make of their acquired capabilities are the basic requirements for the enhancement of their choices and capacity to exercise them.

Strategies for development are generally not designed in favour of or against men or women but the lack of explicit consideration of gender relations in them means in practice that they often tend to neglect women. This absence of gender considerations in the conceptualization of strategies for national development proves to be detrimental to women because the overall national development is likely to have much wider implications for the social, economic and political position of women than specific projects and programmes targeted at women. Moreover, neglect of gender inequality is likely to limit the effectiveness of national development strategies in achieving wider goals such as growth, structural transformation and human development.

This paper seeks to explore some of the conceptual reasons for this failure and suggests a re-conceptualization of development as a gendered structure and of development objectives which integrate the social, economic and gender dimensions of development. It is assumed that a gender-aware perspective on development helps to design more human-centered development strategies.

Development strategies are usually and typically conceptualized by economists in terms of savings, investments, imports, exports and growth with varying roles assigned to markets and prices and state controls and expenditures. Keith Griffin, a well-known development economist, has identified six major development strategies which have been carried out by governments in developing countries. They have been described as the monetarist, the open economy, industrialization, green revolution, redistributive and the socialist strategies (Griffin 1989). Five of these six strategies could be seen relying on five different 'engines of development', i.e., private sector, foreign trade sector, industrial sector, agricultural Sector, and state sector. Each strategy uses a range of policy instruments to harness the power of one of these engines for pulling along the rest of the economy. Though the role of the state Sector varies between strategies, in all cases the strategy is conceptualized as a set of policies which some departments of the state (for instance, the ministry of finance, ministry of trade and industry and pslanning commission) prescribe for the economy on the basis of technical advice. What is missing in this otherwise perceptive analysis is the notion that gender is an important social relation that impinges on all aspects of economic life and may shape the design and outcomes of development strategies.

A gender approach to development is essential to make gender relations visible in the development process. It facilitates the view that 'women' as a general category, can be added to the existing approach to change development outcomes so as to improve women's position. It aids the view that women's issues can not be tackled with out considering the relations of women to men. It also explains that the problem is not women but the disadvantages that women face and that women are not unreasonable in asking for special treatment to redress injustices and to remove distortions which limit their capacities. Moreover, it tends to make it clear that women should not be treated as a homogeneous group with similar interests and identical viewpoints everywhere.

An emphasis on gender highlights the fact that work is gendered; that some tasks are seen as women's 'work' and to do those is considered demeaning for men, while other tasks are 'men's work' and to perform those is not considered womanly. A gender approach encourages a questioning of the supposed unity of the household and examines the notion of the relative power of women and men. A gender approach allows greater flexibility and tends to permit greater awareness of the different ways that different women experience gender.

Therefore, it is essential to understand and underline that any conceptualization of development that does not take account of the care and nurture provided in the home and the community by mothers, sisters, friends and neighbors just because that care is not organised through the cash nexus, is faulty; it ignores the fact that that care is central to human life and it is needed for the very existence of mankind. Though this care is not provided for direct material reward, it nevertheless entails work. The primary/major way in which this work is organised is through social relations, which are explicitly gendered like those of husband and wife, mother and father, daughter and son, sister and brother in contrast to social relations like worker and employee/boss, peasant and landlord, which are not gender-ascriptive. A critical issue for women, thus, is how the work of reproducing and maintaining human resources, raising children and looking after the sick and the old is integrated with getting a living or having an income.

The most crucial aspect of this phenomenon is that the way children are raised may take different forms in different societies. Generally and dominantly, the work of reproducing and maintaining human resources does not carry with it an entitlement to an independent income and those who bear the major responsibility for it must either undertake some additional work to generate an income of their own or become dependent for income transfers on those who are largely free from the unpaid work and engaged in earning for others.

In the Indian context, Government of India has brought out IRDP, TRYSEM, DWACRA and other special programmes for the development of women. Women's development began mainly as a welfare oriented programme in the First Five Year Plan (1951-56). The Central Social Welfare Board (CSWB), set up in 1953, undertook a number of welfare measures through the voluntary sector. The Second Five Year Plan (1956-61) organised women into Mahila Mandals to act as focal points at the grassroots levels for the development of women. The Third, Fourth and other interim plans (1961- 74) accorded high priority to education of women and introduced measures to improve maternal and child health services, including supplementary feeding for children and nursing mothers etc. The Fifth Plan (1974-78) saw a shift in the approach for women's development from "welfare" to "development" to cope with several problems of the family and the role of women; the new approach aimed at an integration of welfare with development services. A landmark in the history of women's development took place during the Sixth Five Year Plan (1930-85) by including a separate chapter and adopting a multidisciplinary approach with a three pronged thrust on health, education and employment.

The developmental programmes for women continued in the Seventh Plan (1985-90) with the major objective of raising their economic and social status to bring them into the mainstream of national development. A significant step in this direction was to identify/promote the beneficiary-oriented programme for women in different developmental sectors which extended direct benefits to women. The Eighth Five Year Plan (1992-97) which was launched in 1992, marked a shift from development to empowerment in the approach to women development schemes. It promised to "ensure that the benefits of development from different sectors do not bypass women" and women must be enabled to function as equal partners and participants in the development process. The report of the committee on the status of women exposed the hyperbolic character of women's welfare programmes. That the constitutional safeguards and legislative enactments were a mockery of democracy was evident from the compiled data of criminal violence and other atrocities committed on women in families and social setup and in the different economic development structures. In the Ninth Five Year Plan (1997-2002) two major steps towards gender justice have been taken for the first time in the history of planning. The first is the listing of empowerment of women as a major plan objective. The other is to propose inclusion of a women's component plan in the plan of all central Ministries/ Departments and of state governments/Union Territories' Administration.

A number of studies during the eighties indicated the irrelevance of developmental policies at grassroots because those policies failed to stir the patriarchal hold over rural assets which has contributed to the marginalization of women creating a wide wage differential between men and women in addition to the latter's low status, low literacy and low work conditions. The process has also led to the gradual draining out of rural resources to the market forces. So much so that women have been unable to hold on to the benefits that flow out of the various poverty eradication schemes of income generation, like IRDP, TRYSEM, NREP, RLBGP or programmes for special areas like D&DP or DDP or programmes of giving back up support like MNP. Thus, women have continued to sink into a disempowered and dependent existence.

Almost three decades have passed since then and women

seem to have crossed over the 'mother child syndrome' of policy makers. It seems more and more obvious to policy planners now that grassroots agricultural economies, which employ 70% of working population of which 84% are women, cannot continue with those growth oriented policies which marginalize women.

Today, the Indian state has accepted women's empowerment as its major policy goal. It has also accepted women as active agents, participating in and guiding their own development. Happily in the Ninth Plan, as mentioned above, there was a veritable sea change in plan perspectives. Until then women's development, to quote the document, was primarily 'welfare oriented'. The focus was always on health, nutrition, education and in the early nineties, on training for employment. The demands that there was a need to recognize women as participants in development made little headway. The approach during the earlier period was patronizing and chauvinistic. The draft was therefore significant in promising, as it did, "to create an enabling environment where women can truly exercise their rights in and outside homes as equal partners along with men." The Ninth Plan directed both the Centre and the states to adopt the 'Women's Component Plan' through which no less than 30 per cent of funds and benefits are earmarked to the women-related sectors. There is no doubt that women's development is directly related to national development. The effective management and development of women's resources i.e., their abilities, interests, skills and other potentialities are of paramount importance for the mobilization and development of human resources.

Continuing it further in the Tenth Plan and the approach paper to the Eleventh Plan have envisioned a growth strategy that would be "much more roadways and inclusive, bring about a faster reduction in property and helping bridge the divides" which are challenging the harmonies of development. The plan paper recognizes the need for gender balancing by taking care of the special needs of women and planning special measures for gender empowerment and equity. The plan's strategies focus on three aspects particularly—violence against women, women's economic empowerment and women's health.

If development is about people, it is essential to increase their capabilities to develop themselves; if women are in a state of social, economic, political and knowledge disempowerment, the imperative is to reverse this process. Instead of merely adding a gender agenda to a development plan drawn up by a gender insensitive system, the goal should be to redraw it by mainstreaming women's perspectives. It is this empowerment strategy which has emerged as India's response to the challenges of equality, development and peace. For women to be truly empowered it is necessary to provide an expanding network of services so that they are freed from some of their gender related shackles of a practical nature and are also enabled to aspire to the actualization of their strategic gender needs.

The concept of "Empowerment" is often understood by different people in different ways. There is a need for conceptual clarity to ensure its suitability in approach and method. Part of the problem with understanding and implementing empowerment is the difficulty of defining precisely what empowerment is. It is necessary to decipher empowerment properly, in stead of making it a catchword in the political circle while deciding a policy and implementing a plan. Otherwise the concept of empowerment will be shrouded with many ambiguities. Empowerment, too often, can simply mean shouldering more responsibility with less reward. This type of interpretation will never serve the purpose of having empowerment.

Power in the social context, implies a process of governance, regulation, direction and influence for the sake of protection and uplift of the people both individually and collectively in a symbiotic manner. Empowerment is considered a little more than delegation: some see it simply as an element of some other change in existing programme, while some others define it in terms of encouraging and allowing individuals to take personal responsibility for improving the way they do their job and contribute to the common goals. It requires the creation of a culture which not only encourages people at all levels to feel that they can make a difference but also helps them to acquire the confidence and skills to do so. Development of women in terms of their empowerment in its simplest form means the readjustment of distribution of power.

Despite the proclaimed policy of encouraging and involving the different sections of people for a greater participation for overall development, a large number of people in India continue to be excluded from the benefits of development; especially, the weaker sections of society including women still remain noninvolved in the development process.

After five decades of planning in India, women are far below their counterparts. The main reason for such a plight of women has been their non-involvement and non-participation while decisions are made in governance and development.

When Balwant Rai Mehta Committee Report suggested co-option of two women members along with one SC and one ST member and later when Ashok Mehta Committee Report suggested election of these two women obtaining highest votes, it was largely felt that 'co-option by election' would be a form of reservation for women and would answer all aspects of women miseries at the village level. However, much of this structural sensitization was considered without micro surveys involving identification of the problems, study of feasibility planning and assessment of the women participants at the implementation and evaluation stages of public policy. The result was a very weak representation of only one or two co-opted or nominated women members in a village panchayat of 15 to 19 members.

One recommendation of Ashok Mehta Committee Report that later accelerated the process of empowerment of women was to elevate the village panchayat from the level of a mere development institution to a political institution. It may be seen that this suggestion in no way came as a concern for women but as an indispensable requirement for designing a self-reliant grassroots structure. It was only in the G.K.V. Rao Committee Report (1985) that a sub-committee, constituted exclusively of women members, was suggested at the intermediary Panchayat or Mandal/Samiti Level to look into the problem of women and children.

Ironically, women were never considered for any role beyond the women and child welfare activities. To pursue a policy where women could participate in the local planning was beyond the comprehension of not only Ashok Mehta Committee but also of the Dantwala Working Group appointed by the Janata Government. Although Ashok Mehta suggested a close association of Panchayati Raj Institutions with planning at every step and Dantwala group suggested a complete detachment from district planning, there was little to highlight the importance of women in village planning.

The 73rd Constitution Amendment Act empowers women to take part in decision making in decentralized governance and development. Women have been trying their best to make themselves assertive in local governance. But the ground realities such as illiteracy, poverty, unemployment and ignorance, inhibit them from assertion.

The outcome of these elections in terms of women's participation has been very encouraging. Elections in Karnataka, Orissa and West Bengal earlier had witnessed appreciable number of women turnout as voters as well as candidates. Not merely in the reserved constituencies, even in the general constituencies, women had stood with great confidence. In many states, the percentage of women who got elected to PRIs exceeded the reserved positions. Thus, it can be said that in all these above instances, the participation of women went beyond expectations.

As a result of this mighty revolution, Tamil Nadu elected around 40,000 women. In Rajasthan, 33,566 women were elected out of which 1741 women were Sarpanchs. In Karnataka, instead of 33 per cent, women cornered 42 per cent seats in village panchayats, which was 9 per cent more than the mandatory 33 per cent reservation. This favorable change for women took place despite the fact that literacy is quite low in Karnataka. The most heartening aspect was to come across many 'all women panchayats'. There were the areas where a new thrust was felt for women welfare programmes. Most of these PRIs widened the areas of District Rural Development Agency, SC and ST Tribal Cooperative Societies, Minorities Financial Cooperation and the National

Rural Employment Programme (NREP) and Rural Landless Employment Guarantee Programme (RLEGP).

The experiences gathered about women's participation in Panchayats show that a woman leader has been projected as somebody's mother or wife or sister or widow and not as a people's representative. On the other hand, there are cases where the women have played a leading role in local development. After having been elected as members or chairpersons or vice-chairpersons of different Panchayat bodies, the women leaders have made many constructive contributions and their own lives have been affected positively.

Examples show that women initially were not participating in the meetings of Panchayats, but started participating later on. Not only this, in Karnataka, when panchayats were handed over to the bureaucracy, women's groups in Bijapur district formed the committees to monitor the bureaucrats' performance. Those, who were shy earlier even in attending meetings, had later on become assertive; the reason for this change was the opportunity given to women for participation in the decision making process. The basic disabilities before women are illiteracy, assetlessness and ignorance. If these disabilities are removed, they could perform their role no less effectively than their counterparts.

The new panchayat configurations have led to the unfolding of innumerable issues, which can be handled by women very successfully. The politics of uncertainty and colonial governance has created a lot of confusion over the allocation of functions to each level of Panchayat inherent in Article 243(G). Similarly, the power of the state government regarding the allocation of functions under the Eleventh Schedule has been usurping the power of the panchayats. The Dalit women Sarpanchs face an additional problem of suffering the wrath of the dominant castes at the village level that under no circumstances are ready to surrender their control over the village matters. All these women have to be trained to use their rights and positions in the Panchayats.

Several NGOs have undertaken programmes of systematically training the women. Arivoli Iyakkam in Tamil Nadu, Satyamurti Centre for Democratic Studies, Makkal Sakthi Iyakkam (Madras), Gandhi Gram Rural Institute

(Gujarat), Empowerment and Sustainable Development Institute (ESDI, UP), Indian Social Institute (Delhi) and All India Women's Conference (AIWC) along with National Commission for Women (NCW) have assumed training programmes for women Panchayat Members and chairpersons all over India. It was manifested in the activities of these women that despite the handicap of village literacy level as low as 3 to 4 percent, they could sweep off several unfair decisions imposed upon their villages and could also successfully direct action against the connivances of corrupt bureaucrats with dishonest contractors under the chaperoning of local politicians having vested interests.

People's participation is a necessary pre-condition for the successful implementation of any plan programme. This is based on the assumption that the process of people's development is not likely to strike very deep roots unless the target groups themselves are part of it. Participation is a means of reducing power differences and is, therefore, contributory to equalization and social justice. Participation in public life has many facets.

It includes activities which have strong bearing on a group and the community, the power to effectively influence the elected representatives, decision-making process as well as policies and actually altering the existing situations wherever they are found to be clearly disadvantageous. While women should be positioned in large number at crucial levels for significant and effective exercise of power, they need to be equipped with suitable means to shoulder these responsibilities. Otherwise their representation would end up as mere tokenism.

The key instruments of the strategy for women's development both as the beneficiaries and as the participants are, therefore, grass-root level organizations of women for learning and being engaged in a productive activity. This would help to (i) draw them into the mainstream of development; (ii) promote self-reliance and collective action; (iii) strengthen their participation and increase their voice in the development process; (iv) assist them to achieve economic viability as well as knowledge for their personal growth; (v) provide forums to enable women, especially from the poorer sections, to participate freely and fully in decisions that affect their lives and that of the community; (vi) enable them to acquire full access to development of resources and services; and (vii) enable them to function as instruments of social change.

The process of empowerment is multi-dimensional and it enables women to realize their full potentiality and powers in all spheres of life. Women empowerment begins with the perceptions of a woman of herself and her rights and her capabilities and her potentials. It makes her aware of how gender and socio-cultural and political forces affect her. Political empowerment, economic development and social uplift of women are necessary and desirable to fight myriad forms of patriarchal domination and discrimination at every stage. In fact, women's empowerment is central to the achievement of the triple goals of equality development and social justice. And for that political participation is needed. In a democratic system, women participation may be viewed at two levels, (i) awareness and assertion of women's political rights and (ii) acquisition and exercise of power.

Women have a distinct role to play in the development of the nation. In the role of a mother, a woman shapes the personality and character of her children and hence, the character of the nation. As a housewife, she maintains the productivity of human capital within the household through proper management of home. Apart from this, a woman herself represents a unit of human capital and is, therefore, capable of making a contribution to the economy of the nation. For a country like ours, people, both male and female, are the only abundant asset. Women constitute nearly half of the population. There can not be true development or growth of a nation with half its population living in ignorance, withdrawn from the mainstream, unrecognized and unaccounted for. With this background, women rank as the very important resource in the nation's development.

The UN Development Report puts it thus, "Development must be participatory and for this, people must have the opportunity to participate and to invest in the development of their capacities. All the citizens must have the opportunity to put their capabilities to use, to be fully involved in all aspects of life, to express themselves freely and collectively."

Mega projects in the Development Sector introduced by world organizations virtually dictate identification of women as partners in development and roping in the NGOs as mobilizers. The attractive terms of reference have created new ambitions among the GOs to grasp the opportunity to become NGOs by opting for voluntary retirement. It is important that the world organizations also prescribe the essential quality of the NGO in terms of number of years of experience of working at the grassroots levels.

Women as partners in the process of development need to be empowered in terms of information update and skills in correct choice and decision making. They will also be required to take an independent stand in case of oppressive and unjust forces acting in self-interest than for the benefit of the project. One more asset of women force is that they adapt to changes quite easily. They do not take long to adjust to a new role. The monitoring agency of a plan ought to consider fresh inputs to ensure continued role enhancement and prevention of stagnation.

"Participation" means direct involvement of the masses individually or through their representatives. Participation cannot be imposed on the people from above. It should be voluntary and based on the will to participate. People's participation in (i) decision-making; (ii) implementation of development programmes and projects; (iii) monitoring and evaluation of development programmes and projects and most importantly, (iv) sharing the benefits of development, is most essential for the success of a development project.

The participation of women in the PRIs is considered necessary not only for ensuring political participation in the democratic process but also for realizing the developmental goals for women. Participation of women in PRIs involves: (i) Women as voters; (ii) Women as members of political parties; (iii) Women as candidates; (iv) Women as elected members of PRIs taking part in decision-making, planning, implementation and evaluation and (v) Women as members of Mahila Mandals and their association with the voluntary organizations.

Therefore, programmes to help women can have much wider impact; they can reveal family poverty, improve the quality of human resources and reduce population growth rate. Women should be the main forces in the stream of development, since they are responsible to the community as a whole for further generation. Once the active participation of women is established, a community can and will be a cohesive and really representative unit.

Although participation in economic production is the base to improve the lot of women, it is not enough by itself. Women must be involved as men in the struggle against poverty and injustice; without such involvement, poverty may be overcome, but exploitation and oppression of women would remain unchanged. In addition, it is important for women to participate in political decision-making as it is politics which determines the direction and pace of most development plans.

A fuller participation of women in development, requires an all round transformation in the consciousness of both men and women as also in the socio-cultural norms, the mass media and the pattern of education. All of which at present tend to perpetuate a passive and unequal role for women in social, economic and political affairs.

Effective participation of all women in development as intellectuals, policy makers and decision-makers, planners, contributors and beneficiaries should be strengthened according to specific problems of women in different regions and the needs of different categories of women in them. That commitment on the part of the policy-makers should guide the formulation and implementation of strategies, policies, plans, programmes and projects. This Innovative approach towards strategizing must rest on the awareness and belief that development prospects will improve and society will advance through the full and effective participation of women.

References

Books

1. Boserup, Ester (1970), *Women's Role in Economic Development*, London, Allen and Unwin.

2. Boserup, Ester and Christian Liljencrantz (1975), *Integration of Women in Development: Why, When, and How?*, New York, United Nations, Department of Public Information, UN.
3. Elliott, Carlyn M., "Theories of Development: An Assessment" in *Women and National Development* (1977) edited by Wellesley Editorial Committee, Chicago, Chicago University Press.
4. Gupta, AK. (Ed.), (1979) *Women and Society, The Developmental Perspective,* New Delhi, Criterion Publications.
5. Karl, Marilee (1995), *Women and Empowerment, Participation and Decision Making,* London and New Jersey, Zed Books Ltd.
6. Kolhar, Suman (1993), *Decentralization, of Power and Role of Women in Panchayati Raj System,* New Delhi, NIEPA.
7. Mishra, Anil Dutta (Ed.) (1999), *Gender Perspective: Participation, Empowerment and Development,* New Delhi, Radha Publications.
8. Mishra, S.N. and Kumar Lokesh, (1996), *New Panchayat Raj in Action,* New Delhi, Mittal Publications.
9. Mukherjee, Neela (1993) *Participation, Rural Appraisal, Methodology and Applications,* New Delhi, Concept.
10. National Perspective Plan for Women 1988-2000 AD, Report of the Core Group Set up by the Department of Women and Child Development, Ministry of Human Resources Development, Government of India.
11. Nirmala Buch (2005), "Women and Panchayats: Opportunities, Challenges and Supports", L.C. Jain ed., *Decentralisation and Local Governance,* Orient Longman, New Delhi.
12. Nussbaum, M. and Glover J. (ed.) (1995), *Women, Culture, and Development: A Study of Human Capabilities,* Oxford, Clarendon Press.
13. Rounaq Jahan, (1995), *The Elusive Agenda: Mainstreaming Women in Development,* London, Zed Books.
14. Yadav Sushma & Mishra, Anil Dutta, *Gender Issues in India,* Radha Publication, New Delhi, 2003.

9

National Policy for the Empowerment of Women 2001—An Appraisal

M.V.S. Koteswara Rao & B.P.C. Bose

> "You can tell the condition of a nation by looking at the status of its women."
>
> —Jawaharlal Nehru

Empowerment of women is an on-going concern of the academicians, researchers, policy makers, bureaucracy and political executives, NGOs, Civil Society Organisations and the important components of the society and the stake holders themselves—Women activist groups, both at the Union and state levels in India and all over the world. Both the Union and State governments in this regard have initiated several measures covering the multiple dimensions of issues relating to women since independence. Over the years, several expert committees and commissions have been appointed to look into the problems and issues connected with women apart from the initiatives in the form of various enactments by the Union and State governments.

The focus of these expert bodies is mainly on improving the status of women through different methods, such as, institutional arrangements, allocation of proper role and status to women, allocation of resources to specific policies and programmes concerning women, etc. These efforts, no doubt, have aimed at correcting the limitations and inadequacies of women and strengthening and revitalizing their role and status in the country.

However, many observers and analysts have expressed an opinion to the contrary and hold the view that most of the efforts directed towards empowerment of women have not been translated into reality.

In spite of the proclaimed commitment to the issues and problems relating to women, the post independence scenario indicates that the condition and the status of women is one of negligence, discrimination, subjugation and marginalization. They suffer from hunger, poverty, malnutrition, ill health, lack of education, overwork, and mistreatment in greater numbers and to a greater degree.

The women have become so unwanted and undesirable that according to one estimation deaths of young girls in India exceed those of young boys by over 3,00,000 each year, and every sixth infant death is specifically due to gender discrimination. Of the 15 million baby girls born in India each year, nearly 25 per cent will not live to see their 15th birth day (see, www.thp.org. / reports, p. 4). The same is proved to be correct in a study conducted by UNICEF in 1996.

Social institutions all over the world are in a transition. So are the nature, role and status of women in various societies. The Indian situation is no exception to this. The paper is addressed to the efforts of empowering women in the post-Independence period in India, especially in the light of National Policy on Empowerment of Women (2001). The paper also presents the limitations of the policy.

The term empowerment has different meanings in different political and social contexts. The contextual meanings associated with empowerment include—self-strength, self-control, self-power, self-reliance, having one's own choice, leading a life of dignity in accordance with one's values, capable of fighting for one's rights, having one's independence, having one's own decision making power, one being free, awakening and having a right to acquire capability. Empowerment has an intrinsic value. It also has an instrumental value. Empowerment is relevant both at the individual and collective levels.

There are obviously many passing definitions of empowerment. In its broadest sense, empowerment is the expansion of freedom of choice and action. It means increasing one's authority and control over the resources and decisions those affect one's life. As people exercise real choice, they have increased control over their own life. In essence, empowerment is the expansion of the assets and capabilities of the marginalized and disadvantaged sections of society to enable them to participate in the social process in an equitable manner. Empowerment gives an opportunity to the deprived people to negotiate with the social system and influence and control the situations which affect their life.

Empowerment of women was sought to be achieved through several methods in different respects. They are: Typology and size; Electoral representation; Institutional existence and autonomy; role and status; resources etc. They can be further categorized as there are two constitutional methods of empowerment of women through conferment – namely coordinate status and independent status. The constitutional spirit of social welfare seeks to establish a social order in which freedom, equality and social justice are the central values. Government is expected to plan and implement programmes meant for the various sections—especially the vulnerable and disadvantaged sections of society.

In the post independence period in India, different policies are being adopted through the planning process for rapid economic growth, which would ultimately result in the well being of all citizens. In tune with the stated goals and objectives of the Constitution, a number of social legislations and policies have been initiated. To bring positive changes in the social situation attempts are being made to improve the conditions of the different deprived sections of society. In the same vein, the recognition of the need to bring women into the mainstream of the development process has underpinned national policy and planning since independence. For example, as early as the late 1950s, Mahila Mandals or grassroots women's organizations were promoted to ensure better implementation of the welfare schemes run by the Government.

The issues connected with empowerment of women come under the purview of several ministries both at the Central and State levels. Institutional arrangements were made through the Department of Social Security in 1964. Women welfare was one of the subjects assigned to it. The Department of Social Security was later redesigned as Department of Social Welfare. The same was further divided in 1985 into the Ministry of Welfare and the Department of Women and Child Development.

The Department of Women and Child Development is currently located under the Ministry of HRD covering the following subjects:

a) Family welfare
b) Women and Child Welfare
c) International affairs relating to women and children.
d) Promotion of voluntary effort pertaining to women.
e) Administration of SITA Act, 1956.
f) Dowry Prohibition Act, 1961.

Various programmes were launched for the welfare of women with incremental outlays from the First Five Year Plan to the current Plan. Major programmes under this scheme include rescue homes, protection homes, service women's homes, working women's hostels, vocation training, crèches for working women, socio-economic production groups, self-help groups, DWCRA, DWCUA, etc. In spite of these efforts, the development/empowerment of women in most of the stated objectives were mainly on paper and they were not translated into concrete actions or programmes of reality.

Ironically, men treat women as burdens, even though women work more than men. The presence of many women, for example, Mrs. Indira Gandhi and others, in powerful positions for a long time did not change the condition of women. The programmes announced for the betterment of their position, particularly from 7th Plan remained only on paper. It was not until the Sixth Five Year Plan (1980-85) that women's advancement received recognition as a specific development sector. In later Five Year Plans, there has been a gradual shift in favour of women's empowerment programmes as compared to the women's development approach of the earlier plans. The ninth Five Year Plan (1998-2002) identifies the empowerment of women and other socially disadvantaged groups as crucial to socio-economic change. The plan seeks to promote their participation in local government and in people's organizations.

A joint committee has been constituted to keep women's concerns under constant review and to monitor progress in pursuance of plans of action developed at national and international levels. A constitutional amendment which came into effect in 1993 reserves 30% of the seats in Panchayati Raj (local government) Institutions for women, bringing thousands of grassroots women into the country's political life. Women's Development Corporations have been set up in about 18 states of India to channel financial assistance to women's economic enterprises. In order to soften the impact of structural adjustment programmes on poor women's lives, a special fund has been established under the social safety net to offer credit to women for self-employment and for setting up micro-enterprises.

National Policy 2001

Thus, the National Policy for the Empowerment of Women assumed significance, even before it was formally approved. Most of the concerned eagerly awaited its declaration. The policy proposes, among other things, a system of regularly collecting sex-desegregated data on resource allocation, specializes sectoral policies and the performance of different development programmes for the advancement of women. Four Indian states, Andhra Pradesh, Madhya Pradesh, Maharashtra and Tamilnadu, have also issued policies or plans of action for women.

The National Policy document is divided into 17 small sections[1]. The introduction reminds us that gender equality and positive discrimination were guaranteed by the Constitution. Beginning from the fifth Five Year Plan, informs the policy, to the 73rd and 74th amendments, a number of steps were taken to build a strong foundation for empowering women and making them participate in decision making.

The first section deals with various international conventions and India's declared commitment to innumerable declrations[2] and appreciates the steps taken by non-government organizations and the spirit of the 9th Five Year Plan. This section rightly concludes that there is a wide gap between the declared goals and the situational reality in India[3]. The same section identified goals and objectives of the policy as:

i. Creating an environment through positive economic and social policies for full development of women to enable them to realize their full potential.

ii. The de-jure and de-facto enjoyment of all human rights and fundamental freedom by women on equal basis with men in all spheres—political, economic, social, cultural and civil.

iii. Equal access to participation and decision making of women in social, political and economic life of the nation.

iv. Equal access to women to health care, quality education at all levels, career and vocational guidance, employment, equal remuneration, occupational health and safety, social security and public office etc.

v. Strengthening legal systems aimed at elimination of all forms of discrimination against women.

vi. Changing societal attitudes and community practices by active participation and involvement of both men and women.

vii. Mainstreaming a gender perspective in the development process.

viii. Elimination of discrimination and all forms of violence against women and the girl child; and

ix. Building and strengthening partnerships with civil society, particularly women's organizations" (1:11).

The second section underlines the necessity of introducing the required changes in the judicial legal system to make it gender sensitive and more responsive. The third section promises to take all measures to guarantee equal access to decision-making bodies. The fourth section talks about the mainstreaming a gender perspective in the development process. The fifth section unfolds various ideas to ensure the economic empowerment and eradication of poverty. They include micro credit, reinterpretation and redefinition of conventional concepts of work, preparation of satellite and national accounts, training the women in soil conservation, social forestry, poultry, fisheries etc. While inviting the process of globalization this sections wants to design strategies to enhance the "capacity to meet the negative social and economic impacts, which may flow from the globalization process" (5:4).

The sixth section is about the social empowerment of women. Equal access to education, holistic approach to health and recognition to the traditional knowledge of women on health care etc. are stressed in this section. The problems of intra-household discrimination in nutritional matters, safe drinking water, sanitation, housing, shelter, environment etc., are given special importance. The next two sections, seventh and eighth, deal with the violence against women and rights of girl child respectively. Section nine is on mass media and it is for using the media to portray images that are consistent with the human dignity of girls. Section ten is about action plans and the next section is on institutional mechanisms at central, state and district levels[4]. Section twelve touches upon the key issue—issue of resources and says that the necessary resources to implement the policy will have to be managed by the concerned departments, society as a whole and connected/concerned institution. It assigns the responsibility of monitoring and reviewing the implementation to Department of Women and Child Development. Section thirteen repeats the theme of second section, which deals with the Judicial–legal efforts. While the 14th section deals with the need for gender sensitization of personnel, the 15th section hopes that the 73rd and 74th amendments (reservation to women in Panchayati Raj and urban local bodies) will play a key role in enhancing women participation.

The 16th section assures the voluntary organizations of appropriate support. The last section reaffirms its will to implement international obligations and commitments in all sectors of empowerment of women.

It is highly appreciable that a national policy on empowerment of women, who constitute half of the country, is formulated. As the document rightly puts it, right from nutritious and equal share in square meal to equal status, everything is a scarce commodity to women. Though it is very late[5], late by at least 54 years, finally we have a policy now. The wise say "better late than never".

This policy document is successful in identifying the areas where extra inputs are needed to ensure the empowerment. The importance given in it to the micro-credit warrants a special appreciation; it has been used for preparing a national account to calculate the contribution of women in generating the domestic product. Identifying various strata among women and exclusive attention to their problems is another novel feature of this policy because the feminist attitude of projecting women as a homogeneous group proved to be less useful to women from poorer sections (Sahell, Sabala Sangh, 1991).

However, this policy document did disappoint the people who had been waiting for it[6] on many counts. The text and spirit of the policy appears like a statement of promise. Each paragraph positively promises something or the other. Though the policies carry assurances, assurances themselves don't become a policy. A policy is an attempt to set something right or to achieve something. For that purpose it has to overcome the hurdles created and utilize the opportunities provided by the social environment[7]. The policy makers have to strive hard to identify the opportunities and ways of overcoming hurdles. From this flow the necessary strategies and programmes with a thorough understanding about alternatives. Being a policy on a vital or most important segment with social consequences, a policy of this nature is supposed to be rational rather than populist or all-promising one.

The readers of the policy are at a loss to understand how so many wonderful changes could be possible, when nothing substantial was achieved in the 54 year history of independent India. The policy acknowledges that a wide gap exists "between the goals enunciated in the Constitution, legislation, policies, plans, programs and related mechanisms on the one hand and the situational reality of the status of women in India on the other." But it did not try to identify the reasons for failure. Perhaps, this is a vital overlook on the part of the policy formulators. One has to remember that this policy was formulated after 54 years of experience in development effort. The question that naturally arises is what factors prevented or downsized the expected development. The failure of the policy to address this point is a major drawback.

A fatal mistake of the policy is to treat the elders (old members of the household) as obstacles to empowerment. Consequently the policy proposed to "expand and improve" homes for the aged and disabled to ensure full cooperation of women in social, political and economic life.[8] This implies that old and disabled are hurdles for women participation in public affairs or productive activities. This is an erroneous conclusion. Otherwise this leads to a situation where every other member of family is treated as a hurdle for women participation in social affairs or her empowerment. As the American experience demonstrates, breakdown of emotional relationship in the family automatically leads to the breakdown of social life, paving the way for "pleasure seeking" individualism.

The stand taken by policy on globalization vis-à-vis women needs a debate. There is a considerable section of academicians who feel that structural adjustment programs cause more harm to women. A good number of case studies also proved the same (Maithreyi, 1993; Krishnaswami, 1993 and Sujaya, C.P., 1993)[9] Even the policy document accepts that globalization has presented new challenges for the realization of the goal of women equality and growing global economy leads to feminization of poverty. Still the policy assured that the "strategies will be designed to enhance the capacity of women and empower them to meet the negative social and economic impacts, which may flow from the globalization process". The rest of the document or other documents released later by the Department of Women and Child Development did not come out with any strategy till date.

The policy document is completely silent on the need for developing a counter culture as an essential precondition for achieving gender equality. The existing cultural values run counter to gender equality. It is quite natural for everybody to treat women as inferior beings[10]. Most of the religions[11] and the education system, particularly at the elementary level, perpetuate this feeling. Unless appropriate counter strategies are developed, gender equality remains as a theme of academic discussion. The need of the hour is for a secular outlook and an education system, which project the women as an essential subsystem of a wider social system. The realization that any injury or inadequacy of a subsystem ultimately becomes an injury or inadequacy of the total system is a prerequisite for gender equality. It is the hope of this paper that a serious attention to the above mentioned issues makes the women policy more comprehensive.

Experience during the last decades since 1947 indicates that empowerment of women has several positive and negative aspects. Positive aspects include building institutional framework, raising expectations, realization for the need to establish integration and linkages, facilitation of opportunities for democratization etc. In spite of these positive aspects, women continue to be discriminated and the issues relating to women have received low priority for a long period. The tragedy has been that these positive features have remained confined to only some selected areas in a few states. By and large, if we look at the overall picture of the process of empowerment of women and its actual impact on socio-economic situation and social transformation the achievement has been dismal. While the states are very keen about promoting empowerment of women they are not always equally keen to promote and support their cause. The gap between promise and performance has been widening. There is perhaps no alternative to making statutory arrangements in this regard. The establishment of a National Commission for Women and the state level commissions has, however, fallen short of the expectations.

It is to be noted that statutory reforms on their own can't bring out the desired changes. But it is the mind set of the stake holders involved in the empowerment of women, for example, the public, political representatives, policy makers at the state and union levels, bureaucracy and civil society organizations, play a significant role in the empowerment of women. Features of the initiatives undertaken till now compels one to be skeptical and substantiates the apprehension that problems have really been compounded because of lack of commitment with wholehearted political determination. The growing expectations will essentially widen the gulf between promise and performance.

When in opposition our political leaders are extremely vocal about empowerment of women. All major political parties have promised to empower women in their manifestoes during the election seasons. The moment they come to power, they change their colour. It is such lip service to women that tends to undermine their cause. The idea that 'empowerment of women should not depend at the sweet will and pleasure of the government in power' is central to a functioning democracy. The larger interests of the society within the over-all framework of national interest should guide them. It is a fact that the empowerment of women is mainly correlated to the political game plan of ruling political parties. Experience in India shows that progress only takes place when the political executives decide so for what ever reasons; now it is for them to understand that empowerment of women is most important not only for the improvement of the condition of women but also for the development of the whole country. Support of the political head is not the only sufficient necessary condition for progress. Positive and supportive guidance from the higher civil service is another necessary condition. On the whole, the available evidence points to achievements that are 'nominal' or 'sub-optimal'.

In an appraisal of the achievements so far in a different context, it is noted that enfranchisement, empowerment and ethical functioning with a moral code of conduct, are the three elements of democratic decentralization. If democratic decentralization is viewed as a 'stages approach' in transformation, it can be safely asserted that India has successfully crossed the first stage of enfranchisement and has partially moved towards the second stage of empowerment with limited success. But what has been called the third wave of democratic transformation, which is the 'ethical mode of functioning', is yet to be addressed in its totality (Sundaram, 2000: 298). One of the major impediments to the empowerment of women is the "dependency syndrome" created by the society as a whole and partly due to the policies of the Union and state governments.

There are several aspects of the Constitution that require changes to empower women in India. They include removal of contradictions within the Constitution itself and between constitutional provisions and international conventions adopted.

In this context several questions can be raised.

Questions

- Have the last fifty years initiatives lent credibility, continuity and strength to them?
- Whether the national policy is an innovative and comprehensive improvement?
- Whether the present status of women is different from the past?
- To what extent statutory efforts to plug the proverbial pitfalls, imparting a new lease of life, have indeed provided impetus to the process of women empowerment?
- How and when women come out of discrimination and gender bias?
- Whether and to what extent national policies clinch genuine departure from the earlier thrust?
- Whether and how far state efforts and practice precipitate improvement in the status of women?
- Whether the policies and programmes have resulted in artificial dichotomy between rural and urban women within the region.
- Whether, in view of their social backwardness, illiteracy and conditions of deprivation and as a consequence of the reservation provided to them, the rural women, SCs/STs will be able to shoulder the responsibilities of governance? Will they not become pawns at the hands of the local elite/political parties?

Notes

1. Though this was the first ever policy, certainly not the first attempt in the direction of ensuring empowerment of women. This is just the culmination of a prolonged effort. The first attempt was made in 1974 when an official document entitled "Towards Equality: Report of the Committee on the Status of Women in India" was published by Department of Social Welfare, Ministry of Education and Social Welfare, Government of India. This was a report by the Committee on the Status of Women in India. The Ministry of Education and Social Welfare Constituted this Committee in 1971. There was a National Perspective Plans for Women 1988-2000, published in 1988 and Sharamashakti Report, a report on the condition of women working in unorganized sector.
2. The policy statement that "India ratified .... Convention on Elimination of All Forms of Discrimination Against Women (CEDAW, 1993)" was not correct. In fact the Government of India did not become a party to Art. 16(1) and 16(2) of CEDAW that dealt with uniform code of marriage and compulsory registration of marriage respectively. The Government also rejected Art 29(1), which imposed compulsory arbitration in International Court of Justice in gender discrimination cases (see Empowerment women through Self Help Groups, a report published by the Department of Women and Child Development, 2000, p.2).
3. To be clear, the problem of empowerment of women is not only an Indian one, but almost universal. For a brilliant presentation of the status of women world over see, "Further Actions and Initiatives to Implement the Beijing Declaration and the Platform for Action" document adopted by the 23rd special session of the UN General Assembly entitled "Women 2000: Gender Equality, Development, and Peace for The 21st Century". For the place of women in decision making process see "50-50 by 2005: Get The Balance Right", and Sushila Ramaswami, "Women in Parliament: A Global Glimpse".
4. The Prime Minister and the Chief Minister act as heads of the Councils at center and state levels. Besides representatives from the concerned departments, chairpersons of National and State Commissions for Women, social welfare boards, representatives of non-government organizations, women's organizations, corporate sector, trade unions, financing institutions, academics, experts and social activists also serve on these councils.

5. It may be recalled that the vital issue of women empowerment had been on the agenda way back in 1942; the National Planning Committee's sub-committee on women prepared a policy note entitled "Women in Planned Economy". It reminded the nation about the necessity of involving women on equal status in economy and decision making (see Empowerment of Women through Self Help Groups, a report published by the Department of Women and Child Development, 2000, p.2, p.12).
6. It is appropriate to recall here that the whole nation in general and the clientele groups in particular waited for four years for this document. Inspired by the Beijing Conference (1995), a draft national policy was formulated. A serious of consultations with members of Parliament, state government, Non-governmental organizations, women organizations, social activists, researchers and other experts delayed the finalization of the policy. The policy in its finalized form was sent to the Cabinet around February 1998 (see, Asha Das, 1998). The political uncertainty and other factors delayed the policy announcement for two more years.
7. For a detailed discussions on this point see, Anderson, James E (1979), Anderson Walt (1975) and Easton David (1965).
8. As early as 1910s and 20s a Feminist, Alexandra Kollontai argued that child–rearing and children education is the responsibility of the state. She also argued that the precondition for women participation in collective affairs is liberating her from private responsibilities. Neither Kollontai nor feminists of her school bothered to make their better–halves as equal partners in household affairs, so that private and personal remains as private and yet women get more time and space to contribute to collective affairs (see Holt, Alix 1977 and Lokaneeta Jinu, 2001).
9. There are another set of writers who argue that the structural adjustment programme helps the economic empowerment. A representative example is Sudha and LK Deshpande (1992, Nandita Shah *et al* 2001 and Rohini Hensman 2001).
10. It pains to see that even the leaders of the feminist movement and academicians who champion the cause of gender equality like to be recognized by the names of their better-halves or fathers.
11. For a thought provoking debate on this issue see Agnes, Flavia 1995, Omvedt, Gail 1994, Sangari 1995 and Engineer, Asghar Ali 1994.

References

1. Anderson, James, E. 1979, *Public Policy Making*, New York: Rinehart.
2. Anderson Walt, 1975. *Politics and Environment*, California: Goodyear.
3. Asha Das, 1998, Secretary, Department of Women and Child Development. *Statement to the Commission on the Status of Women*, U.N.O.
4. Department of Women and Child Development, 2001. *Women's Empowerment Year*, Delhi: Ministry of Human Resource Development.
5. Department of Women and Child Development, 2000. *Epowering Women Through Self Help Groups*.
6. Easton David, 1965. *A Framework of Political Analysis*, New Jersey: Prentice Hall.
7. Holt, Alix, 1977. *Selected Writing of Alexandra Kollontai*, London: Alison.
8. Krishnaswamy, 1993. 'Notes on Issues Regarding Women and the New Economic Policy".
9. Lokaneeta Jinee, 2001. "Alexandra Kollontai and Marxist Feminism", *Economic and Political Weekly*, April, 28.
10. Maithreyi, Krishna Raj, 1993. "The New Economic Policy: Safeguarding Women Interests" in the *New Economic Policy and Women: A Collection of Background Papers to Sixth National Conference 1993*. Bombay: Indian Association for Women Studies.
11. Nandita Shah *et al.*, 2001. "Structural Adjustment, Feminisation of Labour Force and Organisational Strategies" in Nivedita Menon (ed.), *Gender and Politics in India*.
12. Rohini Hensman, 2001. "Impact of Technological Change on Industrial Women Workers".
13. Saheli, Sabala Sangh, 1991. "Development for WhomA Critique of Women's Development Programmes" Delhi: Action India.
14. Sudha and L.K. Deshpande, 1992. "New Economic Policy and Female Employment", *Economic and Political Weekly*, 10 October.
15. Sujaya, C.P., 1993. Effects of Adjustment: A Review of Experience.
16. Sundaram, K.V. 2000. "From Top-Down Planning to Decentralised Regional and Local Development in India—Vision and Reality: Challenges and Perspectives", *Indian Social Science Review*, 2(2):275-300.
17. UNICEF: (1996) "The Asian Enigma".

10

Strategies for Empowerment of Women in India: A Review

K. Chandra Kumar

Poverty and chronic deprivation of certain sections have long been a tragic aspect of human society. Globally 1.5 billion people live in extreme poverty. Roughly more than two thirds of them are in Asia and more particularly in South Asia alone. Three quarters of these poor live and work in rural areas, while more than half of them are expected to do so by 2025. Seventy per cent of the poor work and live in rural areas. Recent projections suggest that over 60 per cent of the population will continue to be so even by 2025. Most of them in this category are women and they are considered on par with the other sex. In India, there are also several important initiatives to emancipate the women and end discrimination in all the spheres of life. The UNDP Report for 1995 presented a gender–related development index (GDT) which ranked countries according to the extent of gender disparity in development. According to the index gender discrimination and gender gaps are ubiquitous in different spheres of life in almost all the countries in the world.

Generalizations about India's women always seem to be an over simplification. Nevertheless, the problem is lessened by the invisible threat of value–orientation provided by the country's classical traditions. Traditionally, Indian women were denied access to several facilities including equality with men with regard to education. They have lived in a male dominated system right from the ancient period. According to the latest estimates women are 495.7 million in number and they cônstitute 48.26 per cent as against the total population of 1027.01 million.

In view of the fact that the women constitute nearly half of the population of the country, it is widely and also aptly remarked that without the development of women the development of the country is impossible. Against this back-drop that the development of women assumed greater significance right from the Independence of the Country. The rapid development of women in different fields was also mandated by the Constitution through its various Provisions. In order to fulfill the constitutional mandate, the Government in free India has evolved several policy approaches and strategies for the all round development of women.

Under these strategies, a variety of programmes, and schemes were being implemented during various Five Year Plan periods with huge investments. All these women development strategies laid emphasis mainly on the elimination of inequalities between women and men and also provision of special opportunities and measures to enable them to progress equally with men. These special measures are required in view of the fact that the Indian women are lagging far behind men and are subjected to several disabilities throughout the nation's history.

Further, the Government has also laid more emphasis on the welfare of the rural women in view of severity of their situation. Most of the rural women participate in various economic activities but this fact does not find place in the Indian Census Reports. Rural women participate in agricultural activities like sowing, weeding, transplantation, manuring, harvesting, winnowing, shelling and storing of crops. According to official statistics out of the total work force of 374.39 million in the country in 1993-94, 121.63 million

(32.5%) are women. The rural work force has increased by more than 50 per cent during the last two decades from 69.2 million in 1972-73 to 104.29 million in 1993-94, while the rural female working population has increased at a much lower rate by 43 per cent during the same period. The same is reflected in their work participation rates also.

Evidently, absolute Poverty and economic compulsions have forced the women, particularly those belonging to the Scheduled Castes, Scheduled Tribes and other backward classes and also economically poorer sections of the rural society, to take up unskilled and menial works requiring more labour hours for which they earn a petty sum. The glaring gender difference in the field of employment is also evident in the field of education. A look into the census data reveals that the literacy rate, as per 2001 census is around 78.0 per cent for males, while it is 54.16 per cent for females. Although there is a dramatic increase in the female literacy rate from mere 7.93 per cent in 1951 to 54.16 percent in 2001, the disparity between the male and female literacy rates has remained constant during the period between 1951 and 2001. At the same time, the gender gap which was 17.02 per cent in 1951 rose to 22 per cent in 2001.

The Indian National Commission on Self Employment (1987) in its Report envisaged that in wage employment, more than half of the rural women labour receives wages below the subsistence level. It further reveals that the jobs in which they are usually appointed are generally irregular, uncertain, seasonal and discretionary and characterized by malpractices in payment, non-payment of the wages in time, signature on an inflated amount and extraction of commission on payments. In 1991, the World Bank remarked that the participation of women in such activities do not increase their control over family resources.

Government Policies Towards Women Welfare after Independence

It is estimated that above 30 different programmes for rural development have been implemented for the alleviation of poverty and wellbeing of rural poor during the post-independence period by the State. When India adopted a planed strategy for its socio-economic development during early 1950s, it was realized that the uplift of women was an equally important factor in the nation's development. The principle of welfare was the earliest policy approach towards women, which is still prevalent in all the welfare policies of the Government.

The First Five-Year Plan (1951-56) envisaged various welfare schemes for women which aimed at the development of maternal and child health through family planning services. In 1953, the Central Social Welfare Board (CSWB) was set up to chalk out various welfare programmes for the development of women. It symbolized the approach of the Government towards the welfare of women. The Community Development Programme (1952), for the first time, emphasized the need for mobilization of women through Mahila Mandals or Women's Clubs for promoting their welfare. In 1956, the CSWB started a scheme of Condensed Courses of Education for Adult Women and a scheme for socio-economic programmes for Women.

The Second Five Year Plan (1956-61) while emphasizing the overall development of rural women mainly focused on the protection of women against various types of exploitation and atrocities. It also stressed that women should be provided maternity benefits and crèches for their children. It also suggested speedy implementation of the principle of equal pay for equal work and provision of training for women to enable them to compete even for higher level jobs along with men. The Maternity Benefits Act, 1961 was enacted at the end of this Plan.

The Third Five Year Plan (1961-66) pinpointed female education as a major welfare strategy. In social welfare sector, the largest share in the financial outlays was provided for expanding rural welfare services and condensed courses of education. The Fourth Five Year Plan (1969-74) continued the emphasis on women's education. It gave high priority to the immunization of pre-school children and provision of supplementary feeding for children, expectant and nursing mothers. In 1972, the central scheme of Assistance for Construction of Hostel Buildings for Working Women was introduced by the Central Government. The scope of the scheme was widened in 1980 by including a provision for day care centers for children.

It was in the early 1970s that Crash Schemes like Rural Employment, Food for Work Programme, Drought Prone Area Programme, and Desert Development Programme were initiated, aiming at strengthening the rural base of the economy. Though these schemes seemed to be gender neutral, they were male biased. They were targeted at the men as the heads/main earners of the families, with the assumption that benefits to men will trickle down to the rest of the family members.

The Fifth Five Year Plan (1974-79) continued emphasis on the need to train women who were in need of income and protection. A major thrust of the plan was women's employment which was seen as the "critical entry point" for women's integration into the process of the nation development. The International Women's Decade (1975-85) in India, witnessed unprecedented efforts by various agencies to reassess the role of women, to enlarge the information base, to search for alternative strategies for promoting equality and development of women and to evolve policies and programmes addressed to women's specific needs and problems. In the light of these policy concerns the Fifth Plan (1974-79) showed a shift from welfare to development. It emphasized the need to train women who were in need of special protection. Accordingly, the CSWB started the Scheme of Assistance to Voluntary Organisations for Crèches for Working and Ailing Women's Children and the Scheme for Vocational Training and Adult Women.

The Ministry of Social Welfare also started a massive scheme, called as the Functional Literacy for Adult Women in the same year and a Scheme for Setting up Women's Training Centers for rehabilitation of Women in distress in 1977-78. In 1976, the Welfare and Development Bureau was set up in the Ministry of Social Welfare for looking after the implementation of women welfare programmes and schemes. In the same year, the Equal Remuneration Act was enacted to benefit the working women.

The various development schemes launched parallel to the welfare schemes during the 1970s were gender neutral. Initiating the Integrated Rural Development Programme (IRDP), the Government launched a direct attack on poverty in 1978-79. Under this programme credit from banking institutions and subsidy from the Government were given to the rural families below the poverty line for self-employment and income generation activities. In this programme a special place was accorded to the policy of Training Rural Unemployed Youth for Self-Employment (TRYSEM). Further, the National Rural Employment Programme (NREP) was introduced in 1980 and also the Rural Landless Employment Guarantee Programme (RLEGP) in 1983. But in all these employment programmes rural women were only marginally helped, as they were mainly targeted for men.

The National Plan of Action (NPA) for women was an immediate consequence of the CSWB Report submitted in 1980s. It identified the areas of health, family planning, nutrition, education, employment, legislation and social welfare for the formulation and implementation of action programme for women and called for planned intervention to improve the conditions of women. The National Machinery for Women was set up in 1975 which consisted of: (a) national committee; (b) a steering committee of the national committee; (c) an inter-department coordination committee; and (d) a women's welfare and development bureau.

The various welfare programmes taken up in 1960s and 1970s made no discrimination among the urban and rural women, among the rich and poor women and also among the not so poor and extremely poor women. As a result, most of the benefits of all these schemes were cornered by the urban middle class women. In the late 70s, it was revealed by the Government sponsored studies that the improvement in the conditions of women remains confined to the urban and economically affluent families. In the rural areas, there was minimum impact of various schemes, and women belonging to the socially backward and poor classes were further relegated to the background.

These facts caused serious concern to Government which started improving its policy frame and also instituting mechanisms and framing programmes for women welfare. In the beginning of 1980s, there was a change in the administrative framework for planning and monitoring of women-based programmes implemented by the Central Government. In 1985, the Department of Women and Child Development was set up at the center based on the appreciation of women's productive role in the development process rather than as mere beneficiaries of various programmes of the Government.

In the Sixth Five Year Plan a shift was made from welfare to development in the approach for the welfare of women. The Plan recognized the inaccessibility of women to resources as a critical hindrance impeding their development. Hence it adopted a three-pronged thrust on the wealth, education and employment of women in accordance with the sub-themes of the International Decade for Women. This approach led to the initiation of several schemes exclusively for women beneficiaries, such as the Employment and Income generating Programmes, Training-cum Production Centers for Women and Non-formal Education for Girls and so on. As the coverage of women in the main Anti-Poverty Programmes of IRDP was very poor, a sub-scheme was launched within the IRDP called 'Development of Women and Children in Rural Areas' (DWCRA), 1982 in few selected areas but later extended all over the country. In 1990s, it was made as a pivotal scheme aiming at the socio-economic empowerment of rural poor women.

The manifest failure of the IRDP to reach the poor women, more particularly those living in the rural areas, led to the launching of the DWCRA under the Self-Help Group strategy with the UNICEF assistance. Initially started as a pilot project in 50 selected Districts in a few States, it has been extended to several other districts in the Country by 1995. Gradually, it has been introduced in all most all the States. Aimed to address some of the implications of IRDP the DWCRA is intended to bring about overall improvement in the quality of life of women by creating credit based opportunities for self employment for the poor women and by improving their access to the basic services like health, education, drinking water, sanitation and so on. The DWCRA has achieved spectacular result in improving the lot of rural women in several states. The DWCRA groups have become empowered in several spheres and playing an active role in the development process at the grassroots.

The Department of Women and Child Development created at the Centre in 1985, funds the CSWB that sponsors welfare and developmental schemes for women and children. The Seventh Five Year Plan (1985-90) operationalised the concern for equity and employment for women as articulated by the International Decade for Women. For the first time, the emphasis in the plan was focused on inculcating confidence among women, generating awareness about their rights and privileges and providing them training in various economic activities and employment. The National Policy on Education, 1986 truly began the women's empowerment phase in India. In the subsequent years access of women to critical inputs and productive resources such as land was expanded to include support through credit, marketing, training in skills/management and technology. Priority were given to women headed households and efforts were made to enhance the share of women in the fruits of development process under the anti-poverty programmes of IRDP, TRYSEM, NREP and RLEGP.

The National Commission for Women was set up in 1980s as a national apex level statutory body to review the implementation of the Constitutional and legal safeguards provided for women. The commission recommended several remedial legislative measures to facilitate redress of grievances of women and it was to advise the Government on all policy matters affecting women.

In the light of various developments taken place during the 1980s, the Eighth Plan (1992-97) shifted the focus from development to empowerment. In 1990, the National Commission for Women Act was enacted. In 1991, a National Plan of Action for SAARC Decades of the Girl child (1991-2000) was formulated for the development of women and Children. In 1996, the Draft of the National Policy for the Empowerment of Women was finalized. The Ninth Five Year

Plan, (1997-2002) has its objectives evolved from the Common Minimum Programme (CMP) of the Government and the Chief Ministers' Conference on basic minimum services. Based on the objectives of this program emphasis has been laid on the empowerment of women and socially disadvantaged groups like the Scheduled Castes, Scheduled Tribes, Backward Classes and Minorities.

The Ninth Five Year Plan attempted to consolidate the women empowerment strategies adopted by the earlier Plans through creating an enabling environment which provide women ample opportunities to realize their potential through exercising their rights as equal partners with men. The Ninth Plan adopted specific strategies for empowering women to play their role as the agents of socio-economic development. These strategies include:

i. to create an enabling environment to exercise their rights equally with men;
ii. to provide reservation for women to the extent of 33 per cent in the Lok Sabha as well as the State Legislative Assemblies to ensure them adequate role in the decision making process;
iii. to adopt an integrated approach for empowering women through effective convergence of the services, resources, structures and man power in related sectors;
iv. to organize women into self-help groups for empowering them;
v. to accord high priority to the child health services;
vi. to equip women with modern skills in modern ventures to make them economically independent and self reliance.
vii. to take steps to provide equality to women in educational institutions for eliminating gender bias in the field of education.

The Central Government initiated several steps to translate the strategy of women empowerment into a concrete reality. It has constituted a committee on empowerment of women in March 1997 to review the progress of various programmes taken up for the empowerment of women from time to time. The Planning Commission required the various Ministries of

Central and State Governments to draw up special component plans exclusive for women in the programmes of their respective Ministries. Further, the nodal Department of Women and Child Development, responsible for women welfare has initiated several innovative programmes for the promotion of women welfare. These programmes are in the fields of: (i) empowerment; (ii) employment generation, (iii) welfare and support services; (iv) awareness generation and gender sensitization; and (v) creating enabling environment.

Conclusions

The various development initiatives, strategies, schemes and programmes which were implemented during different Plan periods with huge outlays for the all-round development of women produced substantial results which improved their socio-economic conditions to a great extent. Particularly, the women welfare interventions have brought about radical transformation in the conditions of women of both rural and urban areas. The strategy of special component Plan for women development highlighted in the programmes and schemes included in the Five Year Plans resulted in the mobilization and convergence orchestrated by the women's groups. The mobilization of women under these strategies is expected to empower them in different spheres and provide them a forum for articulating their needs and also contributing their perspectives to the nation's development. This will also enable them to participate in the decision-making process which will result in the building of grassroots leadership, capable of participating in the governance at the local level and also at the higher levels.

Needless to point out that the women specific development interventions over the last five decades have created an enabling atmosphere which sensitized women about their rights and responsibilities and also increased their awareness about their inherent potentialities and capabilities. Consequently, the participation of women in the development process has increased and now they are playing a role equal to the men in indifferent spheres of national life. In particular, the political empowerment of women consequent of the 73rd and 74th Constitutional Amendment Acts along with their social and economic empowerment resulted from the Self Help Groups and other innovative strategies have greater impact on the economic position and psychological outlook of women.

As a result, the Indian women are now standing at the crossroads of their destiny. There has been tremendous urge among them for empowerment, development and emancipation in all spheres of life. They are considering the space now they occupy in politics as the space in development. They are equipped to play their role in the society as equal partners with men. They are prepared to take up any responsibility and accept challenges and convert these challenges and responsibilities into opportunities for the achievement of development in their life as well as of the society as a whole.

References

Mira Seth, *Women and Development*, New Delhi, Sage, 2001.

Sakuntala Narasimhan, *Empowering Women*, New Delhi, Sage, 2001.

Asha Das, "Child Development and Empowering Women in India", *The Indian Journal of Public Administration*, Vol. XVII, No. 3, July, September, 1997.

Government of India, *Five Year Plan Documents, 1950-1977*, New Delhi, Planning Commission.

Sahay, Sushma, *Women and Empowerment: Approaches and Strategies*, New Delhi, Discovery Publishing House, 1998.

Bipin Chandra *et al*, India After Independence 1947 – 2000, New Delhi, Penguin Books, 2000.

11

Women Empowerment: New Initiatives in Voluntary Action

V. Divya Thejo Murthy

Several events have occurred during the last few centuries which are now, part of History and well known. A Nation which was leading in Culture, Civilization and Prosperity slid and slipped into the status of a "Developing Nation" with 25 crores of population being below poverty line out of the total population of 102 crores at the dawn of 21st century. How to facilitate conversion of majority of 102 crores of population into productive assets and capital should be our approach towards development.

We have witnessed tremendous development in the last five decades since the dawn of Independence in terms of Infrastructure, transport, Communication, Employment and in several other areas of Development. China which was on part with India 50 years ago is on the way to become a super power at present. What bare foot doctors, bare foot teachers, bare foot social workers and bare foot technocrats have achieved in China is what India had missed in the last five decades. China's model of development of population stabilization, family welfare, Harvesting of Natural resources, work culture and community development are worth emulating with relevant modifications suited to our country.

Ours is one of the very few countries which have gone through the second doubling of population in less than a century. We were 20 crores at 1901, reaching to 45 crores by 1951 and crossing of 100 crores by 1999, with a projected population of 120 crores by 2011. It was only in 1999, four decades after Independence, the rulers could announce a "National Population Policy". We must commit and work for a campaign mode of family welfare, one child norm, and population stabilization.

Through the Five Year Plans, focus on several areas was given during the last 5 decades. In the fifties focus was on Agriculture, in the sixties it was on Industries, in the seventies it was on combination of Agriculture, Industries, Services and Community Development. In the eighties it was on poverty alleviation schemes, integrated rural development and Natural and Human resource development. In the nineties it was on Human development. The nineties have also seen approaches of Social Mobilisation, Empowerment of the poor, Empowerment of Women and other weaker sections of the society.

The approaches at the dawn of 21st century is on Right based campaigns for Human Rights, Rights of Women, Rights of Children, Rights of Disabled, Rights of Senior Citizens, Right to Information, Right to Participation and people centered campaigns for environmental Rights.

The dawn of 21st century made people to increasingly realize that they are in a Global village, as any and every developmental issue which may be local has its linkages throughout the globe. It has become imminent to be a part of "VASUDHAIVA KUTUMBAKAM", the age-old Indian philosophical idea of regarding whole mankind as one family. Increased use of Remote Sensing Applications through Geographical Information Systems (GIS), Geographical Positioning Systems (GPS) and Information Technology Applications have made people to realize that the day to day problems affecting people in large and more so, the poor in developing countries, can only be best addressed by networking the efforts of various countries and collectively approaching the problems such as poverty, drought, hunger, health and environment.

Voluntary action for development of rural communities is claimed to be in vogue from the historic past; but more deliberate, planned and organizational attempts for rural reconstruction are traced to the last decades of the 19th century. The most active role in the field of rural regeneration, largely in the inaccessible parts of the country, was played by Christian missionaries since the middle of the century, who aimed at an all round development (secular and spiritual) of their converts.

In the post-Independence era, voluntary organizations are playing a greater role for the needy and destitute, particularly women, children and the disabled. They initiated several programmes touching all the fields like health, education, sanitation and nutrition. The activities of voluntary organizations are not only confined to their own activities but also supplement and support the central and state sponsored schemes like I.R.D.P., N.R.E.P., D.W.C.R.A., T.R.Y.S.E.M., P.M.R.Y. etc.

The setting up of agencies like All India Women's Organisations, Child Welfare Council, All India Panchayat Parishad, Association of Voluntary Agencies for rural development etc., manifested and enlarged the role of voluntary agencies.

Voluntary Social Work in India is as old as our country itself. The entire freedom struggle for our independence is an excellent example of voluntary social work and sacrifices for the sake of our mother land. The foundations for several policies, programmes and schemes of the Government are in voluntary social work. Several innovative approaches, more so the participatory approaches of development have their roots in voluntary social work. Voluntary social workers, grassroots level workers, unorganized and organized social workers, registered and unregistered social organizations and several trusts constitute a wide range of role players in women empowerment.

In recent decades, we have witnessed the outbreak of many issue based micro movements. There is also an increasing role of civil society (its various facets) in giving birth to several micro movements and carving out a niche for its interests which could mainly be attributed to the state's passive role in mitigating the complex mode of deprivation and to the growing activism displayed by the middle classes. The emergence of new social movements synchronises with an active civil society stimulated by the NGOs. In other words, the growing importance of civil society and its agents coupled with growing rate of dissidents against the state have generated a new commotion by developmental perspectives. The macro development strategies are being replaced by micro development mechanisms. The rise and growth of popular grassroots initiatives, often engineered by the grassroots NGOs and the subsequent emergence of a new strategy particularly the bottom-up approach (putting people first) unleashed by them seem to have augured well for the society.

Voluntary organizations are required to be involved in a bigger way by various Government departments as per the approaches laid down as per the Tenth Five Year Plan. States like Andhra Pradesh, Tamil Nadu, Karnataka, Maharashtra, Madhya Pradesh, Bihar and Delhi have significant number of Voluntary organizations campaigning for women empowerment. Co-ordination and collaboration among village communities, voluntary organizations and Government are improving over the years.

At the dawn of 21st century "Participatory of Women Rights Based Campaign Mode of Development" has become an imminent need of the hour. There are seven freedoms which are very important as parts of Human Rights and Human Development. Those are:

§ Freedom from discrimination—for equality

§ Freedom from want—for a decent standard of living

§ Freedom for the realization of one's human potential

§ Freedom from fear—with no threats to personal security

§ Freedom from injustice

§ Freedom of participation, expression and association

§ Freedom for decent work—without exploitation.

Majority of population of our Nation as well as of several other Nations are not even having one of the seven freedoms in full. Voluntary Social Organisations have a great role to play in sensitizing the people regarding seven freedoms and initiating campaigns for Human Rights.

- § The mark of all civilizations is the respect they accord to human dignity and freedom.
- § In short, human development is essential for realizing human rights and human rights are essential for full human development.
- § Without the rule of law and fair administration of justice, human rights laws are no more than paper.
- § A decent standard of living, adequate nutrition, health care, education, decent work and protection against calamities are not just development goal—they are also human rights.
- § Struggles for human freedoms have transformed the global landscape.
- § Instruments of political oppression still threaten many thousands of people.

Voluntary organizations can play a great role in Women's Empowerment Campaigns. There are constitutional guarantees, Legislative measures, programmes and Policies as shown below for women's Empowerment. But several States in the country are not able to implement various policies in this regard. The blatant violations of Women's Rights, day in and day out in various parts of our country is very evident.

Constitutional Guarantees

Art. 14-Equal Right & Opportunities (Political, Economic & Social)

Art. 15-Prohibits Discrimination (on Religion, Race, Caste, Sex etc.)

Art. 15(3)-Special Provision for State to make affirmation regarding discrimination in favour of women.

Art. 16-Equality of opportunities in matter of public appointments

Art. 39(A)-Equating both Men and Women regarding their Right to Means of Livelihood.

Art. 39(C)-Equal Pay for Equal Work for both men and women

Art. 42-Ensuring Humane conditions of work & Maternity relief

Art.51(a,e)-To Renounce practices derogatory to dignity of women

Legislative Measures

§ Equal Remuneration Act of 1976

§ The Hindu Marriage Act 1955 (amendment) in 1976

§ The Immoral Traffic (Prevention) Act of 1956 (amendment) in 1986

§ Dowry Prohibition Act, 1961 (amendments) in 1984, 1986

§ Child Marriage Restraint Act, 1976

§ The Factories Act of 1948 (amendment) in 1976

§ The Medical Termination of Pregnancy Act, 1971

§ Amendment to Criminal Law, 1983

§ 7 years RI in Rape Cases; 10 years for custodial rapes

§ Indecent Representation of Women (Prohibition) Act, 1986.

Policies Advocating Women's Concerns

National Plan of Action for Women 1976

National Perspective Plan 1998-2000

Shrama Shakti—National Commission on self-employed Women & Women informal sector, 1998.

The National Expert Committee on Women Prisoners, 1986

The National Policy for Children, 1974

The National Nutrition Policy

The National Plan of Action for Girl Child 1991-2000

NEP 1986

NHP 1983

NPP 1993

NPEW

Andhra Pradesh is leading in campaigning for Women's Rights through Self Help Groups and DWCRA groups. Several developmental linkages for promotion of literacy, health and hygiene, nutrition, income, small family norm and empowerment have been established in a sustainable manner during the past one decade.

The metamorphosis of the women's groups from thrift to service delivery has been remarkable. Empowerment of the poor has been a key in such a transformation. I believe a new revolution is taking place in the countryside in which poor, rural women are leading the change. Few people in the cities and in the halls of power are aware of the existence of these groups, what they have achieved, and what their potential is. Throughout India, there are about 1 (one) million such self-help groups, about half of them are in Andhra Pradesh with a membership base of 5 million women. The potential of these women and their groups, if adequately empowered and supported, is enormous.

The Andhra Pradesh government has been quick to tap this enormous potential by emphasizing the formation of these groups in the development agenda of the state. Through supportive policies, collaboration with the private sector, and partnership with NGOs, the government has been able to increase the membership of these groups and extend the scope of their activities. The government is keen that all poor women in rural areas become members of Self-Help Groups (SHGs) within the 5 years. SHGs are being encouraged to federate at mandal and district levels to improve social mobilization and increase access to credit from financial Institutions. Some 200 NGOs are said to be involved with forming SHGs and Federations.

As per National Human Development Report, 2002 some states viz., Kerala, Tamil Nadu, Karnataka, Andhra Pradesh, Maharashtra and Himachal Pradesh have a gender equality index of 0.75 and above; some other states for example, Orissa, Madhya Pradesh, Rajasthan, Gujarat, West Bengal, Punjab and Haryana have gender equality index of 0.600 – 0.749 and still some other states have an index of 0.5 – 0.59 and Bihar is separately in the range of 0 – 0.49.

The success of Women Empowerment campaigns in Andhra Pradesh is due to the work of a large number of voluntary organizations in the state and networking of the efforts of village communities and Government and Non-Governmental approaches on a campaign mode of Empowerment of Women. The success of Women's Empowerment Campaigns is evident in the decrease of decadal growth rate of population during the last one decade in Andhra Pradesh compared to increase of the growth rate in Bihar.

Voluntary organization has a great role to play in campaigning for Women's Rights as well as for sustainability for Women's Rights Campaigns.

Due to successful implementation of Women's Rights Campaigns, the sex ratios which are constantly declining during the last several decades have shown an upward trend during the last decade.

Further, several developed countries have a very favorable sex ratio which is shown as below. We may aim for equality of women at par with the developed nations in a gradual manner.

Table 1

Gender related Development Index

Country	*Gender related development index(GDI) 1998*		*Life expectancy at birth(years) 1998*	
	Rank	*Value*	*Female*	*Male*
United States	4	0.927	80.20	73.50
Australia	3	0.927	81.20	75.60
Croatia	45	0.790	76.70	69.00
Sri Lanka	68	0.727	75.60	71.10
India	108	0.545	63.30	62.50
Bangladesh	121	0.441	58.70	58.60

The field experiences and social innovations mentioned here mean in the context of alleviating poverty and improving the livelihood of some 260 million poor people in India. The participation, empowerment and good governance can be powerful means to enable the poor people to reach the benefits of growth and development in socio-economic conditions. Through the different policies efforts can be made to give voice to the powerless and through their participation in DWCRA and SHGs the infrastructural facilities in the rural area can be created. All these have positive impacts on the endeavor for the eradication of poverty and help in reducing unemployment in the primary sector of the rural areas. Another important aspect, the thrift, can serve as an entry point for other development activities of primary and secondary occupations of the middle class and the poor; commodities and the public institutions need to be reoriented to work for the poor and the focus should be on the uplift of the people below the poverty line in the community.

References

1. Government of India; DWCRA Manual, Ministry of Rural Development, April, 2001.
2. Mayonx, Linda, 1998, "Women's Empowerment and Micro-Finance: Programmes, Approaches, Evidence and Ways Forward", Development Policy and Practice Working Paper No.41, Milton Keynes, The Open University.
3. Ministry of Environment and Forests, Government of India, 2002, "A Report", New Delhi.
4. United Nations Development Programmes (UNDP) (1997), Nigeria Human Development Report, 1996, Lagos, UNDP.
5. World Bank (2002), World Development Report: Building Institution for Markets, Washington D.C., The World Bank.

12

Empowerment of Indian Women: The Case of Self Help Groups in Andhra Pradesh

M. Bapuji & Md. Mastanvali

Empowerment of Women—The Concept

Etymologically speaking, empowerment is defined as giving power to create power 'within' and 'enabling'. In this sense, empowerment is a multi-dimensional process, which enables individuals or groups to realize their full potential and powers in all the spheres of life. Empowerment is a process, which helps people to gain control over their own lives through raising their awareness, skills and involvement in the decision-making process. It is also a feeling that activates the psychological energy to accomplish one's goal. In other words, empowerment can be regarded as a process of understanding and capacity building leading to greater participation, better decision-making power and transformative action.

Conceptually, empowerment is the strengthening of capabilities achieved through full participation of people in various processes. In this sense, empowerment envisages competence building and skill development, especially, to make decisions and to organize, manage, and deal with people and institutions. Thus, empowerment is a positive concept concerning the competence of the individuals for self-action and transformation of self. It enables the persons to become active participants in the formulation and implementation of policies and decisions and encourages their involvement in all other processes that affect their lives. Empowerment also makes them to take responsibility for their own choices, decisions and actions. It is an effective answer to oppression, exploitation, injustice and other such maladies; it emphasizes on the building of economic and social capabilities among individuals, groups and even communities to bring out transformation of the societies.

Empowerment requires full participation of people in the decision-making process, which determines the well-being of society. In this sense, empowerment means giving power to certain unprivileged sections of society which hither to have been denied of such power. The economic dimension of empowerment is more important as it benefits all the oppressed sections. The economic wellbeing of people can be achieved through empowerment and they can be provided with material benefits by giving them economic rights.

Empowerment can be discussed at three levels. 'Power to', 'Power with' and 'Power within" levels. 'Power to' connotes empowering the individuals to survive and control their labour, resources and body and have control over the decision-making process within the household and in the broader society. 'Power with' means the power that is derived from people organized together with a common purpose to achieve certain collective goals. 'Power within' implies power derived both at individual and collective levels that has the dimension of involvement, self-awareness, confidence and assertiveness.

In the context of women, power can be understood in relation to caste, class, age, leadership, marital status, etc. Power in the context of women implies collective actions of women to promote their interests through various channels like markets, public institutions, local bodies, political organizations and community. Power in this sense can be measured in terms of various parameters like the women's control over their body, labour, resources etc.

Empowerment of Women in Indian Context

Women in India constitute about half of the population of the Country. According to 2001 Census, the total population of India is 1021 million comprising 531 million males and 490 million females. Women constitute 48.29 per cent of the country's total population. The literacy rate among women increased at a faster rate, as it rose from a mere 8.86 per cent at the time of Independence (1951) to 54.16 per cent in 2001. The corresponding figures for males are 24.95 per cent and 76.1 per cent respectively. The female work participation has grown from 19.7 per cent in 1981 to 22.3 per cent in 1991. The number of female workers in the organized sector has also increased from 27.9 lakh (12.2%) in 1981 to 42.3 lakh (15.4%) in 1991. In 1991, the participation of women in the Central Government services is about 8 per cent. The number of women IAS and IPS Officers is 631 (1991).

Position of Indian Women

When compared with men, women in India always have occupied a lower space in all respects. In the spheres of politics and economy they have occupied a subordinate position. Their representation in the legislative bodies has been consistently marginal. In the social sphere also they are subjected to a number of disabilities and hardships in the name of traditions and customs. The gender inequalities are glaring in the country, as is the case all over the globe. They lag much behind men in terms of every set of socio-economic indices, in spite of the fact that the gender equality is the mandate of the Indian Constitution, which is manifested in many of its parts. The plight of rural women and women belonging to weaker sections is still more deplorable. Empowerment in such a context calls for modalities other than mere economic uplift because backwardness among women stems not merely from poor economic position but also from dismal social conditions and inequalities because of the societal system characterized by male domination. Conventional strategies of development address only economic poverty, but conveniently ignore the social realities. Hence alternative strategies, which focus not only on economic issues but also on non-economic factors, are necessary to deal with the poverty of Indian women.

Right from independence, the representation of women in the representative bodies such as the Parliament and Legislative Assemblies has been extremely marginal. The number of women contesting the Lok Sabha and Assembly elections is also extremely low. In general, all the political parties without any exception are reluctant to field women in elections. In all the Lok Sabhas so far, out of the total membership of 543, the number of women members has always been below 30. They constituted a meager 8 per cent of the total members of the House. The representation of women in Rajya Sabha is equally dismal. Their share has never exceeded 15 per cent of the total membership of 250 in the House. So far, the highest number of women members in Rajya Sabha was 38, but generally it is les than 16. In the State Assemblies the position of women is still worse. According to available data, in the State Assemblies the women members account for only 2-3 per cent of the total members.

Earlier Women Empowerment Strategies

After Independence, the Government has evinced keen interest in the welfare of women along with other weaker sections of the country. From the very beginning the guiding principle of the Government in the formulation of policies and programmes for the advancement of women is that if the women, who constitute half of the nation's population and also the very kernel for social transformation, are bypassed, no real development is possible. Accordingly, the Government started concerted efforts to improve the plight of the teeming millions of women and to ensure them equal status along with men. The Government adopted a multi-pronged approach to promote the welfare of women. Besides introducing many legislative measures, it initiated several policies and programmes for the all round development of women. These policies and programmes were implemented through the Five-Year Plans. Each Five Year Plan implemented a number of special schemes and programmes for the advancement of women in different fields like education, health, employment and so on with huge outlays. The National Plan on Action for Women (1974) set a guiding policy for the uplift of women. The National Perspective Plan for Women adopted in 1988 mainstreamed the women's issues in the Public Policies making a long-term perspective for both safeguarding their rights and promoting their socio-economic development. The Plan envisages an alternative strategy while enjoining special space for women in all the policies and programmes of the Government in order to create a democratic, egalitarian and secular fabric in the country. The Plan also proposed several measures for achieving the development of women within the existing framework of development parameters.

During 1980s, the Central and State Governments exhibited increased concern for the development of women. In 1985 the Women and Child Development Department was set up in the Ministry of Human Resource Development exclusively for the promotion of welfare of women and children. In 1992, the National Commission for Women was set up for protecting the rights of the women. The Rastriya Mahila Kosh was started in 1993 to extend credit to the poor women for meeting their different needs. In the same year the Mahila Samridhi Yojana was launched to help women for promoting self-reliance and economic independence among the rural poor women by encouraging thrift. The Indira Mahila Yojana is another scheme launched in 1995 to coordinate and integrate the components of all sectoral programmes for facilitating the empowerment of women.

The Eighth Five Year Plan (1992-1997) marked a shift from the development to empowerment approach for the sustainable development of women. The most significant contribution of this Plan is the creation of a separate component plan for women in all related development programmes. Empowerment of Women has received further thrust in the Ninth Five Year Plan (1997-2002). Empowerment of women has become one of the core objectives of this Plan. The Plan stressed on the need for empowering women as the agents of change and development. For the first time, the Plan raised the issue of reservation of seats for women in the national and state legislatures. The Plan also proposed for the reservation of 30 per cent of the jobs for women in the public services. It emphasized as usual on the promotion of health and education among women. Against this background, the National Policy on Women Empowerment was initiated in 2001. This Policy seeks to bring about advancement, development and empowerment of women through various means. It emphasized on the creation of a suitable environment through positive socio-economic measures in which women can have their total development and realize their inherent potentialities so that they can play an active role in the progress of society.

The landmark effort made by the Government in the direction of women empowerment is the enactment of 73rd and 74th Constitutional Amendment Acts of 1992, which sought to revolutionize both the rural and urban local bodies, namely the Panchayati Raj Institutions and Municipal bodies. These two Acts provided for reservation of 33.3 per cent of the total elected offices in the Panchayati Raj Institutions and Municipalities and Municipal Corporations for women. As a result, about 0.8 million women have emerged as leaders at the grassroots and entered into political arena through 0.2 million local bodies existing all over the country. The various research studies conducted on the implementation of these two Acts in different states reveal that there has been a considerable awakening among the women after the implementation of these Acts. There is also significant increase in the participation of women in the political process at the grassroots level. The political empowerment affected by these Acts among women has its impact on their socio-economic conditions.

Self Help Groups Intervention

During the various Plan Periods, the Central Government has initiated several programmes to provide employment to the rural poor women to bring them into the mainstream of the Nation's development. The Integrated Rural Development Programme (IRDP) which is the major anti-poverty programme introduced during the Fifth Five Year Plan provides for 40 per cent share for the female beneficiaries in the benefit of all developmental programmes. The Programme of Training of Rural Youth for Self Employment provides a share for the female trainees. The wage employment programmes such as the Jawahar Samridhi Yojana (JSY) and the Employment Assurance Scheme (EAS) also provided wage employment to women to the extent of 40 per cent. The Women Development Corporation was set up to give the necessary thrust to the states with a view to enable them to play the role of catalysts to create sustainable income generating opportunities for women and for attaining economically independent and self-reliant status.

Even though, all these programmes were implemented with huge outlays for the amelioration of the problems of women there was no perceptible change in the conditions of women. The Government of India constituted a working committee to study the impact of various developmental programmes on the conditions of women. The Committee felt that the programmes initiated for the development of women could not cover the majority of rural women and only few women were benefited by these programmes. The Committee emphasized on evolving a comprehensive strategy that addresses the problems of rural women in an integrated manner.

In 1980s, there was a considerable rethinking among the policy makers in India about the existing approaches and strategies towards women welfare. It was found that the strategies for development of women are multi-sectoral and there is no coordination among the various departments and ministries implementing the schemes and programmes intended for the welfare of women. Hence they attempted to evolve a holistic strategy to provide various services to the women in a cohesive manner. This rethinking among the policy makers resulted in the formulation of a novel programme in the name of Development of Women and Children of Rural Areas (DWCRA), which is essentially an employment programme. Started in 1982 in about 50 districts on a pilot basis, the DWCRA was gradually extended to cover all the districts in the country. It was estimated that about 112 lakhs women were covered under this programme by the end of the 9th Five Year Plan. Apart from providing assistance to take up income generating activities, the DWCRA programme encourages the habit of thrift and saving among the targeted women. It also provides its beneficiaries access to various basic services such as education, health, nutrition, child care, sanitation and so on. However, the main objective of this programme is to provide women greater access to institutional credit, particularly, the banks for meeting their productive as well as consumption needs.

The Self Help Groups in Andhra Pradesh

According to Census of India 2001, the total population of Andhra Pradesh accounts for 72,727,541. Of them, 38,368,811 are males and 34,358,730 females. Thus, women constitute slightly less than half of the total population. The male-female ratio is 1000:947. The literacy rate among women in the state is 51.17%, according to 2001 census. The State ranks 13th in the entire country in the matter of women literacy. The female literacy in the state showed a remarkable rise during the last two decades, as it increased from 24.16 per cent in 1981 to 32.72 per cent in 1991, which rose to 51.17 per cent in 2001. Even though the state has improved in terms of female literacy it occupies lowest position in the country in some other respects.

The State Government has adopted social mobilization through the Self Help Groups as a strategy for addressing poverty; particularly among the rural women Social inclusion and participation in the political process is the important aim of SHGs. Besides group moblisation, the programme focuses on expanding the assets of poor women and creating economic opportunities for their livelihood. This process uses social mobilization as an institutional mechanism to help the poor women interact with the governmental machinery so that the public resources and services are better accessed. Under this strategy the Government has started in 1980s Self Help

Groups to eradicate poverty among the women in rural areas. This strategy is sought to provide self-employment to the poor women in order to incorporate them into the development process. Under this programme the homogeneous groups of women would choose and collectively undertake different economic activities suited to their skills and local conditions, supplemented by the Government's matching grant. Following their initial success, the State Government significantly increased the number of SHGs throughout the state. As a consequence the number of these groups shot up. These groups have targeted mainly the women because they have more credit than the men. Hence women groups are considered as an entry point for the formation of men groups, youth groups, groups of the physically handicapped and so on.

The women SHGs approach has become a central theme of the State Government's approach towards the welfare of women in Andhra Pradesh. It has become a key element in the state's Women empowerment strategy for eradication of poverty among the rural women. Under this approach three different types of Self Help Groups were formed in the State. These models are Development of Women and Children in Rural Areas (DWCRA), South Asian Poverty Alleviation Programme (SAPRP) and Cooperative Development Federation (CDF). The basic assumption of these models is that social capital or group efforts can contribute to the eradication of poverty, particularly, among the poor women. Further, these models are rooted in the premise that lack of access to the credit has resulted in the perpetuation of poverty among the rural poor, particularly, among women. Hence social capital and empowerment eliminate general as well as gender poverty.

The DWCRA is the main model with a large number of groups formed under it. According to the Official Statistics there are about 4.75 lakh SHGs in Andhra Pradesh by the end of December 2003. These Groups consist of about 60 lakhs women members. Of these Groups, about 1.90 lakh Groups are DWCRA Groups with a membership of about 25 lakhs while 5201 groups are SAPPP Groups with 34600 members and 200 groups are CDF Groups with a membership of 45605.

Table 1 projects that there has been remarkable growth in the number of SHGs in Andhra Pradesh. The progress is more conspicuous after 1999. In 1995-96 there were about 40 thousand Self Help Groups in the state which have steeply increased to 4.75 lakhs within a period of a decade which implies a manifold growth. A similar trend can also be found in the revolving fund of these groups which increased from Rs.90 Crores in 1995-96 to the staggering figure of Rs.1625 Crores in 2003-2004. These SHGs are operating in 48567 villages and in a few towns throughout the 23 Districts in the State.

Table 1

Progress of Self Help Groups in Andhra Pradesh

Year	*No. of Self Help Groups*	*Corpus Fund (In Rs. In Crores)*
1995-1996	40,154	80.00
1996-1997	73,678	122.00
1997-1998	85,415	240.00
1998-1999	99,243	310.00
1999-2000	20,010	520.00
2000-2001	3,10,100	808.00
2001-2002	4,22,366	1201.94
2002-2003	4,51,248	1432.18
2003-2004	4,75,646	1624.95

Source: Collected from the Reports of the Department of Rural Development, Government of Andhra Pradesh, Hyderabad.

The SHGs in Andhra Pradesh are taking up number activities for generation of income. These groups are manufacturing about 450 articles and goods. These groups are engaged in the production of cloth, garments, fancy goods, pickles and other edible items, handicrafts, toys, leather bags, Kitchenware and so on. The goods are marketed through various means. There are DWCRA Bazars which were started specifically to market the various items and goods manufactured by these Groups. These Bazars were formed in almost all important villages, towns and cities in the State.

The current financial position of SHGs given in Table 2 speaks about their successful functioning.

Table 2

Financial Position of Self Help Groups 2003

No. of SH Groups	4,75,646
No. of Members	65.40 (Rs. In Lakhs)
Savings	904.42 (Rs. In Crores)
Government Assistance	720.53 (Rs. In Crores)
Total Corpus Fund	1624.95 (Rs. In Crores)
Average Savings of Each Group	19,105 (Rs.)

Source: Collected from the Reports of the Department of Rural Development, Government of Andhra Pradesh, Hyderabad.

The Women belonging to the weaker sections like the SCs, STs and BCs are the main targets of SHGs Programme. They are the main beneficiaries of these programmes. About 90 per cent of the members of various SHGs belong to various weaker sections. Only 10 per cent of the members of these Groups belong to the upper castes. A glance at the Table 3 reflects this fact.

Table 3

The Social Background of the Self Help Groups Members in Andhra Pradesh

S. No.	*Social Category*	*No. of Members*	*Percentage*
1.	Scheduled Castes	21,80,150	33.33
2.	Scheduled Tribes	9,93,593	15.9
3.	Backward Classes	27,48,074	15.19
4.	Other Castes	6,18,788	9.64
	Total Members	65,41,105	100.00

Source: Collected from the Reports of the Department of Rural Development, Government of Andhra Pradesh, Hyderabad.

The DWCRA Programme in Andhra Pradesh

The DWCRA Programme was initiated in Andhra Pradesh in 1982 along with other states in the country for providing self-employment on a sustained basis for the rural poor women. Under this programme, the women living in the same village with similar socio-economic background united into groups. The size of each group ranges from 10–15 members. The DWCRA Groups are federated to the Mahila Banks under the Andhra Pradesh Mutually Aided Cooperative Societies Act of 1995 for credit purposes. The DWCRA Groups take up varieties of economic activities suited to their skills and local conditions for income generation. The members of the Groups are provided training by the Government in leadership, attitudinal change, production skills and so on. Each DWCRA Group is sanctioned Rs.25, 000 by the Government as revolving fund for undertaking the economic activities. This fund is a common group fund revolved periodically. In addition to this fund, the members are provided IRDP subsidies and bank loans on liberal terms for undertaking the economic activities. Apart from these funds, the groups members mobilize funds through their monthly savings for meeting consumption needs. The members are provided with various channels to market their finished products. As already stated the DWCRA Bazars are the main channels for marketing of these goods. Along with these credit services, the DWCRA members are also provided with basic services like education, health, child care, nutrition, drinking water and so on. Thus, organizing the women around thrift and credit services, along with various social services, results in the enhancement of their bargaining power and the power to resist exploitation in all forms. The socio-economic empowerment of women is the crux of the DWCRA.

The DWCRA in Andhra Pradesh made a steady progress in different aspects. Started in 1982 in a few selected districts on experimental basis, gradually it was expanded to cover the entire state. At present, the DWCRA groups exist in almost all the villages in the state; the number of these Groups increased from a few hundred in 1982 to 1.90 lakhs in 2003. They constitute about 45 per cent of the total Self Help Groups (4.25 Lakhs) functioning in the state. There about 25.10 lakh members in the DWCRA groups. Of these members, 84 per cent belong to the weaker sections like Scheduled Castes (34%), Scheduled Tribes (10%) and Backward Classes (40%). These

Groups have saved Rs. 316 Crores while the Government provided them Rs.590 Crores as corpus fund.

The Impact of Self Help Groups

Various Institutions like the Universities, NGOs, NABARD etc. evaluated the impact of Self Help Groups on the rural women of Andhra Pradesh. The main findings of these studies can be summed up as follows:

1) About 98 per cent of the Self Help Groups save regularly according to the norms.
2) The members of all Groups meet regularly and discuss matters relating to their activities along with other matters relating to their life.
3) About 98 per cent of the members of the SHGs have adopted Family Planning.
4) The children of the members of SHGs have availed the immunization services against diseases.
5) Among 80 per cent of the SHGs have got access to the financial institutions like the Banks for meeting their credit needs.
6) About the 98 per cent of the members of SHGs who took loans from the Banks and other institutions have repaid their loans.
7) A considerable number of SHGs members have got elected to various offices in the Panchayati Raj Bodies.
8) The dependence upon the private moneylenders has declined considerably due to the increased access to credit through the SHGs.

Apart from the above findings these studies also revealed that the Self Help Groups members have gained awareness about the society and its problems. This awareness motivated them to participate in the several community welfare programmes like laying roads, planting trees, conducting health and awareness programmes, prevention of crimes against women and girl children, eradication of social evils like casteism and dowry, rescue and rehabilitation of orphan children, support to destitute women and so on. Apart from this, they are actively taking part in the Government sponsored programmes like the literacy promotion programmes, family planning programmes, Janmabhoomi and such other Programmes.

According to some independent studies, the SHGs have improved the socio-economic conditions of women to a large extent. As a result, they have gained control over their labour and economic resources to some extent. They are freely moving and interacting with the officials and other women for different purposes. Besides, the DWCRA women assumed leadership roles in various political organizations at the grassroots. The adoption of family planning techniques by these women indicates their control over the reproductive choice. Thus, the DWCRA women have gained control over their labour, reproductive choice, resources, freedom to move and interact with others, assumed leadership and so on. It can be said that there is empowerment of women in different spheres as result of the formation of the Self Help Groups.

These studies, however, suggest that even though there is improvement with regard to the 'power to' dimension of empowerment, there is no improvement in the 'power with' dimension of empowerment. But, there is improvement in 'power within' dimension of empowerment because these women are able to manage some of their issues independently without the help of others. As one study highlights, the political potential of Self Help Groups is powerful. These Groups are serving as training ground to train the women to become leaders and potential aspirants of political power. These women have potential to work for the development of their areas as people's representatives.

A few other studies underline that the DWCRA programme has brought about considerable improvement in certain important issues like consumption, which has led to enhancement in the nutritional status of the children, pregnant women and old women in the families of DWCRA members. These members are spending considerably on health care of their family members. It is also mentioned in these studies that the state has achieved impressive reduction in the growth rate of population, from 2.4 during 1980s to 1.3 per cent in 1990s. The dramatic decline in the decaderal growth rate of population has also been attributed to the impact of Self Help Groups in the state.

However, the single most important benefit to the rural poor women accrued from the DWCRA as revealed by all these studies, is that the DWCRA members have gained access to institutional credit for both production and consumption purposes which relieved them from the clutches of the money lenders. They are now in a position to get loans from the Banks without the help of others for meeting their various needs.

Thus, the SHGs in Andhra Pradesh is a success story and became a key element of the strategy for the removal of rural poverty by means of social mobilization, empowerment and capacity building among the women folk. The Government of Andhra Pradesh has provided large space for SHGs in its poverty eradication strategies. This strategy succeeded to a large extent in achieving its objective of empowering rural women in different spheres.

Then, the issue is whether the SHGs strategy, particularly, the DWCRA model adopted by the State Government sustains the process of women empowerment. These Groups have succeeded in placing the rural poor women into the ambit of institutional credit, which enabled them to undertake productive and income generating activities, which they could not do in the past. The resultant improvement in their economic condition coupled with increased control over their labour and resources improved the consciousness and promoted capacity building among the rural women to some extent. How far this empowerment has uplifted the rural poor women is another important aspect to be examined. The Andhra Pradesh experience proved that the Self Help Group is valuable as an anti-poverty strategy. However, one has to understand its lapses and rectify them to get much more out of this model. There is tremendous potential in this strategy if its vision is expanded beyond the economic concerns to social and political concerns, for transforming it as one of the most potential empowerment interventions.

References

1. Seth, Mira, *Women and Development*, New Delhi: Sage, 2001.
2. Narsimham, Sakuntala, *Empowering Women*, New Delhi, Sage, 1999.
3. Galeb, S. and N. Chandra Sekhar Rao, "Women's Self Help Groups Poverty Alleviation and Empowerment", *Economic and Political Weekly*, Vol: XXXVIII, No. 12 and 13, March 22–28/29, April 4, 2003, pp.1274-1283.
4. *Government of Andhra Pradesh, DWCRA and Women's Empowerment: A Success Story of Self Help Groups Movement in Andhra Pradesh, Hyderabad.* Panchayati Raj and Rural Development Department, 1999, UNDP, South Asia Poverty Alleviation Programme, Progress Report, 1996-1998, Hyderabad: 1998.
5. Rajya Lakshmi, C.S., "Empowerment Through Self Help Groups", *EPW*, Vol: XXXVIII, No.12 and 13, March 22-28/29, April 4, 2003, pp. 1302.
6. Shanta Kohili Chandra, "Women and Empowerment", *The Indian Journal of Public Administration*, Vol: XLIII, No. 3, July–September 1997.
7. Government of India, Planning Commission, Various Five Year Plan Documents (Sixth Five Year Plan to Ninth Five Year Plan), New Delhi.
8. Karmakar, K.G., *Credit for Self help Groups*, New Delhi: Sage, 1999.

13

Empowerment through Political Participation

Anil Dutta Mishra

Introduction

A.S. Altekar has rightly remarked "the degree of freedom given to women to move about in society and to take part in its public gives a good idea of the nature of its administration and enables us to know how far it had realized the difficult truth that women too have a contribution of their own to make to its development and progress".[1] In fact, if we wish to cure the traditional diseases of the Indian society, family and individual, if the attainment of equality, freedom and justice is our goal and if the future generations are to be nurtured in peace, harmony and brotherhood, our social consciousness has to be restructured in a manner, free from the masculine arrogance and social prejudices.

Despite their vast numerical strength, women occupy a marginalised position in Indian society due to several socio-economic constraints. Social evils like dowry deaths, polygamy, child-marriage, female infanticide, forced prostitution and crime against women have not been uprooted from our country. This has inhibited the effective participation of women in the political processes and institutional structures of democracy.

According to the Document on Women's Development (1985), women's role in political process has virtually remained unchanged, despite the rapid growth of their informal political activities. Wide-ranging political participation of women has been severely limited due to various traditional factors such as caste, religion, feudal attitudes and family status. As a result, women have been left on the periphery of political life.

Of late, several steps have been taken to improve women's representation in political decision making centres and enable them to be equal partners in the country's political affairs. The most notable one in this regard is the policy of reservation for women at the grassroots institutions of Indian democracy which has been incorporated in the 73rd and 74th Amendments of the Constitution. Reservation of seats for women in the Panchayati Raj Institutions (PRIs) and municipal bodies will provide them with an opportunity to ventilate their grievances and to take an active part in the formal political arena which deals with the local level social and economic problems.

The system of Panchayati Raj, which was initiated mainly for people's participation in political and economic processes at the grassroots level, has not been successful in ensuring women's participation to the expected extent. The champions of the Panchayati Raj system desired that rural women should not only become the beneficiaries of development, but also, more importantly, the contributors to it. The Balwantrai Mehta Committee was particular that women should find representation in the rural political institutions and recommended that two women should be co-opted in Panchayat Samiti. As a consequence of this recommendation, a few states did make provision for women's representation. But the system of nomination or co-option resulted in sheer patronage of the dominant political or social groups and the women who got nominated had practically no knowledge on the functioning of Panchayats nor any experience in working for women. Women's representation on these bodies came to be symbolized by 'tokenism' and not by a meaningful association.

Therefore, some states gave up nomination or co-option and resorted to reservation as the only way of ensuring women's participation in the PRIs. But in the recent years, special efforts are being made to ensure women's representation in the PRIs in the wake of the 73rd Constitutional Amendment Act which reserves one-third of the seats for women in PRIs. The participation of women in PRIs is considered essential not only for ensuring their political participation in the democratic process but also for realising the developmental goals for women.

Participation and Empowerment: Women's Perspective

People's participation is a necessary pre-condition for the successful implementation of any plan programme. This is based on the assumption that the process of people's development is not likely to strike very deep roots unless the target groups themselves are part of it. Participation is a means of reducing power differences and is, therefore, contributory to equalization and social justice.

Participation in public life has many facets. It includes activities which have a strong bearing on a group and the community, the power to effectively influence the elected representatives, decision-making process as well as the policies and actually alter existing situations wherever they are found to be clearly disadvantageous. While women should be positioned in large number at crucial levels for significant and effective exercise of power, they need to be equipped with suitable means to shoulder these responsibilities. Otherwise their representation would end up as mere tokenism.[2] Political participation manifests itself in actual participation in those voluntary activities by which members of a society share in the selection of rulers and, directly or indirectly, in the formulation of public policy. It also includes such activities as voting, seeking information, contributing financially, discussing and proselytizing, attending meetings, communicating with representatives, enrolment in a party, canvassing and registering voters, speech writing and speech making, campaigning and competing for public and party office.[3]

Participation of women in politics involves: *(i)* women as voters; *(ii)* women as members of political parties, trade unions/pressure groups; *(iii)* women as elected members of Parliament, State Assemblies and various bodies of local self-government and taking part in decision-making, planning, implementation and evaluation; *(iv)* women as members of women's organization and their association with voluntary organisations and NGOs. The concept of political participation of women is broader than the one covering women's participation only in the electoral and administration processes. It includes the gamut of voluntary activities with a bearing on the political processes, including voting, support of political groups, communication with legislator, dissemination of political views and opinions among the electorate and other related activities. However, political participation can be considered to include an involvement in any form of organized activity that effects, or seeks to affect, these power relationships. It refers broadly also to "activities by those not formally empowered to make decision, these activities being mainly intended to influence the attitudes and behaviour of those who have powers for decision making".[4] In fact, protests and demonstrations against those in power also form part of political participation. Women's participation has covered a range of activities including movements, protest and support meetings on all issues connected with labour, dowry, rape, domestic violence, and pressurize against food adulteration and deforestation, as also movements for the promotion of peace.[5]

Explaining the importance of participation in politics, Milbrath and Goel argue that the citizens must at least participate in the choice of their public officials in order to keep public action responsive to the wishes and desires of the people.[6] In fact "participation in politics and in public debate helps to build a better and more noble character in the people... People would be better human beings if they, so participated". Similarly McClosky said participation benefits the participants as well as the larger community. According to N.D. Palmer, participation helps the individual to be effective and it associates him or her with the political system. The higher the rate and levels, the more varied the forms of participation, the healthier is the democratic system.[7]

Participation enables women by giving them a sense of their own dignity and value. For women participation has three roles: educative, integrative and empowering. Women constitute half the society and belong to all classes and all sections. So, the women's empowerment is not the question of one section only. It is ultimately the question of the entire society. It is an integral part of the entire social phenomenon. Human society cannot move forward without stirring half of its body, the women. Thus, it is in the social and national interest to draw womenfolk into the social and political process.

Today women are connected directly or indirectly to the operation of society at every level and at the same time occupy the aggregate position of outsiders. No one can deny today the fact that for women's empowerment, participation at every level and in every field is essential.

The political space belongs to all citizens; politics is everyone's business and affects the lives of each of us... the more women are associated, in numbers corresponding to their percentage of the population, in the political decision making process, in parties, in elected bodies, in government and in international bodies, the more they can be associated with this process as protagonists and more they can change the modalities and outcomes of politics. Only then will the concept of democracy find concrete and tangible expression democracy and the participation of women go hand in hand and promote each other mutually.[8]

Twentieth century has brought a great change in the life of women all over the world, influencing their attitudes, values, inspirations, ways of feeling, standards of behaviour and acting for effective participation in all walks of life. Women's quest for equality with men has become a global phenomenon. It is particularly relevant in the societies which have deep roots of patriarchy and subjugation of women. In these societies gender division is found in all walks of life. This division influences the family, division of labour, class structure and the nation state. Now, women are involved in politics, developmental programmes, movements etc., and are throwing a challenge to patriarchy. They are now coming out of their insulated enclosures and expressing their equality with men and demanding freedom and dignity. They are resisting the control of their sexuality by men. Caste, class and gender-based oppression of women are being opposed in several quarters in Indian society. Women's rights over land and property are being acknowledged as instruments of their empowerment. The 73rd constitutional amendment has initiated a process of empowerment of women in India in general and the women of the countryside in particular. It is realized that women empowerment is the need of the hour.

Although women are participating in greater numbers in politics and in other aspects of public life all over the world, they still remain largely outside the realms of power and decision making in government. The gap between men and women's participation in political life have narrowed somewhat but remain huge, as figures on women as head of governments, holders of ministerial positions and member of parliaments show.[9]

In fact, women's participation in elections depends on the mobilization by the political parties, general awareness among the people of the community of the importance of voting and the overall political culture prevailing in the country. No serious effort has as yet been made to mobilise women as a political constituency by any political party and women are often projected as not being interested in and uninformed about matters political. Women are also not perceived as an organised interest or pressure group, so their needs are not taken into consideration. However, these stereotypes are not borne out by facts.[10]

It is difficult, nonetheless, to generalise about the links between any single factor and political behaviour. They vary and are influenced by factors such as the social status of women, their economic position, cultural norms and above all, the regional outlook towards women's participation in public affairs.[11] The number of women contestants in parliamentary elections has not increased over years. Political parties are still reluctant to field women candidates. The high cost of election campaigning is a deterrent to women candidates.[12] In spite of these facts, woman in decision making and leadership roles at the grass-roots, regional and national level is a major change factor.[13]

The key instruments of the strategy for women's development both as beneficiaries and as participants are, therefore grass-root level organizations of women for learning and productive activity, which would help: *(i)* to draw them into the mainstreams of development; *(ii)* promote self-reliance and collective action; *(iii)* strengthen their participation and voice in the development process; *(iv)* assist them to achieve economic viability as well as knowledge for their personal growth; *(v)* provide forums to enable women especially from the poorer sections to participate freely and fully in decisions that affect their lives and that of the community; *(vi)* enable them to acquire full access to development resources and services; and *(vii)* enable them to function as instruments of social change.[14]

The process of empowerment is multi-dimensional and it enables women to realize their full destiny and powers in all spheres of life. A woman's empowerment begins with her perceptions of herself and her rights and her capabilities and her potentials; it depends on her awareness of how gender and socio-cultural and political forces affect her. Political empowerment, economic development and social uplift of women are necessary and desirable to fight myriad forms of patriarchal domination and discrimination at every stage. In fact, women's empowerment is central to the achievement of the triple goals of equality, development and social justice. And for that political participation is needed. In a democratic system, women participation may be viewed at two levels, *(i)* awareness and assertion by women of political rights and *(ii)* acquisition and exercise of power by them.

Improving the political status of women in India is an integral aspect of the overall problem of socio-economic change. Do women politicians have different concerns or behave differently from men in politics and does women's participation make a difference to political issues and the way politics are carried out? Drude Dhalerup, who has carried out extensive research on women in politics, says: Don't expect us to make much difference as long as we are only a few women in politics. It takes a critical mass of women to make a fundamental change in politics.[15]

When a significant number of women are in politics, as in the Nordic countries where women hold a relatively high percentage of elective positions in government, studies show that they do make a difference. As Dahlerup says, women politicians are just as powerless when it comes to the global economic changes as are the male politicians. But the many women in politics in the Scandinavian countries have to some extent changed people's attitude towards women as leaders, have changed the political discourse somewhat, have placed women's issues on the agenda and have to some extent changed the political culture.[16] It is argued that if women in good number enter the corridors of power they will be able to take up women's issues within state structures and also effect changes in the party and local bodies. They will have access to state resources which can support women's groups and provide services to them. Their positions and actions can legitimise the women's cause in the eyes of the people and parties.

Women Participation in Indian Politics

The active participation of women in the freedom struggle simultaneously developed among them an increasing sense of awareness to organise and lead the cause of their liberation from oppression and subordination. After independence, a large number of legal and socio-economic measures have been taken to elevate the status of women. Women too, have become politically conscious as they have started participating in national and state politics.

Independence of India opened the doors for the women of the country to find their due place in society and partake in the political, social and administrative life of the country. The advent of democracy in India brought forth the spectacle of women moving up along in the corridors of political power, which has brought them new opportunities both as voters and candidates. They entered the two houses of the Indian parliament in their own way and some of them made a mark therein.[17]

Voting is the basic activity by which the citizens get assimilated in the political process. Women's participation in formal elections is to a great extent dependent on the mobilization efforts of the political parties, general awareness among the community of the importance of increasing franchise and the overall political culture. It is a common experience that the percentage of non-voters is usually higher among women than men. But the recent studies indicate that the sex differences in political participation are diminishing.[18] Reference may be made in this connection, about a study undertaken by Usha Mehta. She has examined the voting trend of men and women of the General Elections in India from 1952 to 1977. Her study shows that the gender gap is diminishing.[19]

Voting Turnout 1952-1977[20]

		Voted	
Year	*Men (%)*	*Women (%)*	*Difference (%)*
1952	55.00	31.1	17.9
1957	56.00	39.6	14.4
1962	62.1	46.6	15.5
1967	66.7	55.5	11.2
1971	69.7	60.0	9.71
1977	65.62	54.91	10.71

Studies on political participation show that there is still gender gap in the level of political information and perception regarding implications of various political issues (e.g. the right to franchise both quantitatively and qualitatively). The committee on the status of women has attributed this to the lack of interest shown by political parties in improving the political knowledge of women.[21] It is generally held that in spite of the growing equality between men and women in society, political participation is taken as more natural to men than to women. It is assumed that women voters vote as the male members of the family desire and as such no separate and special effort is usually made to mobilize them as participants in the voting act.[22]

Women are increasingly participating in the political

process, as indicated by the shrinking gap of per cent of actual voters by sex. In 1962 the gap was more than 15 per cent. This declined steadily over different elections. In 1980, the gap was little over six per cent, but in 1984, it again went up to about 10 per cent.

The number of women contestants to the Lok Sabha rose steadily between 1962 and 1980, but the number of successful female candidates progressively declined till 1997 (from 33 in 1962 to 19 in 1977).

But in the elections of 1980 and 1984 the number of successful female candidates again increased to 28 in 1980 and 42 in 1984. However, women members now constitute less than 10 per cent of the Lok Sabha. The picture is not better in the states.[23]

Women Contestants: Lok Sabha

Year	*Total No. of seats*	*No. of Women contestants*	*Percentage*
1952	487	43	8.8
1937	494	45	9.1
1962	491	69	14.0
1967	515	67	13.0
1971	518	85	16.4
1977	542	71	11.07
1980	542	142	26.2
1984	542	173	32.3
1989	543	189	34.8

These increasing figures are indicative of the fact that after independence more and more political consciousness and desire for greater political clout has grown among Indian women. However, this increasing participation of women is insignificant when we view this fact in the light of male participation. The participation of male members far exceeds the participation of women. The table given below testifies this generalization.

Women Contestants and Elected in General Elections

Year	*Contestants*		*Elected*	
	Total	*Women*	*Total*	*Women*
1952	1974	43 (2.3)	489	14 (2.3)
1957	1519	45 (3.0)	494	27 (2.5)
1962	1938	69 (3.5)	494	33 (6.7)
1967	2369	67 (2.8)	520	30 (5.8)
1971	2784	85 (3.1)	518	21 (4.1)
1977	4371	71 (1.6)	542	18 (3.3)
1980		142	542	28 (5.1)
1984		142	542	43 (7.9)
1989		189	543	28 (5.1)
1996	13353	599 (4.4)	543	39 (7.1)

However, when we look at the number of women candidates actually elected to Lok Sabha in the various General Elections, we find their percentage increasing upto the 1962 elections and then it started declining. This indicates that the presence of women at the highest political level coexists with a generally low rate of overall participation in the political life of the country. The table gives the number of women M.Ps and their representation in each of the Eight Lok Sabhas. The Eighth Lok Sabha had the maximum and the Sixth Lok Sabha had the minimum representation of women members.[24]

As far as women's membership in the upper house as against the male membership is concerned, the number of women in the upper house reached an all time high in 1977. In 1977, the number of women M.Ps was 25 (10.2%) of the total membership of Rajya Sabha; except in 1957 and 1962, the percentage of women's representation in Rajya Sabha remained higher than that in the Lok Sabha.

It must, however, be noted that most women in the rural as well as urban areas are still not fully participating in the political field and decision making processes of the nation. It does not mean that the status of women in India has not improved after Independence and that there is no social consciousness at all towards the social reality. When one reflects upon the presence of women representatives in the centers of power, one can not ignore the fact that we had a woman Prime Minister who had an Olympiən position in her nation's political system.

Number of Women Members in Lok Sabha

Name of the Lok Sabha	*Year*	*Total no. of seats*	*No. of Women Members*	*Percentage*
1st Lok Sabha	1952	499	22	4.4
2nd Lok Sabha	1957	500	27	5.4
3rd Lok Sabha	1962	503	34	6.7
4th Lok Sabha	1967	523	31	5.9
5th Lok Sabha	1971	521	22	4.2
6th Lok Sabha	1977	544	20	3.4
7th Lok Sabha	1980	544	28	5.5
8th Lok Sabha	1984	545	45	8.9
9th Lok Sabha	1989	543	28	5.1

Obstacles Coming in the Way of Women's Participation

The participation of women is influenced by many inter-related factors like the social status of women, their economic position, the cultural norms and above all the regional outlook towards women's participation in the wider society. Access to significant decision-making position in the political parties continues to elude women. Women in the political world face some peculiar problems which are totally unknown to their male counterparts. These inhibit their performance in the legislative and party work not only in India but also in the so-called emancipated societies of the developed countries.

A variety of reasons account for women's diminished role in the political arena. They include tradition, physiology, lack of vertical mobility, concern for home and family, psychology and lack of patronage, particularly, from senior women politicians. In other words, political participation of women in India is severely limited due to a nexus of several traditional factors; Indian politics is dominated by the factors like caste, class, religion, feudalism and family status etc., all of which are parochial and essentially patriarchal forces that work in favour of men against women. Consequently, women are still left on the periphery of the mainstream political process of the country and their political participation remains limited to mainly voting at the time of elections and they fail to capture of seats of power and influence. At the same time, there are several other socio-economic constraints by which women have been marginalised. The number of women in leadership positions at the local, village, district and national level is still not commensurate with their number in society. The reason is that a stone can not be different from the rock from which it comes. A woman in public life at the different levels is as much a part of the Indian Society as her sister who is confined to her home and family. Styles of functioning of such women in the three tier system of Panchayati Raj, or the State Assemblies or Parliament are bound to be shaped by the cultural mosaic which is studded with the prescriptive and descriptive elements, codes of conduct, role models, political goals, values and ideals in transitions.

The United Nations Divisions for the Advancement of Women (DAW) has identified a number of obstacles to women's participation in politics which prevent them from reaching parliamentary and ministerial positions:

- the relatively short historical tradition of women's political participation and lack of experience in campaigning, public debate, exposure to media;
- prevailing negative attitudes towards women's participation in public life, lack of confidence and support for female candidates and politicians on the part of the electorate, including women;
- the difficulty women experience in combining a political career with the traditional women's role in the family and often in society;
- economic dependency or lack of financial means; insufficient education in general and political education in particular;
- women's reluctance or diffidence to participate in politics, particularly at a high level.[25]

Mechanism to Increase Women's Participation

Empowerment is not a technocratic goal; it is a wholesale Political commitment. Achieving it requires a long term process in which all cultural, social, political and economic norms undergo a fundamental change. It also requires an entirely new way of thinking, in which the stereotyping of women and men no longer limits their choices, but gives way to a new philosophy that regards all people as essential agents of change and that views development as a process of enlarging the choice of both sexes, just not one. Stages of emancipation of women, in any given country, lie in the mind of man and in the attitudes of their leadership. And these two factors nave mostly favoured women in India.

Training is one of the most important mechanisms for improving women's participation in politics, particularly for increasing women's access to the higher levels in national decision making bodies. Whilst training can be directed for improving women's skills in specific areas, particularly in management, gender sensitivity training can be directed to both men and women to build awareness among them and demolish the attitudinal barriers to women's participation, advancement and empowerment. Nehru held that women "must" be trained to participate "in every department of human activity" and play an active part in all professions and spheres.

In some countries quotas have been successfully used to increase women's participation in the leadership of political parties and in party lists for public election. For instance, the Norwegian Labour Party stipulates that at least 40 percent of all candidates for election must be women. The Danish Social Democratic party has a similar provision for municipal and county elections. According to the Norwegian Labour Party's Secretariat, "Quotas for Women are the most efficient strategy we ever used to increase women's political representation".[26] The constitutions or legislations of only a few countries provide for quotas for women in parliament, including those of Angola, the former USSR and Nepal. In addition, the 1991 electoral law of Argentina establishes a compulsory 30 percent quota for women candidates for all elective posts. Related to the quota system is the mechanism of reserved seats: Bangladesh, Egypt, Nepal, Pakistan and the United Republic of Tanzania are the countries that have or have had in the past earmarked a certain number of seats in their national parliaments reserved for women.[27]

The under representation of women in political decision making bodies is the key reason for the backwardness of Indian women. To ensure the women's participation the 73rd and 74th Amendments of the Constitution mandated 1/3 reservation of seats for women in all local level elected bodies. Similarly there is a need of reservation of seats in Parliament and State Assemblies. Reservation of seats in a legislative body for women will alter the very character of the legislative body and will compel the political parties to change their strategies and tactics and induce them to give women their due. If the women enter the legislative bodies in larger number, inhibitions that result from their minority position in these institutions may disappear fast and give them greater freedom to articulate their views. A system of reservation may also increase the women legislators' sense of responsibility and concern for the problems affecting women, this ensuring the presence of a body of spokesmen of the women's cause in the representative bodies of the states. Such a system would also help to increase the degree of political modernization of women both in the electorate and within the parties.[28]

Political education and awareness building is intended to promote women's representation in the electoral process, to establish and lobby for a women's agenda and to sensitize both women and men to women's issues and the role of women in politics. For that it is necessary to organize from time to time a series of seminars, workshops and conferences all across India to involve women in the political debate and present their views. These workshops will reach a wide cross section of women.

An expert group meeting on Equality in Political Participation and Decision-making organized by DAW made the following recommendations to women's status in political parties:

- as an interim measure, substantial targets, such as

quotas or similar forms of positive action to ensure women's candidacy for office and participation in political posts should be applied;

- training programmes should be developed to increase the political and management skills of women in politics, both as candidates and as elected or appointed officials, especially making use of the experience of other women who have achieved public office;
- women's sections of parties should be evaluated and strengthened to enable them to influence party policy and promote female candidacy;
- information on potential women candidates should be compiled, maintained on a systematic basis and made available when candidacy or appointments are considered;
- parties should be encouraged to examine the criteria used to select persons for political functions to ensure that the varieties of experience possessed by women are taken into account in selection;
- training activities should be developed to sensitize party members to the needs and potentials of female members;
- as an interim measure where the electoral system might make it useful, parties should undertake special measures to provide funding for women candidates for office.[29]

Other important mechanisms include networking, participation in the campaigns of other politicians, lobbying, and membership in some clubs, professional and academic associations.[30]

The corrective mechanisms are to be viewed holistically and not as isolated piecemeal actions. Only then women will be at par with men in all fields.

Conclusion

Manu's dictum that she should do nothing independently even in her own house—in childhood a subject to her father, in youth to her husband and when her husband is dead to her sons, she should never enjoy independence—has proved to be wrong. Now women have come out of their isolation, got themselves educated, stormed the male bastions in jobs and services and also have the backing of constitutional safeguards and social legislation. Women need to make themselves politically visible and politically important in order to change the direction of development, empowerment and gender justice.

Unless the deep-rooted changes in the power relations among people and between men and women are brought about things are not going to change. Rays of hope are gradually becoming brighter; radical changes in and through participation in social and political processes will be instrumental to women's empowerment. Women's empowerment is essential and desirable for societal development. A society attempting to develop without the full participation of women is like bird trying to fly with only one wing. It is bound to go off course.

Let women realize their immense potentialities for social change, rise up and excell like men as the builders the nation. Women must take upon themselves the task of participating in political and economic affairs with commitment and a sense of challenge. At the same time, men must accept women in their new roles. They must welcome the emerging trend of having more women leaders in different fields. It must be realized that both men and women are the equal partners in the process of nation building. Only then there will be true empowerment of women and greater participation of women in the affairs of the state.

Notes and References

1. Altekar, A.S., *The Position of Women* in *Hindu Civilisation*, Varanasi, Motilal Banarsidass, 1962, p. 9.
2. Country Report, Fourth World Conference on Women, Beijing, 1955, New Delhi, Government of India, 11195, p. 66.
3. Vir, Dharam and Mahajan, Kamlesh, "Contemporary Indian Women," *Collected Works*, Vol. 4, *Politics, Awareness and Women's Movements*, Delhi, New Academic Publishers, 1969, p. 121.
4. Gupta, Sunita and Gupta, Mukta, (eds.), *Role of Women in the Twenty-first Century*, Delhi, Anmol Publications, 1966, p. 63.

5. *Ibid.*, p. 64.
6. Milbrath, L.W., and *Goel*, M.L., *Political Participation: How and Wiry, Do People Get Involved* in *Politics?*, Chicago, Rand McNally, 1977, p.2.
7. Palmer, N.D. *Elections and Political Development in India*, New Delhi, Vikas, 1976, pp. 59-61.
8. Inter-Parliamentary Union (IPU), Women and Political Power Survey Carried Out Among the ISO National Parliaments as of 31 October, 1991, *Reports and Documents*, No. 19, 1992, p. 1.
9. Karl, Marilee, *Women and Empowerment, Participation and Decision Making*, London and New Jersey, Zed Books Ltd., 1955, p. 59.
10. Country Report, *op. cit.*, p. 68.
11. *Ibid.*
12. *Ibid.*
13. *Ibid.*, p. 73.
14. Gaur, K.D., "Women and Governmental Programmes", in Dharam Vir and Kamlesh Mahajan (eds.), *Contemporary Indian Women, Collected Works*, Vol. 4, New Delhi, Academic Publishers, 1996, p. 177.
15. Dahlerup, Drude, "From a Small to a Large Majority: Women in Scandinavian Politics", quoted in Virginia Willis, "Public Life: Women make a difference", paper for the Expert Group Meeting on the Role of Women in Public Life, DAW, Vienna, 1996, p. 10.
16. Karl, Marilee, *Women and Empowerment, Participation and Decision Making*, London and New Jersey, Zed Books, 1995, p.63.
17. Bhall, Shanta, *Women Parliamentarians of India*, Udaipur, Shiva Publishers and Distributors, 1995, p. 44.
18. Baxter, S. and Lansing, M., *Women and Politics: Tile Invisible Majority*, Ann Arbor, University of Michigan Press, 1980, pp. 24-27; S. Welch "Women as Political Animals: A Test of Some Explanations from Male-Female Political Participation Differences," *American Journal of Political Science;* 21 November, 1977, pp. 711-33; K. Anderson "Working Women and Political Participation 1952-1972", *American Journal of Political Science*, 19 (August) 1975, pp. 433-53.
19. Chaudhuri, Sanghamitra Sen, *Women al1d Politics: West Bengal a Case Study*, Calcutta, Minerva Associates, 1955, p. 24.
20. Reports of Election Commission of India as compiled by Usha Mehta in "Indian Women and their Participation in Politics", *Social Change*, Vol. 8, No. 3, September 1978, p. 32.

21. Chaudhuri, Sanghamitra Sen *op. cit.*, p. 76.
22. *Ibid.*, p. 14.
23. Gupta, Sunita, and Gupta, Mukta, (eds.), *Role of Women in the Twentyfirst Century*, Delhi, Anmol Publications, 1996, pp. 46-47.
24. Bhall, Shanta, *op. cit.*, p. 46.
25. Karl, Marilee, *op. cit.*, pp. 64-5.
26. *Ibid.*, p. 69.
27. *Ibid.*, p. 70.
28. Chaudhuri, Sanghamitra Sen, *op. cit*, p. 126.
29. Karl, Marilee, *op. cit.*, pp. 68-69.
30. *Ibid.*

14

Political Participation of Women in Local Administration in India and Globalisation

Rajendra Bharti

Women, nearly half of the human race, are suffering from inequality in every walk of life. They have been considered as second rate citizens in one way or the other. If we analyse the participation of women in the social, political, cultural, economic and religious fields, we find that their participation is not equal to their male counterparts. But modernization has opened the floodgates for women in every area. Democracy and globalization have given them voice and ample space to express their views about the society, polity, culture, economy and religion. Democracy has provided equal opportunity to them to elect the representatives of their choice, who in turn from the government.

But in spite this right to equality given to women civil societies in all countries also present another picture where women are less represented in the decision making process at every level and in every sphere. Thus, the policy of affirmative action in the form of reservation of seats in the legislative bodies, are opted in many countries. In an era of globalization and openness, there is a growing need to associate all sections of society in the processes of nation building and development. Especially, the involvement of women is needed at local level administration because of the challenges posed by different issues like globalization, environmental degradation and social turmoil.

This is why in India the Constitution through its 73rd Constitutional Amendment Act (CAA) 1992 w.e.f. 1993 and 74th C.A.A. 1992 w.e.f. 1993, makes provisions of 30% for reservation of 1/3rd of the seats for women in Panchayats & Urban Local Administration.

One of the positive aspects of Panchayati Raj Institutions (PRIs) is the empowerment of women. About one million women have entered into the Panchayat bodies in different capacities after the first election has taken place on the basis of 73rd CAA. Among them about 40% of the elected women belong to the marginalised sections of society. However, out of the total women representatives, nearly 70% are illiterate and most of them have no previous political experience; but this very entry of women in local administration has deep impact on gender equality. Initially, there was an apprehension that these women representatives would work like puppets at the hands of the male members of their families, but the experience of their work has disapproved it.

Political Participation

Political Participation is a very important function in every political system; particularly in democratic political system it has an added dimension. It provides a scope to the people to ventilate their discontentment and opposition against any policy. The aspirations of the people are translated into policies through their participation in the political system. Political participation can be helpful in the long run to release the energy of the people, evolved through the method of expressing discontent, opposition to repression or demand. It is, in fact, a positive action for the involvement of all sections of society in the processes of making of laws, policies, regulations etc. within the system. Therefore, every nation state provides for people's participation via constitutional laws and policies.

Political participation is a voluntary activity. It is a means by which people directly and sometimes indirectly communicate their political opinion. In fact, political participation is the involvement of groups and individuals at various levels in the political system. Structurally, the orbit of political participation includes those legal activities by private citizens which are more or less directly aimed at influencing the selection of government personnel and their actions.

A political system has emerged in the human society because man is basically a social and political animal and he wants to live a community life. The feeling of enjoying a community life results in the creation of a political system. In absolute terms, politics is a struggle for power; but power has many connotations, from political to cultural, social, economic or religious. The inception of civil society creates a sense among the people towards understanding the very concept of power in the form of authority, decision etc. in their family or in any social organization. Politics, thus, paves the way for understanding the structure of decision making, both formally and informally.

Political participation (PP) of the people is very important in a democratic system of governance, where it (pp) provides scopes to people to express their views on any political matters related to them directly or indirectly. This helps people to give their verdict on any issue related to the decision and action of the government. There is a need of political participation of people in any democratic process because it prevents discontentment among people and ultimately restricts any kind of revolution; one may conclude that this would help towards the continuance of the system. Political participation has been encouraged in non-democratic polities to some extent to know about the desires and aspirations of the people and their expectations from the government. Participation of people in an election is not the only way of political participation; it also means mobilization of people on any decision of the government or expression of their views in the forms of *dharna, pradarshan* (agitation) or through their writings.

Historically, political participation of people in one form or other has its references in the recorded history of India and Greece. In Vedic period, the institutions like "Sabha and Samiti" reflect the concept participation of people in public affairs; even women were allowed to take part in the deliberations related to public matters. In Ancient Greece, it was considered that a citizen, who did not actively participate in any political activity, was not a man but an animal or an idiot. Political participation is a continuous process which accelerates political actions, political measures and political opportunities.

Local Administration

Local administration occupies an important place in almost all systems of the government. It deals with those areas and functions which have a direct bearing on the life of citizens. The local institutions perform very important functions as well as crucial roles towards the welfare of human beings residing in the areas within their jurisdiction.

Local administration is often regarded as being basis of local self government. The argument is that national self government requires certain habits of minds and way of public behaviour and that the great training ground is in local council.[1] Local Administration (L.A.) is essentially a method of getting various services run for the benefit of the community. It is true that local administration concentrate locally but its area of performance is nationalistic. In the era of globalization and liberalization its sphere of functioning has become wider. It is also a fact that local administration is basically suffering from parochial views; but the onslaught of the electronic gadget, Information technology (I.T) etc. has compelled it to reconsider its orientation and modernity has influenced its outlook. In the changing modern scenario local administration needs to orient itself for meeting the changing needs of the people and bringing their socio-economic-cultural development.

Local administration in India is of two types i.e. Rural Local self government or Panchayati Raj Institutions (PRI) and Urban Local Self government. They have been given a unique position in the three tire structure of government via 73rd and 74th Constitutional Amendment Acts.

Evolution of the PRIs and urban local bodies (ULBs)in India has its own historical background. The ULBs in their present form may be said to have their origin in 1687 when a Municipal Corporation in Madras was first set up by the East India Company. Lord Ripon's famous but largely abortive resolution of 1882 invested in local government (l.g.) with a distinct philosophy, but it was not until the inauguration in 1921 of Government India Act, 1919, that it began to acquire the character of self governing institution and to be taken with a greater measure of seriousness.[2]

During Ancient period, India had the record of possessing local self governing institutions and those local bodies enjoyed greater freedom in managing their affairs. This can be sufficed by the statement made by Met Cafe. "The village communities are little republics having nearly everything they can within themselves and (are) almost independent of any foreign relations. They seem to last where nothing else lasts, dynasty after dynasty tumbles down; revolution succeeds to revolutions... The union of village communities continue, each forming a separate little state in itself. It has contributed more than any other cause to the preservation of the peoples of India through all the revolutions and changes which they have suffered. And is in a high degree conducive to the happiness and to the enjoyment of a great portion of freedom and independence". The picture which is painted by Met Cafe has been an idealistic one, but it reflects the nature, purpose and function of such institutions in old times.

During Vedic period, village was the basic unit of administration because of the agrarian economy. An important functionary of the village was called "Gamini". He was a respectable officer who played a vital role during the coronation ceremony of the king. There was the reference of "Samiti" (Assembly) and Sabha where discussions were taking place on issues related to public matters. In Samiti women were also given representation. The Jataka stories of this period and even Jain literatures and Kautilya's *Asthashastra,* provide the vast sources related to function, role and purpose of local administration for rural and urban local institutions. During medieval period, new pattern of local administration was evolved, but local institution still continued to function. However, the village communities were completely broken down during British rule; they also ruined the age old economic self-sufficiency of village life.

Post independent India strived towards local government and administration through the Constitution of India which became operational on 26th January 1950 after great deliberation in the Constituent Assembly. Article 40 was inserted into it as a part of Directive Principles of State Policy. This was basically based on the philosophy and desire of Mahatma Gandhi, who was of the opinion that villages should be self-sufficient units not only economically but also in political and administrative affairs.

Gandhi was not in favour of people always looking towards the government for anything and everything. According to him, village Panchayat should be elected on the basis of adult suffrage and the control of the state agencies over it is to be minimum. During the implementation of Community Development Programmes and Five Years Plans it was thought that village Panchayats & urban local bodies should have a constitutional status. Thus, Balwant Rai Mehta Committee, Ashok Mehta Committee and many other such committees were constituted. On the basis of reports and advices of different committees and commissions 73rd and 74th Constitution Amendment Acts 1992 (w.e.f. 1993) came into force for rural local government and urban local government respectively. The chapter IX and schedule XI were inserted into the Constitution for Panchayats and chapter IX A and schedule XII were inserted for urban local bodies.

73rd C.A.A. describes the definition, purpose, function of local administration in rural areas. Art.243 gives the definition of Panchayat while Art. 243A and 243C stipulate the provisions of Panchayat at three different levels. Art 243D provides the scope for reservation of S.Cs., STs. & OBCs, at different levels in the Panchayatiraj system through the Rules made by the state government. According to Art 243E the duration of Panchayat is fixed for five years from its first constitution and it should be reconstituted before the expiry of the duration and in case of dissolution election should take place within six months. Art 243G speaks about the powers, authority and responsibility of the Panchayat through the Acts and rules framed by state government. Art. 224H speaks about powers to impose taxes by, and fund of the Panchayat by state laws. 73rd CAA provides financial powers to the Panchayat via Art. 243I by the constitution of a financial commission by the state government to review the financial position of Panchayat. This has been supplemented by Art 245 to take audit of accounts of Panchayat through the laws enacted by the state government. The continuation of Panchayat with out any hindrance by way dissolution, suspension or vacancy can be solved by Art 243K, which empowers the state to constitute State Election Commission which would have the power of superintendence, direction and control of the preparation of electoral roll for and the conduct of all election to the Panchayats.[3]

For Urban Local Administration 74th CAA 1992 (w.e.f. 1993) provides a chapter called Part IXA in which Art 243P, 243Q, 243R and 243S describe the definition, constitution of municipalities and constitution and composition of ward committees etc. respectively. Art.243T speaks about reservation for seats in municipalities for SCs. STs and OBCs and women and prescribes that not less than 1/3rd seats are reserved for women of every categories. Art 243Y speaks about constitution and function of State Financial Commission. Art. 243Z provides scope for audit of the municipalities. Art. 243ZA creates space for State Election Commission which has been empowered for superintendence and conduct of all the elections of municipalities. Art.243ZD speaks about the committee for district planning and Art. 243ZE is related to committee for metropolitan planning. There is a schedule XII which describes the power, authorities and responsibilities of Municipalities etc.[4]

Panchayati Raj System is also extended to the scheduled areas by the providing Panchayat (Extension of Scheduled Areas Act 1996) with 73rd CAA. There were only 4944 elected people representatives in the union and state and union territories in pre-73rd CAA period of Indian democracy. Now the world's most popular working democracy has constitutionally mandated 2,32,1332 village Panchayats, 6000 intermediate Panchayats and 534 Zila Panchayats. The three tiers of these elected bodies consist of as many as 27, 75,858 village Panchayat members and 15,067 members of Zila Parishad. This has been the broadest representative-based democracy, which does not exist anywhere else in the world. (Indian Panchayati Raj Report 2001 NRD)[5]

Woman and Political Participation

There is a struggle ongoing all over the world launched by women to get equal share not only in social, religious and cultural spheres but also in political sphere. To realise the goal of ending the existing inequalities in gender relationship it is necessary to create women leadership in the state and civil society—the key centres of power in the present globalised economy. It is, therefore, imperative for women to be in the corridors of power and utilise power to negotiate a better deal for themselves, if they are to influence policy decisions which have been an impact upon them. Empowerment of women in all areas, in particular the political area, is crucial for their advancement and for the foundation of society based on gender equality. It is central to the achievement of the goals of equality, development and peace.[6] It is also a fact that participation of women in politics is based upon three fundamentals and nonnegotiable principles:

a. The equality between women and men;
b. Women's right to the self development of their potentials;
c. Women's right to the self representation and self determinations.[7]

It is also a truth that representation of women in political areas is some how, very thin; under representation or invisibility of women in decision making enforces their deprivation, leading to an unequal distribution of resources, neglect of their interests, needs, perspectives and priorities and no say in policy making.[8] This is why Alida Brill vehemently insisted, "without our own voices being heard inside the government areas and hall of public policies and debate we are without the right of accountability—a basic entitlement of those who are governed."[9] On this belief a struggle for women's participation in political areas was carried on in the past and is being carried on now also for more representation in State Assemblies and Parliament in India.

It is a fact that the question of reservation of seats was left to National Perspective plan for women to take up. It is recognized that political participation of women is severely restricted and it is suggested that 30 percent quota for women be introduced at all levels of elective bodies to encourage women participation in politics. Women's organizations too favoured introduction of reservation though initially it is only at Panchayat (village council) level with the passing of 73rd CAA and 74th CAA 1992 which introduced 1/3rd reservation of seats for women in Panchayat and urban local bodies at every level.

The power to make rules for Panchayat and ULB has been vested in state legislature via 73rd CAA and 74th CAA. Thus, a major initiative was taken by the state of Bihar when it reserved 50% of the posts at every level of Panchayat for women for every section of society i.e. general, OBCs, Scs, and STs via Bihar Panchayati Raj Act 2006. At about 155 writs were filed in Patna High Court against the reservation in a single post. But all such writs were declared as null and void on the basis of the system of horizontal reservation for women.[10] There is a support for and against the reservation of seats in Parliament and State Assemblies. The pro-reservation groups demand for reservation for women and other demands quota in quota for the women in SCs, STs and OBCs. as in Panchayats. The leaders of most of the women groups are in the hands of the upper caste and class of society. They are of the opinion that caste issue is a divisive one for women but the real picture is somewhat different when we see reservation in Panchayats. The women representatives belonging to SCs, STs, & OBCs work more vigorously for women and society than the women of other groups. The women of these (SCs, STs, OBCs) groups have suffered much and have been exploited more in comparison to the general categories women; since their childhood they have been discriminated against in all fields, from education to employment and even in media. They (SCs, STs & OBCs women) have been more prone to be exploited economically, sexually, socially and religiously than the general categories women. On the present scheme of reservation Madhu Kiswar argues that the scheme of reservation will "ghettoise" women's politics confining them to contesting from the reserved constituencies. She further maintains that the lottery system of gender based reservation would inhibit women from nursing their constituencies, which could damage the legitimacy of women's participation.[11] The idea of multimember constituencies has also been mooted in opposition to reservation for women. On the other hand, it is contended that women's entry will change the texture of the present day politics and bring women's values, preferences and perspectives into the political area. Reservation itself is needed in order to break the hold of the patriarchal structure. But it should be in the tune with the constitutional norms as has been done at Panchayat & U.L.B. Political representation encourages participatory role of women in the political field and it would be helpful to shape the political system in such a way that the system would become more compassionate, human, ecologically balanced and even free from violence, criminalization and corruption. The experience at the grass-roots level clearly vindicates the claim that if women are given the opportunities and level playing field they can lead the nation.

It does not suffice for women to be just members of the legislative bodies. They should occupy positions where they can bring their power and knowledge to bear on changing the direction of society in order to make it more inclusive and just.[12] As Georgia Asworth observes, "A critical mass of women is necessary within a given institution or structure if real change is to occur but it is important to understand that "critical" refers not just to the sufficient numerical presence of women , but also to the women having an active share in decision making through legitimate influence or numerical leadership."[13] It is also a fact that more increased representation of woman not only increases the interests of women but also increases the various interests of society due to the basic character of women. As every human being possesses soul and the soul is beyond the gender, each soul has within it those qualities typically associated with male or "masculine qualities" and those qualities typically associated with female or "feminine qualities". A soul in a male body can learn to transcend over-identification with the body and then express feminine qualities as well as masculine ones. Mahatma Gandhi was an example of this. He not only had powerful determination and dynamism but also the gentleness of non-violence ... while Mother Teresa was a combination of both the feminine and masculine qualities; she was being caring and serving while having the courage and power to overcome many obstacles and challenges .[14]

The public private domain theory has been used by Vicky Randall who observes "ideologically to justify women's exclusion from public-politics while women's actual confinement to narrow domestic areas has been major break upon effective political participation. At the same time the public-private convention has masked the crucial interdependence of these spheres. Not only women's private roles limited but largely defined their public contribution but public policies have confirmed their 'private' obligations."[15]

Globalization and Cultural Identity

Globalization is a process in which a nation state integrates itself with the world economically, politically, culturally and technologically. The unification process not only breaks down the barrier of nation-state boundaries but also strives towards betterment of its subjects as well as the whole world. Globalization promotes specialization not only in economy but also in technology, which would be helpful for alleviation of poverty through trickle-down theory. It unifies different people by sharing prosperity as well as common miseries there by reducing the incidence of wars that are now capable of annihilating mankind due to advances made in weapon technology through atomic, chemical and biological sciences... Globalization is also being pursued by many nations as it is considered to be in furtherance of democracy and freedom of the individuals.[16]

The flip side of globalization unleashes the market forces.

It is an important tool of modern state for not only governance but also for distribution of goods and services. In its functioning it is ruthless because it obeys the command of money power...globalization tries to perpetuate a system where the poor are always kept deprived and craving for more.[17] The lopsided development leads to rural urban divide, regional disparities and tensions over economic issues in developing countries like India. This process also paves the way for more role for the MNCs which ultimately hammers traditional values and traditional way of economic relationship. But it is also true that one can not keep oneself away from the process of globalization.

There has been different forms of globalization i e political, economic, cultural and technological. Economic globalization believes in the principle where all economies have to be absorbed into global economy. The Economic Cooperation and Development (OECD) defines it (globalization) as "a shift from a world of distinct national economies to a global economy in which production is internationalized and financial capital flows freely and instantly between countries".[18] The increasing roles of World Bank, IMF, WTO etc. are glaring examples of it.

Political globalization has been reflected in the international political organization where nation states have accepted the will of international political organization for the purpose of international peace, security and development and national sovereignty has become secondary to the international order. International organizations like UNO, NATO, EEC, SAARC etc. provide mechanisms that enable states, at least in theory, to take concerted action without sacrificing national sovereignty.

Cultural globalization is the process where by information, commodities and images which are produced or evolved in one part of world can be easily transferred to the other parts of world and affect it. Global village is the concept derived by the mixture of cultural globalization and technological globalization. In the global village technical know-how has been transferred from one country to another or from one corner of the world to another corner either by legal way or through an illegal path. The nuclear program and it technical know-how and the patent regime are the clear examples of it.

There is a global trend towards the breakdown of communitarianism and community values. This is also reflected in contemporary India. In fact it is not the product of post industrialization but is the consequence of over politicizing without accompaniments of material benefits that a post industrial society offers to its citizen.[19]

Some "universal of culture" common to all mankind have been a reality ever since the beginning of human history. This should not be confused with the sharing of cultures resulting from globalization. It had its own basis in the similarity of man's nature at a certain level which led anthropologists to conclude "a man is like all other men" even though recognizing differences at other levels where they postulated "man is like some other man and man is like no other man".[20] Similarly, the cultural reality of contemporary processes of globalization also did not exist in the past when intercultural contacts were established between societies either on the basis of imperial domination or colonization. The most important reasons for the distinctive historical phenomenon of globalization of cultures or the new challenges that it poses for the humanity can be traced to its unique technological base which has revolutionized the concept and quality of the system of production, communication and social organization and the various processes of acculturation and symbolization in societies.[21]

It is also a fact that globalization does not contribute cultural, social and economical integration of people in the society through equity access to the fruits of developments available through globalization. Cultural conflicts or contradictions sharpen in society due to unlimited exposure of people to foreign cultural and entertainment packages beamed from television and other mass media.[22]

The cultural treat that globalization poses to this society are not displacement of the traditional moral norms of society due to exposure to "dehumanizing and retrogressive cultural products" in the form of entertainment, consumerism, exposure to new style of life etc. leading to high incidence of crime and moral deviance such as prostitution, cult of money and loss of traditional humanistic values like care of elderly and emotional bond among the members of family.[23]

Challenges to Local Administration

The process of globalization and its impact on culture, both local and national give it a new urgency. As the process of economic and social development have expanded, the importance of local cultures and particularistic expression of ideology and sentiment have been taken note of information of the public policies as well as in the analysis of nation-state.

The Indian society is comforted today with the lack of secular rational principles of membership based on the unity of cultural, social, political and economic interests to form associative groups which could effectively mediate between the state and the people for realization of goals and redress of grievances. The rise in ethnic movements and new social movements related to ecology, gender and human rights etc. results from a heartless manner in which the operative structures of domination in society, such as the state corporations and multinationals, encroach upon the rights of the weak and vulnerable sections of society.

These are following challenges against the PRIs & ULBs in India :

(i) The nature of people's participation (pp) in PRIs & ULBs is just managing the affairs at the local level or one can say, is related to attending the meetings of Panchayats & Urban bodies. But in real sense it (pp) should be in the direction of presentation of people's aspirations and to make the bureaucratic structure more accountable for the desire and need of the people.

(ii) The task of planning at grass root level and implementation of policies so framed has to be done by the local leaders.

(iii) The negative approach of bureaucracies towards PRIs & ULBs and to some extent support from the people in general to the bureaucracy is also a challenge. In fact, bureaucratic approach needs to be changed in such a manner so that they can realize the need of the hour and the basic principles of parliamentary democracy where the permanent executive (civil servants) always work under the cloak of ministerial responsibilities (political executive or temporary executives)

(iv) There is a struggle of power between the politicians at local level and those at the state level for the implementation as well as formulation of developmental programmes.

(v) The income of Panchayats & Municipalities is from house tax, water tax, octorai, etc. which is very meagre and this is due to lack of political will as well as of administrative support. The taxation has been one of the major constraints towards revenue mobilization at local level. Local bodies can play a genuine role in the local development and self rule only if they enjoy some degree of financial autonomy. Though some local bodies rely on innovative resources mobilization, most of them do not experience a fair amount of financial autonomy. The fiscal decentralization is not yet reality. Fiscal autonomy can not be built in a regime of grants-in-aid.[24] Tax collection responsibility is also a permanent challenge. The possibility of achieving higher revenues through increased rates of taxes is both undesirable and infeasible. Higher tax revenues can be achieved only through buoyancy and expansion of the tax base. Thus, the main instruments for achieving a sustained increase in over all revenues are (a) Expansion tax base (b) wide spread and bold imposition of users charges on all non-merit goods (c) wide spread and bold privatizing.[25]

(vi) The institutional challenge from local government to deal with the need to review the complicated and absolute legal frame work and planning roles that hinder any possibility of introducing rationality to the local administration.[26]

(vii) The design and implementation of local municipal information systems seem to be of utmost importance. The production and hence, democratization of knowledge through the discourse and the free access to the basic information, is a kind of challenge that local governments predominantly overlook.[27]

(viii) The challenge of globalization i.e. political, economical, cultural and technological, has been glaring to make the l.a. in tune with these changes and values.

(ix) At local level, enactment of 'Right to Information Act', is a great challenge for the Panchayats and municipalities to satisfy the desire and queries related to developmental plans.

Conclusion

It is crystal clear that local administration is very closely linked with the local people. It can create a wave, just as the throwing a stone in calm water. It can be able to provide required impetus to the ongoing process of development, social justice and social quality. The problem related to social and physical ecology is very crucial for local administration particularly in an era of globalization. In such a situation women can play major role towards environment protection and ecological sustenance; because they have the basic instinct of having the feeling of nurturing, preservation and protection. Participation of women in large number in different movements such as Chipko, Narmada Bachao, Prohibition etc., are the few examples of it.

Local Administration needs to be revamped structurally and functionally by means of training, education, and legal instruments so that it can be able to preserve country's bio-diversities, traditional values, freedom for subjects and environment protection for future generations. In this context, the association of women in local institutions will be of much value.

Notes and References

1. Jackson, R.M. *The Machinery of Local Government,* Macmillan New York, 1967, second (ed.) p. 2.
2. Maheshwari, S.R., *State Government in India,* Macmillan, Delhi 1979, p. 245
3. Bakshi, P.M.; "The Constitution of India", Universal Law Publishing Pvt. Ltd. Delhi, 2002, pp. 208-12.

4. *Ibid*, pp. 214-18.
5. Singh, M.K.; *Jharkhand Development and Politics, Avenues and Challenges*, Gangadeep Publications, Delhi, 2006, p 228.
6. Pam Rajput, "Women's Political Participation in India: An agenda for Empowerment" in Pramilla Kapur ed. *Empowering the Indian Women*, Publication Division, New Delhi, 2001, p. 223.
7. CAPWIP, "Issues in Women's Political Empowerment in 'Asia-pacific Region', Proceedings of Women in India and Pacific: High Level Intergovernmental Meeting to Review Regional Implementation of the Beijing Platform for Action, Escap, Manila Oct.26-29 p. 281.
8. Pam Rajput, p. 224.
9. Brill Alida (ed.) *A Rising Public Voice: Women in Politics World Wide*, New York N.K. 120 Ferminist Press 1995, p. 1.
10. Kuman Gaurav, " Nateeze Zamini Satta Sanrachana Badal Dange" in Chetanshi Year - 2 vol. 3-4 April - Sept. 2006 p. 13.
11. Madhu Kiswar in *Manushi*, http:..www.freespeech.org. manushi.96.zenana.html.
12. Pam Rajput, p. 237.
13. Georgia Asworth, Gendered Governance: Agenda for change UNDP: Gender in Development Monograph series # 3, Bureau for Development Policy, March 1996, p. 5.
14. Jayanti, B.K, "Spirituality for Women's Empowerment" in Pramilla Kapur ed. *Empowering Indian Women*, Publication Division, New Delhi, 2001, pp. 401-402.
15. Pam Rajput, p. 239.
16. Ramashwaram P.R "The Challenges of Globalization for Civil Services", *IJPA*, vol.XLVIII No.1, Jan-March 2002, p. 51.
17. *Ibid*, p. 53.
18. Quoted in Hey Wood, Andrew, *Politics*, 2nd edn. (New York; Palgrave Foundations, 2002), p. 139.
19. Singh, Yogendra, *Cultural Change in India: Identity and Globaization*, Rawat Publications, Jaipur, 2000, p214
20. Singh Yogendra, p. 71.
21. *Ibid*, p. 71.
22. *Ibid*, p. 73.
23. *Ibid*, p. 74.
24. Majumdar, Paramita, "Decentralization: Challenges to Urban Local Government." *Nagarlok*, vol. XXX VIII, July – Sept., 2006, No. 3, p. 5.
25. *Ibid*, p. 5.
26. *Ibid*, p. 6.
27. *Ibid*, p. 7.

15

Women and Political Participation in India

Sweta Mishra

The plight of women, in India, is no better than that of women in other developing countries. Despite the honour and reverence accorded to them as deities in religion and mythology and tributes paid to them in the country as personified in the Taj Mahal, the ground realities have a different tale to tell. In a patriarchal society such as ours, there exists the unfounded belief that man is the bread-earner of the family. Consequently, the male child gets the best of whatever facilities and resources available in the family. Despite the fact that women are massively involved in agriculture, food production and the like, their work counts for nothing. Their activities as producers are not reflected in statistics, thus making their contribution invisible.

The attainment of independence in 1947 and the promulgation of the Constitution in 1950 brought women at par with the traditionally dominant men. They got equal rights to participate in the political process and to enter high political offices. The experience of the last fifty-five years clearly shows that women in India have largely been marginalized in the political field and remained inactive and indifferent towards politics. Politics is one field where the evidence of participation by women is still not very impressive.

Twentieth century has brought a significant change in the life of women all over the world, influencing their attitudes, values, inspirations, ways of feeling, standards of behaviour and effective participation in all walks of life. It is particularly relevant in the societies, which have deep roots of patriarchy and subjugation of women. Especially, there has been a remarkable change in their involvement in the political field. It was thought that if women enter the legislative\decision-making bodies in large numbers, inhibitions that result from their minority status in these institutions, may disappear faster giving them greater freedom to articulate their views. It may also increase the legislators' concern for the problems affecting women.[1]

With this introductory background, the paper provides a conceptual analysis of the term participation. It then examines political participation of women in its historical perspective. Finally, it analyses in detail political participation of women with regard to parliament, cabinet, political parties, etc. and suggests ways of ensuring greater political participation of women in India.

Participation: The Concept

In plain and simple words, participation means to share or take part in. In the political context, the word takes on a more specialized meaning. Participation refers to actions through which ordinary members of a political system influence or attempt to influence outcomes.[2] "Participation" means direct involvement of the masses individually or through their representatives. Participation cannot be imposed on the people from above, it should be voluntary and based on the will to participate.[3] It is a means of reducing power differences and is, therefore, contributory to equalization and social justice.

Participation is a necessary pre-condition for the successful implementation of any plan programme. Participation in public life has many facets. It includes activities which have a strong bearing on a group and the community, the power to effectively influence elected representatives, decision-making process as well as policies and actually alter existing situations wherever they are found to be clearly disadvantageous.[4]

Political participation can be considered to include an involvement in any form of organised activity that affects, or seeks to affect, the power relationships. It refers broadly also to "activities being mainly intended to influence the attitudes and behaviour of those who have powers for decision-making".[5] It is a process by which people take part in political activity with more or less a clear choice or preference of their own. Attendance at public meetings, taking part in agitational activities, attendance at study circles of political parties, voting in elections, participation in election campaign, membership of a political party and membership in representative bodies are some of the important indicators of political participation.[6]

Political participation manifests itself in actual participation in those voluntary activities by which members of society share in the selection of rulers and, directly or indirectly, in the formulation of public policy. In fact, protest and demonstrations against those in power also form a part of political participation.

Explaining the importance of participation in politics, Milbrath and Goel argue that the citizens must at least participate in the choice of their public officials in order to keep public action responsive to the wishes and desires of the people.[7] According to N.D. Palmer, participation helps the individual to be effective and it associates him or her with the political system. The higher the rate and levels, the more varied the forms of participation, the healthier is the democratic system.[8]

Women and Political Participation

So far as women are concerned, political participation has been conceived of in a narrow sense. It has been mostly conceived of in relation to party politics. But it is not the only expression of political participation. Women's participation does not mean only the mobilization of power to solve their problems. It is much more. It is necessary to apply the women's point of view in policy-making which affects the whole society.[9]

Participation of women in politics involves: (i) women as voters; (ii) women as members of political parties, trade unions\pressure groups; (iii) women as elected members of Parliament, state Assemblies and various bodies of local self-government and taking part in decision-making, planning, implementation and evaluation; (iv) women as members of women's organization and their association with voluntary organizations and NGOs. Thus, the participation of women includes the gamut of voluntary activities with an effect on the political process, including voting, support of political groups, communication with legislators, dissemination of political views and opinions among the electorate and other related activities. Women's participation has covered a range of activities including movements, protest and support meetings on all issues connected with labour, dowry, rape, domestic violence, food adulteration and deforestation, as also movements for the promotion of peace.[10]

Historical Background

The founding fathers of the nation recognized that a freedom gained without the active involvement of women would be a hallow and fragile freedom and called upon women to place the nation above family and faith and enter the struggle as crusaders in a sacred cause.[11] Taking the historical development of women's participation into account, in the first three decades of the history of the Indian National Congress women's participation in its activities was peripheral and negligible. As Margaret E. Cousins remarked, "Perhaps in those early days women went to those Congress sessions more as the helpmates of their husbands, to see after their food and comforts. So I have heard it said—than because of their own individual interest in the debates".[12]

The agitation against the partition of Bengal and the Swadeshi Movement attracted the attention of women in many parts of India. As a result, women started taking active part in the Satyagraha campaigns, took out processions and organized demonstrations in front of liquor-shops and shops selling imported cloth.

The participation of women in the National Movement was mainly due to Gandhiji's influence. It was Gandhiji who realized that without the active participation of women real 'Swaraj' was impossible. He encouraged women to participate in all aspects and phases of nationalist activity, particularly in his constructive programmes and the non-voilent Satyagrahas. He believed that women, being an oppressed unequal group, would be the best fighters against social inequalities of all kinds.

Under Gandhiji's leadership, women played a very important role in the freedom movement. Women from all walks of life participated in the movement. An American journalist who came specially to witness the Dandi march, on seeing the participation of women commented that Mr. Gandhi might not achieve independence but he has been able to do miracle in releasing women and making them play an effective role in the national life.[13] Thus, the freedom movement, especially non-violent movement led by Gandhiji brought women to the forefront in every walk of life. He was successful in stirring the national conscience among the women.

Apart from participating in the non-violent movement, women took part in the trade union movement by organizing strikes and agitating for the workers' rights. Women also participated in the Dalit liberation movement launched by Dr. B.R. Ambedkar. There are examples of women being sent to jails during the freedom movement and they did not lag behind their male counterparts even in this respect.

During the freedom movement educated women provided leadership to the hitherto unmobilised women of India and organized them to fight for national independence. However, the basic concern of prominent women leaders of this period was to seek legislative enactments for women's uplift and gender equality in every field of human activity, besides demanding adult suffrage. The most outstanding of these women were Sarojini Naidu, Annie Besant and Bi Amma, the mother of Muhammad Ali. Both Annie Besant and Sarojini Naidu, addressed meetings in Bombay to educate women in the nature of Satyagraha.[14] Kasturba Gandhi and Kamaladevi Chattopadhyay were other great women who sold proscribed literature in the streets.[15] Manibehn Patel, took initiative to organize Gujarat women under the banner of Swadeshi. Rajkumari Amrit Kaur extensively promoted the use of khadi and organized a spinner Association in Punjab.[16]

Women Since Independence

After independence, while the Constitution of India was adopted and enacted several provisions were incorporated into it to emancipate the Indian women and many legal measures were taken by Parliament and Government of India to improve the status of women in India. The Constitution guaranteed to all women equal rights of participation in the political process along with equal opportunity and rights in education and employment. The right to vote was granted to men and women who were above 21 years of age. The principle of equal pay for equal work was also recognized by the Constitution. But the Constitution also does not prevent the government from passing separate Acts for protecting the interests of women and children. Moreover, the Constitution provides for right to an adequate means of livelihood for men and women equally [Article 39(a)]. During 1954-56, Special Marriage Act, Hindu Marriage Act, Hindu Succession Act, Hindu Minority and Guardianship Act and Hindu Adoptions and Maintenance Act were passed which legalized inter-caste marriage, ensured monogamy and conceded the right to divorce and equal share of property to Hindu women making women self-confident to stand equal to the men in the family and society.

In 1971, the Government of India appointed a Committee to examine all questions relating to the rights and status of women in the context of changing social and economic conditions in the country. The report of the Committee stressed the need for special temporary measures to transform the equality granted by the Constitution into equality in practice, in other words, to convert the de-jure equality into de-facto equality. A significant outcome of these policy debates in the seventies was a shift in paradigms, from viewing women as targets of welfare policies in the social sector to regarding them as critical groups for development.[17]

Women in Legislatures

Though few in number, women have always been a constant presence in the Indian Parliament. They encompass a wide section of this country's enterprising political aspirants and stalwarts, whose qualitative, if not quantitative, contribution can be ranked as significant in the annals of Parliament's history. Although out-numbered by their male counterparts, they have, with great spirit, made an impressive mark and left indelible impressions on the sands of time.

They have been playing a remarkable role in the political field as well since the framing of the Constitution. They have served in both Houses of Parliament and in the State legislatures, been Governors and Chief Ministers of states and served at the national level as ambassadors, cabinet ministers and of course, in the case of Indira Gandhi, as Prime Minister. As politicians and parliamentarians, they have done commendable work in eliminating evils and in conservation as also in the development of the country.

In 1946, when elections for the Constituent Assembly were held, many prominent women of India like Sarojini Naidu, Hansa Mehta, Durga Bai, Renuka Bai and others were elected. Sarojini Naidu was the first woman to be appointed in 1947 as the Governor of United Provinces, the biggest state in India, and Rajkumari Amrit Kaur was the first woman in the Union Cabinet to be the Minister of Health.

However, despite the achievements of an elite few, women as a whole have been underrepresented throughout India in both appointed and elected positions; they have minimal power within the parties; and they participate in elections as candidates and as voters with less frequency than men.[18] This is clearly visible from the Table No. 1 given below.

Table 1
Women Members in Lok Sabha

Year	*Total No. of elective seats*	*Total No. of seats filled*	*Total No. of women candidates*	*Percentage*
1952-57	489	489	22	4.49
1957-62	494	494	27	5.46
1962-67	494	494	35	6.88
1967-71	520	520	30	5.76
1971-77	518	518	21	4.05
1977-78	542	542	19	3.50
1980-1984	542	529	28	5.29
1984-89	542	542	42	7.74
1989-91	543	528	27	5.11
1991-96	543	521	39	7.48
1996-97	543	543	39	7.18
1998-99	543	543	43	7.91
1999-till date	543	543	49	9.02

Source: M.S. Rana, *India Votes Lok Sabha and Vidhan Sabha Elections, 1999, 2000,* B.R. Publishing Corporation, New Delhi, 2000, p. 74.

The above data on the representation of women from the first to the thirteenth Lok Sabha indicates that in spite of all good intentions on the part of the political parties, they were no where nearer to the expected number. Their representation has all through been between 4 to 9 per cent of the total strength of the House.[19] In the first general elections, out of 489 seats, as many as 22 women were elected to Lok Sabha. The latest figures (1999) show that out of 543 seats, women have been successful in 49. This means that their representation is increasing in the subsequent elections. These increasing figures indicate that after independence more political consciousness and a desire for greater political clout have grown among Indian women.

After the second general elections, women began to assert their position in political matters. The women parliamentarians actively participated in the legislative business of\in the House and contributed their best talent in shaping and moulding policy formulations during this period.

A shift in the role of women members was witnessed during the fourth general elections. Now they were no longer according priority only to women problems. Their domain of interests covered the vexed political questions of parliamentary polity, planning and development and the foreign policy of India. One of the interesting features of this period was the stabilization of leadership of a woman Prime Minister, Smt. Indira Gandhi, both in the Congress Party as well as the then political process of the country.[20]

The representation of women members in the sixth Lok Sabha was numerically the lowest. It was for the first time that the Congress Party was voted out of power at the centre. During this period, Smt. Indira Gandhi played the role of a constructive and vigilant leader of the opposition. If the sixth Lok Sabha witnessed the lowest number of women MPs, the thirteenth Lok Sabha had the distinction of having the largest ever representation of women members.

These figures and analysis clearly reveal that despite the steadily expanding participation of women in successive general elections, their numerical strength has never exceeded ten per cent of the total membership of Lok Sabha. In the legislative assemblies, their number is even less. However, the fact of the thinness of their representation has not inhibited women parliamentarians and legislators from making their presence felt. And of late, women have shown themselves capable of matching their male colleagues even in the display of lung power.

Despite being very few in number, they have always been a constant presence in Parliament. Many of the earlier women MPs, within a short span of time, introduced not only many, but important, private members bills like the Dowry Restraint Bill, Hindu Marriage Amendment Bill, Indian Adoption of Children Bill, Suppression of Immoral Traffic and Brothels Bill, Women's and Children's Institutions Bill, to name a few. Most of these Bills were put up for discussion and passed, enhancing both the position of women in India and the reputation of the women MPs.

During the time, when Jawahar Lal Nehru and Lal Bahadur Shastri were the Prime Ministers, women parliamentarians tend to be restrained and self-effacing, barring a few occasions when they participated in debates or piloted some private Bills. With the emergence of Smt. Indira Gandhi, as the India's first woman Prime Minister, the role played by women parliamentarians underwent a qualitative change.

In case of Rajya Sabha too, the women members have played an important role. Their membership has been on the increase even in this House. Many women have either been elected or nominated to this august House. Some of the eminent women members of this House include Violet Alva, Uma Nehru, Nargis Dutt, Pratibha Devisingh Patil, Najma Heptullah, Jayanthi Natarajan, Sarla Maheshwari, Saroj Khaparde, Renuka Choudhary, Margaret Alva, and others. Some of these women have also held important legislative positions like the Deputy Chairmanship of the Rajya Sabha. Until now, three women who have become the Deputy Chairpersons are: (i) Smt. Violet Alva; (ii) Smt. Pratibha Devisingh Patil; and (iii) Dr. Najma Heptullah.[22]

In Rajya Sabha too, the women members have had been very active in pioneering important legislative enactments not only for the welfare of Indian women but for the overall socio-economic development of Indian society. They have moved resolutions on subjects like women's development, tribal welfare, economic issues and constitutional aspects like fixing of some time-limit for granting of President's assent to the Bills sent to him by the State Legislatures, reorganization of States, etc.

On the basis of above analysis, one can say that the contributions of women parliamentarians are in no way less significant than those of their male counterparts in the Indian Parliament or State Legislature. They have pioneered social legislations which have important bearing on the structural aspects of Indian society.

Women at Ministerial Level

Worldwide women held only four per cent of ministerial level positions in 1990.[23] In case of India, there has been a dismal state of women's incumbency to ministerial portfolios at the centre. The number of women in the council of ministers has not improved over the years, the maximum being eight in 1984.[24]

Between the first general election in 1952 and 1975 there were thirteen women ministers in the union government of whom one became Prime Minister and one attained cabinet rank, five became Ministers of State and six became Deputy Ministers.[25] In case of Ministries too, women's representation as Cabinet Ministers is well below eight per cent.[26] In the ninth Lok Sabha out of the 58 Ministers in the Union Cabinet, only six were women including one with Cabinet rank.[27] Similarly, in the twelfth Lok Sabha there were four ministers with one of them holding a Cabinet rank.

One finds a sorry picture of the scope available to women to become Ministers of State and Deputy Ministers. Stigmatic status of weaker sex is also reflected in the portfolios assigned to them. They usually get soft portfolios like health, education, social welfare and women and child development. They have never been assigned independent charge of challenging and more important portfolios like defence, finance, home, etc. However, a significant shift is visible in the present NDA government where women have been given the charge of Information and Broadcasting (cabinet rank), Human Resource Development (minister of state) and Foreign Affairs (minister of state).[28]

Women in Political Parties

Political parties are a major path to participation in elected and appointed political bodies. Whilst women comprise a substantial part of the membership of political parties in many countries, they are regularly excluded from leadership. Women in India are no doubt regarded as an emancipated lot, but political parties have always been seen to be reluctant to field women candidates. No political party wants to take the risk of fielding a 'housewife' who is neither seasoned nor mentally prepared for a hectic political life. In comparison to men, the 'winnability' factor is very much low in case of women candidates.[29] It is commonly believed that women generally do not succeed in winning a seat except when they carry the banner of some popular male figure. Although at the time of election, declarations are made of granting 15-20 per cent seats to women, no party has been able to achieve the target. This is clear from the ticket distribution done by various national parties in 1999 elections to the Lok Sabha (Table no. 2). Women received only 7.37 per cent of the total BJP tickets, 11.25 per cent of the Congress tickets, 4.88 per cent of the BSP tickets, 7.40 per cent of the CPI tickets, 6.94 per cent of the CPM tickets, 5.20 per cent of JD (S) tickets and 5.00 per cent of the JD(U) tickets.[30] As one MP puts it "when it comes to getting tickets they say, *yeh to lady haiji, yeh kamjor hai* (after all, she is a women sir, she is weak)". "The argument is that the women won't win, so why invest in woman candidates".[31]

In India, even the best of our women parliamentarians feel sidelined and powerless within their respective parties. The few women leaders who exist in various parties have not been able to facilitate the entry of greater number of women in electoral and party politics and therefore are an ineffective minority within their own respective parties.[32] The argument that women lack 'winnability' is used by political parties to deny tickets to women candidates. This statement is not true as Ms. Veena Nayyar, President of the Women's Political Watch, rightly argues. Citing the 1999 Lok Sabha polls as a case study, she reports that "11.38 per cent of women candidates, who contested the elections, made it to the lower House compared to 5.77 per cent of males. In fact, only 484 out of total 8699 male contestants in the fray won the battle of ballots".[33]

Many studies have shown that before the women's decade, political parties were not even stressing on women's issues, in their campaigns or mobilizing rallies. In the last decade all political parties have shown greater interest in women's problems as a result of various developments but primarily due to the pressure of women's group. The very same male party leaders who compete with one another in announcing special quotas for women have shown little willingness to include women in the decision-making process within the

Table 2

State-wise and Party-wise Representation of Women in the 13th Lok Sabha

States	*INC*	*BJP*	*CPI*	*CPI(M)*	*JD(U)*	*SS*	*NCP*	*BSP*	*RJD*	*TC*	*TDP*	*AIADMK*	*SF*	*INLD*	*IND.*	*TOTAL*
Andhra Pradesh	01										03					04
Assam	01	01														02
Bihar	01	02			01				01							05
Gujarat	01	02														03
Haryana		01												01		02
Karnataka	02															02
Kerala				01												01
Madhya Pradesh		03														03
Maharashtra	01	01				01	01									04
Orissa	01	01														02
Punjab	02															02
Rajasthan	01	02														03
Tamil Nadu												01				01
Uttar Pradesh	03	01						01					03		01	09
West Bengal			01	02						02						05
NCT of Delhi		01														01
Total	14	15	01	03	01	01	01	01	01	02	03	01	03	01	01	49

Source: M.S. Rana, *India Votes Lok Sabha and Vidhan Sabha Elections, 1999, 2000*, B.R. Publishing Corporation, New Delhi, 2000, p. 74.

party or even to create a conducive atmosphere for women's participation in politics. Women's representation within the decision-making fora of various political parties is even lower than their representation in Parliament, as it is evident from the table no. 3. The figures reveal that women in the decision-making bodies of the major political parties range from 5.1 per cent in the CPI(M) to 12.5 per cent in BJP. The other parties lie in between.

Table 3

Women's Presence in Top Decision-Making Committees

Party	*Committee*	*No. of women*	*Total Members*	*% of Women*
CPI(M)	(i) Politburo	0	15	0
	(ii) Central Committee	3	58	5.1
CPI	(i) Secretariat	0	9	0
	(ii) National Executive	2	18	10.1
	(iii) National Council	6-7*	125	5
JD	(i) Political Affairs Committee	0	15	0
	(ii) Parliamentary Board	0**	15	0
	(iii) National Executive	11	75	15
	(iv) Central Office Bearers	3	25	12
UF	Steering Committee	0	15-17***	0
BJP	(i) Parliamentary Board	1	9	11
	(ii) Election Committee	2	17	12
	(iii) National Executive	8	62	12.5
Congress	Working Committee	2	19	11

* The 7th member is a candidate member who participates in discussion but does not vote.

** Normally the state President of the Janata Dal's women's wing is invited to attend and offer suggestions, but she does not have a vote. Even this invitation depends upon the wishes of the party President or of the President of the Parliamentary Board.

*** Total number of members varies due to visitors.

Source: i) *Manushi*, No.96, September-October, 1996, p. 27.

ii) Party Officers of Respective Parties.

Suggestions for Increasing Women Participation

Women's political participation can be increased by creating social awareness and consciousness among women, by removing gender bias and providing family life education for all, by preventing atrocities and exploitation against women, by assessing the psychological needs, aspirations and anxiety of the masses, especially the women folk and by providing these to the extent possible.[34]

The DAW in its expert group meeting on Equality in Political Participation and Decision-Making, made the following recommendations in order to improve the status of women in political parties.[35]

(i) as an interim measure, substantial targets, such as quotas or similar forms of positive action to ensure women's candidacy for office and participation in political posts should be applied;

(ii) training programmes should be developed to increase the political and management skills of women in politics, both as candidates and as elected or appointed officials, especially making use of the experience of other women who have achieved public office;

(iii) information on potential women candidates should be compiled, maintained on a systematic basis and made available when candidacy or appointments are considered;

(iv) training activities should be developed to sensitize party members to the needs and potentials of female members; and

(v) as an interim measure where the electoral system might make it useful, parties should undertake special measures to provide funding for women candidates for office.

Reservation for Women

Reservation for women in the most efficient strategy to increase women's participation in the leadership of political parties and in party lists for public elections. The Constitutions or legislations of a few countries provide for quotas for women in Parliament, including those of Angola, the former USSR and Nepal. In addition, the 1991 electoral law of Argentina establishes a compulsory 30 per cent quota for women candidates for all elective posts.[36]

So far as India is concerned, the demand for reservation is not new. In 1920, Sarojini Naidu and Margaret Cousins had led a small delegation of women demanding rights of representation. The Indian National Congress at the Karachi session, in 1931, committed itself to political equality of women regardless of their status and qualifications in response to women's organizations' memorandum demanding total adult franchise.[37] The Constitution, already provides for thirty three per cent reservation to women in the Panchayats and Municipalities. As a result of this, hundreds and thousands of women have emerged from the seclusion of their homes into the public arena at the local level. In fact, this experiment was cited vociferously by those who favour reservation for women in legislative bodies.

In 1996 all political parties arrived at a consensus that thirty three per cent reservation for women should be made in the legislature. Accordingly, the Women Resrvation Bill, (81st Amendment) 1996, providing for reservations of one-third of the seats in State Assemblies and the Lok Sabha for women, was tabled\introduced in the Lok Sabha on September 13, 1996. The Government was able to reintroduce the bill several times (1997, 1998, 1999, 2000, 2002), but till date it could not be passed for some reason or the other.

The campaign for women's reservation had now been going on for the last eight years with a view to establish political equality which is guaranteed in our Constitution. It seems that this campaign will continue for another couple of years as the political parties have still not decided whether to give reservation to women or not. Even the two political parties, the Trinamool Congress and the AIADMK, headed by women stalwarts Mamta Banerjee and Jayalalitha, have not honoured their much publicized preference for adequate representation to women candidates in the Lok Sabha elections.[38]

Summing Up

Thus one finds that after independence, with the removal of socio-legal disabilities and by availing themselves of the opportunities in the field of education and employment, women are now actively participating in politics. Despite the disadvantage of inadequate numerical strength, women MPs have discharged their responsibilities as elected popular representatives with as much commitment and dedication, if not more, as their male colleagues. They did not confine themselves only to issues affecting women, but also evinced keen interest in politics and administration. As is evident, women parliamentarians have pioneered social legislations which have an important bearing on the structural aspects of Indian society. They have succeeded in protecting the rights of Indian women and in promoting their interests and general welfare.

To ensure effective participation of women it is imperative that they are allowed to play an active role in day-to-day functioning of the parties, otherwise powerful male politicians will corner the women's quota by presenting their own wives and daughters for ticket allocation at the election time. It is hoped that with the passing of the Women's Reservation Bill, women's participation will increase and they will play a more active role in politics.

References

1. Sushma Yadav and Anil Dutta Mishra, *Gender Issues in India Some Reflections*, Radha Publications, New Delhi, 2003, pp. 10-11.
2. Jack H. Nagel, *Participation*, Prentice Hall Inc., New Jersey, 1987, p. 1.
3. Sweta Mishra and S.N. Mishra, "Women and Political Process in India", in *Kurukshetra*, Vol. XLIII, No. 11, August, 1995, p. 40.
4. Anil Dutta Mishra, "Empowerment through Political Participation", in Anil Dutta Mishra (ed.), *Gender Perspective Participation, Empowermnet and Development*, Radha Publications, New Delhi, 1999, p. 49.
5. Ashok Kumar, "Political Participation of Women", in Sunit Gupta and Mukta Gupta (eds.), *Role of Women in the Twenty*

First Century, Anmol Publications, New Delhi, 1996, p. 64.
6. D.M. Shukla, "Politicization of Women in Gujarat", in Vina Majumdar (ed.), *Symbols of Power*, Allied Publishers, Bombay, 1979, p. 93.
7. L.W. Milbrath and M.L. Goel, *Political Participation: How and Why, Do People Get Involved in Politics?*, Rand McNally, Chicago, 1977, p. 2.
8. N.D. Parmer, *Elections and Political Development in India*, Vikas, New Delhi, 1976, pp. 59-61.
9. Surat Singh, *Women Panchayati Raj Representatives: A Study of a District in Haryana*, Haryana Institute of Rural Development, Nilokheri, 1997.
10. Ashok Kumar, *op.cit.*, p.63.
11. S.L. Amin, " A Paradigm Shift from Welfare", in *Social Welfare*, Vol. 42, No. 8, November, 1995, p. 26.
12. Premlata Pujari and V.K. Kaushik, *Women Power in India*, Vol. I, Kanishka Publishers, Delhi, 1994, p. 9.
13. Nirmala Deshpande, "Participation of Women in Political System", in *Kurukshetra*, Vol. XXXVII, NO. 5, February, 1989, p.56.
14. *The Bombay Chronicle*, February 17, 1919.
15. Kamaladevi Chattopadhyay, *I Remember, 1921 Reminiscences*, Ministry of Information and Broadcasting, Government of India, Delhi.
16. M.K. Gandhi, *Letters to Rajkumari Amrit Kaur*, Navjivan Publishing House, 1961, p. vi.
17. S.L. Amin, op.cit., p. 27.
18. Leslie J. Calman, *Toward Empowerment – Women and Movement Politics in India*, Westview Press, USA, 1992, p. 60.
19. M.S. Rana, *India Votes Lok Sabha and Vidhan Sabha Elections, 1999, 2000*, B.R. Publishing Corporation, New Delhi, 2000, p. 74.
20. C.K. Jain, *Women Parliamentarians in India*, Surjeet Publications, Delhi, 1993, p. 37.
21. Tarkeshwari Sinha, "Women in Parliament", in C.K. Jain, *op.cit.*, p. 151.
22. C.K. Jain, *op.cit.*, p. 54.
23. Marilee Karl, *Women and Empowerment: Participation and Decision-Making*, Zed Books Ltd., London and New Jersey, 1995, p. 61.
24. Aparna Srivastava, "Reasons for Low Participation of Women in Politics", in *Social Welfare*, Vol. 45, No. 12, March, 1999, p. 13.

25. Mary Fainsod Katzenstein, "Towards Equality? Cause and Consequence of the Political Prominence of Women in India", in Gail Minault (ed.), *The Extended Family Women and Political Participation in India and Pakistan*, Chanakya Puplications, Delhi, 1981, p. 288.
26. Sanjay Sharma, "Political Status of Women in Lok Sabha", in Dharam Vir and Kamlesh Mahajan (eds.), *Contemporary Indian Women*, Vol. 4, New Academic Publishers, Delhi, 1996, p.
27. B.S. Bhargava and K.C. Vidya, "Position of Women in Political Institutions", in *Journal of Rural Development*, Vol. II, No. 5, September, 1992, p. 603.
28. Aparna Srivastava, *op.cit.*, pp. 13-14.
29. M.S. Rana, *op.cit.*, p. 74.
30. *Ibid.*, p. 70.
31. *Ibid.*, p. 75.
32. Madhu Kishwar, "Out of the Zenana Dabba", in *Manushi*, No. 96, September-October, 1996, p. 27.
33. M.S. Rana, *op.cit.*, p. 75.
34. Aparna Chattopadhyay, "Empowering Women", in *The Hindustan Times – The* Metropolitan, February 5, 1997, p. 5.
35. Marilee Karl, *op. cit.*, pp. 68-69.
36. *Ibid.*, p. 70.
37. M.S. Rana, *op.cit.*, p. 70.
38. *Ibid.*, p. 73.

16

Voting Participation of Women in India: A Case Study of Uttaranchal with a Special Reference to Garhwal

M.M.S. Negi

A politically aware and active citizenry is the sinews of democracy. Election is the indices of the political maturity attained by the citizens of a democratic country. Consequently, it is through the evaluation of the voting participation of people that the strength of the democratic tradition of their political system may best be measured.

The Indian scene has its own peculiarities. Culturally diverse, geographically extensive and economically as well as educationally unevenly distributed, the Indian people from different regions provide not only an example of social variation but also great divergence of political attitude and behavior.

Women Enfranchisement and India

On 18th December, 1917, a delegation of Indian women waited upon Lord Montague to convey the need of women enfranchisement, a matter completely ignored in the constitutional reforms of 1892 and 1909. However, their request could not find place in Montague–Chelmsford recommendation. Even the Southborough Committee (1918), while observing that circumstances were not ripe for general women enfranchisement, made provision for voting rights of educated women only. This provoked a wave of protest from women's associations in India. Some prominent Indian women also gave evidence before the Joint Parliamentary Committee, which was discussing the Government of India Bill 1919, in support of the demand. Even this proved futile. Though the Indian National Congress came out in support of the extension of franchise to women, a resolution to this effect could not be passed in the Calcutta Session (1921) for want of time.

The highly inadequate recommendation of the Southborough Committee giving voting rights to educated women only was accepted by some provincial governments like those of Bombay, Madras , Punjab, United Province and Central provinces. Meanwhile, support for women enfranchisement kept gaining ground. In 1927, the Simon Commission recognized the need for women enfranchisement in India and stated in its report that it was essential for the development of India. In the thirties Ramsay Muir constituted the Lothian Committee to go in to the subject. It made two specific recommendations:

(1) an adequate number of women should be placed on the electoral rolls to compel candidates to consider their interests and opinions, to awaken political interest among women and to make their vote an effective level particularly in providing reforms of special concern to women and children,

(2) to protect women representation, two to five percent of the seats in the provincial councils should be reserved for them for the first ten years[1].

But despite making such sweeping recommendations, the Lothian Committee also attached special qualifications for women voters such as those relating to property, education and wifehood and excluded the unmarried and widows to a large extent. Most of the provincial governments rejected these recommendations.

The Government of India Act, 1935, while accepting educational qualification, reserved seats for women. It removed the qualification for appointment to civil services on ground of sex and extended suffrage to the following categories of women over 21 year: (a) those who possessed property and taxation qualifications as men (b) those who were able to read and write any Indian Language or dialect, (c) those who were wives or widows of those possessing or who would have possessed the necessary property qualifications, (d) those who were wives or widows of those assessed to be income tax payees in the previous financial year, (e) those who were pensioned widows or mothers of persons who were in the armed forces, and (f) those who were wives or widows of retired, pensioned or discharged officers or soldiers of armed forces.[2]

Complete sex equality in the matter of voting could ultimately be established only after the promulgation of universal franchise by the Constitution of free India, enforced on January 26, 1950.

Concept of Voting Participation

Elections provide the individual with the most accessible means of political participation in a democratic system. They link the individual in the most direct form with the political system. In fact, the nature of an individual's interest and involvement with the electoral process can be treated as an index of his actual political interest and attitudes. In this sense, even the strength and maturity of a political system can be measured by attempting and understanding patterns of voting participation of its members. In other words, since elections have an important system-maintenance function in a democracy, the system's capability for self-preservation may well be assessed in terms of the voting behavior of its constituents. "Participation in elections, particularly in an open society, helps to strengthen the people's sense of belonging while also shaping and influencing the nature and working of the political system. In developing societies, where primordial and parochial loyalties are generally quite strong, involvement in politics through free and fair elections enable them to be not merely co-participants with the different and diverse groups in the struggle of 'who gets what and how' but also co-partner in the existing adventure of social and political transformation of a traditional and backward society so as to secure to all the citizens without distinctions and/ or discrimination the blessings of justice, liberty and equality."[3]

Almond and Verba, viewing the subject from the point of view of the participant's capabilities, suggest it as a "belief in one's competence. The self confident citizen appears to be a democratic citizen. Not only does he think that he can participate, he thinks that others ought to participate as well. Furthermore, he does not merely think he can take part in politics, he is likely to be more active and perhaps most significant of all. The self-confident citizen is also likely to be the more satisfied and loyal citizen".[4]

Lazersfeld defines voting participation as "Political attitudes and their sources, party selection and candidate preference, source of political information and the process by which the voter makes his political decisions."[5] While engaging himself in voting participation, the individual is directly or indirectly affected by the political developments around him as also by the influences "of parents, of environment, of communication media, of personality identification, etc."[6] To these may be added other factors like religion, caste, community, language, money, policy or ideology, purpose of poll, extent of franchise and the like. The special characteristics of the Indian electoral scene can be attributed to the fact that voting participation in India is exposed to diverse influences through various agencies over a period of time. Political parties and pressure groups are among the most prominent of these agencies.

Ironically, sometimes, as Krishnamurty suggests, "illiterate, backward, poverty stricken and uncommunicative turn up at the polls in large numbers and hence exhibit the inability to distinguish and discriminate between candidate and parties and different policies adopted by the parties".[7]

No doubt, voting attitudes are significant and have a strong bearing on voting participation; yet, nonvoting cannot always be thought of as a negative parameter. Many a time physical constraints of ill-health, lack of time, absence from the scene and the like may thwart an elector's use of his voting right. In addition, the frequency with which a voter casts his vote must essentially be viewed against a background of diverse social factors. As suggested by social scientists, these factors have a varying degree of impact upon the voters' decision to exercise their franchise. For instance, according to Lipset, "men vote more than women, the better educated more than less educated, urban residents more than rural, those between 35 and 55 years more than younger or older voters, married persons more than unmarried, higher status persons more than lower, members of organisations more than non- members." [8] However, all these observations are not likely to be true in the Indian context.

Garhwal and the Voting Participation of Women

The people of Uttaranchal have peculiarities of their own. Their socio-economic environment is not comparable to that of the plains and even of other hilly areas of the country. Barring the contacts with parts of Nainital, Haridwar and Dehradun districts, the region has largely remained isolated. It was only after independence and more particularly after the 1962 Chinese aggression that the area attracted the attention of the government. This has left Garhwal and Kumaun lagging far behind the rest of the country in the matter of development. As a result, the people of this area have a special socio–political attitude of their own.

The women of this region shoulder a more crucial socio–economic responsibility than the men and unlike the women of other areas. This is because of a negative sex ratio, as shown in the Table 1, resulting from a drain of able–bodied local men towards the major urban centers in search of work since enough employment opportunities are not available back at home.

Table 1 Population and Sex Ratio in Uttaranchal

S.No.	*Districts*	*Total population in lakhs*	*%*	*Sex ratio*
1.	Uuttarkashi	2.94	3.47	941
2.	Chamoli	3.69	4.35	1017
3.	Rudraprayag	2.28	2.68	1117
4.	Tehri Garhwal	6.05	7.13	1051
5.	Dehradun	12.79	15.08	893
6.	Pauri Garhwal	6.97	8.22	1104
7.	Pethorragar	4.62	5.45	1031
8.	Champawat	2.25	2.65	1024
9.	Almora	6.30	7.43	1147
10.	Bageshwer	2.49	2.94	1110
11.	Nainital	7.63	9.00	906
12.	Uddamsinghnagar	12.35	14.56	902
13.	Haridwar	4.44	17.03	868
	Uttaranchal	84.80	100.00	964

Source: Director, Census, Uttaranchal.

The women are left behind to struggle economically; they mainly depend on non–profitable agriculture and supplement their income with the money-orders from their male folk. The burdens of agriculture as well as domestic works fall on women's shoulders. All these works leave them with little time to think of anything else apart from their daily routine.

This, however, is not to say that the women of Garhwal have no interest in socio-political affairs. On the contrary, growing standard of education, increasing exposure to mass media like radio and television, rising influence of modernization and implementation of Panchayati Raj Act have made them fairly conscious of political matters. Especially during an election they get keenly involved in the political process. They are not only anxious to cast their vote but also active in the various areas of election campaign like distributing handbills and door-to-door canvassing.

Two more factors make the voting participation of the hill women still more important. Firstly, since they account for the majority of the electorate, they are in a strong position to influence the election outcome. Secondly, since in most cases, their husbands, brothers and fathers are normally away form home, they are comparatively more free from family influences and more exposed to external influences in making their election decision.

The Research Design

The Uttaranchal is a state spread over 60,000 sq. km. with a population of 84,79562. 63.69% of its total area is covered by forest and 10 out of 13 districts are hilly districts. The state comprises of Almora, Bageswar, Champawat, Chamoli, Dehradun, Garhwal, Haridwar, Nainital, Pithoragarh, Rudraprayag, Tehri, US Nagar and Uttarkashi districts. The whole state is divided into five Parliamentary constituencies and 70 Assembly segments; Garhwal parliamentary constituency, falling within the administrative area of Garhwal district, has been selected as the universe of the study.

Geographically, Garhwal district is spread over an area of 5440 sq. km. and lies between $78^{0}10^{1}$-$79^{0}10^{1}$E longitude and $29^{0}20^{1}$-$30^{0}15^{1}$ N. latitude. It shares the boundaries with the districts of Bijnor, Chamoli, D.Dun, Nainital and Saharanpur. The terrain is largely mountainous with attendant ruggedness. The topography of the district imposes limitations on communication, transportation and exposure to the external world. The economy is highly fragile for want of industrialization and domestication of productive forces. The people of the district are simple, honest and often poor, characterized by a strong caste and class consciousness. They are divided into three principal castes, the Brahmins, the Kshatriyas and the Harijans (S.C.). The principal productive function of all these communities has conventionally been agriculture, which suffers from the limitation of terrace forming. As a result, the income at home remains low forcing most able bodied men to migrate to plains in search of jobs and leaving women and children behind. Consequently, women have assumed an important role in all walks of local life, whether social, economic or political.

To conduct a comprehensive study of the entire region the researcher decided on a sample design. Random sampling method was used for collection of data in rural and urban areas of the universe of study through interview schedule.

Data Analysis of Voting Participation

Voting is the simplest form of political participation. It is at this level that maximum numbers of citizens interact with the political system. It is the means by which sovereignty is referred back to the masses. However, all those qualified to vote are not equally enthusiastic towards it. Some await elections eagerly and look forward impatiently to cast their vote while others are passive and apathetic in this regard. These interpersonal variations have often been attributed to differences in bio-social background or the level of political maturity determinable in the context of what has been called in this study, acquired personality attributes. The present paper seeks to discover how far such a contention is true in the case of the women of Garhwal.

Voting and Non-voting

Though all the respondents selected for the study were technically qualified voters only 88.5 percent of them had actually cast their votes. More of the women in rural area (96%) were active in this regard than those of the urban area (81%). 7.29 percent of rural voting women and 7.40 percent of the urban voting women reported having failed to cast their votes in elections. The women in rural area who had not voted had missed only the parliamentary elections, while among the urban women 66.67 percent of non-voters had missed the parliamentary elections and 33.3 percent missed the Assembly elections. For their failure to vote, 42.85 percent of the rural women attributed to their ill-health on the day of polling, a like percent to their absence and 14.3 percent to various domestic reasons. In urban area, 66.67 percent of the women could not vote due to absence while the remaining 33.33 percent because of ill-health. In all, 89.0 percent of rural women and 75 percent of the urban women reported that they had been casting their vote regularly at every election ever since they qualified to vote.

In the case of the rural women it was found that exclusion

from the voters' lists was the only reason responsible for non-voting. The same was largely, though not wholly, true of the urban non-voting women of whom 89.4 percent had failed to exercise their voting right for this reason; pronounced disinterest in political affairs and unwillingness to go to crowded places were responsible for the abstention of the remaining 11.6 percent of them.

This would generally show that circumstantial factors including registration inaccuracies, ill-health, absence from the election scene and not political apathy are the primary causes for the marginal non-voting incidents among the women of Garhwal.

Age and Voting Participation

Age has important influence over voting participation. Voting eagerness may tend to decline due to repeated exposure to election or with an advance in age one will be more mature and motivated to express one's political views.

Table 2 A

Age and Voting Frequency

S. No.	*Age Group*	*HVF*		*AVF*		*LVF*		*Total*	
		f	*%*	*f*	*%*	*f*	*%*	*f*	*%*
1.	Young	-	-	2	4.8	15	88.2	17	17.7
2.	Middle	6	11.5	26	50.0	20	38.5	52	54.2
3.	Old	8	29.6	17	63.0	2	7.4	27	28.1
	TOTAL	14	15.6	45	46.9	37	38.5	96	100.0

Table 2 B

Age and Urban Voting Frequency

S. No.	*Age Group*	*HVF*		*AVF*		*LVF*		*Total*	
		f	*%*	*f*	*%*	*f*	*%*	*f*	*%*
1.	Young	-	-	-	-	17	100.0	17	21.0
2.	Middle	2	4.3	22	46.8	23	48.9	47	58.0
3.	Old	4	23.5	10	58.8	3	17.7	17	21.0
	TOTAL	6	7.4	32	39.5	43	53.1	81	100.0

On the basis of data given in these tables it can be concluded that the women belonging to the middle age group are considerably ahead of others in voting frequency. The women belonging to the younger age group show less frequency.

The second contention i.e., voting eagerness tends to decline in age was, however, not found to be perfectly true. The data for the study computed for both the voters and non-voters showed that age has a curvilinear relationship with voting eagerness. It was noted that the middle aged as, shown in Tables 3 A& B, are ahead of their younger and older counterparts with respect to high voting eagerness in both the rural and urban areas.

Table 3 A

Age and Rural Voting Eagerness

S. No.	*Age Group*	*HVE*		*AVE*		*LVE*		*Total*	
		f	*%*	*f*	*%*	*f*	*%*	*f*	*%*
1.	YOUNG	17	89.5	2	10.5	-	-	19	19.0
2.	MIDDLE	48	92.3	3	5.8	1	1.9	52	52.0
3.	OLD	26	89.3	2	7.1	1	3.6	29	29.0
	TOTAL	91	91.0	7	7.0	2	2.0	100	100.0

Table 3 B

Age and Urban Voting Eagerness

S. No.	*Age Group*	*HVE*		*AVE*		*LVE*		*Total*	
		f	*%*	*f*	*%*	*f*	*%*	*f*	*%*
1.	YOUNG	19	63.3	9	30.7	2	6.7	30	30.0
2.	MIDDLE	43	82.7	6	11.5	4	7.6	53	53.0
3.	OLD	12	70.5	4	23.5	1	5.9	17	17.0
	TOTAL	74	74.0	19	19.0	7	7.0	100	100.0

At the AVE level, the young are in the lead with the old following them in the cases of both rural and urban women. Further, it may also be noted here that voting frequency is at higher ebb in the rural areas.

The contention that closer association between voting motivation and expression of political views commensurate with age, was not found to be perfectly true of Garhwal. In fact, as may be seen from Table 4 A, the reverse is actually true of the rural women.

Table 4 A

Age and Rural Political Motivation

S. No.	*Age group*	*Political motivation*				*Total*	
		CR		*EPV*			
		F	*%*	*F*	*%*	*F*	*%*
1.	Young	13	76.5	4	23.5	17	17.7
2.	Middle	41	78.8	11	21.2	52	54.2
3.	Old	22	81.5	05	18.5	27	28.1
	Total	76	79.2	20	20.8	96	100.0

Table 4 B

Age and Urban Political Motivation

S. No.	*Age group*	*Political motivation*				*Total*	
		CR		*EPV*			
		F	*%*	*F*	*%*	*F*	*%*
1.	Young	15	88	2	11.8	17	21.0
2.	Middle	42	89.4	5	10.6	47	58.0
3.	Old	14	82.4	3	17.6	17	21.0
	Total	71	87.6	10	12.4	81	100.0

The situation is somewhat different in the urban areas. It may be seen from Table 4 B that with a slight aversion among the middle aged, who lag behind the rest, the desire for expressing political views tends to become a greater motivating force for voting with an increase in age. This fact could be attributed to a comparative lack of political interest among the urban young.

Marital Status and Voting Participation

Marital status could prove to be a significant arbiter of voting participation among women, for in their cases marriage does not only account for a change in circumstances, influences and loyalties, but also for a change in physical surrounding and social environment. Further, marital status also causes differences in the nature of responsibilities to be shouldered by women.

Table 5A

Marital Status and Rural Voting Frequency

S. No.	*Marital Status*	*HVF* *F*	*%*	*AVF* *F*	*%*	*LVF* *F*	*%*	*Total* *F*	*%*
1.	Married	14	15.1	45	48.4	34	36.5	93	96.9
2.	Unmarried	-	-	-	-	3	100.0	3	3.1
	Total	14	15.6	45	46.9	37	38.5	96	100.0

Table 5B

Marital Status and Urban Voting Frequency

S. No.	*Marital Status*	*HVF* *F*	*%*	*AVF* *F*	*%*	*LVF* *F*	*%*	*Total* *F*	*%*
1.	Married	6	8.0	31	41.3	38	50.7	75	92.6
2.	Unmarried	-	-	1	16.7	5	83.3	6	7.4
	Total	6	7.4	32	39.5	43	53.1	81	100.0

To find out the variation of the extent of the influence of this factor on the rural and urban women data have been collected and presented in Tables 5 A& B. With respect to voting frequency, it is noticed that the married are far ahead of the unmarried.

However, as may be concluded from the comparison of the two tables the urban unmarried women show higher voting frequency scores then their rural counterparts, a fact proved by their being ahead at the average voting frequency level. The prime reason for this could be that women in rural areas usually get married at a much younger age than those in the urban areas. Nonetheless, the over all balance is tilted in favour of the rural women on account of the pronounced lead of their married number over their urban counterparts at both the HVF and AVF levels.

Rather interesting results have been obtained on the relationship of voting eagerness and marital status as presented in Tables 6 A & B.

Table 6 A

Marital Status and Rural Voting Eagerness

S. No.	*Marital Status*	*HVE*		*AVE*		*LVE*		*Total*	
		F	*%*	*F*	*%*	*F*	*%*	*F*	*%*
1.	Married	87	90.6	7	7.3	2	2.1	96	96.0
2.	Unmarried	4	100.0	-	-	-	-	4	4.0
	TOTAL	91	91.0	7	7.0	2	2.0	100	100.0

As may be seen from, the unmarried women in the rural areas are emphatically more eager in the matter than their married counterparts.

Table 6 B

Marital Status and Urban Voting Eagerness

S. No.	*Marital Status*	*HVE*		*AVE*		*LVE*		*Total*	
		F	*%*	*F*	*%*	*F*	*%*	*F*	*%*
1.	Married	65	75.6	15	17.3	6	6.9	86	86.0
2.	Unmarried	9	64.0	4	28.6	1	7.1	14	14.0
	TOTAL	74	74.0	1.9	19.0	7	7.0	100	100.0

On the contrary, among the urban women the lead on this count belongs to the married women.

Tables 7A and B describe the link between motivation and marital status.

Table 7A

Marital Status and Rural Voting Motivation

S. No.	*Marital Status*	*CR*		*EPV*		*Total*	
		F	*%*	*F*	*%*	*F*	*%*
1.	Married	74	79.6	19	20.4	93	96.9
2.	Unmarried	2	66.7	1	33.3	3	3.1
	TOTAL	76	79.2	20	20.8	96	100.0

Table 7 B

Marital Status and Urban Voting Motivation

S. No.	*Marital Status*	*CR*		*EPV*		*Total*	
		F	*%*	*F*	*%*	*F*	*%*
1.	Married	67	88.2	9	11.8	76	93.8
2.	Unmarried	4	80.0	1	20.0	5	6.2
	TOTAL	71	87.6	10	12.4	81	100.0

It may be seen that the married women outnumber the unmarried ones in both rural and urban areas.

Caste and Voting Participation

Caste being a very peculiar feature of the Indian society, exercises a strong influence in the political process of this country. It assumes a still more important role in Garhwal where caste divisions are prominent. Although it is true that it influences voting choice consideration more than voting participation yet it has important implications for the latter too. For example, its relation with voting frequency could bring out the probable caste lobby effects on an election out come. This makes caste relevant to study voting participation.

In this respect, the study discovered that caste and voting frequency are related differently to each other in rural and urban areas.

Table 8 A

Caste and Rural Voting Frequency

S. No.	*Caste Group*	*HVF*		*AVF*		*LVF*		*Total*	
		F	*%*	*F*	*%*	*F*	*%*	*F*	*%*
1.	Kahatriyas	6	15.8	21	55.3	11	28.9	38	39.6
2.	Brahmins	3	8.8	16	47.0	15	44.2	34	35.4
3.	SCs	2	15.4	4	30.8	7	53.8	13	13.5
4.	Others	3	27.2	4	36.4	4	36.4	11	11.5
	TOTAL	14	15.6	45	46.9	37	38.5	96	100.0

As may be seen from Table 8 A, the Kshatriyas are in the

lead at the overall levels followed by the Brahmins who also take the second highest lead at the HVF level. The scheduled castes occupy the third place at the overall level as also HVF levels.

The picture changes considerably in the context of urban areas. Here, as may be seen from Table 8 B, the Kshatriyas, continue their lead at the HVF level, LVF level and the overall level. The 'other castes' despite being in the second place at the HVF and AVF levels are relegated to the third place at the over all and LVF levels. The Brahmins, however, move up to the second place at the overall. Ironically, the scheduled castes even without representation at the HVF level goes fourth place at the overall level because of their supremacy at the AVF level, this would generally shows that the scheduled castes are being used as 'vote bank much more effectively in the urban areas of Garhwal.

Table 8 B

Caste and Urban Voting Frequency

S. No.	*Caste Group*	*HVF* F	%	*AVF* F	%	*LVF* F	%	*Total* F	%
1.	Kahatriyas	4	15.8	13	33.3	22	56.4	38	48.1
2.	Brahmins	1	4.0	10	40.0	14	56.0	25	30.9
3.	SCs	-	-	2	66.6	1	33.3	3	3.7
4.	Others	1	7.1	7	50.0	6	42.9	14	17.3
	TOTAL	6	7.4	32	39.5	43	53.1	81	100.0

The voting eagerness patterns for both the rural and urabn areas do not conform to voting frequency pattern in relation to caste. As may be seen from Table 9 A, in the rural areas it is only the Kshatriya women whose voting frquency is compatible with their voting eagerenss. The Brahmins retain the second place at the HVE level. Similarly, the scheduled castes and 'other castes' despite being different in the voting frequency display similarity at the HVE level of voting eagerness.

Table 9 A

Caste and Rural Voting Eagerness

S. No.	Caste Group	HVE		AVE		LVE		Total	
		F	%	F	%	F	%	F	%
1.	Kshatriyas	36	94.7	2	5.3	-	-	38	38.0
2.	Brahmins	33	91.7	3	8.3	-	-	36	36.0
3.	SCs	11	84.6	2	15.4	-	-	13	13.0
4.	Others	11	84.6	1	7.7	1	7.7	13	13.0
	TOTAL	91	91.0	8	8.0	1	1.0	100	100.0

Table 9 B

Caste and Urban Voting Eagerness

S. No.	Caste Group	HVE		AVE		LVE		Total	
		F	%	F	%	F	%	F	%
1.	Kshatriyas	36	81.8	6	13.6	2	4.5	44	44.0
2.	Brahmins	23	69.7	8	24.2	2	6.1	33	33.0
3.	SCs	5	100.0	-	-	-	-	5	5.0
4.	Others	14	77.8	1	5.5	3	16.7	18	18.0
	TOTAL	78	78.0	15	15.0	7	7.0	100	100.0

Again in the urban areas as shown in table 9 B, the Kshatriyas and the other castes, who occupy the top two places with respect to high voting frequency can be seen moving to the first and third places of voting eagerness at the HVE level. Although the HVE scores and the overall voting eagerness scores could be used to project a different picture more compatible with voting frequency patterns, yet it could be concluded that a considerable gap is visible between the voting frequency and voting eagerness of the women of Garhwal when viewed from the point of caste.

The data on motivation for voting is given in Tables 10 A and B.

Table 10 A

Caste and Rural Political Motivation

S. No.	Caste Group	CR		EPV		Total	
		F	%	F	%	F	%
1.	Kshatriyas	30	78.9	8	21.1	38	39.6
2.	Brahmins	31	91.2	3	8.8	34	35.4
3.	Scheduled	8	61.5	5	38.5	13	13.5
4.	Others	7	63.6	4	36.4	11	11.5
	TOTAL	76	79.2	20	20.8	96	100.0

It may be seen that in rural areas the desire for expressing political views weighs most heavily with the Scheduled caste and the 'other castes'.

In the urban areas, it is the 'other castes' who take a pronounced lead in this matter relegating the Scheduled Castes to the fourth place at the overall level. This shows that the rural Scheduled caste women are politically more motivated than the urban scheduled caste women. The 'other castes' are fairly vocal being in an acute minority in the region.

Table 10 B

Caste and Urban Political Motivation

S. No.	Caste Group	CR		EPV		Total	
		F	%	F	%	F	%
1.	Kshatriyas	37	94.9	2	5.1	9	48.1
2.	Brahmins	23	92.0	2	8.0	25	30.9
3.	Scheduled	3	100.0	-	-	3	3.7
4.	Others	8	57.1	6	42.9	14	17.3
	TOTAL	71	87.6	10	12.4	81	100.0

Education and Voting Participation

Tables 11 A & B describe the link between education and voting frequency.

Table 11 A: Education and Rural Voting Frequency

S. No.	Educational Status	HVF F	HVF %	AVF F	AVF %	LVF F	LVF %	Total F	Total %
1.	Illiterate	10	19.3	27	51.9	15	28.8	52	54.2
2.	Literate	4	16.7	12	50.0	8	33.3	24	25.0
3.	Semi-educated	-	-	4	30.7	9	69.3	13	13.5
4.	Educated	-	-	2	33.3	4	66.7	6	6.3
5.	Highly educated	-	-	-	-	1	100.0	1	1.0
	TOTAL	14	15.6	5	46.9	37	38.5	96	100.0

Table 11 B: Education and Urban Voting Frequency

S. No.	Educational Status	HVF F	HVF %	AVF F	AVF %	LVF F	LVF %	Total F	Total %
1.	Illiterate	3	13.7	12	54.5	7	31.8	22	27.1
2.	Literate	2	33.3	2	33.3	2	33.3	6	7.4
3.	Semi-educated	1	5.3	10	52.6	8	42.1	19	23.5
4.	Educated	-	-	4	20.0	16	80.0	20	24.7
5.	Highly educated	-	-	4	28.6	10	71.4	14	17.3
	TOTAL	6	7.432	39.5	43		53.1	81	100.0

As can be seen from the above two tables voting frequency is related to education negatively in both rural and urban areas.

The link of education with voting eagerness is given in Tables 12 A & B.

Table 12A: Education and Rural Voting Eagerness

S. No.	Educational Status	HVE F	HVE %	AVE F	AVE %	LVE F	LVE %	Total F	Total %
1.	Illiterate	49	92.4	3	5.7	1	1.9	53	53.0
2.	Literate	23	95.8	1	4.2	-	-	24	24.0
3.	Semi-educated	13	86.7	2	13.3	-	-	15	15.0
4.	Educated	5	71.4	2	28.6	-	-	7	7.0
5.	Highly educated	1	100.0	-	-	-	-	1	1.0
	TOTAL	91	91.0	8	8.0	1	1.0	100	100.0

Table 12B: Education and Urban Voting Eagerness

S. No.	Educational Status	HVE F	HVE %	AVE F	AVE %	LVE F	LVE %	Total F	Total %
1.	Illiterate	17	73.9	5	21.7	1	4.4	23	23.0
2.	Literate	5	83.3	1	16.7	-	-	6	6.0
3.	Semi-educated	19	96.4	2	9.1	1	4.1	22	22.0
4.	Educated	23	71.9	5	15.6	4	12.5	32	32.0
5.	Highly educated	14	82.4	2	-	11.8	15.8	17	17.0
	TOTAL	78	78.0	15	15.5	7	7.0	100	100.0

Noticeably, most educational strata of one area differ from their counterparts in the other area with regard to voting eagerness. In the rural areas, the highly educated take the lead at the HVE level of voting eagerness. They are followed by the literate, the illiterate, the semi-educated and the educated, respectively. In urban areas, the lead at the HVE levels is taken by the semi-educated. They are followed by the literate, the highly educated, the illiterate and the educated respectively at the HVE level and by the educated, the illiterate, the semi-educated, the highly educated and the literate respectively at the overall level. It is generally assumed that education, being an important agent of awareness, should have a positive relation with voting participation. This can, at times, produce negative effects as well. In the context of woman of Garhwal the latter proves true with respect to voting frequency.

Similarly, as is obvious from Tables 13 A &.B there does not seem to be any significant relationship between education and voting motivation.

Table 13 A: Education and Rural Political Motivation

S. No.	Educational Status	CR F	CR %	EPV F	EPV %	Total F	Total %
1.	Illiterate	41	78.8	11	21.2	52	54.2
2.	Literate	18	75.0	6	25.0	24	25.0
3.	Semi-educated	10	76.9	3	23.1	13	13.5
4.	Educated	6	100.0	-	-	6	6.3
5.	Highly educated	1	100.0	-	-	1	1.0
	TOTAL	76	79.2	20	20.8	96	100.0

Table 13 B: Education and Urban Political Motivation

S. No.	Educational Status	CR F	CR %	EPV F	EPV %	Total F	Total %
1.	Illiterate	21	95.5	1	4.5	22	27.2
2.	Literate	5	83.3	1	16.7	6	7.4
3.	Semi-educated	14	73.7	5	26.3	19	23.4
4.	Educated	19	95	1	5.0	20	24.7
5.	Highly educated	1	85.7	2	14.3	14	17.3
	TOTAL	71	87.6	10	12.0	81	100

It can be concluded that all of the educated and highly educated in the rural areas are less motivated towards voting and it is left to their semi-educated, literate and illiterate counterparts to express their political views through voting.

In the urban areas the picture, though some what different, is no better. Here the semi-educated women take the lead in being motivated towards voting by a desire for expressing political views. Here, they are followed by the literate, the highly educated, the educated and the illiterate, respectively. It is clear that among the women of Garhwal education can be seen to have a negative relationship with voting frequency.

Family Income and Voting Participation

As a key determinant of the socio-economic status, income plays an important role in molding one's political attitudes. Consequently it may also have significant bearing on voting participation. The circumstances and thinking of people from different income strata differ causing them to participate in voting more or less actively. The present study also found this to be true in Garhwal.

It was found that income is negatively related to voting frequency. As shown in Tables 14 A&B, in both the rural and urban areas overall voting frequency keeps on declining with an increase in income.This is equally true of the AVF level in rural area. This relationship is somewhat curvilinear at both the AVF and LVF levels in both rural and urban areas with the curve tending to rise among the middle income group. This shows that economic well being has generally tended to breed political disinterest among the women of Garhwal.

Table 14 A
Income and Rural Voting Frequency

S. No.	Income Group	HVF F	HVF %	AVF F	AVF %	LVF F	LVF %	Total F	Total %
1.	Low	5	13.2	22	57.9	11	28.9	38	39.6
2.	Middle	9	20.5	17	38.6	18	40.9	44	45.8
3.	High	-	-	6	42.8	8	57.2	14	14.6
	TOTAL	14	15.6	45	46.9	37	38.5	96	100.0

Table 14 B
Income and Urban Voting Frequency

S. No.	Income Group	HVF F	HVF %	AVF F	AVF %	LVF F	LVF %	Total F	Total %
1.	Low	2	11.1	9	50.0	11	28.9	38	22.2
2.	Middle	2	5.4	15	40.0	18	40.9	37	44.7
3.	High	2	7.7	8	8	8	57.2	26	32.1
	TOTAL	6	7.4	32	39.5	43	53.1	81	100.0

Voting eagerness was found to be related to income in ways different from one another in rural and urban areas. As is obvious from Tables 15 A & B, this relation curvilinear in the rural areas with the curve clearly rising among the middle income group women at both the overall voting eagerness and the HVF levels. On the contrary, in the urban areas this relationship, as in the case of voting frequency, is fairly negative with voting eagerness registering a clear decline both the HVF and the overall voting eagerness levels with an increase in income. These findings reinforce the contention that increase in income leads to a lowering of political interest towards voting among the women of Garhwal.

Table 15 A: Income and Rural Voting Eagerness

S. No.	Income Group	HVE		AVE		LVE		Total	
		F	%	F	%	F	%	F	%
1.	Low	35	89.7	3	7.7	1	2.6	39	39.0
2.	Middle	42	95.5	2	4.5	-	-	44	44.0
3.	High	14	82.3	3	17.7	-	-	17	17.0
	TOTAL	91	91.0	8	8.0	1	1.0	100	100.0

Table 15 B: Income and Urban Voting Eagerness

S. No.	Income Group	HVE		AVE		LVE		Total	
		F	%	F	%	F	%	F	%
1.	Low	15	83.3	2	11.1	1	5.6	18	18.0
2.	Middle	40	87.0	3	6.5	3	6.5	4	46.0
3.	High	23	63.9	10	27.5	3	8.3	3	36.0
	TOTAL	78	78.0	15	15.0	7	7.0	100	100.0

The relationship between motivation for voting and income also follows an almost similar trend. It can be seen from Table 16A that the motivation for voting keeps on declining with an increase in income in rural areas. However, the picture is different in the urban areas as may be concluded from Table 16 B.

Table 16 A

Income and Rural Political Motivation

S. No.	Income Group	CR		EPV		Total	
		F	%	F	%	F	%
1.	Low	28	73.7	10	26.3	38	39.6
2.	Middle	36	81.8	8	18.2	44	45.8
3.	High	12	85.7	2	14.3	14	14.6
	TOTAL	76	79.2	20	20.8	96	100.0

Table 16 B: Income and Urban Political Motivation

S. No.	Income Group	CR F	CR %	EPV F	EPV %	Total F	Total %
1.	Low	16	88.9	2	11.1	18	22.2
2.	Middle	33	89.2	4	10.8	37	45.7
3.	High	22	84.6	4	15.4	26	32.1
	TOTAL	71	87.6	10	12.4	81	100.0

Occupation and Voting Pattern

Occupation often determines the extent of the availability of time for political thinking and action. As a result, it can have far reaching effects on the nature of an individual's voting participation. This factor assumes greater importance in the context of Garhwal where women, particularly in the rural area, being engaged in agricultural and other productive activities, are left with less time to questions other then those related to daily bread.

As may be seen from Table 17 A, the agriculturists in the rural areas, despite being the busiest, are in a clear lead with respect to voting frequency not only on account of their superior voting frequency score, but also by virtue of being the only class which figures at the HVF level. Further, it may also be seen that the housewives who would supposedly have the greatest leisure return the lowest voting frequency percentages at the AVF level. The employed women stand in the last place at the overall level with no rural respondent falling in the miscellaneous category.

Table 17 A: Occupation and Rural Voting Frequency

S. No.	Occupational Group	HVF F	HVF %	AVF F	AVF %	LVF F	LVF %	Total F	Total %
1.	Agriculture	14	15.4	43	47.3	34	37.3	91	94.8
2.	Employment	-	-	1	50.3	1	50.0	2	2.1
3.	Housewives	-	-	1	33.3	2	66.7	3	3.1
4.	Miscellaneous	-	-	-	-	-	-	-	-
	TOTAL	14	15.6	45	46.9	37	38.5	96	100.0

The position with respect to urban women is somewhat different. As may be seen from table 17 B, the housewives, in confirmation of the hypothesis of time availability takes a lead at the HVF and overall voting frequency levels. They are followed by the employed women with the miscellaneous lying in the third place and the agriculturists naturally not figuring in the list.

Table 17 B: Occupation and Urban Voting Frequency

S. No.	*Occupational Group*	*HVF*		*AVF*		*LVF*		*Total*	
		F	*%*	*F*	*%*	*F*	*%*	*F*	*%*
1.	Agriculture	-	-	-	-	-	-	-	-
2.	Employment	1	5.6	8	44.4	9	50.0	18	22.2
3.	Housewives	5	8.9	24	42.9	27	48.2	56	69.2
4.	Miscellaneous	-	-	-	-	7	100.0	81	100.0
	TOTAL	6	7.4	32	39.5	43	53.1	91	100.0

Table 18 A: Occupation and Rural Voting Eagerness

S. No.	*Occupational Group*	*HVE*		*AVE*		*LVE*		*Total*	
		F	*%*	*F*	*%*	*F*	*%*	*F*	*%*
1.	Agriculture	86	91.5	7	7.4	1	1.1	94	94.0
2.	Employed women	1	50.0	1	1	50.0	-	2	2.0
3.	Housewives	3	100.0	-	-	-	-	-	-
4.	Miscellaneous	1	100.0	-	-	-	-	-	-
	TOTAL	91	91.0	8	8.0	1	1.0	100	100.0

In voting eagerness, as indicated by Table 18 A the housewives and women having miscellaneous occupations are jointly ahead in the rural areas followed by the Agriculturists and the employed women.

As shown by Table 18B, in the urban areas, the employed women follow the housewives at the HVF level, while the women with miscellaneous occupations come in the last.

Table 18 B: Occupation and Urban Voting Eagerness

S. No.	Occupational Group	HVE F	HVE %	AVE F	AVE %	LVE F	LVE %	Total F	Total %
1.	Agriculture	-	-	-	-	-	-	-	-
2.	Employed women	16	80.0	1	5.0	3	15.0	2	20.0
3.	Housewives	52	78.8	11	16.7	3	4.5	6	66.0
4.	Miscellaneous	10	71.4	3	21	1	7.2	14	14.0
	TOTAL	78	78.0	15	15.0	7	7.0	100	100.0

With regard to voting motivation, as may be seen from Tables 19A& B in rural areas, the agriculturists take a lead in expressing political view as a motivation for voting. In urban areas the lead position is occupied by the housewives. Thus, as the occupational background of the respondents varies the degree of motivation also varies. But in the urban areas the availability of time is also a determining factor for motivation.

Table 19 A: Occupation and Rural Political Motivation

S. No.	Occupational Group	CR F	CR %	EPV F	EPV %	Total F	Total %
1	Agriculture	72	79.1	19	20.9	91	94.8
2.	Employed women	2	100.0	-	-	2	2.1
3.	Housewives	2	66.7	1	33.3	3	3.1
4.	Miscellaneous	-	-	-	-	-	-
	TOTAL	76	79.2	20	20.8	96	100.0

Table 19 B: Occupation and Urban Political Motivation

S. No.	Occupational Group	CR F	CR %	EPV F	EPV %	Total F	Total %
1.	Agriculture	-	-	-	-	-	-
2.	Employed women	15	83.3	3	16.7	18	22.2
3.	Housewives	50	89.3	6	10.7	56	69.2
4.	Miscellaneous	6	85.7	1	14.3	7	8.6
	TOTAL	71	87.6	10	12.4	81	100.0

Family Structure and Voting Participation

Since family is a very powerful institution of Indian society its influence on voting participation cannot be ignored. This influence is, however, liable to variation in the context of the structure of the family. Evaluating the effect of this variable becomes more deserving for comparison in the context of Garhwal, since here the order of the day is much more in favour of the nuclear family in both the rural and urban areas.

Table 20 A: Family Structure and Rural Voting Frequency

S. No.	Family Structure	HVF F	HVF %	AVF F	AVF %	LVF F	LVF %	Total F	Total %
1.	Nuclear	11	15.7	31	44.3	28	40.0	70	72.9
2.	Joint	3	11.6	14	53.8	9	34.6	26	27.1
	TOTAL	14	14.6	45	46.8	37	38.5	96	100.0

Table 20 B: Family Structure and Urban Voting Frequency

S. No.	Family Structure	HVF F	HVF %	AVF F	AVF %	LVF F	LVF %	Total F	Total %
1.	Nuclear	6	7.7	32	41.0	40	51.3	78	96.3
2.	Joint	-	-	-	-	3	100.0	3	3.7
	TOTAL	6	7.4	32	39.5	43	53.1	81	100.0

As may be seen from Tables 20 A & B, the women from the nuclear families outnumber those from joint families in both rural areas and urban areas.

The picture with respect to the relation of voting eagerness and family structure is much more straightforward. It is obvious from Tables 21 A&B that those from the nuclear families are far ahead of those from the joint-families at HVE as well as the overall voting eagerness levels in both the rural and urban areas. The difference may, however, be said to be much more sharp and pronounced among the urban women.

Table 21 A: Family Structure and Rural Voting Eagerness

S. No.	Family Structure	HVE F	HVE %	AVE F	AVE %	LVE F	LVE %	Total F	Total %
1.	Nuclear	67	94.4	4	5.6	-	-	71	71.0
2.	Joint	24	82.8	4	13.8	1	3.4	29	29.0
	TOTAL	91	91.0	8	8.0	1	1.0	100	100.0

Table 21 B: Family Structure and Urban Voting Eagerness

S. No.	Family Structure	HVE F	HVE %	AVE F	AVE %	LVE F	LVE %	Total F	Total %
1.	Nuclear	76	80.0	14	14.7	5	5.3	95	95.0
2.	Joint	2	40.0	1	20.0	2	40.0	5	5.0
	TOTAL	78	78.0	15	15.0	7	7.0	100	100.0

As may be seen from Tables 22 A&B, those from the joint-families show a fair amount of motivation though those from the nuclear families show a desire for expressing political views to be the prime motivation for voting; it is true in cases of both rural and urban women. The findings with respect to the impact of family structure on voting participation may, however, not be considered to be conclusive, since, particularly in the urban areas, those from the joint-families do not find satisfactory representation in the sample.

Table 22 A: Family Structure and Rural Political Motivation

S. No.	Family Structure	CR F	CR %	EPV F	EPV %	Total F	Total %
1.	Nuclear	57	81.4	13	18.6	70	72.9
2.	Joint	19	73.1	7	26.9	26	27.1
	TOTAL	76	79.2	20	20.8	96	100.0

Table 22 B: Family Structure and Urban Political Motivation

S. No.	Family Structure	CR F	CR %	EPV F	EPV %	Total F	Total %
1.	Nuclear	69	88.5	9	11.5	78	97.0
2.	Joint	2	66.7	1	33.3	3	3.0
	TOTAL	71	87.6	10	12.4	81	100.0

Political Socialization and Voting Participation

Political socialization is an attribute of individual personality, which may not exactly be treated as a part of his bio-social background but which is one of the most powerful influences over his political behavior. The effect of this factor assumes added importance in case of the Indian women, particularly those from hills, who do not appear to be highly politically socialized. It is against this background that the relationship of political socialization with voting participation in Garhwal shall be viewed.

The relation between the political socialization and voting frequency is neither consistent nor systematic in Garhwal. Table 23 A shows a partially negative curvy-liner pattern at the overall level and partially positive curvilinear pattern at the HVF level among the rural women. The women with an average political socialization are much more sublime and those with a high political socialization fall behind those with a low political socialization level at the overall level while taking the lead at the HVF level. AVF scores were, however, found to be varying inversely with a rise in the political socialization levels.

Table 23 A: Political Socialization & Rural Voting Frequency

S. No.	Pol. Socialization Level	HVF F	HVF %	AVF F	AVF %	LVF F	LVF %	Total F	Total %
1.	Low	5	18.5	14	51.9	8	29.6	27	28.1
2.	Average	7	11.5	28	45.9	26	42.6	61	63.6
3.	High	2	25.0	3	37.5	3	37.5	8	8.3
	TOTAL	14	15.6	45	46.9	37	38.5	96	100.0

The position is somewhat different in the case of the urban women. Among them, political socialization seems to be having a strongly negative curvilinear relationship at the overall level. Here, while those with average political socialization scores continue to lag behind, those with high political socialization scores take a pronounced lead over the rest. Furthermore, voting frequency appears to vary directly though not harmonically, with a rise in political socialization levels. This tends to show that there does not exist any coherent and systematic relationship between the voting frequency patterns of the women of Garhwal and the extent of their political socialization.

Table 23 B: Political Socialization & Urban Voting Frequency

S. No.	*Pol. Socialization Level*	*HVF F*	*HVF %*	*AVF F*	*AVF %*	*LVF F*	*LVF %*	*Total F*	*Total %*
1.	Low	1	3.8	10	39.5	15	57.7	26	32.1
2.	Average	2	4.7	17	39.5	24	55.8	43	53.1
3.	High	3	25.0	5	41.7	4	33.3	12	14.0
	TOTAL	6	7.4	32	39.5	43	53.1	81	100.0

The findings of the study with regard to the relation of political socialization with voting eagerness are not consistent with those regarding the relationship between political socialization and voting frequency. As may be seen from Tables 24 A&B, voting eagerness tends to vary directly with an increase in the extent of political socialization in both the rural and urban areas. This would suggest that the inconsistencies registered with respect to the relation of political socialization with voting frequency may well be a product of the effect of the age configuration of the different categories.

Table 24 A: Political Socialization & Rural Voting Eagerness

S. No.	*Pol. Socialization Level*	*HVE F*	*HVE %*	*AVE F*	*AVE %*	*LVE F*	*LVE %*	*Total F*	*Total %*
1.	Low	24	85.7	3	10.7	1	3.6	28	28.0
2.	Average	59	92.2	5	7.8	-	-	64	64.0
3.	High	8	100.0	-	-	-	-	8	8.0
	TOTAL	91	9.1.0	8	8.0	1	1.0	100	100.0

Table 24 B: Political Socialization & Urban Voting Eagerness

S. No.	Pol. Socialization Level	HVE F	HVE %	AVE F	AVE %	LVE F	LVE %	Total F	Total %
1.	Low	23	67.6	7	20.6	4	11.8	34	34.0
2.	Average	41	78.8	8	15.4	3	5.8	52	52.0
3.	High	14	100.0	-	-	-	-	14	14.0
	TOTAL	78	78.0	15	15.0	7	7.0	100	100.0

The picture changes ones again when political socialization levels are plotted against voting motivation. In this context, as shown by Tables 25 A and B, it may be noted that a desire for expressing political views varies curvilinearly with an increase in political socialization among the rural women with the curve rising among those having an average political socialization, while this variation follows a reverse trend if voting is regarded as the fulfillment of a right and the principal motivation.

Table 25 A: Political Socialization and Rural Political Motivation

S. No.	Pol. Socialization Level	CR F	CR %	EPV F	EPV %	Total F	Total %
1.	Low	23	85.2	4	14.8	27	28.1
2.	Average	46	75.4	15	24.6	61	63.6
3.	High	7	87.5	1	12.5	8	8.3
	Total	76	79.2	20	20.8	96	100.0

On the contrary, in case of the urban women the desire for expressing the political views as the prime motivation tends to vary inversely with an increase in political socialization while the drive for treating voting to be a right in its motivational capacity tends to vary directly with political socialization enhancement. This shows that political socialization does not clearly establish any linkage between the political views of the women of Garhwal and their voting motivation.

Table 25 B: Political Socialization and Urban Political Motivation

S. No.	Pol. Socialization Level	CR		EPV		Total	
		F	%	F	%	F	%
1.	Low	20	76.9	6	23.1	26	32.1
2.	Average	39	90.7	4	9.3	43	53.1
3.	High	12	100.0	-	-	12	14.8
	Total	71	87.6	10	12.4	81	100.0

Political Awareness and Voting Participation

Possession of significant political awareness is a sine qua non of all meaningful political activity. It becomes a key arbiter of voting frequency and other related questions since it disseminates crucial knowledge which not only evokes political interest but also helps in the formation of voting preference and decisions. This makes it essential to evaluate its relation with the voting participation of the women of Garhwal, whose political awareness is not satisfactorily high since the effects of the modern communication exposure have not fully reached them.

It was found that the patterns of the relationship between political awareness and voting frequency follow opposite trends. As may be seen from the Tables 26 A&B this relationship is more or less negative in case the rural women and positive in case of urban women.

Table 26 A: Political Awareness and Rural Voting Frequency

S. No.	Political Awareness	HVF		AVF		LVF		Total	
		F	%	F	%	F	%	F	%
1.	Low	10	26.6	20	52.6	8	21.1	38	39.6
2.	Average	4	7.4	23	42.6	27	50.0	54	56.2
3.	High	-	-	2	50.0	2	50.0	4	4.2
	Total	14	15.6	45	46.9	37	38.5	96	100.0

Table 26 B: Political Awareness and Urban Voting Frequency

S. No.	Political Awareness	HVF F	HVF %	AVF F	AVF %	LVF F	LVF %	Total F	Total %
1.	Low	-	-	1	16.7	8	83.3	6	7.4
2.	Average	2	5.4	17	54.9	18	48.7	37	45.7
3.	High	4	10.6	14	36.8	20	52.6	38	46.9
	Total	6	7.4	32	39.5	43	53.1	81	100.0

So for as the relation of political awareness and voting eagerness is concerned, the study discovered that the rural and urban women do not differ significantly.

Table 27 A: Political Awareness and Rural Voting Eagerness

S. No.	Political Awareness	HVE F	HVE %	AVE F	AVE %	LVE F	LVE %	Total F	Total %
1.	Low	36	92.3	2	5.1	1	2.6	39	39.0
2.	Average	51	91.1	5	8.9	-	-	56	56.0
3.	High	4	80.0	1	20.0	-	-	5	5.0
	Total	91	91.0	8	8.0	1	1.0	100	100.0

Table 27 B: Political Awareness and Urban Voting Eagerness

S. No.	Political Awareness	HVE F	HVE %	AVE F	AVE %	LVE F	LVE %	Total F	Total %
1.	Low	6	85.7	1	14.3	-	-	7	7.0
2.	Average	34	79.1	7	16.3	2	4.6	43	43.0
3.	High	38	76.0	7	14.0	5	10.0	50	50.0
	Total	78	78.0	15	15.0	7	7.0	100	100.0

The relationship in the rural areas is negatively curvilinear at the over all voting eagerness level and negative at the high voting eagerness. In the urban areas the relationship of political awareness with voting eagerness tends to be negative at the HVE levels. It may then be concluded that voting eagerness among the women of Garhwal generally tends to vary inversely with an increase in political awareness.

Similarly the study found political awareness to be negatively related to the desire for expression political views as motivation for voting. Tables 28 A & B present the relationship between political awareness and political motivation.

Table 28 A: Political Awareness and Rural Political Motivation

S. No.	*Pol. Socialization Level*	*CR*		*EPV*		*Total*	
		F	*%*	*F*	*%*	*F*	*%*
1.	Low	27	71.1	11	28.9	38	39.5
2.	Average	45	83.3	9	16.7	54	56.3
3.	High	4	100.0	-	-	4	4.2
	Total	76	79.2	10	20.8	96	100.0

As may be seen from Table 28 A the desire for expressing political views tend to weaken as voting motivation while the drive for treating voting to be the fulfillment of a right tends to be strengthened with a rise in political awareness among the rural women of Garhwal.

Table 28 B: Political Awareness and Urban Political Motivation

S. No.	*Pol. Socialization Level*	*CR*		*EPV*		*Total*	
		F	*%*	*F*	*%*	*F*	*%*
1.	Low	3	50.0	3	50.0	6	7.4
2.	Average	34	91.9	3	8.1	37	45.7
3.	High	34	89.5	4	10.5	38	46.9
	Total	71	87.6	10	12.4	81	100.0

The relationship follows an almost similar pattern in the urban areas with a marginal breach of the trend among the women with high political awareness, as presented in Table 28 B. This rather unbelievably show that political awareness tends to dissuade the women of Garhwal from using their voting right as an instrument of expressing political views.

Conclusion

The present study has measured voting participation in the context of its three key areas namely voting frequency, voting eagerness and the desire for expressing political views as a motivation for voting. Though the rural and urban women of Garhwal broadly speaking do not appear to be much different from one another, yet in minute detail subtitle variation along bio-social lines may be noted, voting frequency in rural and urban areas varies positively with age negatively with education, income and political awareness. Voting eagerness in the sample tends to vary positively with political socialization, expression of political views as voting motivation in rural and urban areas tends to vary with age, political socialization and political awareness in Garhwal.

Notes and References

1. Indian Franchise Committee, 1932, vol. 1, Para 213.
2. S. Sarswati, *Women in Political Life in India*, Delhi; I.C.S.S.R published thesis, pp. 59-60.
3. S.A.H.Haqqi, *Political Behaviour: Empirical Study*, Delhi; I.C.S.S.R. published project report, p. 94.
4. Almond and Verba, *The Civic Culture*, New Jersey: Princeton, 1963, p. 25.
5. Paul F. Lazersfeld, et al. *The People's Choice*, New York, Columbia University Press, 1944, p. 5.
6. Angus Campbell, *The Voter Decides*, Evanston, Illinois press, New York, 1954, and Hymn, H.H., *Political Socialization*, New York, The Macmillan Company, Free Press, 1959.
7. K.G. Krishanamurti and G. Laxman Rao, "Socio-economic and demographic factors and voting behaviour", *Political Science Review*, April-June 1969, pp. 279-80.
8. S.A.H. Haqqi, *Political Behavior: Empirical Study*, Delhi; I.C.S.S.R. published project report, p. 115.

17

Political Participation of Women Leaders: A Case Study in Orissa

Gayatri Mishra & A.N. Panda

Democracy is one of the most cherished ideals of the world. It may be considered as the best possible form of government as it insists on exercising power by the rulers with the consent of the ruled. In a democracy, political power is controlled by people and decisions are taken with their active involvement. As the decision making system in a democratic state operates with the continuing support of people the interests of people have a greater chance of being protected. Hence, it has become the most acceptable and desirable form of government in the world today.

Democracy occupies a pride of place among the different ideologies because it emphasizes on sovereignty of people. Sovereignty of people becomes meaningful only when there is active involvement of all people at different levels of the decision making structures. "If democracy is interpreted as rule by the people, then the question of who participates in political decisions becomes the question of the nature of democracy in a society."[1] The successful working of democracy can not be ensured without the active and continuous participation of the different sections of people in different activities which have a direct bearing on the political process of the country. Therefore, in a democratic polity there is an imperative need for maintaining a condition which is conducive for the keen political participation of the citizens of the country.

Political Participation as a Concept

Participation is an essential element of democracy. It completely makes people a part of the political process of a country and motivates them to think and act for the country's political system. A country's political authority gets its legitimacy and can be assured of its stability only through the political participation of its people. Moreover, political participation enhances the self esteem of people and gives them a sense of achievement, apart from imparting political education to the citizens of a state and making them aware of their responsibilities.

Thus, the concept of political participation has always invited the attention of scholars who have made many studies on the involvement of people in the decision making process of their respective countries. The researchers have probed the behavior of people while the latter exercise their supreme power in selecting the rulers of their own countries.

Different academics have forwarded different definitions of political participation and all have defined it from their own points of view. But all have emphasized on the association of people in the affairs of the state and the performance of different activities by individuals towards that end. Hence, political participation can be defined as "comprising all those activities that, one way or another, are intended to affect the workings of and outcomes in the political system."[2]

Participation always presupposes taking decisions and showing preferences. It implies selecting the right people and taking the right decisions. "Political participation refers to those activities by private citizens that are more or less directly aimed at influencing the selection of governmental personnel and/ or actions they take."[3] Through their participation, common men control the selection and functioning of the political leadership in their own countries. Political participation means "those activities of citizens that attempt to influence the structure of government, the selection of government authorities, or the policies of government."[4] Participation includes the performance of many functions, ranging from the simple function of voting in an election to the intricate job of protesting against the incumbent rulers. "Participation consists of many things, such as voting, conducting revolutions, forming political parties and leading them, managing bureaucracies and rioting."[5]

Though the participation of common people is important in a democracy, participation in the political system reaches its fullest magnitude only in the case of the leaders because only the leaders are more directly involved in the decision making process. "They often have more information; they are more likely than others to hold public office; they are likely to have more financial resources and more access to the public media."[6] Only the leaders have a greater chance of influencing the decision making process and policies of the government. Therefore, the leaders' participation has its own significance in a democratic polity.

Political Participation in India

A democratic government must be supplemented by a democratic society and a democratic way of life for its proper working which in turn implies the prevalence of justice, equality and respect for the capacity and individuality of all beings. All these are possible if all the sections of society get associated in the course of decision making in the country.

In India, political participation is a major problem. Even though it is the largest democracy in the world, the low political participation of people is a matter of great concern. Even after more than five long decades of enforcement of the Constitution and adoption of the principle of universal adult franchise in India, a large chunk of people have not been able to be a part of the democratic system of the country. 'If the voting percentage in different elections to Lok Sabha is taken into account it can be observed that since the election of 1952 up to the election of 2004 the total voting percentage is never more than 63.56 that too it was in the year 1984. The number of voters has increased from 173,213,635 in 1952 to 671,524,575 in 2004, but the voting percentage has decreased from 61.2 in 1952 to 57.82 in 2004, though there has been variation in between.'[7]

In this context, participation of the Indian women in the political process assumes great significance. Women constitute about fifty per cent of the total population of India. If women do not evince any interest in the political affairs of the country and they drift away from the mainstream political process, the political system of the country itself suffers for their non-involvement. If women are politically alienated, neither they would be able to solve their own problems, such as safety and security, access to education, employment, health care and other such difficulties, which directly concern them nor the country would be able to utilize their potentiality and take advantage of their contributions for its own progress. Therefore, it is vital to make women more engaged and active in the affairs of the country.

If the participation of people in general is not satisfactory, the participation of women in particular is pathetic. The percentage of female voters in the elections to Lok Sabha has remained lower than the percentage of male voters or the percentage of total voters. 'In 1984 election the percentage of female voters was 58.60, the highest female voting percentage in any Lok Sabha election, against the male percentage of 68.18 and the total percentage of 63.56.'[8]

While the participation of women in general is not very encouraging in India, that of women in Orissa is also no better. They lag much behind their male counterparts in the political arena. For example, in the election to the State Legislative Assembly in 2004, there were in total 802 contestants out of them only 55 were women candidates.[9] Particularly in those districts which have large number of backward people among their inhabitants, there is less chance of political participation for women.

There has been an increasing demand to involve more and more women in the democratic process of the country and make them integral parts of the decision making bodies. In this context their participation at the grassroots level acquires special importance because of the roles played by grassroots institutions in grooming women as the leaders and representatives of the people in general and women in particular. With this background, an enquiry into the theme political participation of women in Orissa will make a very fascinating study. In this paper such an endeavor has been made.

Panchayatiraj in Orissa

As in the case of other states of India, Panchayatiraj system has also been introduced in Orissa on the recommendation of the Balbantrai Mehta Committee. But the first legislation which was passed in Orissa to introduce local self government was known by the name of Bihar Orissa Local Self Government Act. After independence Gram Panchayats have been functioning in the state since 1950 according to the Orissa Gram Panchayat Act, 1948. The Zilla Parishad and Panchayat Samiti Act of 1959 in Orissa introduced Panchayat Samiti at the Block level and Zilla Parishad at the district level. According to the Act of 1959 Panchayat Samitis were constituted at the Block level on 26 January 1961 and Zilla Parishads were constituted at the district level by the middle of March 1961.

The Orissa Panchayat Samiti and Zilla Parishad Act was further amended in 1968 and Zilla Parishad was abolished and in its place a District Advisory Council was constituted in each district with the Collector as the Convener and a non-official member as the President. The District Advisory Council was superseded by the District Development and Planning Board in 1970 with a minister as Chairman.[10] It was again revived in 1991 and later modified in accordance with the 73rd Constitutional Amendment in 1993.

At present there is a three tier Panchayati Raj system operating in Orissa. The three tiers are the Panchayats at the village level, the Panchayat Samitis at the Block level and the Zilla Parishads at the district level. Though the 73rd Amendment of the Constitution introduced one third reservation for women in the rural grassroots level institutions in India, Orissa had already introduced the move to have reservation for women in its Panchayatiraj system in 1992. Thus, "Orissa became the first state to introduce one-third reservation for women in Panchayats."[11]

The present system of Panchayatiraj in Orissa prescribes

for constitution of a Zilla Parishad in each district in the state. The existing system makes provision for greater involvement of women in the functioning of Zilla Parishad. As required by the Orissa Zilla Parishad Act out of the total seats in Zilla Parishad, one third seats are reserved for women.[12]

The Chairman/President of Zilla Parishad shall be directly elected by the people. However, not less than one third of the total number of offices of the Chairman/President in Parishads shall be reserved for women[13] and if the office of the President is not reserved for women and if a woman is not elected as President, the post of Vice-President shall be reserved for women.[14]

In this paper a modest attempt has been made to study political participation of the district level women leaders by making a case study of the participation of positional women leaders of the Zilla Parishad in Sundargarh district of Orissa.

Universe of Study

The present district of Sundargarh is the new shape of the erstwhile princely states of Gangpur and Bonaigarh. It is surrounded by the borders of two other states, Jharkhand and Chhattishgarh and two districts of Orissa, Jharsuguda and Keonjhar. It has a geographical area of 9712 square kilo meters.[15]

The district has 'a total population of 18, 31,000 out which 48.88 per cent are women. The Scheduled Caste and Scheduled Tribe people account for 18.61 and 50.18 per cent of the total population respectively. The male literacy rate is 75.34 where as the female literacy rate is 53.88.'[16]

The district has a peculiarity of being one of the most backward districts of Orissa and paradoxically, it is also one of the economically developed areas of the state due to large scale industrialization which has resulted because of the establishment of different industries like Hindustan Steel Ltd., Orissa Cement Ltd., Mahanadi Coal Ltd., etc.

The district is constituted by three subdivisions and in different grassroots institutions as many as 262 Panchayat Samiti members and 262 Sarpanchs, besides 35 Zilla Parisad members[17] function as the office bearers. Out of about four thousand representatives of people in the district one third is women. Out of the 35 total members of Zilla Parishad in Sundargarh, 23 are males and 12 are females.[18]

The district offers a suitable area for field study for women leadership, a sizable part of which is also constituted by tribal women.

Participation of women in the tribal district of Sundargarh presents an interesting picture. Many women leaders have occupied different political positions in the district such as memberships in Orissa Legislative Assembly and Lok Sabha and political posts in the district level body. 'In the past Ms. Frida Topno had won an Assembly seat in Raghunathpali constituency in 1985 and had also become a minister. Also she had won the Lok Sabha seat of Sundargarh twice in 1991 and 1996. The present MLA of Sundargarh Smt. Susama Patel is also a woman. In the Sundargarh municipality Smt. Padmini Shekhar Deo had served a term as the Chairperson.'[19] These are but a few examples of women leadership in the district. But in spite of these successes women participation in politics has still a long way to go.

Research Design

The present study is based on the responses of the elected positional women leaders of the Zilla Parishad in the district to varieties of questions. The questionnaire has been prepared and responses have been collected from the women leaders in such a manner so as to elicit information on different aspects of their political participation and other related matters. The questionnaire was formulated in a simple manner to enable the respondents for understanding the questions and forming their responses. Due care has been taken to have a proper perspective on the subject.

The Zilla Parishad of Sundargarh consists of 35 members; out of the total seats 12 are reserved the women. At the time of election, in total 43 women contested for these seats and out them 12 were declared elected.[20]

Data Analysis

The various activities related to political participation can be broadly divided into two categories, those performed at the time of election and those performed at a time when there is no election. In the case of leaders another category can added which will reveal their participation as decision makers. To know the political participation of women leaders several questions have been asked to the respondents and information on their participation during election and at a time when there is no election being held as well as their association in the decision making system has been gathered; after analyzing their responses conclusions have been drawn and presented in a tabular form.

(a) Participation of women leaders during election

(i) Voting in election

Voting is the simplest and most vital form of political participation. It gives an opportunity to maximum number of people to involve themselves directly in the political process of the country and use their decision making power in selecting their representatives who in turn take policy decisions on behalf of the people and decide the fate of the country. Therefore, the first question was on participation of the women leaders as voters during the time of election. The respondents were asked whether they were regular voters in all elections. Their responses are presented in Table 1.

Table 1

Distribution of Women Leaders by Voting during Elections

S. No.	*Voting participation*	*No. of Leaders*	*Percentage*
1	Regularly voting	10	83.33
2	Not regularly voting	02	16.67
3	TOTAL	12	100

As Table 1 shows all the women leaders have voted in different elections but 83.33 per cent women leaders vote regularly whereas 16.67 are irregular in voting.

(ii) Encouraging others to vote in elections

One kind of getting involved and making others involved in the political process is to encourage others to take part in the political process of the country. To make the political system vibrant one has to not only involve oneself in the political process but also initiate others by encouraging them to involve themselves in the political process. So a question has been asked to know whether the women leaders encourage others to cast their votes in elections.

Table 2

Distribution of Women Leaders by their act of encouraging others to vote

S. No.	*Encouraging others*	*No. of Leaders*	*Percentage*
1	YES	11	91.67
2	NO	01	8.33
3	TOTAL	12	100

As the table shows most of the women leaders understand the importance of voting. 91.67% of women leaders not only vote in the elections but also encourage others to vote. This shows that those women leaders are helping others to get initiated in the process of election.

(iii) Acting as polling agents

One of the activities which are performed during election is doing the job of a polling agent. A polling agent helps the voters in the polling station to cast their votes. He also assists the polling officers to perform their duties in a better manner by helping them in their duties in different ways such as helping the officers to identify the voters or checking malpractices inside the booth. As the target group of the study consists of the elite women of their areas they are expected to be approached by the candidates and political parties to act as their polling agents and they are likely to have acted as polling agents. So they have been asked a question on their association in the election process as polling agents. Their responses are given in Table 3.

Table 3: Distribution of Women Leaders by their acting as the Polling Agents

S. No.	Responses	No. of Leaders	Percentage
1	YES	04	33.33
2	NO	08	66.67
3	TOTAL	12	100

As the data presented in table shows out of the total women leaders 33.33% have acted as polling agents whereas 66.67% have never acted as polling agents. When a question was further asked to the respondents who replied the previous question in the affirmative to specify how many times they had acted as polling agents all of them replied that they had performed the work of polling agents only once.

(iv) Participation in Parliamentary elections

In India, elections are held at regular intervals to the lower house of Parliament, i.e. Lok Sabha and as the Lok Sabha election is a direct election people get an opportunity to elect their representatives who in turn form government at the centre. Therefore, participation in the Parliamentary elections forms an integral part of political participation in India.

A question has been asked to the respondents to state the manner of their involvement in the democratic process of the country, i.e. how they have been involved in the Parliamentary elections. Their responses have been presented in Table 4.

Table 4: Distribution of Leaders by their Participation in Parliamentary Elections

S. No.	Activity	No. of Leaders	Percentage
1	Voting	09	75.00
2	Campaigning	-	-
3	Candidacy	-	-
4	Voting, Campaigning	03	25.00
5	All activities	-	-
6	TOTAL	12	100

As the data reflects the participation of the women leaders in Parliamentary elections was limited to only to voting and campaigning, that too only 25% of women leaders have acted as campaigners. The majority of the leaders have participated only as voters. As the table shows 75% of the leaders have acted only as voters and only 25 percent of the respondents have performed other works apart from the job of voting, i.e. campaigning. No woman leader has ever contested the election as a candidate. Thus, the participation of the women leaders in the Parliamentary elections is limited.

(v) Participation in Assembly elections

Likewise, to know the involvement of the women leaders in the political process another question was asked to them on the manner of their participation in the Assembly elections held in the state. Assembly elections give another opportunity to the adult citizens to be directly engaged in the election process. The responses of the women leaders are given in Table 5.

Table 5: Distribution of Women leaders by their participation in Assembly Elections

S. No.	*Activity*	*No. of Leaders*	*Percentage*
1	Voting	09	75.00
2	Campaigning	-	-
3	Candidacy	-	-
4	Voting, Campaigning	03	25.00
5	All activities	-	-
6	TOTAL	12	100

As it is known from the above table, in the Assembly elections 75% women leaders participated only as voters and 25% leaders, besides voting also took part in campaigning. None of the women leaders had ever contested the elections to the Assembly as a candidate.

(vi) Participation in earlier Panchayat elections

The Panchayatiraj system has been adopted in India to spread democracy at the grassroots level. It is believed that democracy is possible only if the people are given a scope to take the local decisions locally and this scope is given to them through their involvement in the formation and functioning of the Panchayatiraj institutions. Thus, political participation in grassroots politics is possible mainly through the participation of women in the Panchayatiraj system. Hence, a question has been asked on the manner of their participation in the democratic process at the lowest level of the political system in the country.

Table 6: Distribution of Women Leaders by their Participation in Earlier Panchayat Elections

S. No.	*Activity*	*No. of Leaders*	*Percentage*
1	Voting	04	33.33
2	Campaigning	-	-
3	Candidacy	-	-
4	Voting, Campaigning	01	8.33
5	All activities	07	58.33
6	TOTAL	12	99.99

As the data presented in the above table shows, participation of the respondents in the Panchayat elections is more than either the Parliamentary election or the Assembly election. 33.33 percent leaders have participated only as voters where as 8.33 per cent women leaders have participated both as voters and as campaigners. The remaining leaders i.e. 58.33 have participated as campaigners and candidates, besides voting in the elections. The women leaders have shown more interest in the political process at the local level.

However, it can also be said that contesting for a seat in the Assembly or in the Lok Sabha is considered more prestigious and only the top level leaders in the state or districts contest in such elections. As the women leaders are grassroots level leaders they do not get an opportunity to contest for a seat either in the Assembly or in the Lok Sabha.

(vii) Participation in election campaign

During the time of election one of the major activities is campaigning and taking part in election campaign is also an important political activity. A campaigner propagates in favor of a political agenda, convinces the people of the worthiness of candidate or a party and canvasses for votes in favor of a candidate and/or a party. Therefore, the importance of campaigning can not be ignored at the time of election.

As the respondents are the political leaders of their localities they are likely to be approached by political parties and candidates to campaign for them. It is important to know whether the women leaders have participated in campaigning and if they have, then the manner of their participation. The responses of the leaders have been presented in Tables 7 and 8.

Table 7: Distribution of Women Leaders by their Participation in Campaign Activities

S. No.	*Options*	*No. of Leaders*	*Percentage*
1	YES	08	66.67
2	NO	04	33.33
3	TOTAL	12	100

As Table 7 shows 66.67% participated in campaign activities while 33.33 did not.

While a person participates in campaigning he performs varieties of functions such as preparation of election materials, distribution of election materials, organizing election rallies and canvassing for votes. The women leaders were further asked to specify the nature of their campaign activities.

In response to the question on the manner of their participation in the campaign activity during elections the women leaders specified the kind of work they had done during campaigning. The answers of the women leaders on the nature of their participation have been given in Table 8.

Table 8: Distribution of Leaders by the Nature of their Participation in Campaigning

S. No.	*Type of Activity*	*No. of Leaders*	*Percentage*
1	Preparation of election materials	-	-
2	Distribution of election materials	-	-
3	Organizing election rallies	-	-
4	Door to door canvassing	06	75.00

5	All activities	-	-
6	Organizing rallies & canvassing	01	12.50
7	Material distribution & canvassing	01	12.50
8	TOTAL	08	100

It can be seen from Table 8 that out of the total women leaders involved in campaigning most of them, i.e. 75% have been engaged in door to door campaigning while 12.50% have been engaged in organizing rallies and canvassing and an equal percentage of leaders has been engaged in material distribution and canvassing.

(b) Participation of women leaders when there is no election

Political participation does not end with participation in various election activities. Even when there is no election one can be politically active. In fact, it is more worthwhile to study the political participation of leaders because they remain active politically at a time even when there is no election. The leaders do so in a number of ways such as propagating for a political cause, discussing political issues with others, keeping contacts with their followers, organizing public meetings to protest or support some political issue, etc.

(i) Propagating for a political cause

As the elites of their locality, the women leaders have an important role to play in deciding many political issues in their localities. They may take sides in a political debate. They may have to propagate for or against a political cause. To know such activities of the women leaders a question has been asked to the respondents whether they take part in propagating for or against a political cause; the answers of the leaders are presented in Table 9.

Table 9: Distribution of Women Leaders by their Propagating for or against a Political Cause

S. No.	*Responses*	*No. of Leaders*	*Percentage*
1	YES	08	66.67
2	NO	04	33.33
3	TOTAL	12	100

Out of the total respondents 66.67 percent leaders engage themselves in propagating for or against a political cause while 33.33 percent do not.

(ii) Discussing political issues with others

Discussion can be regarded as a mode of interaction among different actors and it is one of the different ways of political communication. While deliberating an issue the various participants in the discussion exchange their own thoughts among themselves. One way of propagating for or against a political cause is discussing the issue with others and arrive at a conclusion. Discussing with others also helps in socializing others in political matters by spreading political information among them. As the women leaders have comparatively more exposure than other people of their areas they help in politically socializing others. To know whether the women leaders are engaged in this activity a question has been included in the questionnaire. The answers of the women leaders are given in Table 10.

Table 10: Distribution of Women Leaders by their discussing Political Issues with Others

S. No.	*Responses*	*No. of Leaders*	*Percentage*
1	YES	08	66.67
2	NO	04	33.33
3	TOTAL	12	100

It can be seen from the table that 66.67 per cent of women leaders discuss political issues with others while 33.33 per cent do not do so.

(iii) Meeting the followers

It is necessary for a leader to keep contacts with his followers. A leader keeps contact with his followers in an effective manner through his meetings with his followers. As the representatives of the people the women leaders have to be aware of the problems of the electorate. It can be done if the leaders keep regular contacts with their followers. Meeting serves the purpose of having a two way communication. So meeting is important for both the leaders and their followers.

To know this activity of the positional leaders a question has been asked to the women leaders whether they are in regular touch with their constituents through their meetings with them. Their responses are presented in Table 11.

Table 11: Distribution of Women Leaders by their meeting with their Electorate Regularly

S. No.	*Responses*	*No. of Leaders*	*Percentage*
1	YES	11	91.67
2	NO	01	8.33
3	TOTAL	12	100

As table 11 shows out of the total respondents 91.67 percent meet their electorate regularly and 8.33 percent do not meet their followers regularly.

While meeting their followers the leaders can themselves go to the latter or expect the latter to come to them or they both can exchange visits and keep the communication in tact. It is sometimes complained that the leaders do not visit their electorates and remain isolated from them. Therefore, another related question has been asked to the women leaders on how they meet their followers; whether their followers come to the leaders or the leaders go to their followers or it is a two way affair. The responses of the women leaders have been given in Table 12.

Table 12: Distribution of Women Leaders by the mode of meeting their Electorate

S. No.	*Responses*	*No. of Leaders*	*Percentage*
1	Going to the electorate	-	-
2	Coming of the electorate to the leader	-	-
3	Both	11	100
4	TOTAL	11	100

As it can be seen from Table 12 all the women leaders who meet their followers regularly keep contacts with them either by going to their followers or the followers coming to the leaders. It is a two way communication between them and their followers.

(iv) Organizing public meetings

People get politically involved when they take part in a public meeting. They mix with other people, exchange their opinions, try to influence others and also get influenced by others. Therefore, attending and organizing public meetings can also be regarded as a kind of political participation.

Another kind of political activity a leader performs is to organize public meetings for different purposes. Through public meeting discussions are held and issues are decided and messages are spread among the people. It is also a way of keeping in touch with the electorate. To know this kind of activity of the leaders a question has been asked to them and their responses have been presented in Table 13.

Table 13: Distribution of Women Leaders by their Organizing Public Meetings

S. No.	*Responses*	*No. of Leaders*	*Percentage*
1	YES	08	66.67
2	NO	04	33.33
3	TOTAL	12	100

Out of the total leaders 66.67 per cent leaders organize public meetings whereas 33.33 per cent do not do so.

(v) Taking part in procession

Still another kind of political activity when there is no election is to take part in a procession to support or oppose an issue. Therefore, a question was asked to the respondents if they had participated in any procession for or against any cause. A related question was asked to the leaders on their participation in such procession and whether it was inside or outside the district. The answers of the leaders have been given in Tables 14 and 15.

Table 14: Distribution of Women Leaders by their Participation in Processions

S. No.	*Responses*	*No. of Leaders*	*Percentage*
1	YES	09	75.00
2	NO	03	25.00
3	TOTAL	12	100

Table 15: Distribution of Leaders by the Place of their Participation in Processions

S. No.	*Responses*	*No. of Leaders*	*Percentage*
1	Only Inside	08	88.89
2	Only Outside	-	-
3	Both	01	11.11
4	TOTAL	09	100

It can be seen from Table 14 that 75 per cent leaders have taken part in processions and 25 per cent have not. Out of the leaders who have taken part in the processions, 88.89 per cent have participated only inside the districts whereas only 11.11 per cent have participated both inside and outside the district; no leader is found who has participated only outside the district.

(c) Participation of women leaders in decision making

Political participation reaches its fullest form only in the case of the decision makers because certain scopes are available only to the decision makers and not to the ordinary citizens. The ordinary citizens get the opportunity to participate politically to a limited extent; but the leaders do something more apart from performing all those political activities which are performed by the ordinary citizens. Even when there is no election the leaders are actively involved in the political process of the country. The leaders take different decisions as the representatives of the people. Therefore, it is more fruitful to know the participation of leaders as decision makers. As the study is concerned with the participation of the women decision makers it is worthwhile to enquire into the nature of their association in the decision making system. With this purpose in mind several questions have been asked to the women leaders and their responses are presented in the following tables.

(i) Attending the local body meetings

The first question has been on the attendance of the women leaders in the local body meetings. It is to know whether the leaders attend the local body meetings or not.

Table 16: Distribution of Women Leaders by their attendance in Local Body Meetings

S. No.	*Responses*	*No. of Leaders*	*Percentage*
1	YES	12	100
2	NO	-	-
3	TOTAL	12	100

As the responses of the women leaders show all the leaders attend the meetings of the local body. This shows their interest in public affairs and their eagerness to do their duty as leaders.

At the same time, it is necessary to know the number of meetings the leaders have attended. So, the second question in this regard is to find out the number of meetings the leaders have attended.

Table 17: Distribution of Women Leaders by their Attendance in Number of Meetings of the Local Body

S. No.	*Responses*	*No. of Leaders*	*Percentage*
1	ALL	08	66.67
2	SOME	04	33.33
3	NONE	-	-
4 .	TOTAL	12	100

As the table shows 66.67 per cent leaders have attended all meetings and 33.33 per cent leaders have attended some meetings. It is clear that two-third leaders have attended all meetings of the local body.

(ii) Raising the local problems in local body meetings

Attending the meetings only does not serve the real purpose of representation. A representative has to raise the problems of the area he or she represents and try to get the cooperation of others to solve those problems. As the local bodies are the best forums at the grassroots level for such a purpose the women leaders have to raise the issues of their localities in the local bodies. To know whether the women leaders have been performing their responsibility properly in this regard a question has been asked to them. The question is, "Have you ever raised the problems of your area in the local body meetings?" The responses of the leaders are given in Table 18.

Table 18: Distribution of leaders by their act of raising the problems of the local areas in the local body meetings

S. No.	*Responses*	*No. of Leaders*	*Percentage*
1	YES	09	75.00
2	NO	03	25.00
3	TOTAL	12	100

As it is seen from the above table 75 per cent leaders have raised the problems of their areas whereas 25 per cent have not done so. It is clear that there are still some women leaders who do not perform their duty as representatives of the people properly.

Another related question asked to the women leaders is to know how many times the women leaders have raised the problems of the people in the local body meetings. Their answers are given in Table 19.

Table 19: Distribution of Leaders by their act of raising local issues the number of times in the local bodies

S. No.	*No. of Times*	*No. of Leaders*	*Percentage*
1	1-5	01	11.11
2	6-10	04	44.44
3	11-15	01	11.11
4	16-20	01	11.11
5	More than 20	02	22.22
6	TOTAL	09	99.99

As the table shows, more number of leaders has raised the problems of the people for 6 to 10 times, but their number is less than fifty per cent of the total respondents who say that they raise the problems of the people in the local body meetings. Only 22.22 per cent of these leaders raise the problems for more than 20 times. There are some leaders, 11.11 per cent of them, who raise the problems for less than 5 times in the local body meetings.

(iii) Protesting when ignored

Another question asked to the leaders is to know whether they protest if their opinion is not given due importance i.e. whether they raise their voice if they are ignored. The responses of the leaders have been tabulated in the following table, Table 20.

Table 20: Distribution of Women Leaders by their Protest when their Opinion is Ignored

S. No.	*Responses*	*No. of Leaders*	*Percentage*
1	YES	05	55.55
2	NO	04	44.44
3	TOTAL	09	99.99

It is clear from Table 20 that 55.55 per cent women leaders protest whereas 44.44 per cent do not if their opinion is ignored.

(iv) Meeting Government officers

One of the functions the leaders perform as representatives of the people is to keep contact with the government officers to make the latter aware of the problems of the people. They have to communicate with the officers for ventilating the grievances of the people and therefore, the leaders have to meet the officers concerned for doing so. So the women leaders have been asked to state whether they meet the government officers to solve the problems of the people. Their responses have been collected and given in the following table, i.e. Table 21.

Table 21: Distribution of the Leaders by their Meeting with Government Officers to solve the Problems of People

S. No.	*Responses*	*No. of Leaders*	*Percentage*
1	YES	07	58.33
2	NO	05	41.67
3	TOTAL	12	100

Out of the total respondents 58.33 per cent leaders meet the government officers while 41.67 per cent leaders do not meet them. It is clear that a substantial section of the leaders do not try to solve the problems of the people through meeting the officers concerned.

(v) Complaining against Government officers when they do not act

Sometimes the officers ignore the suggestions of public representatives. In that case the representatives should protest against such acts of the officers. To know whether the women leaders protest against such actions of the officers a question has been added to the questionnaire. The answers of the women leaders to this question are given in Table 22.

Table 22: Distribution of Leaders by their Complain when Local Officers do not act

S. No.	*Responses*	*No. of Leaders*	*Percentage*
1	YES	04	57.14
2	NO	03	42.86
3	TOTAL	07	100

As Table 22 shows, 57.14 per cent leaders protest and 42.86 per cent leaders do not protest if the government officers ignore their suggestions.

(vi) Meeting higher political leaders

As the positional women leaders are political leaders of their areas it is natural for them to have contacts with other higher political leaders. With their political connections they might be able to solve the problems of their electorates. So to know the link of the women leaders with higher political leaders a question is asked to them and their responses are given in Table 23.

Table 23: Distribution of Women Leaders by their Contacts with Higher Political Leaders

S. No.	*Responses*	*No. of Leaders*	*Percentage*
1	YES	08	66.67
2	NO	04	33.33
3	TOTAL	12	100

As the table shows 66.67 per cent leaders have such connections and 33.33 per cent do not have links with higher level leaders.

Related to the above question another question has been asked to the women leaders who do have such links; they have been asked whether they raise the problems of the people before the higher political leaders and the replies of the women leaders are tabulated in Table 24.

Table 24: Distribution of Women Leaders by their Communicating Problems of the areas to the Higher Leaders

S. No.	*Responses*	*No. of Leaders*	*Percentage*
1	YES	08	100
2	NO	-	-
3	TOTAL	08	100

As the above table shows all the women leaders, who have links with the higher political leaders, tell the problems of their areas to the higher leaders.

When the leaders' opinions are ignored generally they complain against such disregard. Therefore, such a question has been included in the questionnaire. They have been asked if they complain to the higher leaders if their opinion is ignored either in the local body or by the officers concerned. The answers of the women leaders are given in Table 25.

Table 25: Distribution of Leaders by their Complain to Higher Leaders when their Opinion is Ignored

S. No.	*Responses*	*No. of Leaders*	*Percentage*
1	YES	08	100
2	NO	-	-
3	TOTAL	08	100

As Table 25 shows all the women leaders having links with higher leaders make complaints in such situations.

At the same time a question is asked to the women leaders to know whether they lead the people to meet the higher political leaders to pressurize the latter for some favorable decision. The replies of the respondents are given in Table 26.

Table 26: Distribution of Women Leaders by their Leading the People to Meet the Higher Leaders

S. No.	*Responses*	*No. of Leaders*	*Percentage*
1	YES	05	62.50
2	NO	03	37.50
3	TOTAL	08	100

Out of the total leaders who have links with the higher leaders 62.50 per cent also lead people to meet the higher leaders whereas 37.50 do not.

(vii) Talking to media

Another way of ventilating the problems of the people is talking to the media and making others aware of the problems of a locality. A question is asked to the women leaders to know this fact. The replies of the women leaders have been tabulated in Table 27.

Table 27: Distribution of Leaders by their Talking to Media

S. No.	*Responses*	*No. of Leaders*	*Percentage*
1	YES	07	58.33
2	NO	05	41.67
3	TOTAL	12	100

It is clear from the Table that 58.33 per cent talk to the media whereas 41.67 do not talk.

(viii) Willingness for future involvement in politics

One normally wants to continue one's present role in future if one is satisfied with it. If there is professional satisfaction one is likely to be engaged in that activity in future. So to know the job satisfaction of the women leaders a question has been asked to them if they would continue their involvement in politics in future. The replies of the leaders are presented in Table 28.

Table 28: Distribution of leaders by their desire to continue their further involvement in the political process

S. No.	*Responses*	*No. of Leaders*	*Percentage*
1	YES	10	83.33
2	NO	02	16.67
3	TOTAL	12	100

As the above table shows most of the women leaders say that they want to continue their involvement. Out of the total leaders 83.33 per cent want to continue their association in politics while 16.67 refuse to continue. This shows most of them are satisfied with their present assignment.

Conclusions

It can be seen from the analysis of the above tables that the women leaders are, in general, active in the political process of the country. Most of them are regular voters in the elections and also encourage others to vote in the elections. However, the women leaders are more active in the elections to the local bodies than either the Parliamentary elections or the Assembly elections. The women leaders are active even when there is no election to be held. Most of them take part in discussion, propagation and also in organizing meetings. Most of them keep regular contact with their electorates. While acting as decision makers most of them are effectively performing their duties and not only attending meetings of the local body but also raising the various issues of their localities in them. Many of them even meet the higher leaders and government officers to solve the problems of the people and protest when their opinion is not given due importance. One heartening fact is that most of the women leaders have shown their willingness to continue their involvement in the political process of the country. One does not want to continue one's involvement in some activity unless one is willingly associated with that activity. This proves the fact that women can be willing participants and active agents in the democratic process, if given an opportunity. If the women are given a scope they can prove to be effective leaders of the country.

References

1. Verba, Sidney; Nie, Norman H., *Participation in America*, The University of Chicago Press, Chicago, 1972, p. 1.
2. Goel, M. Lal and Smith, David Horton, "Political Activities" in Smith, David Horton; Macaulay, Jacqueline and Associates, *Participation in Social and Political Activities*, Jossey-Bass Publishers, San Francisco, 1980, p. 76.
3. Verba, Sidney; Nie, Norman H., *Participation in America*, The University of Chicago Press, Chicago, 1972, p. 2.
4. Conway, M. Margaret, *Political Participation in the United States*, Congressional Quarterly, Washington, 1985, p. 2.
5. Riker, William H.; Ordeshook, Peter C., *An Introduction to Positive Political Theory*, Prentice-Hall Inc., New Jersey, 1973, p. 45.
6. Ibid., p. 76.
7. Election Commission of India.
8. *Ibid.*
9. *Ibid.*
10. Mishra, Rashmi, "Devolution of power to women in PanchayatiRaj in Orissa: Challenges and Opportunities", *Kurukshetra*, November 1998, p. 21.
11. Ibid, p. 22.
12. Section 6, *The Orissa Zilla Parishad Act, 1991.*
13. Section 8, Subsection(1) *The Orissa Zilla Parishad Act 1991.*
14. Section 8 Subsection(2) *The Orissa Zilla Parishad Act 1991.*
15. *Districts at a Glance*, 2006, Directorate of Economics and Statistics, Orissa, Bhubaneswar.
16. Ibid.
17. *Information on General Election to Panchayatiraj Institutions in Orissa, 2002*, State Election Commission, Bhubaneswar.
18. District Election Office, Sundargarh.
19. District Election Office, Sundargarh.
20. District Election Office, Sundargarh.

18

The Problems of Working Women in India

Ashu Pasricha

The shifting of the work setting from home, to the factory after the industrial revolution has changed the concept of work drastically. Earlier the whole family worked as one production unit and all the family members were engaged in a craft which was socially ranked and integrated with the social structure. Thus the basis for identification was family occupation and not individual position in the skill hierarchy of the organization. The removal of work setting from home has an adverse- affect on the position of women. Firstly, 'work' has come to be identified as something which is pursued outside the home. Secondly, work has gained an identity specific to the economic system. The work of women at home which produces only use value and which is not remunerated in tangible terms and tied to the day-to-day household chores has come to be regarded as non-work and participation of women is grossly under reported, more so in underdeveloped countries with dual economies than in advanced Western countries.[1]

Along with the emergence of an organizational culture there is also a change in the occupational hierarchy with some occupations attaining an identity of 'professions' or 'elite occupations'. Even the process of professionalization, like the process of industrialization is not in favour of women. Professionalization is basically a process of increased control and power. In the process, women, who are less powerful in the over all social organization, are relegated to the positions which are devoid of power and control, if not through deliberate discrimination at least by the existential exigencies of working women.

Let us very briefly consider the elements of a profession. Professions are occupations based on systematic pursuit of knowledge and skills. Unlike the other occupations, those are distinguishable by their control over the production, distribution and consumption of service provided by them. The exclusiveness of a profession is maintained by stringent admission procedures, a long and highly specialised socialization process and permitting low interference and control by autonomy or self-regulation and monopoly over the market. These are achieved through political manipulation and elite recognition and successfully increasing the social distance between the client and the professional by a process of mystification which has both technological as well as cognitive basis. The members of professional groups are drawn mostly from upper class and dominant ethnic groups and are predominant in the social composition.

There are two points of view from which the relationship between women and professions could be perceived. One is the position of women in full fledged professions, such as medicine, law, academics etc. Another is the position of women in the semi-professions like nursing, teaching, secretarial work etc., and their attempts at professionalization.

Firstly, let us consider the career choices and patterns of women entering the full fledged professions, which are determined to a great extent by their position in the social structure. Silverstone observes that all women use contingency approach in the selection of their career. The contingency approach implies that women choose occupations in which they see the greatest opportunities for flexibility and in which they can respond to any contingency such as marriage, child birth and geographical mobility. To cite an example, practically all over the world medicine and teaching attract more women than the other professions for they provide grater flexibility and are compatible with (a) the image of women as gentle and emotionally responsive and (b) the 'mother' role of women. There are doubts about women's capabilities in professional fields which are derived from the belief that those are opposed to the biological functions of women. A question, which is often asked, is 'Would the women place their commitment to child bearing and rearing to take precedence over the competing demands of the professional life?' The demands of the elder-in-laws as well as the household chores, which are still considered as women's area of responsibility, hamper the uninterrupted pursuit of a career. Silverstone and Ward compare between the career prospects of a man and those of a woman and point out that while for a man a career progresses from education—training—work—retirement, the career of most women follows education—training—work—interruption—retraining—re-employment—retirement. Interruption is accounted for the inevitable period a woman has to spend in child bearing and child rearing as well as the subordination of a woman's career to that of her husband and the consequent geographical mobility. Interruption may sometimes require long periods of retraining. Re-employment may also be difficult in the face of competition from a fresh and younger batch of professionals. For those women who are involved in highly specialized areas such as microwaves in electronics and surgery in medicine mobility is limited, as it is difficult to find suitable employers everywhere and self employment is expensive in most cases. A compromise between the roles means sacrificing one in-toto which is wastage of the investment made in the training process.[2]

There are two facets of the strategy to meet the basic needs of the women in developing countries. One is to enable them to contribute more effectively to the satisfaction of their families' basic needs, within the framework of their traditional responsibilities. The other, which is a fundamental need of the women themselves, is to ease their work burden while furthering their economic independence and their more equitable integration into the community, beyond the narrow circle of the family.

Especially in the rural areas, most women in developing countries are overworked rather than underemployed, and a more appropriate technology for the tasks they perform implies labour saving, in order to improve the quality of their employment, rather than employment creation.[3]

Demographers are interested in work or more narrowly, in labour force participation because it interacts with so many demographic variables. For both males and females there are strong causal links between both occupations and work status with marriage, fertility, migration and mortality. In order to understand the nature of these causal relationships it is necessary to have reliable data on the working behaviour of individuals. There is also the practical factor that demographers work with censuses and almost all censuses, except a few, collect data on the economic characteristics of the population.

From the point of view of women and development, one of the biggest barriers preventing women from having adequate recognition and opportunities to participate in development is the acceptance of the myth that women do not work. Thus in Indonesia a Government statement explains that Indonesia faces a heavy dependency burden because it is only the men who work (50 per cent) and if the aged (10 per cent) and children (15 per cent) are subtracted this leaves only 25 per cent of the population to participate in development and to work to support the rest. This perception of women 'not working' is reflected in the Indonesian Government's Family Welfare Education Programme which teaches rural women that they have five major duties as:

(i) Producers of the nation's future generation,
(ii) Wives and faithful companions to their husbands,
(iii) Mothers and educators of their children,
(iv) Managers of the household,
(v) Citizens.[4]

Thus, through lack of understanding of the roles which women actually play, rural women are presented with an inappropriate middle class and urban model to copy. Usually women who serve the state by playing vital but humble roles in agriculture or factory production become heroines and models to be copied only in centrally planned economies such as Russia and China. In Indonesia, the 1971 Census actually showed that formally defined participation rates varied from 20 per cent in the province where women are least visible to 48 percent where they are most active.[5]

The relationship of women to the economy is a special problem area in women's studies. Why do we need to study women's role in the economy separately?

First, because a good deal of women's work remains invisible. Its exact nature, scope, intensity are either not measured at all or partially and erratically measured. Secondly, the valuation of women's work is subject to influences and forces which are different from those of men. Simple laws of supply and demand are not uniformly applicable. Women workers form a special category. The kind of work they do, where, how and under what terms – all these are determined by women's position in society. They have special responsibilities, not shared by others; they face various kinds of cultural taboos and their child-bearing functions place them in a different position. Thirdly, one needs an explanation as to why women's position is a subordinate one. Lastly, changes in society affect men and women differently. As a category of workers, they, therefore, need special focus, attention and analysis because the problems and issues that face them are different.[6]

In colonial India, imperial interests dictated economic policy and their impact in a gender-asymmetric society descended with extra severity on women. In post-independent India, development models adopted and the interests they served within a profit-oriented framework influenced policy options in many directions. The impacts of these on the masses, particularly women, have not been for their benefit. In what precise ways these various forces affected women is described in the following pages.

To gain knowledge of the present, one has to look at the past; but as data or references are practically non-existent, we can only begin with a recent past for which some records are available. These records of the colonial period are subject to many biases and inaccuracies, but when even our present day sophisticated information systems are not free from such shortcomings, there is no harm in using them to get a broad picture. The colonial period is particularly relevant because it was during this time that cataclysmic changes rocked our social, economic and political structure. The exercise at reconstructing women's economic history must be of the nature of informed (and broad) guesses. Later, we use contemporary data to get a profile of the female work force.

Firstly, the most disastrous and ridiculous distortion is the use of the words working women and non-working women in current usage. It is as inappropriate as the terms vegetarians to distinguish between meat eaters and non-meat eaters, because every one eats vegetarian products with or without meat. Men and women both work. The difference lies in the kind of work they do; where it is done, how it is done, for what kind of rewards and so on. If by 'work' we imply broadly 'economic activity', then women have always worked. It cannot but be otherwise. The material requirements for survival demand everyone's cooperation. According to anthropologists, women were the major producers of food, clothing, crafts, and many different tools through most of the human history.[7] In fact, this continues to be so in all those societies of the world where production is mainly for subsistence and not for sale.

In India too, growing food, processing it, spinning and weaving, basket making, clay modeling, extraction of 'soma' juice, preparing perfumes and many other materials for consumption were women's contribution.[8] References to women's economic activities are extremely sparse in Indian history and even for the middle age where much historical research by eminent historians like Irfan Habib or Bipin Chandra have helped to build a composite picture of the economic structure of India. Before British inroads into India, women's roles find no mention and whatever information can be gathered has to be done by inference. Our first records begin with the British. These were traveler's accounts, various administrative documents and finally the Census. In the Census records we get for the first time some rough quantitative estimates that tell us something of the range and degree of the economic involvement of women. These documents are not accurate but they happen to be our only source. The patterns and trends in women's economic activities that became noticeable from the late nineteenth century till the beginning, of the twentieth century excited the attention of scholars like D.R. Gadgil and subsequently others.[9] This interest is, therefore, recent.

Throughout the last hundred years, two very prominent features stand out with regard to women's economic activities: (i) continuous and impressive decline in the number of women reported in the work force; (ii) major shifts in their occupational distribution. These two changes can be attributed to major convulsions induced by colonialism and the development of capitalism but what is significant is the differential impact it had on men and women.[10] This emphasised the different connection that women have with the economy. We need to study the forces that determine the degree of involvement that women have in different economic activities and under what conditions these are altered or become alterable. Research has hardly begun in this area, and hence we have no definitive answers to the many riddles that have surfaced. Nonetheless, we cannot abandon our concern with these issues arising out of a value commitment that women's subordinate position in the economy needs rectifying to enable them to get an equal and fair opportunity for human development. We, therefore, attempt to examine women's position and connection to the economy from this normative stand-point, and not step short at merely describing where they are.

The greatest difficulty in understanding the working women and their problems has been caused by taking them as a homogenous group, while in reality they constitute a heterogeneous group, comprising distinct as well as different categories of women workers. As such, they and their problems cannot be discussed in one stride.

Apart from the fact that due to the processes of technological changes and of the changed economy, the illiterate, unskilled or semi-skilled women labour have been affected adversely as their demand has been greatly reduced, the major problems that they face are that of discrimination, of being under debt and of exploitation.[11] The National Committee on the Status of Women in its report points out that due to these women workers' disabilities, like their being illiterate and lacking skill and training and due to their circumstances which force them to work, the women workers of the unorganised sectors, which forms the large majority of these workers and to a lesser degree even of the organised sector, suffer from poor wages, discrimination, unexplained fines and deductions in pay, insecurity of job and lack of housing, sanitary and welfare facilities.[12] The women workers of the unorganised sector are exploited much more mainly because this sector is not governed and regulated by the Rules and the Laws that are meant to protect the security and working conditions of labour, and provide them with welfare amenities.

The women working in the organised sector also suffer from lack of welfare facilities and are exploited in spite of the enactment of many statutory rules and regulations because these laws are directly or indirectly evaded owing to the workers' ignorance and absence of effective implementing machinery.

Now let us examine the situation of the educated working women. This rather new social group has emerged gradually right from the phase, when it was considered derogatory for a girl and more so for married women of middle and upper class families, to take up paid jobs or professions, to a middle phase when she was permitted to work only under gross economic necessity but in 'respectable' jobs of a teacher and later that of a doctor, to the present stage when in increasing number both unmarried and married women are working in almost all kinds of jobs and professions. Women are now found to be employed even in the jobs which were largely the preserves of men, not only to meet the economic need but also for the satisfaction of their various socio-psychological needs and desires. For example, women work because they would like to have an independent income and individual status of their own, to have opportunities and freedom to mix with people, to fulfill their intellectual needs and sense of achievement, to be engaged in some creative works, to gain recognition and fame, to utilize their education and spare time, or to satisfy the urge to be away from the unhappy atmosphere of home, to overcome frustration in premarital or marital life and so on. They are found to be working also out of love or charm of the profession and also because they are no more contended with carrying out merely the traditional roles of a wife and mother and feel that they must contribute more effectively to the society.

Yet, in spite of all the socio-economic-political changes, including the ones in the attitudes that India has witnessed particularly after Independence and despite the findings of the various studies and experiences that women are no less intelligent and capable workers than men, the number of educated women getting into employment and economic activities is comparatively very small. A large majority of even the employed ones still continue to be at the lower or middle levels. As compared to men, there are still very fewer women found in technical and professional jobs and in top-salaried occupations, more so in top-positions; only a limited number of women are found in top positions compared to the number of women qualified for those posts.

Why is it so? What are the problems that the women face and the obstacles that come in their way of getting into employment and of reaching the higher levels of various occupations and professions? After repeatedly interviewing hundreds of educated working women and after going through other studies, observations and reports brought out by the National Committee and by various scholars, specially during the International Women's Year seminars and conferences, it can be concluded that the problems of working women are multiple and interdependent which vary considerably with the type of jobs they are holding, their marital status, status of family and the atmosphere at home and at work.

However, for purposes of analysis, the problems of working women could be divided mainly into two categories. One may be grouped as the socio-psychological problems and the other as practical problems. These problems are faced both at home and at work place.

Let us first examine briefly the practical problems. While the single women living on their own face the difficulties mainly of inadequate, insecure and inconvenient living accommodation and of proper eating arrangements, the married ones experience many added problems. These additional problems of the married women are created mainly due to the absence of labour minimizing gadgets and declining advantages of having an integrated Joint family and helpful family members to look after the house and children, the increasing scarcity of reliable and trustworthy servants and the unhelpful husbands in carrying out household jobs.

Some of the other problems that the single working women face out-side home are owing to the absence of convenient, cheap and safe transport, lack of centers for vocational, technical and occupational guidance, education and training, lack of opportunities for self-employment, late entry into jobs and lack of facilities for various kinds of pre-marital counseling and assistance. The married working women face the added problems created by the absence of adequate facilities like that of community kitchens or efficiently run cheap canteens, child-care services, part-time jobs, long maternity or parents' leave without its being considered as a break in service, refresher courses and facilities for re-entry into the jobs after a few years gap needed for bearing and rearing of the children. Their problems are intensified by the absence of an effective implementing machinery to see that the workers really get benefits of the legal provisions and welfare schemes.

When we consider the socio-psychological problems the first problem is with regard to marriage and home. There is an emerging trend among the women of middle and upper classes to take up a gainful employment outside their home. This has given rise to certain fears and speculations among the people having a traditional mindset. For example, the practice of working outside one's home goes against the popularly held belief that women should not venture beyond the four walls of their houses. There are popularly endorsed views that educated girls would not want to marry or would reject marriage if they take up jobs or career and that married women's employment would have adverse effects on her marital and family relationships and on her children.

But quite contrary to this, my intensive studies reveal that marriage is very much in vogue among the educated working women and there is hardly any working woman who would not like to marry just because of her job or career. The working women rather prefer to combine the two. More than anything else, the most significant fact that the studies reveal is that a wife's employment in itself does not affect her marital relationship adversely. Even a mother's employment as such has not been found to be having an adverse influence on the mental, emotional and physical development of her children. Yet, these speculations and prejudices do create hindrances for the educated women and do come in the way of their taking up and continuing their job or profession.

However, since the married women have to combine their two major roles they are found to be facing some additional socio-psychological problems which come in their way of achieving success and high positions in occupations and professions. One of these problems is the problem of role conflict which is the consequence of the conflict between the perception of the working women's own roles and the perception of their families and society of a woman's role as the home-maker and a mother. The attitudes towards the traditional role-structure in the family have not undergone much change in spite of the wife's taking up the additional and new role of a wage earner, though her employment helps to improve the life pattern of the working woman as well as her family.

The social norm that the prime role of a woman is that of a wife and mother is still prevalent; it is expected that her career is to be adjusted with her traditional duties at home. But when the women consider their jobs or professions as highly important from their own points of view, intense role-conflict and psychic strain of overload is liable to be felt by the working women because there is a clash between the two full roles and corresponding aspirations of carrying out both the roles very efficiently. This makes the working women torn between their loyalties towards their jobs and those towards their home.

The tension and conflict are also generated by contradictory sex-roles and expectations with regard to the fulfillment of the two roles by the married working women and by the attitudinal lag and the ambivalence in the attitudes of the employed wife, her husband and society towards her being employed. The educated wife likes to be in a job because of the various socio-psycho-economic satisfactions that she derives out of working; yet, she resents it for the stresses and strains it causes. The husband and other members of the family like the wife or daughter-in-law to take up jobs mainly for the different advantages to the family, but at the same time they resent her getting into male dominated prestigious jobs and professions which require her undivided loyalty and attention. This is so as they do not at all like her to neglect her traditional responsibilities towards the house. They also resent her having the opportunity to mix with other men and developing a sense of equality and freedom to take her own decisions with regard to her personal life. The gap between the attitudes of the educated working women and those of their husbands and society towards a woman's role and status creates conflicts in family life. At the same time, the non-acceptance of women as workers and the changed life pattern of the working-wives create multiple socio-psychological problems for the educated working women.

Then there are other significant problems related to women's jobs or professions which come in the way of their progress as working women. The main problems at work are created due to the women's lack of specialized education and training and because of the existence of discrimination and prejudice of men against women, the views of society against women workers and because of sex exploitation. The various studies and the Report of the National Committee point out that in spite of the constitutional guarantee of equal opportunities to men and women for education and employment, in practice subtle, indirect and underhand discrimination is made against women with regard to specialised education and training and more so, in employment at the time of selection, confirmation and particularly, at the time of further promotions for high and prestigious posts even for those women who possess equally high and required qualifications as men have. On analyzing the few surveys carried out to find out the employer's prejudices against employing the educated professional women, it is found that rationally or irrationally the employers, particularly in the private sectors, are reluctant to employ both unmarried and married women and are unwilling to train and promote them to higher and top positions.

The professional and technical women workers suffer from discrimination because of men's negative attitude towards women and the society's prejudice against women as a class and as workers. They continue to believe that women are less efficient and less capable as workers. They distrust the talents and seriousness of women about their career and ability for decision-making. There are still some unfavorable social attitudes of non-acceptance, ridicule, resentment, distrust and of suspicion towards the career women, specially for those who work with men in such jobs and professions which have for long been the preserves of men only. These women have not yet been accepted and even if found successful, they are liable to be labeled as "manly", "selfish and crafty" in case of brilliant but not attractive women and as "immoral" and "getting ahead because of exploiting their sex" in case of the attractive ones.

Another significant problem that the educated working women face is due to the widely prevalent attitude of taking primarily as a sex-object and sex-symbol. An educated working woman feels hurt and frustrated when, even at work, she is viewed as a woman primarily and exclusively and not as a worker or an official or not even as an individual. Being viewed as a woman alone she is also exploited by the male employers, bosses and even colleagues who have to be kept "pleased" if she wants to continue in the job or wants further promotions. Not only this, but on account of the prejudiced attitude of taking women as sex-objects, the women themselves are also found to be liable to deliberately exploit this sex for getting selected, confirmed and promoted in jobs. And this in turn brings moral degeneration in them.

No doubt, it is very essential that many more researches should be carried out about the socio-economic conditions and problems of the working women of various categories. It is also necessary that they are provided in reality with the needed encouragement, support, opportunities and facilities both within and outside home to enable them to combine efficiently and successfully their various roles as home-makers, mothers and socially productive individuals.

References

1. Banaria's article, "Conceptualizing the Labour Force, the Underestimating of Women's Economic Activities" in Jyoti Mitra (ed.) *Women and Society*, New Delhi, Kanishka, 1997, p. 37.
2. *Ibid.*
3. *International Labour Organisation*, ILO, 1978, p. 61.
4. Jyoti Mitra (ed.) *Women and Society*, op. cit., p. 14.
5. *Ibid.*
6. Neera Desai and Maithreyi Krishna Raj, *Women and Society in India*, Delhi, Ajanta Publications, 1987, p. 50.

7. Evelyn Reed, *Women's Evolution*, New York, Pathfinder Press, 1976, p. 203.
8. Padmini Sengupta, *Women in India*, Delhi, Publications Division, Ministry of Information and Broadcasting, Government of India, 1964, p. 42.
9. D. R. Gadgil, *The Industrial Revolution in India in Recent Times*, Bombay, Oxford University Press, 1954.
10. Neera Desai and Maithreyi Krishna Raj, *Women and Society in India*, op. cit.
11. Promila Kapoor, "Working Women in India", in B. K. Vashista (ed.) *Encyclopedia of Women in India*, New Delhi, Praveen Encyclopaedia Publications, 1976, p. 168.
12. *Report of the Committee on the Status of Women in India*, Department of Social Welfare, Ministry of Education and Social Welfare, Government of India, 1974, p. 262.

19

Uniform Civil Code and Gender Justice: A Critical Perspective

Parvathy, A.A.

The implementation of a Uniform Civil Code in India is very intimately connected to the issue of gender justice. But despite its need and importance, the state is not very serious about its implementation. On the other hand, the basic issue of ensuring justice and equality to women is getting enmeshed in many other issues like religion, secularism, and freedom and so on. Today, the BJP has made Uniform Civil Code the part of its election manifesto and thus the issue remains a sensitive one. However, one can not sweep the main issue under the carpet and harp on other connected issues day in and day out. Gender issues need to be addressed very seriously. This paper is an attempt made to link the question of gender justice and equality to the issue of the adoption of Uniform Civil Code.

Constitutional Position of Uniform Civil Code

The need for a Uniform Civil Code is inscribed in Article 44 (Article 35 in the Draft Constitution). This article is included in the Part IV of the Constitution dealing with the Directive

Principles of State Policy. It provides that the State shall endeavour to secure for the citizens a Uniform Civil Code. A new debate has started on the desirability of such a Code. There are some who favour its adoption where as there are others who oppose it very strongly. The Hindutva forces like the BJP and women's groups are vociferously demanding its implementation to bring about national integration and ensure gender justice. However, there are many who oppose it under the pretext that it goes against religious freedom.

It is a known fact that in the personal laws of all the communities gender justice is inbuilt. This is supposed to be the result of the socio-economic conditions under which they have evolved. That is why there is a need to reform the personal laws or bring about a Uniform Civil Code to ensure not only equality between men and women but also bring about gender justice. Women undergo many difficulties and experience sever trauma in matters concerning their marriage, divorce and inheritance. Polygamy, desertion and triple divorce are just a few examples to show the possibilities of harassing women. Indian women have been formally granted equality with regard to enjoyment of political rights by the Indian Constitution. But due to application of different kinds of personal laws women in India experience inequality, deprivation and violence. Within the family their position is pitiable. The question of women's rights as human beings is completely ignored. Elementary human justice and dignity is denied to many of them in India. The personal laws are designed to keep them forever under the control of men. It thus, appears absurd that when all are equal citizens of India, the difference in their personal laws gives different kinds of status to different women.

Indian Constitution as pointed out by Grenville Austin in his book *The Indian Constitution: Cornerstone of a Nation* indicates that it is first and foremost a social document which desires to further its goal of social revolution. According to him, the importance of the Directive Principles can not be overemphasised as they project the ideals which the Constitution aims to achieve. The Directive Principles, in fact, shape the character of freedom exercisable under the Fundamental Rights and hence, closely connected to the issue of citizens' enjoyment of rights. Part III and Part IV together constitute the core and conscience of the Constitution. The Supreme Court in the *Minerva Mills Case* declared so. Part III and Part IV are like the two wheels of a chariot. If you remove one, the other will loose value.

Debate in the Constituent Assembly

In the Constituent Assembly there was sufficient discussion regarding the inclusion of the article dealing with the Uniform Civil Code in the Chapter on Directive Principles.

The Constituent Assembly was a male dominated body with only 15 women members out of the total 296 members. However, women like Rajkumari Amrit Kaur and Hansa Mehta were placed in the important committees and in the sub-committee on Fundamental Rights. The debates in the Constituent Assembly reveal the eagerness of the members to grant women political equality but when it came to the institution of marriage and family, there was a reluctance to grant even a semblance of equality. The main reason pointed out by the members relate to the right being in conflict with the freedom of religion. "There was total reluctance to offend religious sensibilities."[1]

Amrit Kaur and Hansa Mehta anticipated this conflict between freedom of religion and women's rights. They feared that the inclusion of words like "propagation" and "practice" might prevent legislation against child marriage, polygamy, and inheritance laws and so on under the pretext of being considered part of religious practice. That is why they wanted religious freedom to be confined to religious worship.[2]

Many members pointed out that even the British did not interfere in the religious practice. But K.M. Munshi said that even though the British did not interfere, there are certain matters which are fit for secular legislation. Dr. Ambedkar also pointed out "the only province the civil law has not been able to invade so far is marriage and succession. It is this little corner which we have not been able to invade so far and it is the intention of those who desire to have Article 35 as part of the Constitution to bring about that change."[3] Dr. Ambedkar further quoted the example of Common Codes prevalent in other countries having minorities and pointed out that it is purely voluntary. He said that the article in which the State shall endeavour to secure the code implied that it would be implemented if it is acceptable to all and hence purely voluntary. One more issue raised in the Constituent Assembly was regarding the feasibility of the inclusion of Uniform Civil Code in the Directive Principles of State Policy. M.R. Masani, Hansa Mehta and Amrit Kaur pressed for a guarantee to enact this code within a period of 5 to 10 years.[4] But the suggestion was not accepted.

A number of fears and objections were expressed by many members regarding the inclusion of this clause on Uniform Civil Code. Minorities opposed it very strongly. However, K.M. Munshi was in favour of adopting the Uniform Civil Code to bring about the equality of sexes.[5]

The above discussion and also many more details of the discussion on rights clearly indicate that the rights were discussed only in terms of religious identities of minority communities. The question of inequality and injustice prevalent in these personal codes was never taken up for debate. The conflict between the freedom of religion and Uniform Civil Code was discussed but not the conflict between right to equality and personal laws. This indicates the insignificant and casual attitude shown regarding women's rights. It was hoped that the step necessary for rectifying whatever injustice was prevalent in these personal codes was to be taken up as a social reform by the governments in future.

It is under these circumstances that the personal laws based on the principle of inequality have been retained. Subordination of women to male members of family has been inbuilt into it. Even though the Constitution of India gives equality to women in certain areas – legal and social, they are not effective to ensure real equality. Women's labour at home is not recognised as productive labour. Naturally, an equal right over matrimonial property is denied to women. Whatever consideration is shown to women through the Constitution is based on the assumption of treating women as weaker sections which indicates lack of seriousness regarding women's rights. As Sadhna Arya points out, "Thus, if the Constitution treats gender inequality as not a problem needing special attention and care, nor feels the need to create a culture, through its laws and legal ideology—wherein the values of social inequality are accepted in everyday life, it only means that the Constitution quietly and tacitly supports a male dominated society."[6]

All the facts mentioned above, indicate that there is the negation of the principle of justice and equality as enshrined in the Preamble and Articles 14 and 15 of the Constitution for women.

In the Constituent Assembly the discussion on the Uniform Civil Code centred around three aspects. First and foremost it centred on the conflict between freedom of religion and the effort to improve the status of women. Secondly, there was discussion as to the nature of Uniform Civil Code as a Directive Principle trying to take away the identity of minorities. Thirdly, an attempt was made to connect it to the secularisation of law. Five Muslims spoke during the discussion and all the five opposed the article and preferred to maintain the personal law. However, there were wide differences amongst members on the issue of personal laws. The discussion held on the Uniform Civil Code resulted in the following decisions:

1. Demand to protect religious freedom especially for minority interests were respected,
2. To have a Uniform Civil Code for all, based on homogenized citizenship,
3. But since they were unable to arrive at any agreement, Uniform Civil Code was seen as a goal to be implemented and included in the Directive Principles of State Policy.
4. Personal laws were maintained.

Judicial Activism

The Supreme Court in a few judgements has opined that legislation for a common civil code as envisaged by Article 44 of India's Constitution should be enacted. It said so in *Shah Bano's Case* in 1985, in *Sarla Mudgal Case* in 1995 and in *Vallamattam Case* in 2003.

Judicial decisions are important to understand the nature of the Uniform Civil Code and its essence. In the *State of Bombay vs. Narasu Appa Mali*[7] it was considered that personal laws do not fall within the purview of laws in force and therefore, are not void even if they conflict with Fundamental Rights.

However, in 1985, the *Shah Bano* judgement[8] made the Court to think seriously about the Uniform Civil Code and give direction to the State for its implementation. The *Shah Bano Case* concerns an old Muslim woman (65 years old) who went to the Court against the way her husband had divorced her unilaterally. In 1978, she filed a petition demanding alimony from her husband who had abandoned her after 40 years of marriage to marry another woman. As per Muslim law, Shah Bano was entitled to three months maintenance. The Supreme Court, which heard the matter many years later, upheld her right to maintenance. It ruled that Section 125 of the Criminal Procedure Code overrides Muslim Personal Law (*Shariat*) in matters of divorce. The Court meanwhile also referred to the need to enact a Uniform Civil Code to promote social justice.

After this judgement there was widespread protest by the community which made Rajiv Gandhi, the then Prime Minister of India, to enact the *Muslim Women's Protection Bill*. This abrogated the right of the Muslim woman divorcee, the maintenance under Section 125 of the Criminal Procedure Code. This section was considered as interference in their Personal law. The Government had made this Act for the fear of losing the Muslim vote bank. Shah Bano's Case created a furore throughout the length and breadth of India. The position of Muslim woman was exposed. Sympathy for such women poured in from every part of the nation. A sense of indignation was raised against such men who dared to throw out a helpless wife to the streets without providing any kind of maintenance. This indignation is aptly expressed as follows, "It is not a question of maintenance but protection against destitution and vagrancy. This is secular, legal situation. If she has to be saved from begging why can't her husband pay? What personal law is involved? Each personal law, therefore, need to be critiqued from the perspective of social and gender justice. It will mean the modernisation and humanisation of each personal law."[9]

Ever since the *Shah Bano Case*, there is the communalisation of Uniform Civil Code debate. Here, the demand for a woman's right to survive has come into direct conflict with the identity of the minority community. So, the voice of that woman has been suppressed. It also indicates that when the State has to make a choice between personal law and women's rights it has preferred the former to the latter. This has happened even in the Christian personal law.[10]

After Shah Bano's case a sustained and systematic propaganda has been started for deletion of Article 44 along with an amendment of Criminal Procedure Code section 125.

In the 1995 case of Saria Mudgal[11] a Hindu had converted himself to Islam in order to marry a second wife while the first one was living. Once again, the Supreme Court was provoked to ask the Government to implement the Uniform Civil Code. In this case, one of the judges, Justice Kuldip Singh said that Uniform Civil Code would strengthen national integration. In the recent judgement, i.e. July 2003 (John Valla Mathom and Avr. Vs. Union of India)[12] Chief Justice V.N.Khare expressed his regret that Article 44 of the Constitution has not been implemented. Once again the issue of national integration was cited.

All the above judgement should not make us think that the Supreme Court is very much concerned about gender justice. The Supreme Court has not been consistently upholding the principle of gender justice and equality. There are contradictions. For instance, the Court delayed taking up cases questioning the Muslim Women's Protection Bill. Certain statutory enactments regarding personal laws have been kept out of the purview of Article 13.

Legislative Enactments

In 1944 itself the Government appointed a Hindu Law Committee under the Chairmanship of B.N.Rao, the purpose of which was to formulate a code of Hindu Law. According to Derret, the Hindu code is a step in the direction of a Uniform Civil Code.[13] D.E.Smith also felt the same. However, many felt that instead of Hindu Code Bill, Uniform Civil Code should have been adopted. But Nehru was against its adoption. He is reported to have said as follows "If he or anybody else brings a Civil Code Bill, it will have my extreme sympathy. But I confess I do not think that at the present moment, the time is ripe in India to try to push it through. I want to prepare the ground for it and this kind of thing is one method of preparing the ground."[14]

But even in 1947 i.e. prior to the partition of India and also in 1951, the Hindu Code Bill was placed but dropped due to opposition. In 1955 and 1956 the Code was passed in the form of four separate bills – 1.Hindu Marriage Bill, 2.Hindu Succession Bill, 3.Hindu Minority and Guardianship Bill and 4.Hindu Adoptions and Maintenance Bill.

Many members opposed the Hindu Code Bill. The arguments varied widely. Some of them argued that the Bill was opposed to Manu's Code which they equated as God's will. For many Hindus, marriage was a sacrament which should not be interfered. Some other members pointed out that Hindu Law has emerged from the Vedas which should not be altered.

Arguments opposing the Bill pointed out the different obligations of men and women. They also argued that the Bill was against the Hindu Law which would cause disruption in the family. Some men even argued that the women themselves did not want these changes. Hence, with great difficulty, the Bill was passed. Some of the arguments raised during this debate indicated the fact that it is extremely difficult to carry on reforms pertaining to personal laws.

It shows that the Hindu women were also not able to gain equality due to the Hindu orthodox opinion and secondly due to the strong religious and communitarian identity of Hindus as a whole. However, the reforms which were made in the Hindu personal law improved the position of women with regard to divorce and inheritance but did not bring about total equality. The reason was that the objective of reform was to codify Hindu Law. Women's interests were subordinated to the political interests of the state as well as to the interests of men in the family and society.

It is a fact that basic rights of women may be obtained if she is granted equal property rights, custody and guardianship rights etc. This would empower and prevent violence against women. But through the personal laws subordination of women to men is obtained. "The society, family and religion put a number of restrictions on women in the name of 'honour' and with a view to keep women dependent on men and family."[15]

For instance, even in spite of the Hindu Code Bill, the inheritance rights of women according to Hindu personal law shows that equal rights are not given to women on the ground that it would disturb family peace, lead to fight between brothers and sisters, result in fragmentation of land and so on. So a patriarchal order of family is promoted. When a woman is denied the ownership, inheritance and matrimonial rights, it indicates male dominance and non-recognition of women's labour at home. Custody and adoption laws also enforce the notion of father as the natural guardian. A married Hindu woman is not allowed to adopt a child in her own name. Thus, there is a legitimisation of male dominance in a family system. Similarly, the Hindu Succession Law protects the son's rights by keeping the provision of making a will.

General Perspective

A critical look at the Constitutional debate, legislative enactments and judicial decisions very clearly indicate the lack of seriousness in ensuring justice to women. Therefore, it is absolutely necessary that the State should undertake the responsibility of bringing about the Uniform Civil Code in order to reform the society. The State should not take shelter under the pretext that it is hurting the religious sentiments of a particular community. When *Sati* was abolished it hurt religious sentiments. When dowry was abolished it hurt religious sentiments. Such lame excuses should be given up. Law should be used as an instrument of social change. This social change should ensure gender justice and equality. So, a Common Civil Code which gives justice to all communities may be enacted.

Everyone points out that the enactment of Uniform Civil Code should be gradually done and the desire should emerge from the communities themselves. This is very difficult to achieve. Each community is guided by leaders who may not come forward to reform their personal law as they fear the loss of their leadership within the community when the problems are solved or when the community marches ahead. It is, moreover, considered impossible to achieve uniformity in diversity. Thus, there are many hurdles in its implementation.

But a single or uniform civil law can strengthen the unity of the nation and forge the country ahead. The country will be known by the people for their acceptance of progressive laws with inbuilt equality between different communities and also between men and women. However as things go on it is like a mirage for women. A decision on Article 44 should be the concern of the entire nation in general and of women in particular. In case it is implemented it will lay the foundation for women to overcome many social evils like dowry system, bigamy etc. which make a woman feel degraded.

References

1. *Constituent Assembly Debates,* Vol. VII, 1948-49, pp. 511-515, 540-552.
2. B. Shiva Rao (ed.), *The Framing of Indian Constitution,*Vol. II, IIPA, New Delhi, pp. 264-298.
3. *CA Debates,* Vol. VII, 1948-49, pp. 550-51.
4. B. Shiva Rao, op.cit., p. 162.
5. *CA Debates,* Vol. VII, 1948-4, pp. 550-551.
6. Sadhna Arya, *Women, Gender, Equality and the State,* Deep and Deep Publication, New Delhi, 2000, p. 6.
7. State of Bombay vs. Narasu Appa Mali, AIR, 1952, Bombay, 1954.
8. The debate on the Shah Bano Case has been covered in Asghar Ali Engineer (ed.)*The Shah Bano Controversy,* Orient Longman, Bombay, 1987; Zoya Hasan, Minority Identity, Muslim Women Bill Campaign and the Political Process; *EPW,* January 7, 1994, The Shah Bano Affair in Fundamentalism and Gender(OUP, New York, Oxford); Md. Ahmed Khan vs. Shah Bano Begum, 1985, (Sol case No. 85, http://www.supremecourt.online.com)
9. S.P. Sathe, Implications of Supreme Court Intervention, *EPW,* September 2, 1995,p.. 2165.
10. The State showed its inaction regarding the various bills prepared by Christian Women's groups to remove the discrimination aspect of Christian Personal Law.
11. Sarla Mudgal, Smt President, Kalyani and others vs. Union of India, 1995, 3 SCC 635.
12. John Valla Mattom and Avr. S vs. Union of India, 2003 SO.L.Case No.388, http://www.supremecourt.online.com)
13. J.D.M. Derret, *Hindu Law, Past and Present,* A.Mukherjee, Calcutta, 1957, p.v.
14. See P.B. Gajendragadkar, *Secularism and the Constitution of India,* Bombay University Press, 1971, p124.
15. Sadhna, *op.cit.,* p. 258.

20

Women and Politics of Peace Process in North-east India

Dolly Phukon

Conflict situation in the Northeast

The Northeastern region of India consists of eight states, *Arunachal Pradesh, Assam, Meghalaya, Mizoram. Manipur, Nagaland, Tripura and Sikkim*. Because of its location, the region is geo-politically and strategically significant. The Northeast region is rich in its natural resources and is endowed with hydropower potentialities such as oil and natural gas, coal, forest resource etc. But the region has fallen far behind the rest of the country in terms of every yardstick of development. Moreover, the Northeastern region is not a homogenous unit, as it comprises of numerous ethnic groups with distinct identities and with different problems. It is often alleged that the Indian state has never made a sincere attempt to understand the heterogeneity of the northeastern region, but has tried to impose upon the area the homogenous mainstream culture. This imposition has generated resentment among the people of the northeast and has led them to make some radical political demands such as self-determination, complete secession, etc.

Sometimes, these demands have resulted in violence and insurgency in the region.

For so many years there have been many ongoing struggles by people of the different ethnic groups to establish their right to autonomy in most of the seven Northeastern States. For example, Assam has witnessed the anti-foreigners movements, Bodo–adivasi, Karbi-Dimasa and Karbi-Khasi ethnic strifes and the secessionist movement by ULFA (United Liberation Front of Assam) since 1979. Likewise in Manipur, the movement for autonomy took violent turns leading to the application of the draconian acts like Arm Forces Special Power Act. As a consequence, the northeast region is engulfed with political instability, strife and outright violence.

Thus, for the last few decades the North-Eastern Region has witnessed human rights violations due to the ethnic conflicts and militant activities and the resultant response of the state towards these threats. Because of armed conflicts and state sponsored violence the innocent people, especially women, children, elderly persons and the disabled are worst affected. Besides, in the Northeastern societies gender inequalities are deeply inherent and women's condition becomes more vulnerable during these clashes. The continuing armed-conflict in the Northeast has intensified the violence faced by women, which takes the form of sexual, mental or physical abuse and sometimes, killing. Although all the members of communities are affected, the impact on women and girls is far greater because of their status in society and their sex.

At the same time, in a situation where conflict is linked with the question of ethnicity and identity, it leads to more patriarchal control over women. Women are regarded as the custodian of traditional values and culture, which restrict their mobility. One of the most common impacts of armed conflict on women is sexual violence. The bodies of women are regarded as the territory on which each side imprints itself as an assertion of identity, a humiliation of the opposing groups and a means of terrorizing both women and men of the community.

Although women face much causalty because of the armed conflicts, there is lack of literature and media coverage on women's condition and their role during the armed conflicts.

Even when covered, the media projection on women during the armed conflict situation is very stereotyped. While documenting a conflict situation by the media, women are always projected passively often showing them as mourning for their lost children and husbands, looking helpless and worried for their future survival and seeking rehabilitation packages. It would however be wrong to assume that women are passive victims of either state policies or their own traditions. In fact, women have been playing many roles in armed conflict not only as peacemakers or victims but also as perpetrators and supporters of war (Radhika Coomarswamy, Dirukshi Fonseka, 2004).

Women from various ethnic communities have emerged as social actors to fight against the grave social injustices and have developed their own capabilities to actively respond to such situations. Although the women of Northeast India have been playing a very significant role in peace making, either their role is being ignored or their abilities for this purpose are being not utilized.

In most cases it is seen that the government and the rebels don't want to come to the negotiating table due to their apprehension of losing their power positions. The government fears of losing its legitimacy among the people and the rebels fear of losing their gun power. But as women are already in a marginalized position in the society, they view the concept of power and conflict from different angles. This position enables them to act in a very impartial manner and they may foster peace-making efforts and become active peacemakers (*The Assam Tribune,* Nov. 3, 2005).

Moreover, the number of women in representative politics is very low. Sometimes women are given token representation. In many cases, women representation in the decision making bodies is only notional, not substantive. Electoral politics in northeastern states has in no way empowered the women community.

Nevertheless women have proved more successful in gaining a space for themselves in the public sphere and in the politics of the peace process in this region. Women's initiatives for peace negotiations can not only change their own status but also energize them to act as change agents in the society at large. Women have established an active political image by replacing their passive and stereotyped image in the situations of state violence or other kinds of violence.

Impacts of Conflicts on Women

Men and women experience a conflict in different ways. The Beijing Platform for Action highlights the special impact of armed conflict on women and points out that although all sections of society are affected, women and girls are more adversely affected because of their status in society and their sex. In this context, it is important to have an understanding of the perspectives of women and men on peace and violence.

There are different kinds of gender dimensions during the pre-conflict, conflict and post-conflict situation. During the pre-conflict situation, there is increased mobilization of soldiers or army which sometimes leads to increase sexual harassment and loss of privacy even within the four walls of the house (which is considered a so-called safe zone) due to frequent checks and sexual abuse. During the conflict situation, women face psychological trauma, physical violence, causalities and death. Forced displacement from the home land owing to ethnic clashes is also a gendered experience and the process of displacement is more traumatic for women than for men. Moreover, women need special medical facilities and care and extra nutritional requirements during pregnancy and breast feeding which are not provided to them in war and conflict situations. Furthermore, sexual violence perpetrated on women naturally increases the risk of sexually transmitted diseases for the victims and also such women face the risk of unwanted pregnancies (Chabra Satbeer, New Delhi). After the conflict situation, in the reconstruction and rehabilitation policies of government, women are often excluded from formal discussions. Women's unequal access to media also leads to under-recognition of women's concerns.

In the report of the Study of *Women in Armed Conflict Situations*, conducted by the **North East Network**, women are divided into seven different categories in reference to the varied roles played by them during the conflict situations as –women relatives of armed activists, women relatives of State armed forces, women militants or combatants, women as shelter providers, women as victims of sexual and physical abuse, women as peace negotiators and finally, women's rights activists. Thus, women's participation in the peace process should not be seen only in the context of women as victims of war and conflict, but as women playing a proactive role in the process of peace negotiations, peace building and post-conflict activities following the peace agreement.

Contribution of Women towards Resolving Conflicts

Women, individually and collectively have made very important contributions in resolving conflict as care-takers/providers, counselors and negotiators. But women's contributions for peace and human rights are often overlooked. When women participate in peace negotiations, they keep the future of their societies and communities in mind. Women have played significant role both in the domain of women's rights as well as in other domains having implications for human livelihood and democracy. It will not be out of place to make a reference to the role played by Wangari Mathai, the leader of Green Belt Movement in Kenya, where she linked up the poor quality of women's life with that of deterioration of environment. She endeavored to make women the warrior for safeguarding the environment. Reference can also be made to the role of Medha Patker in Narmada Bachao Andolan against the forced displacement of the tribal people in India in the name of development.

The notion of peace as an end of armed conflict or as absence of war situation is the wrong notion. Absence of war situation is not enough condition to ensure non-occurrence of armed conflict. The important step for peace is to end and question all forms of violence in people's lives such as militarization, structural violence of racial and economic injustices, violence against women, etc. A positive peace addresses wider issues that lead to the reduction of all forms of violence. A peace that doesn't address wider issues and is blind to the dynamics of domination or power over 'the other' will be fragile based on injustice and unable to bring an end to the conflicts that are inevitable in militaristic societies (Radhika Coomarswamy, Dirukshi Fonseka, 2004).

Women's peace initiatives are marked by a number of distinct characteristics such as their concerns for food security, access to land, forest, water and other resources. Women negotiate survival strategies like the issue of livelihood, health care, education which are given top priority and are grounded in the notion of justice and human security. Women groups of Northeast India have played varied roles for the cause of positive peace. They have at times addressed the issues of underdevelopment as the root cause of conflict, fought for the restoration of human rights, campaigned against sexual violence and discrimination, negotiated for peace between warring parties and also used the strategy of appealing to maternal consciousness for peace.

Women in Northeast India have played many roles in armed conflict, not only as peace makers or victims but also as perpetrators and supporters of war. Women have been nurses and soldiers, warriors and mothers. Women have mourned and they have celebrated. They have encouraged their children to seek peace and they have supported wars with their time, their money and their voices. Thus, women at different times have contributed towards unmasking multiple domains of domination and subjugation in general and patriarchal domination in particular.

Women have actively participated in organizing a movement for the cause of peace in the north-east. The women of different areas of the northeast have performed proactive roles in negotiating for peace in the region. It is necessary to understand the involvement of women in the peace process in the north-east part of India to know the contribution of women for peace in the area. Also a comparative study can be made of the peace activities of women's groups in Assam, Manipur and Nagaland regarding their different nature of intervention for peace.

Nagaland

The Naga Mother's Association (NMA) is one of the best-known women's organizations for peace in North-East which tried to take an independent stand and negotiate with the state, armies and rebels. The NMA was founded on Feb.14, 1984 out of the Naga Women's concern for the increasing problems of Naga society. The NMA mediated between the Government of Nagaland and the Naga Students' Federation over the age limit for jobs and was successful in this quest. In the year 1994 the NMA formed the peace team with the theme "Shed no more blood" and initiated dialogues with the state government and with the rebel groups to stop the violence and bloodshed. The most important thing about the NMA is that it tried to deal with the root causes of conflicts in order to bring about positive peace. The organization identified underdevelopment of the people as the root cause of any conflict. So the NMA tried to address the issue by undertaking programmes for development and dealt with the issue of health, drug abuse, alcoholism etc. that had paralyzed the development of the people leading them to further drudgery. As the NMA intelligently moved from political to social issues and became involved in developmental activities its effectiveness and acceptance in Naga Society increased. Moreover the NMA was successful in its search for peace as negotiating for peace falls within its traditional scope of action. It is often assumed that peace making in the family is always the duty of the women and is a part of their traditional role. The Naga women have channelized their role by appealing for peace as mothers, wives and sisters without challenging their traditional gender roles. But in doing so, they have already entered into the arena of politics of peace and successfully appropriated a voice in decision-making.

Apart from the NMA, other important peace groups in Nagaland, the Watsu Mongdung and Tangkhul Shanao Long (TSL) are actively participating in discussions on peace and restoration of human rights in Nagaland.

Manipur

In Manipur women are very active and have a certain degree of control over economic resources. The Women's Market of Manipur is exclusively managed by women and besides being a Centre of trade, the market is also a forum for women to meet and discuss social and political issues facilitating space for women's activism in the state of Manipur (The Orient Vision, 2004).The women's movements in Manipur called Nupi Lan, which stood against the injustices of the British with the help of Marwari traders in 1904 and 1939 were famous. The great spirit of the Nupi Lan continued to live on in the Meira Paibies movement. At present the Meira Paibies or the Torch Bearers movement is very active in Manipur. The Meira Paibies started their movement with the campaign to combat alcohol consumption by men and were successful in turning Manipur into a dry state. Their concerns centre on two issues – human rights violations by armed forces and the increasing use of drugs and subsequently the emergence of HIV/AIDS amongst the youth of Manipur. Anytime they hear of a rape, a torture or a death or disappearance of a person, they gather in hundreds and sometimes keep vigil all night (The Hindu, 25th July, 2004). They became more active in 1979 after a period of particularly vicious abuse of power by the Indian armed forces occupying Manipur, which included several cases of rape and indiscriminate arrests and violence.

At present they have been actively campaigning against the atrocities by the security forces and are actively fighting for the repeal of the AFSPA (Armed Forces Special Power Act). The Indian Army and security forces have been given extraordinary powers under the AFSPA 1958 to search, seize arrest and even kill anyone suspected of being an insurgent in order to maintain order. But this Act has triggered resentment, alienation and agitations. These cases were rarely reported by the media to the rest of the country and these problems of northeast remained aloof till the demonstration made by Manipuri women on July 15. The demonstration on 15th July, demanding the withdrawal of AFSPA was triggered by the alleged rape and killing of Thangjam Manorama in the custody of the Assam Rifles leading to the nude protest of womenfolk accompanied by a number of Meira Paibies before Assam Rifles Station (Frontline, 2004). Even the women's protest would have gone unreported had it not been so dramatic. It suggests that they were truly pushed to the end of their tolerance (*The Hindu*, 25th July, 2004). Thus, in this case the women utilized the vulnerability of sex as a decisive weapon of resistance. As due to their resistance against the state agencies they have to suffer lots of physical atrocities like dogs were released against them, rubber bullets, and tear gas shell were thrown at them, etc. (Peace Studies, Paper-2, 2005).

Assam

Assam experienced a number of social movements in the Post-Independence period. Women have played important role in the historic 6 years Assam Movement of 1980s and in many a time women formed human shields between the agitating students and the armed forces. Assam witnessed insurgencies at various scales and within the dominant movements ULFA, NDFB, BLT, etc, regular incidence of violence, killing and atrocities on the sides both of the State and outfits confounded the scenario in the State.

In Assam women's movements retained a sporadic and issue based character. In both pre-independence and post-independence struggles, women are inspired by a sense of nationalism. But when the movement ended they were again pushed back to their traditional sphere. Their participation was never recorded by giving women a voice in institutionalized politics by perpetrating the myth that women were not interested in politics. Their contributions in the movements were kept unreported and women found their share of space in the movements as more victims in any reports on the conflict situation. (Rita Manchanda, 2001). But the interventions of women during conflict situations are varied. The very role women play for peace break away the gender stereotypes and myth that women are not interested in political movements.

In Assam peace initiatives by women groups like Matri Manch, Sajagota Samity, Bodo Women Justice Forum, etc. are of utmost importance. The mothers of those sons who had disappeared and joined the insurgency outfits or were killed during encounter with police and military initially formed the Matri Manch. But of late many women who were not such mothers also joined the movement.

The Matri Manch took up the issue of abuse of women and violence against women by both the state agents and the insurgents. In fact, this group never got the support of either the state or the insurgent groups but instead was threatened to withdraw from active campaigns for peace. Due to this kind pressure, they became either marginalized or the targets of attack.

The Sajagota Mahila Samity often remains in a dormant condition until some incident takes place; therefore, they are politically not so visible. When any issue of violence against women takes place such as a rape or police raids the members of the Samity immediately get organized and lead protest march and agitate for the restoration of human rights. Though they fight for the sake of human rights issue, neither the state nor the rebel groups support their action.

Another women led peace group is the Bodo Women's Justice Forum. This group concerns itself with the issues of peace and human rights and also takes active part in initiating Bodo dialogue on peace. Golapi Basumotary, the founder secretary of the organization initiated and actively acted in negotiating peace through dialogue, but some unknown assassin gunned her down, which led to the end of the peace initiative.

Contribution of Individual Women for Peace

Besides the role of women's groups the efforts of many individuals like Mamoni Raisom Goswami and Biru Bala Rabha of Assam and Irom Sharmila Chanu of Manipur are worth mentioning.

Of late, Mamoni Raisom Goswami, the noted littérateur and Janapith Awardee has taken up the role of a peacemaker in Assam aiming at helping the United Liberation Front of Assam (ULFA) leaders to negotiate peace with the Indian government. ULFA is identified as one of the most powerful militant groups in North East India and since 1979 it has been fighting for a separate homeland. During the last two decades thousands of people died due to the violent struggle. The government of India, in order to suppress this outfit, deployed armed forces in Assam and carried out massive operation such as Operation Rhino, Operation Bajarang etc. which led to massive human rights violations in Assam. In the past, the Indian Govt. persuaded the ULFA for talks but the latter was reluctant to respond positively because of lack of confidence between the government and the insurgent groups.

With the recent initiative of Mamoni Goswami, the peace process in Assam is being expedited. Ms. Goswami appealed the government to deal with the problem by undertaking a humanist approach and to find out why the militants demand for a sovereign state. She hopes that as the discussions goes on other demands of the ULFA will become transparent and if these can be fulfilled then other issues might be compromised. She appealed the government to find out the root causes behind the boys undertaking the path of violence and treat them as our own boys with guns in their hands, not as insurgents. Ms.Goswami too mounted pressure upon New Delhi to control troops engaged in counter insurgency operation against the outlawed ULFA in view of the current peace initiative so as to create a congenial atmosphere to bring the rebels to the negotiating tables. Ms. Goswami too spoke on the role of civil society and also stressed the need of extensive study of the problem to formulate a holistic plan for an amicable settlement of the issue of insurgency. Due to her conscious and untiring efforts the ULFA has agreed to send a nine member people's consultative group to initiate the discussion with the Central Government (Frontline, September 10, 2004). The people of the State saw a ray of hope when the government of India suspended the operations against the ULFA with effect from Aug. 13 and at the initial stage, the ULFA also responded positively. But at later stage, the level of violence in the State has gone up sharply after the peace process to bring the ULFA to the negotiation table ended in a deadlock. But Ms. Goswami is still hopeful of a positive outcome and is assured that she would continue her efforts for restoring peace in Assam.

Biro Bala Rava alias 'Bogi' was born in 1949 in Tridumpur, Goalpara district, Assam. Since 2000, Biro has fought against the *dainy* (witch-hunting) system in close collaboration with the Assam Mahila Samata Society (AMSS). Along with AMSS, Biro organised several *panchayat*-level meetings, where she spoke forcefully against witch-hunts. And since 2001, there has not been a single instance of witch-hunt. Biro saved the lives of six women who had been condemned as *dainys* (www.thehindubusinessline.com). Due to her courageous and untiring effort, she was nominated for the Noble Peace Prize.

Irom Sharmila Chanu of Manipur is one of the six women of the North East who have been nominated for the Nobel Peace Prize, 2005. Irom Sharmila has been protesting against the AFSPA in force in the state and military excesses and atrocities. On Nov. 2, 2002 she went on a fast unto death protesting against the killing of 10 civilians in Malom. The state government promptly arrested her for attempted suicide. Since that day she has been in the security ward of a government hospital (The Assam Tribune July, 10, 2005). The duplicity of the state and gender insensitivity was reflected in the state's action in the arrest of Irom Sharmila who has been fighting for the democratic struggle for justice according to the Gandhian strategy of non-violence and fast –unto death.

Conclusions

The multiplicity of women's responses to conflict in North East proves that women were not inherently pacifist. One of the greatest motivations for women to work for the resolution of conflict is because of the fact that at the time of conflict they are the natural victims. Moreover, during the time of social dislocation and crisis, it becomes their sole responsibility to take care of family. During conflict they face abandonment, isolation, and molestation. Due to constant checks and frisking by police, it rests on the women to bring back normalcy, as men are more vulnerable to police encounters. But it is seen that women who try to negotiate spaces of power in the public sphere pay a heavy price and are killed by the bullets of the insurgents. In the words of Roshmi Goswami, *Women's vulnerability increases depending on the kind of role they choose to play in the peace process. Women are accepted as healers and pacifists but not when they attempt to play a more decisive role and raise questions of peace, linking it with basic concepts of democracy. Women who protest against state oppression are seen as the over ground agents of the underground non-state actors: while women who raise their voices against non-state oppression are branded as state agents and silenced* (Goswami Roshmi, Aug, 2000). Thus viewing women only as passive victims has further made women's situation vulnerable.

So in order to empower women and also to bring enduring peace conflict studies and researches must be done with a gender perspective. At the same time, the media has also to play a more important role to enquire into the basic cause of the situation and project the situation in a gender friendly manner. Thus, it is important to understand the difference between women's and men's perspective of peace. The role of women in peace building needs to be investigated and highlighted as a part of gender analysis of peace support operations so that effective strategies can be developed for incorporating gender perspectives in peace initiatives. Women's right to peace initiatives is based on the principles of justice and democracy. As women constitute about half of the world's population, they have a right to be a part of decision-making on all critical issues that so deeply affect their lives. Gender balance is a democratic principle and should also be applied in peace building activities.

References

Goswami, Roshmi, Sreelekha, M.G, Goswami Meghna (ed), *Women in Armed Conflict Situation: A Study by NEN*, NEN, Guahati, 2005.

Saroj, N. Arambam Parratt, John Parratt., The Second women's war and the Emergence of Democratic Government in Manipur, *The Orient Vision*, Oct.–Nov.–Dec., 2004, Vol. 2 Issue I.

Bunch, Charolettee, Peace, Human rights and Women's peace Activism: Feminist Readings, in Coomaraswami Radhika, Fonseka Dilrukshi (ed), *Peace Work: Women, Armed Conflict and Negotiation*, Women Unlimited, New Delhi, 2004.

Banerjee, Paula, *The Naga Women's Intervention for Peace*, Canadian Women Studies, Vol. 19, No-4.

Arambam, Lokendra, Peace Process in Manipur: Armed Conflict, State repression and women, *Peace Studies Paper-2*, OKD, Guwahati, 2005.

Banerjee, Paula, Between two armed patriarchies: Women in Assam and Nagaland, in Manchanda, Rita (ed), *Women, War and Peace in South Asia: Beyond Victim hood to Agency*, Sage Publications, New Delhi-2001.

Goswami Roshmi, Women and Armed Conflict: Ground Realities in the Northeast, paper presented at the WISCOMP Symposium, *Human Security in the New Millennium*, Aug 2000.

Chabra Satbeer, *Gender Perspective in Peace Initiatives: Opportunities and Challenges*, in, www.articles/genderperspectivesinpeaceoperations.htm

Editorial Notes, in, Ray Ashok & Deb, B.J., (ed.), *Terrorism & Human Rights in Northeast India*, Om Publications, New Delhi, 2007.

Phukon, Dolly, *Women in the Peace Process in Northeast India* , in, Ray Ashok & Deb, B.J., (ed.), *Terrorism & Human Rights in Northeast India*, Om Publications, New Delhi, 2007.

The Assam Tribune, July 10, 2005.

Ibid. August 5, 2005.

Ibid. August 20, 2005.

Ibid, June 5, 2005.

Ibid, June 18, 2005.

Ibid, November 3, 2005

Frontline, September 10, 2004.

21

Prospects for Indian Women

A.N. Panda

Women constitute about half of the population of India. According to the 2001 census out of the total population of 1027 million in India women account for 495.7million. They have contributed for the evolution and continuation of the Indian society and have been active in socio-economic-political field since time immemorial. Their impact on the society is noteworthy not only quantitatively but also qualitatively. Like their male counterparts, women represent the other important segment of the Indian social system.

However, like their counterparts in other countries, Indian women have suffered through the ages. Though sometimes they have been accorded a respectable place in society and regarded as inalienable from their male partners in different respects they have not been given their proper status in society. Gender inequalities, which mean biased opinions and behaviours shown towards women because of their biological features, have permeated various layers of the social system and women have been systematically marginalised in positions of power and the decision making processes. The patriarchal order has neglected their points of views. The control and management of family and social affairs have been at the hands of the male section of society. Very often the patriarchs of society have exerted their power for their own vested interests and exploited women. They have scuttled the progress of women and subjected them to suffer their evil designs. Due to this reason many social evils like female infanticide, child marriage, prohibition of widow remarriage, sati, etc. have taken roots in the India society. Women have been forced to accept discrimination on the basis of sex which has resulted in depriving them of many facilities in the social order. Sometimes women have been treated as mere suppliants by their male equals and considered as dependents and society has assigned them a low status and role. It can be stated that "there has been a constant decline in the status and condition of women during the last two thousand years."[1] This adverse social position of the women folk is reflected in almost all walks of life. They have not been given any importance and their worth has not been properly recognised.

Whenever the cause of women has been acknowledged the attitude of the society in general towards women has been at best protective. Women have been regarded as a target groups and recipients in different socio-economic schemes, but not as active participants or initiators of any new scheme. Whatever positive steps have been taken throughout the ages towards the improvement of women, those have been taken with out the active involvement of women and by some well intentioned individuals of society. As a consequence, the general status of women has remained one of less importance in the social system.

"Status, in pure sociological terms, denotes only the position vis-à-vis others in terms of rights and obligations. In discussion on women's status in any society, the general convention has been to assess their role in relation to men. Two other dimensions have been introduced in recent times to facilitate such assessment, particularly in a period of process of change: (a) the extent of actual control enjoyed by women over their own lives; (b) the extent to which they have access to decision making processes and are effective in positions of power and authority."[2]

As a result of the growing consciousness of women of their low and deprived position in the socio-economic-political orders in almost all countries the movement of feminism began worldwide and women in different countries started the drive to assert themselves and demand due attention from the governments and societies. The feminists challenged the hitherto held notion of male superiority and division of work based on biological consideration. Feminism commenced as a protest against social inequality and discrimination in favour of the male section of society. Feminism led to crystallisation of claims of women and expression of those claims in a systematic way. Feminism encouraged women to insist on leading a dignified life like their fellow men and clamour for equality with them. Feminism inspired women to agitate and struggle for their rights and challenge the wrongly held social notions with regard to women. The echo of this movement was heard in every country of the world, though its intensity varied from one country to another.

Independence of India brought a significant change in the attitude of the Indian society towards women. The active involvement of women in the country's freedom struggle and their positive contributions in it compelled the powerful men in the post independence society to acknowledge the worth of women and accord them a place of importance. Many women leaders also took active role to improve the condition of their fellow sisters by putting forward the demands of women and demanding actins to rectify the hostile situation. As a result, many steps were taken to improve the position of women in society in the post independent India and far reaching changes took place in the status of women in India.

The Indian Constitution opted for a pluralist democracy and adopted a parliamentary system of government for the country. In India, elections are regularly held on the principle of universal adult franchise. Elections in India provide an opportunity to the people to select their representatives and avail the opportunity to get involved in the larger political process of the country. Thus, all Indian citizens get the scope to take part in the democratic process of the country and exercise their power in the recruitment of the rulers. In this respect the Indian women also have the same scope as their male equivalents. Unlike in many other countries where women had to wage a separate struggle to gain voting rights, in India this political right was accorded at a single stroke when the Constitution was adopted and implemented.

The Constitution of independent India affirmed its faith in gender equality and removed discrimination on the ground of sex. It held the view that gender equality is an essential part of social equality and declared both man and woman equal and made provisions for equal opportunities for both male and female. It proclaimed to establish a just social order in order to allow justice to all irrespective of sex difference. All these provisions laid the foundation of a future India and it was hoped that India would have an egalitarian society and a participatory political system where both male and female would get equal chance to take part in the decision making process.

Since independence, many efforts have been made to ameliorate the condition of women in different respects and the positive outcomes have been seen in different areas. Many steps have been taken in India to remove the gender based traditional inequalities from the social system. Many laws have been passed to protect the rights of women and many structural adjustments have been made to strengthen women's social position. The Maternity Benefit Act of 1961, the Equal Remuneration Act of 1976 are the examples of some acts those have been made to protect the rights of women in India. The Pre-Natal Diagnostic Techniques (Regulation and Prevention of Misuse) Act of 1994 which came into effect in 1996 is another such act to check female foeticide. To regulate the marriage system and protect the rights of women the Hindu Marriage Act of 1955 and Special Marriage Act of 1955 have been amended by the Marriage Laws Amendment Act in 1976; accordingly at present a girl has the right to repudiate her marriage if solemnised before her attaining majority. The Child Marriage Restraint Amendment Act of 1978 raises the marriageable age of a girl from 15 to 18. The formation of the Women Commissions at the central and state levels, the constitution of a separate cell, Women Labour Cell, in the Labour Ministry and such other steps have been undertaken with the sole purpose of preserving the rights of women and preventing any discrimination against women. In the field of female literacy there has been an increase from 7.9% in 1951 to 24.82% in 1981 to 39.42% in 1991.

In different Five Year Plans also special importance has been given to women related issues and separate chapters have been incorporated in the Plans to emphasise the interests of women. For example, in the Sixth Five Year Plan (1980-1985) by including a separate chapter entitled "Women and Development" the government "recognised women as more than just passive beneficiaries of government programs and acknowledged them to be equal partners in national development."[3] "Women were also given priority as beneficiaries of government aid programs in rural areas. The Integrated Rural Development Programme accorded preference to women heads of household. Under another program, Training of Rural Youth for Self Employment Management, over 38,000 women, constituting almost 37 percent of the total number of beneficiaries, were trained in 1986 and 1987. In 1982 and 1983 a Development of Women and Children in Rural Areas project was started as a pilot project in 50 blocks (delineated areas for development within a district) around the country. Women below the poverty line, its special targets, were organised into groups of 20 to 30. Each group was provided training in chosen economic activity, such as weaving, fish vending, broom and rope making, and pickle making. Between 1983 and 1985 over 2772 of these groups were formed and trained, benefiting over 36,000 women."[4] The same emphasis continued in other Five Year Plans also.

However, much is needed to be done in respect of improvement of the condition of women. There are many areas, where there is a need to be more concerned. For example, the declining sex ratio indicates the social attitude towards women. The decreasing sex ratio from 972 in 1901 to 933 in 2001 should be viewed more seriously. According to the 2001 census, if the data in different regions are taken into account the dismal position of women is more glaring. The sex ratio is 922 in Maharashtra and as low as 793 in Punjab per 1000 males.

But the most alarming aspect of women's marginalisation in the decision making process in society is their relegation in the political field. Political power is the most important power in society because it is vested in the state and the state is the only organisation which has maximum power of punishment available to it. A share in political power automatically gives advantage to a group as the group can initiate a decision and has effective control while it is made. Therefore, it is believed that participation in political process is vital to the progress of a social group.

An analysis of the involvement of different sections of population in the decision making process reveals that women have lagged much behind the male folks while exercising their power. Even if women constitute about 50 per cent of the total population they have been deprived of an equitable representation in any political body. "The highest representation that women have ever enjoyed was 9.0 per cent in 1999 election."[5] In the political arena, there is still the dominance of the male section and if at all there is association of women in the political process then it is only as the voters. The job of taking actual decision is still left to the male section of society.

In political sphere, like women in other countries, Indian women are no better. The Constitution of India grants formal equality in socio-economic-political sphere but actual equality still eludes women in India. Though the Constitution guarantees legal equality and several laws have been passed to remove many shortcomings of women, in reality, the age old discrimination still continues in many fields. Notwithstanding the favourable enactments women have not been given their due place in the decision making structures. Especially in the political field, women are still considered less capable and not given a chance to be associated in the decision making process. If at any time they are given an opportunity in this respect then it is given not due to their capability, rather it is done for some other reasons; for example, they are allowed to participate because of their family links. Thus, we find many women leaders in India who have been groomed by their parents or other family members and they have reached the position they occupy because they have links with a political heavyweight; there are only a limited number of women leaders who have attained prominence without any such family relationship and because of their own capability.

The opportunity women get in political sphere according to law is not always translated in actual practice. They do not get equal opportunity like their male counterparts and more often than not are sidelined in the decision making process. Moreover, "Political status should be assessed, too, when analyzing women's quest for equality. This status, however, must be observed keeping in mind the caveat that even where women have the same legal and constitutional rights as men, these rights do not constitute or guarantee equality."[6]

On the whole, there has been marginalisation of women in politics. Women face many obstacles while engaging themselves in the political process of the country. Generally political activities are considered as male activities and women are discouraged to delve into it, which results in less number of women in political field. It is also a fact that women are regarded as subordinates to men and this creates structural constraints in their political participation. Women are not allowed to take independent decisions in the family and the same attitude is shown while they are engaged in political activities. It is an irony that there were more women in public life in India during the freedom struggle than in the post independence period, though the Constitution of India guarantees equality in socio-political sphere.

A new impetus took place in the women movement worldwide in 1975 when the United Nations declared 1975 as the 'International Women's Year' and the decade of 1975 to 1985 as the 'International Women Decade'. The resolution of the United Nation emphasised on gender equality, involvement of women in development efforts, employment opportunity and end of discriminations. It created a new initiative throughout world to appreciate the importance of women in different walks of life and remedy their disadvantages to allow them more facilities for enabling them to be equal with their male counterparts in society. Different countries took steps to provide scopes to women in various respects so that they could be in a position to acquire capacity to be truly equal with their male brethren. The attention of the governments was drawn towards women issues.

Another such step was taken in the international field in this direction. The General Assembly of the United Nations passed the Convention on the Elimination of All Forms of Discrimination against Women in December 1979. This charter not only acknowledged the prevalence of discrimination in different countries but also laid emphasis on equal rights of both men and women and called for ending discrimination of any kind. It encouraged member countries to initiate measures to provide employment opportunities to women and enable them to have access to food, health, education, training and opportunities for employment. It also recognised the fact that participation of women was necessary for the welfare of a country and the welfare of the world.

Different countries took different steps to improve the status of women. In India empowerment approach has been adopted to ameliorate the negative condition of Indian women. It is believed that empowerment enables a deprived group to take decisions concerning the group and have a control over the affairs of the group. Through empowerment the disadvantages of the group can be overcome as the group can decide its own affairs and initiate appropriate steps to rectify the defects found in the socio-economic-political system. In the recent years special importance has been given to women related issues and the interests of women. Women themselves have also become vocal in putting forward their demands. They themselves have assumed the responsibility of taking up the leadership to make demands before the decision makers for setting right the long existing disadvantages of women. Efforts were made to develop strategies in the shape of taking proactive administrative decisions and making structural adjustments which were women specific for enabling women to become self reliant and self-confident.

In this context, the 73rd Amendment of the Constitution is a notable milestone. It has enlarged the representation of women in local bodies at the rural level. It has given a chance to women in rural areas to get them involved in the local decision making system. It has allowed them to have a scope for getting knowledge and experience in political matters. It has created an atmosphere where women can get training in leadership quality. They can be associated with grassroots politics and take decisions as the representatives of the rural people. The local institutions can benefit from the involvement of women. Moreover, with their acquired knowledge at the grassroots politics they can be prepared to play a greater role in the politics of higher levels. The 74th Amendment has similar effects for urban women.

But at the higher levels also women need to have scope to participate in the decision making process which is not provided to women; because of the different constraints put in their path they can not be included in the mainstream political process. In this context, the demand for reservation of seats for women in different legislative bodies assumes importance. It is felt that in the normal course women will not be able to occupy political offices or if at all they are able to do so not in the near future. Therefore, there has been a growing demand for reservation of seats for women in the legislatures.

But what will be result of this demand is yet to be ascertained. As women have to operate and gain from the existing political situation the prevailing political condition will determine the success and failure of the women movement towards greater political participation and greater involvement in the decision making process. The attitude of the political parties and their leaders towards the demands of women for more political space will be very crucial for attaining more political power by women. A drastic change is necessary at the structural and attitudinal levels to give women their due importance and rights.

By allowing women a substantial share in political power at the local level the 73rd and 74th Constitutional Amendment Acts have created a new vista for the Indian women. This opportunity will encourage women to prove their might in local politics and be more confident in putting forward their demands before others. They can assert themselves in a more forceful manner in the political field. They have got a chance establish themselves in the political system with strength and create further scope for more political power. It will compel the other actors in the Indian political field to acknowledge the importance of women.

The current debate on the reservation of seats for women in the legislatures proves the fact that there is no sincerity in the intention of the political parties and their leaders. Though the political parties and leaders promise to reserve thirty to forty percent of seats in the legislatures when the time comes for taking the actual decision they dither and forward new arguments justifying why such steps can not be taken. The lack of unanimity among the politicians has hampered any progressive step towards passing the bill. The issues like incorporating a sub-quota for the backward classes or reserving some seats for women of other sections have been causing differences among the political leaders and political parties.

It must be realised that every issue is a women's issue and can not be considered being separated from women because the very fabric of society depends on the involvement of women in any issue. Moreover, as women constitute about fifty percent of society they can not be sidelined in any developmental schemes. Disregarding them will amount to ignoring fifty percent work force of society and not utilising the potentialities of women towards the betterment of society.

Though Indian women have stormed almost all male bastions and venturing into new fields including administration, science, technology, space journey, medicine, journalism and so on they are still considered as a minority group in all these areas and they still lack the importance which is their due. Their marginalisation still continues in different fields, especially with regard to their participation in the decision making processes. There is a gap between the structural incorporations and actual endowment pertaining to women rights. Mere legal enactments will not bring the desired results unless genuine sincerity is shown by the persons who execute the policies and programmes. It has to be realised that more than some lofty slogans, legal enactments and institutional build ups what is urgently necessary is the honest efforts of the decision makers and the policy executors to bring qualitative and quantitative changes in the status of women by allowing them their rightful place in society.

If an integrated approach can be evolved to tackle the multidimensional problems of Indian women there is no doubt that women can shine in any walk of life and prove their mettle in every respect. But the imperative need for the purpose is to bring an attitudinal change in the mindset of people in general and women in particular so that people can accept women in their new role and women can assume their new responsibility with vigour. It is essential that women should be brought into the mainstream of national life and provided scope for more involvement in the decision making process.

There is no doubt that women have started to be more involved in the political process of the country and their impact in the public sphere can no longer be ignored. As a large number of women have already been inducted into the grassroots politics and they have assumed the role of local level leaders they can no longer be sidelined in the mainstream political process. If a political party or a political leader attempts to do so it can be done at its/his own peril.

It has to be realised that reservation policy is not an end in itself. It is a means for achieving gender equality which in turn would result in development of the whole society. Political participation of women is a necessary condition which may lead to achievement of equality by women. "Gaining access to power is, however, only the prelude to using it."[7] Empowerment of women would elevate their social status and help in removing many age old discriminations against women. It will enable the largest neglected section of society to be amalgamated into the mainline socio-economic-political process and contribute for the betterment of the social system as whole. Women reservation should be seen in the larger context of social development. It should be considered from the context of expansion of the democratic values in the social sphere. Political empowerment of women is not an end itself rather a means to attain social justice for which the makers of modern India have made a promise in the Constitution. It is but a small step in the nation building process in India. In this context, the need for greater involvement of women in political and other spheres should be encouraged.

References

1. Singh, Pitam, *Women Legislators in Indian Politics*, Concept Publishing Company, New Delhi, 2003, p. 28.
2. *Ibid*, p. 29.
3. Swarup Hemlata; Sinha, Niroj; Ghosh, Chitra and Rajput, Pam "Women's Political Engagement in India: Some Critical Issues" in Nelson, Barbara J. and Chowdhury, Najma ed. *Women and Politics Worldwide*, Oxford University Press, New Delhi, 1997, p372.
4. Census of India table 8.45 as quoted in Ibid. pp. 372-373.
5. Rana, M.S., *India Votes*, B.R. Publishing Corporation, New Delhi, 2000, p. 74.
6. Palley, Marian Lief, "Women Rights as Human Rights: An International Perspective", *Annals of the American Academy*, 515, May, 1991, p. 169.
7. Antolini, Denise, "Women in Local Government: An Overview" in Flamang, Janet A., ed. *Political Women*, Vol. 8, Sage Publications, New Delhi, 1984, p. 39.

Selected Bibliography

BOOKS

Agnew, Vijaya, *Elite Women in Indian Politics*, Vikash Publishing House, Pvt. Ltd. New Delhi, 1979..

Aiyer, P. S., *Evolution of Hindu Moral Ideals*, Calcutta, 1935.

Almond and Verba, *The Civic Culture*, New jersey; Princeton, 1963

Anderson, James, E. *Public Policy Making*, Rinehart, New York, 1979.

Anderson Walt, *Politics and Environment*, Goodyear, California, 1975.

Altekar, A.S., *The Position of Women in Hindu Civilization*, Motilal Banarsidas, New Delhi, 1966.

Arya, Sadhna, *Women, Gender, Equality and the State*, Deep and Deep Publications, New Delhi, 2000.

Asghar Ali Engineer ed. *The Shah Bano Controversy*, Orient Longman, Bombay, 1987.

Asworth, Georgia, *Gendered Governance: Agenda for Change* UNDP: Gender in Development Monograph series # 3, Bureau for Development Policy, March, 1996.

Avinashalingam, T.S., ed., *Eradication of Rural Poverty*, Sri Ramakrishna Mission Vidyalaya, Coimbattore, 1977.

Bakshi, P.M., *The Constitution of India*, Universal Law Publishing Pvt. Ltd. Delhi, 2002

Basu, Durga Das, *Introduction to the Constitution of India* (19th Edition, Reprint 2004) Wadhwa and Company, New Delhi, 2004.

Bhall, Shanta, *Women Parliamentarians of India*, Shiva Publishers and Distributors, Udaipur, 1995.

Bernard, O.F.M., *Indian Mind*, Gregorian University, Rome,1962.

Biddle, J.J. and Thomas, E.J., *Role Theory: Concepts and Research*, John Wiley and Sons Inc., New York, 1966.

Bipin Chandra *et al*, *India After Independence 1947—2000*, New Delhi, Penguin Books, 2000.

Boserap, Ester, *Women's Role in Economic Development*, St. Martin's Press, New York, 1970.

Boserup, Ester and Christian Liljencrantz (1975), *Integration of Women in Development: Why, When, and How?*, United Nations, Department of Public Information, UN, New York.

Baxter, S. and Lansing, M., *Women and Politics: The Invisible Majority*, University of Michigan Press, Ann Arbor, 1980.

Brill Alida ed. *A Rising Public Voice: Women in Politics World Wide*, Feminist Press, New York, 1995.

Calman, Leslie J., *Toward Empowerment—Women and Movement Politics in India*, Westview Press, USA, 1992,

Campbell, Angus, *The Voter Decides*, Evanston, Illinois Press, New York, 1954.

Chattopadhyay, Kamaladevi, *I Remember, 1921 Reminiscences*, Ministry of Information and Broadcasting, Government of India, Delhi.

Chariton, Sue Ellon M., ed. *Women in Third World Development*, Westerview Press, London, 1984.

Chaudhuri, Sanghamitra Sen, *Women and Politics: West Bengal a Case Study*, Minerva Associates, Calcutta, 1955.

Constituent Assembly Debates, Vol. VII, 1948-49.

Conway, M. Margaret, *Political Participation in the United States*, Congressional Quarterly Press, Washington, 1985.

Conway, M.M.; Ahern, D.A.; Steuernagel, G.A.; *Women and Public Policy*, Congressional Quarterly Press, Washington D.C.

Coomaraswami Radhika, Fonseka Dilrukshi ed. *Peace Work: Women, Armed Conflict and Negotiation*, Women Unlimited, New Delhi, 2004.

Dalton, Russell J., *Citizen Politics*, Chatham House Publishers, Inc., New Jersey, 1988.

Derret, J.D.M., *Hindu Law, Past and Present*, A. Mukherjee, Calcutta, 1957.

De Souza, A., *Women in Contemporary India*, Manohar Book Service, Delhi, 1975.

Desai, Neera and Maithreyi, Krishna Raj, *Women and Society in India*, Ajanta Publications, Delhi, 1987.

Dictionary of Social Sciences, The Free Press, New York, 1967.

Dharam Vir and Mahajan, Kamlesh, "Contemporary Indian Women," *Collected Works*, Vol. 4, *Politics, Awareness and Women's Movements*, Delhi, New Academic Publishers, 1969

Dixon, Ruth B., *Rural Women at Work-Strategies for Development in South Asia*, John Hopkins University Press, London, 1978.

Dube., S.C., *Indian Village*, Routledge and Kegan Paul, London. 1955.

Easton, David, *A Framework of Political Analysis*, Prentice Hall, New Jersey, 1965.

Etienne, Gilbert, *India's Changing Rural Scene: 1963-1979*, Oxford University Press, New Delhi, 1982.

G. Dietrich, *Culture, Religion and Development* by J. Mahakal on behalf of the Centre of Social Action, Madras, 1978.

Gadgil, D. R., *The Industrial Revolution in India in Recent Times*, Oxford University Press, Bombay, 1954.

Gail, Minault ed. *The Extended Family, Women and Political Participation in India and Pakistan*, Chanakya Puplications, Delhi, 1981

Gajendragadkar, P.B., *Secularism and the Constitution of India*, University Press, Bombay, 1971

Gandhi, M.K., *Women and Social Justice*, Navjeevan Publishing House, Ahmedabad, 1968.

Gandhi, M.K., *Letters to Rajkumari Amrit Kaur*, Navjivan Publishing House, Ahmedabad, 1961

Goswami, Roshmi; Sreelekha, M.G.; Goswami, Meghna, ed. *Women in Armed Conflict Situation: A Study by NEN*, NEN, Guahati, 2005.

Gupta, A.K. ed. *Women and Society, The Developmental Perspective*, Criterion Publications, New Delhi, 1979.

Gupta, Sunita, and Gupta, Mukta, ed. *Role of Women in the Twentyfirst Century*, Anmol Publications, Delhi, 1996.

Harlambos, Michael, *Sociology: Themes and Perspectives*, Oxford University Press, New Delhi, 1991.

Hey Wood, Andrew, *Politics*, 2nd edn., Palgrave Foundations, New York, 2002.

Hill, Reuben and Konig, Rene ed. *Families in the East and West*, The Hague Monton and Co, Paris, 1970.

Holt, Alix, *Selected Writing of Alexandra Kollontai*, Alison, London, 1977.

Hymn, H.H., *Political Socialization*, The Macmillan Company, Free press, New York, 1959.

Indra, M.A., *The Status of Women in Ancient India* (second revised ed.) Motilal Banarsidass Publishers, Bombay, 1955.

Jacobson, W. S., *Women in India*, Manohar, New Delhi, 1978.

Jackson R.M. *The Machinery of Local Government*, second edn., Macmillan, New York, 1967.

Jain, C.K., *Women Parliamentarians in India*, Surjeet Publications, Delhi, 1993.

Jain, L.C. ed., *Decentralisation and Local Governance*, Orient Longman, New Delhi, 2005.

Jain, S.P. and Krishna Murthy Reddy, V., *Role of Women in Rural Development (A Study of Mahila Mandals)*, National Institute of Rural Development, Hyderabad, 1977.

James, G.E. and Rolls, M.J., ed., *Progress in Rural Extension and Community Development*. Vol. I, Univesity of Reading, UK, 1982.

Johnston Bruce F. and William, C. Clark, *Redesigning Rural Development—A Strategic Perspective*, The John Hopkins University Press, London, 1982.

Jones, E.E. and Gerard, H.B., *Foundation of Social Psychology*, Wiley, New York, 1967.

Kalidas, *Kumara-Sambhava*.

Kapadia, K. M., *Marriage and Family in India*, Oxford University Press, Calcutta, 1966.

Kapur, Promilla ed. *Empowering Indian Women*, Publication Division, New Delhi, 2001,

Karl, Marilee, *Women and Empowerment, Participation and Decision Making*, Zed Books, London, 1995.

Karmakar, K.G., *Credit for Self help Groups*, Sage, New Delhi, 1999.

Kave, P. V., *History of Dharmasatra*, Vol. II, Part I, Bhandarkar Oriental Research Institute, Poona, 1974.

Kolhar, Suman, *Decentralization, of Power and Role of Women in Panchayati Raj System*, NIEPA, New Delhi, 1993.

Kuppuswamy, B., *Social Change in India*, Konark Publishers Pvt. (Ltd.), Delhi, 1994.

Lazersfeld, Paul F. et al. *The People's Choice*, Columbia University Press, New York, 1944.

Leghorn, Lisa and Parker, Catherine, *Women's Worth: Sexual Economics and the World of Women*, Routledge and Kegan Paul, London, 1981.

Mahabharata Adiparva.

Mahabharata, Anushasana Parva.

Mahabaharata, Aranyaka Parva.

Mahabharata, Shalya Parva.

Mahabharata, Shanti Parva.

Mahabharata, Udyoga Parva.

Maheshwari, S.R, *State Government in India*, Macmillan, Delhi, 1979.

Mahindra, I., *The Rebellions Homemakers*, SNDT Women University, Bombay, 1980.

Majumdar, Vina, *Role of Rural Women in Development*, Allied Publishing Pvt. Ltd., Bombay, 1978.

Majumdar, Vina ed. *Symbols of Power*, Allied Publishers, Bombay, 1979.

Manchanda, Rita ed. *Women, War and Peace in South Asia: Beyond Victim hood to Agency*, Sage Publication, New Delhi, 2001.

Manu III.

Manu IX.

Manu, XII.

Manu-Smrti.

Menon, Lakshmi, *The Position of Women*, Oxford University Press, Bombay, 1944.

Milbrath, L.W. and Goel, M.L., *Political Participation: How and Why, Do People Get Involved in Politics?*, Rand McNally, Chicago, 1977.

Mishra, Anil Dutta ed. *Gender Perspective: Participation, Empowerment and Development*, Radha Publications, New Delhi, 1999.

Mishra, S.N. and Kumar Lokesh, *New Panchayat Raj in Action*, Mittal Publications, New Delhi, 1996.

Mitra, Jyoti ed. *Women and Society*, Kanishka, New Delhi, 1977.

Mukherjee, Neela, *Participation, Rural Appraisal, Methodology and Applications*, Concept, New Delhi, 1993.

Muller, Edward, *Aggressive Political Participation*, Princeton University Press, Princeton, New Jersey, 1979.

Narasimhan, Sakuntala, *Empowering Women*, Sage, New Delhi, 2001.

Nagel, Jack H., *Participation*, Prentice Hall, Inc. New Jersey, 1987.

Nehru, Shyam Kumari ed. *Our Cause*, Kitabistan, Allahabad, 1935.

Nelson, Barbara J. and Chowdhury, Najma edited, *Women and Politics Worldwide*, Oxford University Press, Delhi, 1997.

Nussbaum, M. and Glover J. ed. *Women, Culture, and Development: A Study of Human Capabilities*, Clarendon Press, Oxford, 1995.

Oakely, P. and Marsden, D., *Approaches to Participation in Rural Development*, International Labour Office, Geneva.

Palmer, N.D., *Elections and Political Development in India*, Vikas, New Delhi, 1976.

Pande, G.C., *Dimensions of Ancient Indian Social History*, Books and Books, New Delhi, 1984.

Phadia, Chandrakala, *Feminism Traditions and Modernity*, IIAS, Shimla, 2002.

Prabhu, P.H., *Hindu Social Organisation*, Popular Books, Bombay, 1958.

Pujari, Premlata and Kaushik, V.K., *Women Power in India*, Vol. I, Kanishka Publishers, Delhi, 1994.

Radhakrishnan, S., *Religion and Society*, Allen and Unwin Ltd., London,1947.

Radhakrishnan, S., *Occasional Speeches and Writings*, October 1952-January, 1956.

Rana, M.S., *India Votes Lok Sabha and Vidhan Sabha Elections, 1999, 2000*, B.R. Publishing Corporation, New Delhi, 2000,

Ray, Ashok and Deb, B.J., ed. *Terrorism & Human Rights in Northeast India*, Om Publications, New Delhi, 2007.

Reed, Evelyn, *Women's Evolution*, Pathfinder Press, New York, 1976.

Rig Veda X.

Riker, Wiliam H. and Ordeshook, Peter C., *An Introduction to Positive Political Theory*, Prentice-Hall, Inc., Englewood Cliffs, New Jersey, 1973.

Rounaq Jahan, *The Elusive Agenda: Mainstreaming Women in Development*, Zed Books, London, 1995.

Sahay, Sushma, *Women and Empowerment: Approaches and Strategies*, Discovery Publishing House, New Delhi, 1998.

Saheli, Sabala Sangh, *Development for Whom—A Critique of Women's Development Programmes*, Action India, Delhi. 1991.

Scarlet, *Economic Development and Social Change in South India*, Oxford University Press, India, Delhi, 1962.

Secord, P.F. and Backman, C.W., *Social Psychology*, McGraw Hill, New York, 1964.

Sen, A.K., *Women, Technology and Sexual Divisions*, UNCTAD, Trade and Development, 1986.

Sengupta, Padmini, *Women in India*, Publications Division, Ministry of Information and Broadcasting, Government of India, Delhi, 1964.

Seth, Mira, *Women and Development*, Sage, New Delhi, 2001.

Sharma, Radhakrishna, *Nationalism, Social Reform and Indian Women*, Janaki Prakashan, Patna, 1981.

Shiva Rao, B.ed. *The Framing of Indian Constitution*,Vol.II, IIPA, New Delhi.

Shrivastav, Om and Tandon, R., *Participatory Training for Rural Development*, Society for Participatory Research in Asia, New Delhi, 1982.

Singh M.K., *Jharkhand Development and Politics, Avenues and Challenges* Gangadeep Publications, Delhi, 2006.

Singh, Surat, *Women Panchayati Raj Representatives: A Study of a District in Haryana*, Haryana Institute of Rural Development, Nilokheri, 1997.

Singh, Yogendra, *Cultural Change in India: Identity and Globalization* Rawat Publications, Jaipur, 2000,

Smith, David Horton; Macaulay, Jacqueline and Associates, *Participation in Social and Political Activities*, Jossey-Bass Publishers, San Francisco, 1980

Stifung, Friedrich Ebert, edited *Women in Politics—Forms and Processes*, Har-Anand Publications, New Delhi, 1996.

Thakur, Ramesh, *The Government & Politics of India*, St. Martin's Press, New York, 1995.

Thomas, *Indian women through the Ages*, Asia Publishing House, Bombay, 1964.

Tracey, W.R., *Managing Training and Development Systems*, Taraporevala Publishing Industries.

Varshney, Ashutosh ed. *Essays in Indian Politics*, Sage Publications, New Delhi, 1989.

Vashista, B.K. (ed.) *Encyclopedia of Women in India*, Praveen Encyclopaedia Publications, New Delhi, 1976.

Verba, Sidney and Nie, Norman H., *Participation in America, Political Democracy and Social Equality*, The University Press of Chicago, Chicago, 1987.

Visnu XXII.

Wellesley Editorial Committee, ed. *Women and National Development*, Chicago University Press, Chicago, 1977.

Women Studies Group, Centre for Contemporary Cultural Studies, University of Birmingham edited *Women Take Issue, Aspects of Women Subjugation*, Hutchinson of London, 1978.

Yadav, Sushma & Mishra, Anil Dutta, *Gender Issues in India*, Radha Publication, New Delhi, 2003.

Yates, Gayle Graham, *What Women Want: The Ideas of the Movement*, Havard University Press, Cambridge, 1975.

ARTICLES IN JOURNALS

Anderson, K. "Working Women and Political Participation 1952-1972", *American Journal of Political Science*, 19 August, 1975,

Arambam, Lokendra, "Peace Process in Manipur: Armed Conflict, State Repression and Women", *Peace Studies Paper-2*, OKD, Guwahati ,2005.

Agarwal, Bina, "Work Participation of Rural Women in Third World. Some Data and Conceptual Biases", *Economic and Political Weekly.*

Ahmad, Z.M. and Martha F. Loutfi, "Women Workers in Rural Development", *A Programme of the Rural Employment Policies Branch*, Employment and Development Department, ILO Geneva,1984.

Amin, S.L. "A Paradigm Shift from Welfare", in *Social Welfare*, Vol. 42, No. 8, November, 1995

Anker, Richard, "Female Labour Force Participation in Developing Countries: A Critic of Current Definitions and Data Collection Methods", *International Labour Review*,1983.

Asha Das, "Child Development and Empowering Women in India", *The Indian Journal of Public Administration*, Vol. XVII, No.3, July, September, 1997.

Balasubrahmanyam, Virnal, "Towards Women's Perspective on Family Planning," *Economic and Political Weekly*, 1986.

B.S. Bhargava and K.C. Vidya, "Position of Women in Political Institutions", *Journal of Rural Development*, Vol. II, No. 5, September, 1992.

Banerjee, Paula, "The Naga Women's Intervention for Peace", *Canadian Women Studies*, Vol. 19, No-4.

Batliwala, Srilatha, 'Women in Cooking Energy," *Economic and Political Weekly* ,1983.

Brandtzaeg Brita, "Women, Food and Technology—Case of India", *Economic and Political Weekly*, 1979.

Chandra, Shanta Kohili, "Women and Empowerment", *The Indian Journal of Public Administration*, Vol: XLIII, No.3, July—September 1997.

Colclough, Christopher, "The Impact of Primary Schooling on Economic Development: A Review of the Evidence", *World Development*, 1982.

Deere, Carmen, Diana, "The Division of Labour by Sex in Agriculture: A Peruvian Case Study", *Economic Development and Cultural Change*,1982.

Dhillon, Gurmeet, "Rural Women in Decision-making Action", *Kurukshetra*, 1980.

Deshpande, Nirmala, "Participation of Women in Political System", *Kurukshetra*, Vol. XXXVII, No. 5, February, 1989.

Devi, Rukmini, "Dr. Annie Besant and the Indian Women's Movement", *Women's Indian Association: Golden Jubilee Number, 1917-1967.*

Galeb, S. and Rao, N. Chandra Sekhar, "Women's Self Help Groups Poverty Alleviation and Empowerment", *Economic and Political Weekly*, Vol: XXXVIII, No. 12 and 13, March 22 – 28/29, April 4, 2003.

Good, Barbara J. "Significance of Women's Organisations in the Advancement of Women in the US", *Indian Journal of American Studies*, Vol. 13, No. 2.

Hasan, Zoya, "Minority Identity, Muslim Women Bill Campaign and the Political Process", *Economic Political Weekly*, January 7,1994.

Huntington, Suellen "Issues in Women's Role in Economic Development: Critic and Alternatives", *Journal of Marriage and Family*, 1975.

Iftikar, Ahmad, "Technology and Rural Women in the Third World", *International Labour Review*, 1983.

Kala, C.V., "Female Participation in Farm Work in Central Kerala", *Sociological Bulletin*, 1976.

Kishwar, Madhu, "Out of the Zenana Dabba", *Manushi*, No. 96, September-October, 1996.

Krishanamurti, K.G. and Rao, G. Laxman, "Socio-economic and Demographic Factors and Voting Behaviour", *Political Science Review*, April-June 1969.

Kuman Gaurav, "Nateeze Zamini Satta Sanrachana Badal Dange", *Chetanshi,* Year - 2 vol. 3-4 April - Sept. 2006.

Lakshmi Devi Achanti, "Role of Rural Women in Agricultural Development", *Kurukshetra,* 1982.

Lele, Uma, "Women and Structural Transformation—Economic" *Development and Cultural Change,* 1986.

Lokaneeta, Jinee, "Alexandra Kollontai and Marxist Feminism", *Economic and Political Weekly,* April, 28, 2001.

Majumdar, Paramita, "Decentralization: Challenges to Urban Local Government." *Nagarlok,* Vol. XXX VIII, July–Sept., No. 3, 2006.

Marothia, D.K. and Sharma, S.K., "Female Labour Participation in Rice Farming Systems of Chattisgarh Region", *Indian Journal of Agricultural Economics,* 1985.

Mehta, Usha, "Indian Women and their Participation in Politics", *Social Change,* Vol. 8, No.3, September 1978, p. 32.

Mies, Maria, "Class Struggle or Emancipation: Women's Emancipation Movement in Europe and the US", *Economic and Political Weekly,* 1973.

Mishra, Rashmi, "Devolution of power to women in PanchayatiRaj in Orissa: Challenges and Opportunities", *Kurukshetra,* November 1998.

Mishra, Sweta and Mishra, S.N., "Women and Political Process in India", *Kurukshetra,* Vol. XLIII, No. 11, August, 1995.

Mohanty, K.T., "Empowering Women—A Catalyst in Indian Development", *Employment News* (Weekly) September 16, 2000.

Naik, J.P., "Relevance of Education to Development Especially in Rural Areas" *Education and New International Order,* Concept Publishing House, New Delhi, 1983.

Nagabrahman, D. and Sambrani, Sreekanth. "Women's Drudgery in Firewood Collection", *Economic and Political Weekly,* 1983.

Nieman, L.J. and Hughes, J.W., "The Problem of the Concept of Role: A Resurvey of Literature", *Social Forces,* Vol. 30, 1951-2.

Oppenheimer, Valerie, Kincade, "The Sociology of Women's Economic Role in the Family", *American Sociological Review,* 1977.

Palmer, Ingrid, "Rural Women and the Basic Needs Approach to Development", *International Labour Review,* 1977.

Parratt, Saroj N. Arambam and Parratt, John, "The Second Women's War and the Emergence of Democratic Government in Manipur", *The Orient Vision*, Vol. 2 Issue I, Oct.–Nov.–Dec., 2004.

Poonacha, Veena, *Economic and Political Weekly*, October 9, 1993.

Phukon, Dolly, "Women in the Peace Process in Northeast India" , *The Assam Tribune*, July 10, 2005.

Rajya Lakshmi, C.S., "Empowerment Through Self Help Groups", *Economic and Political Weekly*, Vol: XXXVIII, No.12 and 13, March 22-28/29, April 4, 2003

Ramashwaram, P.R. "The Challenges of Globalization for Civil Services", *Indian Journal Public Administration*, Vol. XLVIII, No.1, Jan-March, 2002.

Rural Women's Organizations, Das, Parimal, "Women under India's Community Development Programme," *International Labour Review*, (July-December), 1959.

Reynolds, Andrew, "Women in the Legislatures and Executives of the World", *World Politics*, John Hopkins University Press, New Jersey, Vol. 51, Issue 4, July, 1999.

Rolthschild, Constantina Safilios, "The Persistence of Women's Invisibility in Agriculture: Theoretical and Policy Lessons from Lesotho and Sierra Leone", *Economic Development and Cultural Change*,1985.

Sathe, S.P., Implications of Supreme Court Intervention, *Economic and Political Weekly*, September 2, 1995.

Sawer, J. Barbara, "Predictors of the Farm Wife's Involvement in General Management and Adoption Decisions", *Rural Sociology*,1973.

Sharma, Miriam, "Caste, Class and Gender Production and Reproduction in Rural North India", *The Journal of Peasant Studies*,1985.

Sisodia, J.S., "Role of Farm Women in Agriculture: A Study of Chambal Command Area of Madhya Pradesh", *Indian Journal of Agricultural Economics*, 1985.

Schwartz, Joel I., "Political Participation and Multi-subjective Understanding: An Interprotivist Approach to the Study of Political Participation", *Journal of Politics*, Vol. 46, 1984.

Sen, A.K. and Sengupta, S. "Malnutrition of Rural Children and the Sex Bias", *Economic and Political Weekly*, 1983.

Sudha and Deshpande, L.K., "New Economic Policy and Female Employment", *Economic and Political Weekly*, 10 October, 1992.

Sundaram, K.V., "From Top-Down Planning to Decentralised Regional and Local Development in India – Vision and Reality: Challenges and Perspectives", *Indian Social Science Review*, 2(2) 2000.

Suryawanshi, S.D. and Kapase, K.M., "Impact of Ghat Irrigation Project on Employment of Female Agricultural Labour", *Indian Journal of Agricultural Economics*, 1985.

Wilson, Fiona, "Women and Agricultural Change in Latin America: Some Concepts Guiding Research", *World Development*, 1985.

Welch, S. "Women as Political Animals: A Test of Some Explanations from Male-Female Political Participation Differences", *American Journal of Political Science;* 21 November, 1977.

REPORTS

A Report, Ministry of Environment and Forests, Government of India, New Delhi, 2002.

Annual Report 1996-97, National Commission for Women, New Delhi.

A Decade of Endeavour (1990-2000), National Commission for Women, New Delhi, 2001

A Decade of Endeavour (1990-2001) Vol. II, National Commission for Women, New Delhi.

Country Report, Fourth World Conference on Women, Beijing, New Delhi, Government of India, 1955.

Department of Women and Child Development, 2001. *Women's Empowerment Year*, Delhi: Ministry of Human Resource Development.

Department of Women and Child Development, 2000. *Empowering Women Through Self Help Groups*.

Department of Women and Child Development. *Statement to the Commission on the Status of Women*, U.N.O., 1998.

Districts at a Glance, 2006, Directorate of Economics and Statistics, Orissa, Bhubaneswar.

Draft Five Year Plan, 1978-83, Government of India, Planning Commission, New Delhi.

DWCRA Manual Government of India, Ministry of Rural Development, April, 2001.

Five Year Plan Documents, 1950-1977, Planning Commission, Government of India, New Delhi.

Gender Equity, National Commission for Women, New Delhi, 2001.

Government of Andhra Pradesh, DWCRA and Women's Empowerment: A Success Story of Self Help Groups Movement in Andhra Pradesh, Hyderabad. Panchayati Raj and Rural Development Department, 1999, UNDP, South Asia Poverty Alleviation Programme, Progress Report, 1996-1998, Hyderabad: 1998.

Haqqi, S.A.H., *Political Behavior; Empirical Study,* Delhi; I.C.S.S.R. published project report.

ILO - ARTEP (1981), Women in the Indian Labour Force, Bangkok.

ILO - (1982), Rural Women Workers in Asia, Geneva.

Legal Awareness Programme, National Commission for Women, New Delhi.

Mayonx, Linda, 1998, "Women's Empowerment and Micro-Finance: Programmes, Approaches, Evidence and Ways Forward", Development Policy and Practice Working Paper No.41, Milton Keynes, The Open University.

National Perspective Plan for Women 1988-2000 AD, Report of the Core Group set up by the Department of women and Child Development, Ministry of Human Resources Development, Government of India.

New Economic Policy and Women: A Collection of Background Papers to Sixth National Conference 1993, Indian Association for Women Studies, Bombay, 1993.

Programmes and Schemes for Women's Development, Ministry of Social Welfare, Government of India, Women's Welfare and Development Bureau, New Delhi, 1979.

Report of the Committee on the Status of Women in India, Department of Social Welfare, Ministry of Education and Social Welfare, Government of India, 1974

Reports and Documents, Inter-Parliamentary Union (IPU), Women and Political Power Survey Carried Out Among the ISO National Parliaments as of 31 October, 1991, No. 19, 1992.

Search for a Vision Statement on Women Empowerment vis-à-vis Legislation & Judicial decisions, National Commission for Women, New Delhi.

Sixth Five Year Plan, Government of India (1980), Planning Commission, New Delhi.

The Approach to the Seventh Five Year Plan 1986-90, Government of India, Planning Commission, New Delhi, p.32.

The Seventh Five Year Plan 1985-90, Vol. II, Government of India, Planning Commission, pp. 322-323.

UNICEF: (1996) "The Asia Enigma".

United Nations Development Programmes (UNDP) (1997), Nigeria Human Development Report, 1996, Lagos, UNDP.

World Bank (2002), World Development Report: Building Institution for Markets, Washington D.C., The World Bank.

Contributors

Anil Dutta Mishra started his career as an Assistant Professor in the Department of Non-violence and Peace Studies, Jain Vishva Bharati Institute (Deemed University), Ladnun, Rajasthan. His areas of specialization include Indian Government and Politics, Grassroots Politics, Women's Studies, Ecology and Human Rights. He has been associated with a number of national and international organizations in various capacities like Secretary of Indian Society of Gandhian Studies, General Secretary of Alliance for Sarvodaya, Secretary General of Human Development Foundation and Member, Board of Studies, Panjab University, Chandigarh. Having completed his PhD he has been engaged in many research and academic works. He has authored/edited 12 books and published a number of research papers in leading professional journals.

A.N. Panda has obtained his Post Graduate degree from Sambalpur University, Orissa and was placed in the Fourth position. He passed his BA from the same university in First class with Distinction and was placed in the Second position. He got his PhD from Sambalpur University in the year 1995. He has been teaching Under Graduate and Post Graduate students ever since he joined the teaching profession in 1981. He has been recognized as research guide by Sambalpur University and has been giving guidance to PhD scholars. Under his guidance two scholars have already completed their research and got their degrees. He has completed one UGC sponsored research project and currently pursuing another project financed by the UGC. He has authored one book and several research articles. He has reviewed six books written by other writers. He is a member of many learned associations such as IIPA, New Delhi; IACIS, Hyderabad; IPSA, OPSA, ISGS and IACS. He has participated in several State, National and International level Seminars/Conferences and presented papers in them.

Archana Pandey is a reseach scholar in Meerut University pursuing her PhD. She has published two of her research articles on "Gandhi and Non-violence" and "Problems of Women in Rural Areas".

Ashutosh Pandey, after passing his Post-Graduation in Political Science from the University of Allahabad in 1996 is working as faculty member in Amar Singh (PG) College, Bulandshahr. He has published several research articles in different journals. He is currently pursuing his D.Phil. in Political Science Department from University of Allahabad. His area of specialization includes Indian Government and Politics, Grassroots politics, Ecology and Human Rights and Public Administration. He has been a member several learned associations such as IPSA, IIPA, ISSA, ISGS. He has participated in several National Seminars and Conferences and presented papers in them. Currently he is pursuing a UGC sponsored research project on "Concerns for Protection of Environment and Rights of Indigenous People".

Ashu Pasrichha is working in the Department of Gandhian Studies, Punjab University, Chandigarh. She is a law graduate and has Master degrees in Public Administration, Gandhian and Peace Studies and Defence and Strategic Studies. She got her M.Phil. and Ph.D. from Punjab University, Chandigarh. Her works "Gandhian Approach to Integrated Rural Development", "Public Administration: Discipline and Dimensions", "Gender Issues in India: Some Reflections (2003)" and "Public Governance and Decentralisation (2003)" have been widely acknowledged as scholarly works of lasting value. Her book "Contemporary Debates in Public Administration" is in the press. She has completed her work on 'Gandhian Concept of State and Power' in twenty volume series, "Rediscovering Gandhi". Currently, she is associated with the Department of Gandhian Studies, Punjab University, Chandigarh. She has published a number of research papers/articles on different subjects in various Indian and foreign journals of repute. She is also a regular contributor to various prestigious newspapers in the country and abroad.

B.P.C. Bose, PhD, is an Associate Professor in the Department of Political Science and Public Administration, Acharya Nagarjuna University, Nagarjuna Nagar, Andhra Pradesh.

Chandra Kumar Konda Reddy, having completed his M.A., joined as a teacher in the Department of Political Science and Public Administration of Nagarjuna University and is working as a Reader at present. He got his Ph.D. from Andhra University in 1996 for his thesis "Tribal Development in India, Policies, Programmes and Structures" in which he made a case study of the ITDA in Andhra Pradesh. He has participated in several National and International Seminars/Conferences and presented papers in them. Also, he has served in different academic and administrative bodies of the University.

Dilip Kumar Padhi has got his Master Degrees in English and Law and PhD in English from CIEFL, Hyderabad. He is a renowned Social Activist and a Reseach Scholar in Archaeology. A member of many associations and societies he has regularly participated in many National and International Seminars and Conferences and presented papers in them.

Dolly Phukon, presently working as a Lecturer at Center for Women's Studies, Dibrugarh University, Assam had a through out first class career during her student days. She has done her Graduation and Post Graduation from Guahati University. She had passed her Graduation with Distinction and stood First in the University and also she was the First class First at her Post Graduation level. She has qualified the NET. She has worked as a Research Assistant and at present she has been engaged in her PhD work. She has published several articles to her credit. She has participated and presented papers in many State, National and International Conferences and Seminars.

Gautam Vir is a Lecturer in the Department of Political Science, D.A.V. (P.G.) College, Bulandshahr. He has completed his PhD and currently pursuing a UGC sponsored research project. He has authored two books on "Foreign Policies of Neighbouring Countries" and "Indian Police Administration". He is a member many learned associations like Indian Political Science Association, Indian Institute of Public Administration and Uttar Pradesh Political Science Association. He has attended several seminars and conferences and presented papers in them.

Gayatri Mishra, presently working as Lecturer in Political Science in Women's College, Bargarh, passed her Political Science BA Hons. Examination from Sambalpur University in First Class with Distinction and was placed in the Second position. She has been teaching Political Science ever since she passed her Post Graduation from Sambalpur University in First Class and taking classes at post graduate and under graduate levels. Currently she is engaged in a research work on 'Political Participation of Women Leaders in Sundargarh District in Orissa' for her Doctoral degree.

H.N.Pradhan has got his Master Degrees in Arts in Political Science and Law and was done his PhD in Law. Presently he is working as Reader in L.R.Law College, Sambalpur. He has a teaching experience of 24 years. He has been guiding PhD students and some of them have already got their degrees. He has completed one UGC research project and currently pursuing another project sponsored by the UGC. He has been a member of several learned associations and participated in State and National level Seminars and Conferences and presented papers in them. He has published several research articles to his credit.

Jai Narain Sharma is a Professor and in the faculty of the Department of Gandhian Studies, Panjab University, Chandigarh. He obtained his Masters Degree from Panjab University, M.Phil from H.P. University, Shimla and Ph.D. from Panjab University, Chandigarh. Dr. Sharma's areas of specialization include Gandhian Economics, Political Power, Human Rights and Human Resource Management. Dr. Sharma has distinguished himself as a management expert and Gandhian Scholar. He is connected with a number of national and international organizations in various capacities. He is a member of Board of Studies, Nagpur University, Nagpur and Mahatma Gandhi Kashividyapeeth, Varanasi and a member of Research Degree Committee of H.P. University, Shimla. He has also served as the General Secretary of Indian Society of Gandhian Studies and presently he is the Editor of the India Journal of Gandhian Studies and the member of the presidium of Alliance for Sarvodaya. He regularly writes for leading newspapers and has published a large number of research papers in various Journals of repute. His books include 'Gandhi's View of Political Power', 'Economics of Defence: A Study of SAARC Countries', 'Economic Thought of Mahatma Gandhi' and 'Human Resource Management'.

M. Bapuji is presently a Professor in the Department of Political Science and Public Administration, Nagarjuna University, Guntur, Andhra Pradesh. He has been teaching Public Administration to the P.G. students. He has authored about 10 Books and 60 Articles in different Journals. He has completed 4 Research Projects funded by the ICSSR and U.G.C. Besides these academic activities, he has also attended more than 20 National level Seminars and Conferences. The areas of his research interest are: Administrative Theory, Tribal Development, Administrative Reforms, etc.

Md. Mastanvali is presently an Associate Professor in the Department of Political Science, Andhra Muslim College, Guntur, Andhra Pradesh. He has been teaching Political Science to the UG students. He has authored 2 books and 12 Articles in different Journals. He has completed 5 research projects funded by different National, State agencies and the UGC. Besides, he has attended more than 10 National level Seminars and Conferences. The areas of his research interest include Women empowerment, Minority and Tribal Development, etc.

M.M.S. Negi has done his D.Phil. from Hemwati Nandan Bahuguna Garhwal University, Srinagar Garhwal, Uttaranchal. At present he is a Reader and Head of the Department in Political Science at H.N.B.G.U. Campus Tehri. Dr. Negi has contributed numerous papers to research Journals. He has also presented a number of papers in the National and International Seminars. His specializations are in Indian Government and Politics and Comparative Politics.

M.V.S. Koteswara Rao, Ph.D., is an Associate Professor in the Department of Politcal Science and Public Administration, Acharya Nagarjuna University , Nagrjuna Nagar, Andhra Pradesh.

Parvathy, A., Ph.D., is a Gold Medalist from Mysore University, Karnataka. She has published her MPhil and PhD theses and written many text books which are well received and have been translated into Kannada. She has been the Coordinator of the Mangalore University Youth Parliament team. She has also been the recipient of a major research project from UGC.

Sushma Yadav (b. 1959) is Professor, Dr. Ambedkar Chair in Social Justice at IIPA, New Delhi. Before joining the present position, she was Reader at Delhi College of Arts and Commerce, University of Delhi. A Gold Medalist from Delhi University and recipient of Rai Bahadur Gori Shankar Memorial Medal and Maharshi Karve Memorial prize she has also availed ICSSR short term Doctoral Fellowship and Associateship at Inter University Center at Indian Institute Advance Studies, Shimla. She has been an elected member of Academic Council of University of Delhi for two consecutive terms i.e. from 1996-2000. She has twenty five years of research and teaching experience. During this period she has authored/co-authored/edited/co-edited about ten books including *Centre-State Relations* (1986); *Secularism and Indian Tradition* (1988); *Political Culture in Post Independent India* (1989); *Issues in Indian Politics* (1994); *Culture and Politics* (1998); *Indian State: Origin and Development* (2000); *Patterns of Gender Violence*

(2002); *Gender Issues in India* (2003); *Jal: Kal, Aaj Aur Kal* (2005); *Gandhian Alternative: Social and Political Structure* (2005); *Social Justice: Ambedkar's Vision* (2006) along with a number of articles published in books and reputed journals. Presently she is working on the philosophy of Dr. B.R. Ambedkar and the issues of Social Justice with special reference to Public Administration and Public Policy for Dalits, Minorities, Women and empowerment of the marginalized sections of the society.

Sweta Mishra is a well-appreciated young and committed researcher and presently teaching Political Science at Shyama Prasad Mukherjee College, University of Delhi. Her areas of specialization are Public Administration and Grassroots Democratic Institutions. Her publications include: *Democratic Decentralization in India* (1994), *Changing patterns of District Administration* (1996), *Theory and Practice of Public Administration* (1998) and *Decentralized Governance* (2002). Besides these, she has to her credit more than two dozen research papers published in reputed professional journals.

Rajendra Bharti is a faculty member in the Department of Political Science, Simdega College, Simdega, Ranchi University, Ranchi, Jharkhand. He is the Head of Political Science Department.

V. Divya Thejo Murthy is working as a faculty member in the Department of Rural Development, Acharya Nagarjuna University, Andhra Pradesh since 1993.